Can't argue with Glenn's critics!

"Only in his wildest dreams could an actual suicide bomber
hope to do as much damage to this country."
—Keith Olbermann

"A half-informed radio blowhard."
—*Vanity Fair*

"Glenn Beck is an idiot."
—*Discover* magazine

"A lying sack of dog mess."
—Whoopi Goldberg

"A vampire . . . a 'death lover.'"
—Roseanne Barr

"Beck likes arguing, but has a deep-seated hatred for logic."
—Stephen Colbert

ARGUING WITH IDIOTS

How to Stop Small Minds and Big Government

WRITTEN & EDITED BY

Glenn Beck ★ Kevin Balfe

WRITERS

Steve "Stu" Burguiere ★ Dan Andros
Brian Sack ★ Alan Gura ★ Pat Gray
David Harsanyi ★ Carol Lynne ★ Carl Williott

CONTRIBUTORS

Claire Calzonetti ★ Evan Cutler ★ Joseph Kerry
Kelly Thompson ★ R. J. Pestritto ★ Tyler Grimm
Darran Foster ★ John Bobey ★ Paul Starke

ILLUSTRATIONS

Paul E. Nunn

THRESHOLD EDITIONS · MERCURY RADIO ARTS

LONDON ★ NEW YORK ★ TORONTO ★ SYDNEY

To my nephew, along with everyone else who has been watching our back in Iraq, Afghanistan, and around the world. We won't let you down—we're watching your back here at home.

THRESHOLD EDITIONS · MERCURY RADIO ARTS

A Division of Simon & Schuster, Inc.
1230 Avenue of the Americas
New York, NY 10020

First Threshold Editions/Mercury Radio Arts trade paperback edition September 2010

THRESHOLD EDITIONS and colophon are trademarks of Simon & Schuster, Inc.

GLENN BECK is a trademark of Mercury Radio Arts, Inc.

For information about special discounts for bulk purchases, please contact Simon & Schuster Special Sales at 1-866-506-1949 or business@simonandschuster.com.

The Simon & Schuster Speakers Bureau can bring authors to your live event. For more information or to book an event contact the Simon & Schuster Speakers Bureau at 1-866-248-3049 or visit our website at www.simonspeakers.com.

Designed by Timothy Shaner, NightandDayDesign.biz

Manufactured in the United States of America

10 9 8 7 6 5 4 3 2 1

ISBN 978-1-4165-9501-4
ISBN 978-1-4165-9502-1 (pbk)
ISBN 978-1-4391-6683-3 (ebook)

ACKNOWLEDGMENTS

SPECIAL THANKS TO...

All of the **VIEWERS, LISTENERS AND READERS,** including the Glenn Beck **INSIDERS**. It goes without saying, but you make it all possible. Together we are getting the message out. ★ My wife, **TANIA,** and all my **CHILDREN** for your endless support. ★ **CHRIS BALFE, KEVIN BALFE, STU BURGUIERE, ADAM CLARKE, JOE KERRY,** and the rest of my extraordinary team at **MERCURY RADIO ARTS** for helping to turn my dreams into reality. ★ **CAROLYN REIDY, LOUISE BURKE, MITCHELL IVERS, LIZ PERL, ANTHONY ZICCARDI, EMILY BESTLER, MARA ANASTAS, EMILY LAWRENCE, TOM SPAIN,** and everyone else at **SIMON & SCHUSTER** for putting up with me and for working so hard to make these projects right. ★ All of my friends at **FOX NEWS,** including **ROGER AILES, BILL SHINE, SUZANNE SCOTT, JOEL CHEATWOOD, BILL O'REILLY, NEIL CAVUTO,** along with my tireless **STAFF** that works so hard every day to get our show on the air. ★ Everyone that makes being in radio a daily dream come true, including **MARK MAYS, JOHN HOGAN, CHARLIE RAHILLY, DAN YUKELSON, JULIE TALBOTT, DAN METTER, KRAIG KITCHIN, BRIAN GLICKLICH AND DOM THEODORE.** ★ My agent, **GEORGE HILTZIK,** for keeping me employed, and his wife, **LINDA,** for making sure that George keeps working. ★ All of my friends, partners, and coworkers who touch my personal or professional life nearly every day, including **MATTHEW HILTZIK, JOSH RAFFEL, JON HUNTSMAN, PAT GRAY, DUANE WARD, STEVE SCHEFFER, GEORGE LANGE, STEPHEN MOORE, M. RUSSELL BALLARD,** along with **ALLEN, CAM, AMY, MARY,** and the whole team at **ISDANER.** ★ Those who helped bring this book to life, including our amazing artist, **PAUL NUNN,** our incredible designer, **TIMOTHY SHANER,** and those at the **CONSTITUTIONAL SOURCES PROJECT,** including **HUGH CHERRY** and **ELEESHA TUCKER,** for their insights and advice. ★ **CITY BAKERY** (1898–2006) for making me understand at a very early age that hard work is the one ingredient you can't buy in a store. ★ **EVERYONE ELSE** whom I couldn't fit in this space . . . sorry, but brevity was never really my strong suit.

CONTENTS

HOW TO USE THIS BOOK

I hardly ever read instruction manuals. I mean, just put everything where it looks like it goes and call it a day. Who cares if there's a mountainous pile of nuts and bolts left over on the floor when you're done? That's what vacuums are for. But, if you'll bear with me for just a minute, there are a few quick things I want to mention before you dive into the book.

First, the title is *Arguing with Idiots*, and I know that implies—

"HEY, WAIT A SECOND! WHO ARE YOU CALLING AN IDIOT! I THOUGHT YOU WERE MR. COMMON SENSE, NON-PARTISAN, BOTH-PARTIES-STINK . . . NOW YOU THINK THAT ALL DEMOCRATS ARE IDIOTS?!"

Say hello to the real star of this book: our Idiot Friend.

As you start reading, you'll quickly notice that each chapter is formatted as an ongoing conversation between the idiot and me. [*Insert your joke about not being able to tell the difference here*]. The idiot's arguments will always appear in the same bold red font you see above, and my (winning) responses follow.

As to the idiot's suggestion that the title of this book somehow proves that I am a partisan-zombie . . . well, let's just say that anyone who makes that argument probably never got past the cover. In this book, "idiots" aren't defined by the way they vote, they're defined by the way they think. Sometimes that means a political activist with an agenda bigger than a brain, sometimes it means a well-intentioned person who's just a little misinformed, and sometimes it means the idiot is, well, me. (Wait until you read the chapter on home ownership. Apparently my 21.4 percent interest-only mortgage was *not* a "VIP deal" reserved only for television hosts.)

By the end of this book you'll hopefully realize that while not all Democrats are idiots, there are plenty of idiots who are Democrats—along with Republicans, Libertarians, Communists, Anarchists, and members of just about every other political party you can imagine. In other words, being an idiot has nothing to do with your party affiliation, it has to do with whether you are able to look *beyond* that affiliation and follow the facts, wherever they may lead.

Speaking of facts, they're the crux of this book. There are plenty of good debates to be had in America, but we often forget that opinions should end where facts begin. Unfortunately, that whole concept is still foreign to a lot of people, so we've included a list of sources at the end of the book. Feel free to consult it whenever you read a statistic, story, or quote that you can't believe is real . . . or just use it as wrapping paper for your Prius-driving cousin's next birthday present.

That's about it—enjoy the book! Oh, and if anyone knows what a "hex wrench" is, would you please give me a ring? I think mine is living in the belly of my Dyson.

IN DEFENSE OF CAPITALISM

Giving the Free Market a Fair Shake

"What I did, when I did it, was honest; now, through changed conditions, what I did may or may not be called honest. Politics demand, therefore, that I be brought to trial; but what is really being brought to trial is the system I represented."

—Samuel Insull, co-founder of Edison General Electric

IN 1881, a young English clerk named Samuel Insull sailed from England to America and took a low-paying job as a private secretary for a determined inventor named Thomas Edison. Insull worked hard, coming in before his boss in the morning and staying until long after Edison, who wasn't exactly lazy himself, had gone home at night.

Over time, Insull's hard work and loyalty did not go unnoticed. He was promoted several times, eventually winding up in charge of Edison's business affairs.

After twelve years absorbing as much knowledge as he could, Insull finally left to pursue his own American dream. He moved to Chicago, took out a personal loan for $250,000, and built the largest power plant in the world.

At the time, electricity was like private jets are today—grossly expensive and available only to those who don't spend much time worrying about their bank account. But Insull had a dream that electricity could be produced on a much larger scale and used by the masses. By developing revolutionary ideas, like variable pricing and inexpensive home wiring, he turned electricity from a luxury into a virtual commodity.

Before long, Insull's new company was servicing over ten million customers in 32 states and had a market value of over $3 billion (somewhere around $66 billion in today's dollars, which is about the size of Amazon.com and Kraft Foods, combined). Insull also benefited personally. At one point, his net worth was estimated to be $100 million. *Time* magazine even celebrated his success by putting him on their cover in 1929. He was a true American success story—a foreigner with virtually nothing to his name who had made it big through hard work and innovation.

Then the world changed.

As the Roaring Twenties morphed into the Great Depression, Insull's business struggled. The debt and equity he'd financed his company's growth with had become virtually worthless, leaving over a million middle-class Americans who'd invested in his stock in financial straits. The public outrage was palpable.

In the matter of a few short years Insull had gone from hero to villain; from the poster boy for everything great about American capitalism to the poster boy for everything wrong with it.

The government, seizing on the public's fury over their lost wealth, charged him with fraud, and though he was acquitted at trial, it didn't matter—the damage was done. Insull was the most hated man in America, the Dick Cheney of the 1930s—and all he'd done to deserve it was to build a remarkable company that, like so many others, suffered during the Depression.

In 1938, Samuel Insull, who'd fled America for France (oh the irony), died of a heart attack in a Paris subway station. He had eight cents in his pocket. It was a sad and lonely ending for a man who exemplified the American dream by bringing affordable electricity to millions.

Like O. J. Simpson, our free-market system seems to be put on trial at regular intervals. People love it until it stops working the way they think it should. Then it becomes the villain.

Wall Street was loved; then it was hated. Alan Greenspan was idolized; then he was demonized. People envied those who flew in private jets; then they despised them. It's amazing how quickly opinions can change, especially when people are looking to blame someone else for their problems.

> "Capitalism is leading humanity and the planet to extinction."
>
> —The Leaders of Bolivia, Cuba, Dominican Republic, Honduras, Nicaragua, and Venezuela

CELEBRITY GUEST IDEEOT

ADVENTURES in CAPITALISM
DECEMBER 12TH   BY BEN GLECK

LEMONADE 2¢

STEVIE OPENS UP A LEMONADE STAND IN FRONT OF HIS HOUSE.

The truth is that capitalism is neither good nor evil, it just is. Capitalism can't get you a job, a bigger house, or a better retirement—*you* have to do all of those things for yourself. But what capitalism *can* do is foster an environment where those with the will to succeed have a better chance of achieving their dreams.

Do hardworking people still fall through the cracks? Absolutely. Are there peaks and valleys as excesses in markets are worked out over time? No doubt. But I defy anyone to show me another system that has done as much to quickly raise the standard of living and quality of life of a country as capitalism has for America.

You can't, because it doesn't exist.

In 1949, someone who worked minimum wage over the summer would have enough money to buy the following items from that year's Sears' catalogue:

A Smith-Corona typewriter; Argus 21 35mm camera; Silvertone AM-FM table radio; and Silvertone 3-speed phonograph.

In 2009, that same person, working the same number of hours at minimum wage, would now be able to purchase:

ADVENTURES in CAPITALISM
JANUARY 27TH   BY BEN GLECK

HAVING OPENED HIS STAND IN DECEMBER, STEVIE'S SALES ARE NOT STRONG. HE GOES TO WASHINGTON TO LOBBY FOR A BAILOUT PACKAGE.

A Dell laptop computer; HP color ink printer, scanner, copier; Canon 8 megapixel digital camera; portable GPS system; 32" LCD HDTV television; 8GB iPod Nano; GE microwave; Haier refrigerator/freezer; Toshiba DVD/VCR combo; RCA home theater system; Uniden cordless phone; RCA AM/FM radio; Camcorder; Sony PlayStation 2; and about seven other things, but I think you get the point: Capitalism promotes innovation and competition—two ingredients necessary for producing things that get progressively better even as they also get progressively cheaper.

The truth is that a minimum-wage worker in America is still one of the wealthiest people in the world. Does that preclude us from trying to make things even better? Absolutely not—but those who favor throwing away the system that made us the envy of the world are either dangerously naive or they have an agenda. You can probably identify which group they belong to by whether they make idiotic arguments like . . .

Special Note for Academics and Crazy People:

When I refer to "capitalism" in this chapter, I'm talking about democratic capitalism—the kind America used to have. Yes, you can technically still have a capitalist economy under a socialist government—but when everyone is paying 85 percent in taxes, the whole "free-market" concept doesn't really work very well.

"YOUR PRECIOUS FREE-MARKET CAPITALISM HAS FAILED."

Capitalism hasn't failed, greed has failed.

Think about it like this: You're a doctor with 50 sick patients, all of whom have the exact same symptoms: 20 of your patients are women, the rest are men. Ten of your patients are Asian, 5 are Arab, 5 are Mexican, 5 are African-American, and the rest are Caucasian. They have varying hair colors and are all different heights and weights. Some smoke and drink, some do neither.

In other words, these fifty people seem to have nothing in common, yet they all have the same disease.

Look around the world right now—virtually every country is sick. Communists, socialists, capitalists, and everything in between, it doesn't matter—the global recession infected everyone. Yet we look at all of these countries, with all of their different styles of government and different views on economic freedom, and we come to one nonsensical conclusion: Capitalism has failed.

CRUISING PAST COMMUNISM

When Haitian refugees pile into rickety boats to flee their corrupt country, they bypass the glorious communist paradise of Cuba (53 miles away), the Turks & Caicos (110 miles), Jamaica (124 miles), and the Cayman Islands (440 miles). Instead, they head for Florida—523 miles away. Why? Do they love "early bird specials" and BINGO night that much? No—it's because the greedy, evil capitalists of America still ensure a far better quality of life than any benevolent dictator.

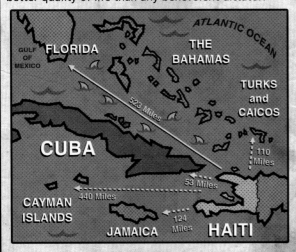

How can that be possible? The only thing those countries have in common is that they all fell victim to the idea that returns could be had without risk. Or, to put it another way, they all succumbed to greed.

If you could trace the economic crisis back to one seminal event, you'd probably point the finger at the collapse of the U.S. housing market. But was that collapse triggered by a failure of capitalism, or by an abuse of it by the government?

Under true free-market capitalism, the government would have no involvement in homeownership whatsoever. They wouldn't encourage it through artificially low interest rates, Fannie and Freddie, tax breaks, or a "Community Reinvestment Act," but they wouldn't discourage it either. Rates would be set by market participants, based on risk, reward, and a clear understanding that making bad loans would result in bankruptcy.

But we've done the *complete opposite* of that. The housing market is manipulated by the government every step of the way. So while some may argue that we need more regulation to prevent these future "excesses," I would argue that it's the existing regulations that created those excesses in the first place. In other words, what has failed isn't the idea of free markets, it's the idea that a market *can* be free when it's run by an increasingly activist government.

"SURE, IT'S ALWAYS THE GOVERNMENT'S FAULT. LET'S PLAY YOUR LITTLE GAME AND GET THE GOVERNMENT OUT OF EVERYTHING—WHO WILL HELP THE POOR? WE HAVE AN OBLIGATION TO TAKE CARE OF OUR WEAKEST, AND ONLY THE GOVERNMENT CAN FILL THAT ROLE."

Great, we (kind of) agree on something! "We" do have an obligation to help . . . but I think I have a different definition of "we" than you do.

The kind of capitalism that has failed is "soulless capitalism," because success without compassion results in greed and excess—and we had plenty of both. But that soullessness didn't come out of nowhere, it was bred by a government that continually tries to step in to do the jobs that individual Americans should be responsible for.

We have never solved problems efficiently from the top down; we solve them from the bottom up. In countries with strong central governments, the people with the money and power are the politicians instead of the businessmen. Are those politicians selfless and charitable? Of course not, they're greedy and corrupt—and the poor are even worse off than they are here.

My point is that capitalism itself is just a vehicle—we're the drivers. Any economic system will inevitably fail if individuals stop caring about the welfare of others. But which economic system is more likely to drive people out of poverty, one that cherishes the slogan "from rags to riches" or one that aims to help the poor via government bureaucracy? If you're struggling to answer that, consider what happened in the aftermath of Hurricane Katrina.

WHO SAID IT?

Sometimes it's scary to think that things have become so twisted that you could reasonably attribute a quote to either a sitting U.S. senator or an America-hating socialist. See if you can figure out who said the following and, if you find it challenging, think about what that means for how immune we've become to attacks on capitalism.

"It's impossible that capitalism can regulate the monster that is the world financial system, it's impossible. Capitalism needs to go down. It has to end."

❏ A. Gordon Brown
❏ B. Hugo Chavez
❏ C. Dmitry Medvedev
❏ D. Bernie Sanders
❏ E. Nicolas Sarkozy

Answer: B. Hugo Chavez, April 3, 2009

Less than one month after the hurricane, private donations surpassed the $1 billion mark, most of which went to private aid organizations that quickly provided relief. Meanwhile, FEMA handed out $6.3 billion in taxpayer money, with nearly a quarter of that going to scammers. According to a GAO report, FEMA gave cash to inmates, sent checks to people who said they lived in cemeteries or post office boxes, and "reimbursed" people for rent even though they were living in hotels that were already being paid for by FEMA.

Oh, and remember those FEMA debit cards? Well, according to the GAO, it turns out they were occasionally used for purchases that (prepare yourself for government-speak) "did not appear to meet legitimate disaster needs." In other words, people spent money meant for food and shelter on jewelry, travel, and porn.

PROFITS=PROGRESS

In January 2006, New Orleans mayor Ray Nagin announced 314 new public projects as part of his rebuilding effort after Katrina. Over two and a half years later, just six of them were complete. Conversely, Wal-Mart had 126 of their stores damaged in the hurricane; 110 of them were up and running within ten days.

Just for good measure, FEMA also reportedly *lost* 381 debit cards worth $762,000.

For some reason, we've become accustomed to the idea that the government must always come to the aid of everyone—but it hasn't always been that way. Those in need used to rely on each other for help.

In 1887, Congress passed a bill appropriating money to Texas farmers who were suffering through a catastrophic drought. These days, that funding would not only be authorized, it would probably be done so under an emergency program that gave more money to the farmers than they ever dreamed of. But not in 1887. Not with Grover Cleveland as president.

Here's how he answered Congress' request:

COUNTING DOWN THE FRAUD

Here are my top five favorite fraudulent purchases using FEMA debit cards:

5 **Vendor:** Hooters; San Antonio, TX
Transaction: *Alcohol, including a $200 bottle of Dom Perignon*
Amount: $300

4 **Vendor:** Vacation Express; Atlanta, GA
Transaction: *All-inclusive 1-week Caribbean vacation resort in Punta Cana, Dominican Republic*
Amount: $2,200

3 **Vendor:** The Pleasure Zone; Houston, TX
Transaction: *Adult erotica products*
Amount: $400

2 **Vendor:** Mark Lipkin; Houston, TX
Transaction: *Divorce lawyer services*
Amount: $1,000

1 **Vendor:** Legends; Houston, TX
Transaction: *Gentleman's club*
Amount: $600

By the way, would you be surprised if the same person who used his card at the strip club and "pleasure zone" also used it for the divorce attorney?

"*I feel obliged to withhold my approval of the plan, as proposed by this bill, to indulge a benevolent and charitable sentiment through the appropriation of public funds for that purpose. I can find no warrant for such an appropriation in the Constitution, and I do not believe that the power and duty of the General Government ought to be extended to the relief of individual suffering*

The right government policies can end poverty!

In 1964 we declared a "War on Poverty."

In 1968 13% of Americans were poor.

From 1968 to 1980 we increased social welfare payments by 400%.

In 1980 13% of Americans were poor.

which is in no manner properly related to the public service or benefit. A prevalent tendency to disregard the limited mission of this power and duty should, I think, be steadfastly resisted, to the end that the lesson should be constantly enforced that though **the people support the Government the Government should not support the people.***"*

Time out. Maybe you need to pause and catch your breath. Go get a glass of water if you need to, and then read that paragraph again. When you're finished, read the rest of his response:

"The friendliness and charity of our countrymen can always be relied upon to relieve their fellow-citizens in misfortune. This has been repeatedly and quite lately demonstrated. Federal aid in such cases encourages the expectation of paternal care on the part of the Government and weakens the sturdiness of our national character, while it prevents the indulgence among our people of that kindly sentiment and conduct which strengthens the bonds of a common brotherhood."

Cleveland vetoed three times more bills than all of his predecessors . . . *combined.*

Wow. Even more impressive was that Cleveland (who was a Democrat!) turned out to be a hundred percent right. Those "fellow-citizens" he put so much trust in donated ten times more money to those farmers than the amount the president had vetoed, once again proving that when individuals personally sacrifice to help each other, it not only makes us better people, it makes us a better country. It forces us to notice need instead of simply hiring corrupt politicians to notice it only when they can exploit, publicize, or politicize it.

Unfortunately, Cleveland's unwavering belief in the individual didn't last long. It was squashed just a few years after his second term when progressive Republican Teddy Roosevelt took over and said idiotic things like: "Every man holds his property subject to the general right of the community to regulate its use to whatever degree the public welfare may require it." (See the "U. S. Presidents" chapter for a lot more on Teddy.)

It just goes to show you that the "R" and the "D" are meaningless—what really matters is whether someone believes in the spirit and unending compassion of the individual, or instead in the destructive power of the collective.

A.D.D. Moment

After reading about his stand for the Constitution and small government, I suddenly became very interested in Mr. Cleveland. Turns out, you didn't want to mess with him when it came to federal money. Time after time President Cleveland turned down seemingly small, harmless requests from people looking for federal handouts. Even better, his denials almost always came with a lecture—like this tongue-lashing he doled out to some poor sap trying to get a new post office built in his town:

> "The care and protection which the Government owes to the people do not embrace the grant of public buildings to decorate thriving and prosperous cities and villages, nor should such buildings be erected upon any principle of fair distribution among localities. The Government is not an almoner of gifts among the people, but an instrumentality by which the people's affairs should be conducted upon business principles, regulated by the public needs."

Here's the definition of "Almoner": *A church officer in charge of distributing the congregation's tithes to the needy.* So, if I may translate, the President was saying that the government is not in charge of redistributing taxpayer money to the poor. Geez, imagine if *Countdown with Keith Olbermann* existed back then? Bill O'Reilly and I would have had a heck of a time beating out Grover for "Worst Person in the World" every night.

ADVENTURES in CAPITALISM
JANUARY 28TH   BY BEN GLECK

SENATOR BILLINGS EXPRESSES SYMPATHY FOR STEVIE. "I LOVE CHILDREN," THE SENATOR EXCLAIMS, "AND THAT'S WHY WE CANNOT ALLOW STEVIE TO FAIL."

"WE NEED A NEW KIND OF CAPITALISM, ONE WHERE THE GOVERNMENT HAS MORE CONTROL."

Thanks for buying the book, Stalin. Actually, if you agree with that statement, your views are closer to those of French President Nicolas Sarkozy than those of Stalin. In January 2009, while hosting a two-day economic conference titled "New World, New Capitalism," Sarkozy said that "in capitalism of the 21st century, there is room for the state."

Now, I'm not exactly sure when America started taking advice on capitalism from socialist France—but plenty of people seem to be listening anyway. From German Chancellor Angela Merkel (If governments "are not in a position to show that we can create a social order for the world in which such crises do not take place then we'll face stronger questions as to whether this is really the right economic system"), to Alan Greenspan ("It may be necessary to temporarily nationalize some banks in order to facilitate a swift and orderly restructuring"), to *Newsweek* magazine's cover ("We Are All Socialists Now"), there seems to be no shortage of voices begging the government to take more control over private markets.

And that's exactly why we should ignore them all. It's easy to get caught up in the headlines and make decisions based on emotion, but it's much harder to objectively look at the decades of evidence that conclusively prove that the state runs things only one way: right into the ground.

The reason why combining the government with private industry always fails is simple: their motives are completely different. Private companies exist to create wealth, the government exists (at least in theory) to provide protections critical to life, liberty, and the pursuit of happiness. Private companies closely manage expenses and ensure every dollar has a return; the government attempts to spend every dollar it's given and measures returns in campaign donations and polling data.

Their constituencies are also different: Corporations serve shareholders and customers; the government (again, at least in theory) serves taxpayers, which means they have to serve politicians, special-interest groups, and the established bureaucracy first.

The incentive to earn a profit goes hand in hand with the ability to operate efficiently and effectively. Take one away and the other will vanish faster than the taxpayer dollars that are continually wasted trying to overcome the simple rules of economics.

Here are four examples of how a few high-profile public/private partnerships have played out in real life:

1 FANNIE MAE & FREDDIE MAC

Fannie Mae was started by FDR in 1938 with a billion dollars and a mission: to buy up mortgages from private lenders so that those banks would have more capital to

You Know You're Turning Socialist When . . .

Sweden, a country internationally known for its cradle-to-grave social programs (free health care, free education, up to 80 percent of your pay for unemployment compensation—and massive tax rates), refuses to do something our government already has: bail out automakers. Responding to the difficult situation their car company, Saab, found itself in, the Swedish enterprise minister said, "The Swedish state is not prepared to own car factories." Ouch.

THE GOVERNMENT "SUGGESTS" THAT FIVE CENTS IS A MORE FAIR PRICE FOR LEMONADE. STEVIE ALSO AGREES TO ACCEPT FOOD STAMPS AND MAKE HIS STAND ADA COMPLIANT.

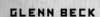

lend. It worked. By 1968 Fannie's loan portfolio had grown so large that it was weighing down the federal budget. So, our politicians did what they always do when faced with something they don't like: They hid it.

President Johnson turned Fannie into a quasi-governmental corporation that would be publicly traded. That allowed him to take Fannie's debt off the government's books, an idea that worked so well they used it to form Freddie Mac two years later.

Unfortunately, there was one big problem: Given their history, size, and importance in the mortgage market, virtually everyone knew the government wouldn't let them fail. That not only gave Fannie and Freddie an unfair advantage over their competition, it also gave them access to things like guaranteed lines of credit and exemption from state and local taxes.

We all know how this story ends. The so-called implicit government guarantee turned into a very explicit one that resulted in the government seizing control of the two companies in September 2008. It also resulted in the $5 trillion in mortgage liabilities they'd racked up moving right back onto the very same books politicians removed them from in the first place.

> ## WHO SAID IT?
>
> "The interaction between government and business will change forever. In a reset economy, the government will be a regulator; and also an industry policy champion, a financier, and a key partner."
>
> ❏ A. Hugo Chavez
> ❏ B. Jeffrey Immelt
> ❏ C. Dmitry Medvedev
> ❏ D. Timothy Geithner
> ❏ E. Nicolas Sarkozy
>
> Answer: B. Jeffrey Immelt, CEO of General Electric

2 AMTRAK

Congress created Amtrak in 1970 (are you starting to detect a trend here?) as a for-profit corporation. They've lost money every single year since.

Despite receiving over $30 billion in federal subsidies (not including another $1.3 billion that they picked up as part of the 2009 stimulus bill), Amtrak has never quite figured out how to fulfill their politically mandated mission *and* make a profit. So they've done neither.

I realize that I'm no choo-choo-train expert, but I am a thinker, so let me take a stab

---

A REGULAR JOE

It's likely that when Joe Biden used to take Amtrak to work he was given a reserved seat in first class. If so, he and other celebrities are the only ones who get that privilege. Yes, despite having fully reserved trains in which Amtrak knows exactly who's getting on and off at each stop, they refuse to assign seats, even for first class.

That moronic policy leads to something that those of us who travel via Penn Station in New York City like to call "The Running of the Idiots" whereby hundreds of nicely dressed businessmen claw past bewildered tourists with the hope of getting a precious seat on an arriving train.

And Amtrak wonders why they can't turn a profit.

---

at fixing Amtrak's problems: First, some of their lines require massive government subsidies because the costs simply don't justify the ridership. For example, the Sunset Limited, which runs from Los Angeles to New Orleans, requires somewhere in the area of $466 in government subsidies for every paying customer. Now, again, I'm a self-educated guy . . . but if that were *my* business and *my* money on the line (oh, wait, it IS) then I might take one look at the old annual report and think to myself, *Huh, I bet if we stopped operating that line and instead moved the trains to a line with, you know, ACTUAL PASSENGERS, we could make a little more money.*

But that kind of common sense doesn't go over well at Amtrak. Their former chief executive, David Gunn, actually warned Congress that they shouldn't be fooled into thinking that the decisions were so black and white. "Do not be misled," Gunn said, "by those who quote huge per-passenger losses on certain routes. Most would conclude that by simply cutting the [Sunset Limited] train you would save tens of millions of dollars." But the actual savings, according to Gunn? "Less than $15 million."

Oh my gosh, *only* $15 million a year—what was I thinking? Why would we even bother closing a route that costs taxpayers *only* $15 million every year?

Of course, while that kind of logic may explain why Mr. Gunn was fired by Amtrak seven months later, it can't explain why I can still go onto the Amtrak.com website and book myself a seat on the Sunset Limited for $133.

And that brings me to Amtrak's second big problem: Pricing is dictated by politics. The Sunset Limited takes 47.5 hours to make the trip from L.A. to The Big Easy. Does anyone else see a problem with charging $133 for 47.5 hours? Here's a hint: That's a rate of $2.80 per hour!

THE AMTRAK RECIPE
Amtrak's problem is that they were created with a recipe straight from hell. Here's how you can re-create it in your very own home.

(Recipe courtesy of the U.S. Congress and Rachael Ray.)

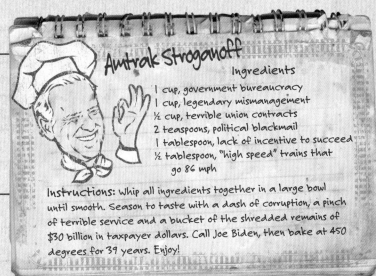

Amtrak Stroganoff

Ingredients

1 cup, government bureaucracy
1 cup, legendary mismanagement
½ cup, terrible union contracts
2 teaspoons, political blackmail
1 tablespoon, lack of incentive to succeed
½ tablespoon, "high speed" trains that go 86 mph

Instructions: Whip all ingredients together in a large bowl until smooth. Season to taste with a dash of corruption, a pinch of terrible service and a bucket of the shredded remains of $30 billion in taxpayer dollars. Call Joe Biden, then bake at 450 degrees for 39 years. Enjoy!

The IRS figures the cost of *driving* one mile at fifty-five cents. So, figuring that you can drive 65 miles per hour in most places, the cost to drive for an hour is about $36—over twelve times more than the cost per mile that Amtrak is charging for this route.

The only reason the Sunset Limited route is still in existence is politics. Amtrak needs subsidies to stay in business, those subsidies have to be approved by Congress; therefore, Amtrak needs to keep certain politicians happy. They can't do that with heavy discounts on their delicious café-car microwave pizzas, so they do it with concessions and favors (like, for instance, keeping a money-losing route open in exchange for votes from the politicians who represent the districts that the train runs through).

Some might argue that that's actually a good thing—America *needs* intercity rail service (even the money-losing kind) and the government is the only entity that can provide it. Fine—but then let's have that debate; let's talk about nationalizing Amtrak and changing its mission. Until then, we're just kidding ourselves that a company reliant on the government for survival can ever produce a profit.

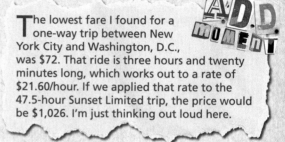

The lowest fare I found for a one-way trip between New York City and Washington, D.C., was $72. That ride is three hours and twenty minutes long, which works out to a rate of $21.60/hour. If we applied that rate to the 47.5-hour Sunset Limited trip, the price would be $1,026. I'm just thinking out loud here.

One More Reason Why Amtrak Stinks

Many airlines offer live satellite television, on-demand movies, music, and interactive games. In addition, most are now also implementing Wi-Fi internet service. Those planes fly 500 mph over 30,000 feet in the air. Meanwhile, Amtrak, which runs on the ground at blinding speeds averaging 70 mph, can't seem to figure out how to offer *any* of those perks.

ADVENTURES in CAPITALISM
JULY 19TH   BY BEN GLECK

STEVIE CLOSES THE STAND FROM JUNE THROUGH SEPTEMBER IN ORDER TO FOCUS ON COMPLETING THE NECESSARY GOVERNMENT FORMS.

3 CITIGROUP

In 2008, Citigroup, along with just about every other major bank in the country, opposed the idea of "cram downs" which would give bankruptcy judges the discretion to modify a borrower's loan. But, on January 7, 2009, news broke that Citigroup had changed their mind—they would support cram-down legislation after all.

Why the one-eighty? I can give you 40 billion good reasons. That, of course, is how much money Citi had taken in federal bailouts at the time they "changed their mind."

So why should you care about any of this? Because when private companies start making decisions based on what's best for their political relationships instead of what's best for their shareholders, we're in big, big trouble. Cram downs are a terrible, awful thing for the banking industry. After all, if some judge can rewrite the terms of a contract, why would a bank ever want to give out another mortgage?

Citigroup's support of this idea means they are acknowledging that their relationship with politicians is more important than their profits. If you're a fan of capitalism, that's a *very* scary prospect.

4 THE POSTAL SERVICE

This might seem like an odd example, but it's actually a great study in how government meddling can prevent an organization from ever reaching its full potential.

In 1971, the "Post Office Department" was turned into a quasi-governmental corporation called the "U.S. Postal Service." The USPS is run by a board of eleven, with nine of those people appointed by the president (meaning they're not exactly independent of the political process).

There are other oddities, too. The USPS receives no government appropriations (good), but they have to adhere to a set of complex regulations that mandate each class of mail pay for itself (bad). They can borrow money by issuing debt (good), but all increases in mailing rates are decided by an independent body called the "Postal Rate Commission" (bad). They don't have to adhere to federal standards on employee pay (good), but they have a federally mandated monopoly on regular mail delivery (bad).

Here's what all of that has added up to: After being semi-privatized, the USPS recognized the need to update their antiquated systems. By issuing debt (and bypassing the ridiculous federal acquisitions process) they adopted bar-code readers and optical scanners that, by 1986, were responsible for processing 90 million pieces of mail each day. Think that would've happened if they were still a government agency?

But it wasn't all sunshine and lollipops. Remember those political appointees? Along with Congress, they wielded tremendous influence over the organization. By simply threatening to hold hearings on the Postal Reorganization Act (translation: "we'll make you a government agency again"), they could influence all major decisions made by the USPS.

In the mid-'70s, the USPS sought to take advantage of their "semi-autonomy" by closing underutilized post offices. Like a national retail chain with underperforming stores, they realized that they could close some locations

ADVENTURES in CAPITALISM
NOVEMBER 12TH   BY BEN GLECK

UNABLE TO SURVIVE, STEVIE HIRES A LOBBYIST AND RETURNS TO WASHINGTON. SENATOR BILLINGS AGREES TO HELP IF STEVIE AGREES TO A LIST OF CONCESSIONS, INCLUDING THE FORMATION OF LEMONADE LOCAL 104.

without impacting service. In fact, a GAO study calculated that they could save $100 million a year by closing 12,000 post offices, some of which served only a few people or were located absurdly close to other post offices.

But politicians liked that idea about as much as they like the idea of closing down a money-losing Amtrak line that runs through their district. To stop it, they amended the Postal Reorganization Act to prohibit the closings, stating that "the rural post office has always been a uniquely American institution" and that "service" is more of a priority than "profit."

A.D.D. MOMENT

New Zealand corporatized their postal service in 1987. As Cornell professor Richard Geddes notes, that change "led to improvements in efficiency, a 40 percent reduction in the system's workforce, a doubling in labor productivity, a decrease in the cost of sending a letter and a decrease in the price of a basic stamp." And they did it all without impacting service in either rural or urban communities.

In 1977 the USPS, under pressure to keep postal rates low, decided to suspend Saturday mail delivery. They calculated that it would save them $400 million a year and wouldn't adversely impact many businesses. In fact, polling indicated that most people *preferred* the loss of Saturday delivery to higher stamp prices. But Congress did not. The House passed a resolution opposing the change and the USPS dropped the idea, even though they knew their budget would suffer.

Being unable to execute either of those business strategies has cost the USPS at least $500 million a year (likely much more given inflation) for the last 30+ years. The result? The USPS lost $2.8 billion in fiscal year 2008 and expects to lose another $3 billion to $6 billion in 2009.

In early 2009, Postmaster General John Potter told Congress that the USPS is once again "facing losses of historic proportion. Our situation is critical." But their hands are tied. The Postal Accountability and Enhancement Act of 2006 mandated the USPS to fund its entire retiree health-benefit fund within ten years— something, as postal officials point out, that no other government agency or private company is required to do. They tried to resurrect the idea of five-day delivery again, but leading politicians with oversight of the USPS, like Senator Susan Collins and Congressman Jose Serrano, have both said they would oppose it. The Postal Service brought back the idea of closing facilities, but politicians don't like that either. (*You* try winning the next election after losing a few post offices in your district.)

That leaves the USPS without very many options. They can't

GOVERNMENT IS GREAT!

Why was Congress so concerned about losing Saturday delivery? The unions. While government agencies aren't allowed to unionize, the USPS is—and those union members were worried about layoffs that might occur if one day of delivery was cut. The unions pressured the politicians, the politicians pressured the USPS, and— poof!—an idea that might've gotten the USPS on secure financial footing was quickly dismissed.

WHAT'S IN STORE FOR AMERICAN BUSINESS

THE U.S. POSTAL SERVICE IS A "QUASI-GOVERNMENTAL AGENCY." WHAT'S THAT? GOOD QUESTION—BUT SEEING THAT OUR LEADERS SEEM TO WANT ALL BUSINESSES TO BE "QUASI-GOVERNMENTAL," IT MIGHT BE HELPFUL TO UNDERSTAND THAT ONCE THE POLITICIANS GET A SEAT AT THE TABLE THEY BRING ALONG A LOT OF UNINVITED GUESTS.

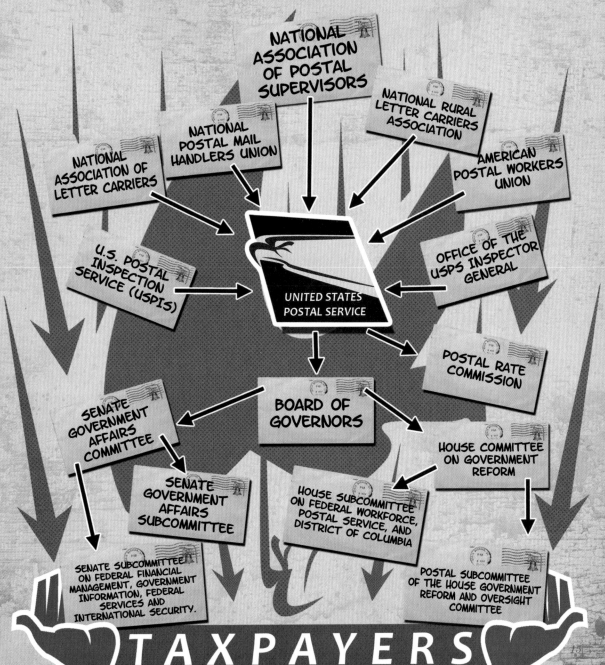

raise rates, close locations, cut employees, reform retirement benefits, or change their service. In fact, about the only thing they *can* do is continue to issue debt and accumulate losses—all of which will have to eventually be paid back by the constituency they serve: the taxpayers.

"SURE, THERE'S A LOT OF BUREAUCRACY IN GOVERNMENT, BUT IT CAN BE STREAMLINED."

The Federal Acquisition Regulation, which provides guidelines for the procedures that government employees must follow when spending taxpayer money, contains over 6,000 pages of rules, and that doesn't even include the addendums created by each individual agency. Why is it so complicated? Because, like our tax code, it serves various competing interests, all of whom spend lots of time and money to make sure the provisions favor them.

Take the 1956 Federal Aid Highway Act, which created the interstate highway system, for example. It appropriated $25 billion for the cause ($188 billion in today's dollars) and was, at the time, the largest public works project in American history.

The entire bill was just 28 pages long.

In 1991 the Federal Aid Highway Act was reauthorized with a bill called the Intermodal Surface Transportation Efficiency Act.

Just how "special" are "special-interest groups"? According to one expert, seven out of 10 Americans belong to an interest group and one in four belong to at least four of them. Best of all, that study was done 15 years ago! Does anyone think there are *fewer* people in interest groups now?

You have to love a country that goes from the "Federal Aid Highway Act" to the "Intermodal Surface Transportation Efficiency Act" yet still has the cojones to put the word "efficiency" in the title.

It was 293 pages long.

Why? Because over those three and a half decades people began to realize that these bills were really nothing more than blank slates upon which they could make their wildest (and most expensive) dreams come true.

James Wilson illustrates this perfectly in his book *Bureaucracy*:

"By 1991 we not only wanted to build more highways, we wanted to build them in ways that would aid mass transit, reduce air pollution, encourage the use of seat belts and motorcycle helmets, preserve historic sites, control erosion and outdoor advertising, use recycled rubber in making asphalt, buy iron and steel from U.S. manufacturers, define women as disadvantaged individuals, and protect Native American reservations—among other things."

Whenever you hear some-
one say that the govern-
ment should run health care
or our banks or . . . well, anything, really, then just read
them this list:

★ Up to 12 different agencies
are responsible for
administering more than
35 food-safety laws.

★ There are 541 clean air,
water, and waste programs
spread out over 29
agencies.

★ 40 different programs
aimed primarily at job
training are administered
by at least 7 different
federal agencies.

★ 50 different programs
to aid the homeless are
administered by at least 8
different federal agencies.

★ 9 different agencies
operate 27 teen-pregnancy
programs and 11 agencies
administer at least 90 early-
childhood programs.

Almost every one of those things was included in the bill because it was promoted by a special-interest group: environmental
groups, safety groups, industry groups, Indian groups, the list goes
on and on. With so many people competing for attention and dollars—and so much complexity added to even the simplest piece
of legislation—how could we ever expect government to run efficiently?

If you think your health-insurance plan is complicated now,
imagine what it would look like after going through months of committee hearings, backroom bargain-
ing sessions, and floor debates. You'd
probably end up being able to visit only
female, minority doctors who run zero-
emission offices located on Indian
reservations. Appointments would
probably cost four times more and you
still wouldn't be able to get any.

My point is that government is not
built for speed, efficiency, or productivity, the very things that make
American business competitive.
So while having a large, lum-
bering, lethargic government
might be the price a country
has to pay for success, allowing those qualities to leak out
into our business community
will undoubtedly mark the
end of that success.

There have been over
51,000 new regulations
put on the books since 1995.

AFTER THE UNION VOTES TO CLOSE
DOWN ON WEEKENDS AND HOLIDAYS,
BUSINESS SUFFERS EVEN MORE.
STEVIE TRIES RAISING HIS PRICES
AND OFFERING GOVERNMENT-
APPROVED SPECIALS IN A LAST-
DITCH EFFORT TO SURVIVE.

REORGANIZING OUR REORGANIZATIONS

It's not as though no one's ever noticed that our government runs about as well as Google (assuming, of course, that Google was being run by hundreds of morally ambivalent elected officials with no particular skill or talent other than getting reelected).

Throughout the twentieth century we've made at least *eleven* (mostly unsuccessful) major attempts at reorganizing/streamlining/modernizing/restructuring our government. A look at just a few of them is below, but my question is this: If we're allowed to reorganize/streamline/modernize/restructure our government so often, why can't we occasionally do the same thing for capitalism instead of declaring it worthless?

1905 "The Keep Commission," created by Teddy Roosevelt.

Roosevelt explained, "It yet remains true that there is a good deal of clumsiness of work, and, above all, the inevitable tendency toward mere bureaucratic methods against which every Government official should be perpetually on his guard."

It's amazing to think that in 1905, with a government infinitesimally smaller than we have today, we'd already created such a mess. (By the way, you might think that Teddy was an early Obama critic, since he once said, "I do not want you in any case to recommend a change simply for the sake of making a change; nothing could be more foolish"—but you'd be wrong. As a progressive, Teddy would've really admired Obama for his ability to get individuals to cede control of nearly every area of their lives to the government.)

1911 "President's Commission on Economy and Efficiency" (haha), created by Howard Taft (haha).

Roosevelt's commission apparently worked so well that we created another one just a few years later. The chairman explained, "After nearly two years of study of the problem, it is my belief that . . . $300,000,000 per annum could be saved if the Government were run on a businesslike basis."

Not surprisingly, Congress ignored the commission's main recommendations, which is too bad considering that $300 million would mean annual savings of $6.4 billion in today's dollars.

1964 & 1966 "Task Force on Government Reorganization," created by Lyndon Johnson.

Nothing like a government "task force" to strip out all of the bureaucracy! You can see how well this one worked by virtue of the fact that Johnson tried it again just two years later.

1969 "Advisory Council on Government Organization," created by Richard Nixon.

Step one of this plan probably should've been: "Find a president who will not be forced to resign."

1970s "Reorganization Project," created by Jimmy Carter.

Despite the super-creative name, all ten of Carter's reorganization attempts were approved by Congress, a first for any American president. It's just too bad that none of that legislation focused on a better way to rescue hostages or prevent oil shocks.

1982 "The Grace Commission," created by Ronald Reagan.

This commission was tasked to work "like tireless bloodhounds" looking for ways to get the government "off the backs" of the American people. Their report to President Reagan summarized their findings:

> *"We came up with 2,478 separate, distinct, and specific recommendations. . . . For practical purposes, these savings, if fully implemented, could virtually eliminate the reported deficit by the 1990s versus an alternative deficit of $10.2 trillion in the decade of the 1990s if no action is taken.*
>
> *"Equally important, the 2,478 cost-cutting, revenue-enhancing recommendations we have made can be achieved without raising taxes, without weakening America's needed defense build-up, and without in any way harming necessary social welfare programs."*

And? What happened? Hellooooo? Was anyone in Congress listening or were they all too busy looking for ways to spend more money?

I think it might be time for Grace Commission Part II . . . and I nominate Ted Nugent and Chuck Norris to head it up. I dare Congress to get in their way.

> **Bonus!** *We could rework some of those famous Chuck Norris facts to be "Nugent/Norris Committee Facts." For example: "There's no such thing as government bureaucrats— just a list of politicians Nugent and Norris have allowed to live."*

1993 "National Performance Review," aka "National Partnership for Reinventing Government," aka "REGO," created by Bill Clinton.

If the number of different names this effort had are any indication, efficiency was not a priority.

"WE JUST NEED TO CHANGE THINGS TEMPORARILY, UNTIL WE GET BACK ON OUR FEET."

In 1936, Johnstown, Pennsylvania, was hit by its second devastating flood in less than 50 years. The water rose 14 feet in some areas, over two dozen people were killed, and 77 buildings were destroyed—resulting in total property damage estimated at over $40 million.

To help the town rebuild, the government levied a temporary 10 percent tax on all alcohol sales across the state, with the proceeds earmarked to help flood victims get back on their feet.

It worked. A lot of money was raised and the town eventually began to recover.

Seventy-three years later, many of the Johnstown flood victims have long since died . . . but the Johnstown flood tax never did. In fact, over the years, greedy legislators have actually *raised* the rate (twice), bringing it to an absurd 18 percent.

Since 1936, Pennsylvania has collected over $15.4 billion from this tax. The 2009–10 Pennsylvania Governor's Executive Budget projects the tax will net about $283 million for the state next year alone, from a "temporary" tax originally imposed to pay for $40 million in damages.

The lesson should be obvious: Be very careful about giving the government any additional power or authority. No matter how temporary it may seem, it never is.

You Know You're Turning Socialist When . . .

The French president is less interested in redistributing wealth than the American one:

President Sarkozy, March 2009: "I was not elected to raise taxes [but] to reconcile France with the workplace and factory."

President Obama, February 2009: "The past eight years have discredited once and for all the philosophy of trickle-down economics—that tax breaks, income gains, and wealth creation among the wealthy eventually will work their way down to the middle class. In its place, we need economic opportunity to trickle up."

A.D.D. Moment

Since the president brought up "trickle-up" economics, I'd love for him to explain how that works in practice. I think about it as though our economy is a mountain. The top is covered in snow, which melts and results in fresh cold water trickling all the way down to a stream in the valley below. Villagers use that water to drink, cook, and bathe.

To keep life good for the villagers, trickle-down economics would say that we should focus our energy on keeping the snow pack at the top thick. More snow at the summit inevitably means more fresh water for the villagers, right? But trickle-up economics says that we should cut off the top of the mountain, bring the water down to the village, and watch as it magically defies gravity and somehow trickles back up to the top. I'm open to new ways of thinking, but . . . huh?

"YOU'RE OUT OF YOUR MIND. WE'RE CALLING FOR MORE REGULATION—THAT'S A LOT DIFFERENT THAN CALLING FOR NEW TAXES OR ANOTHER PATRIOT ACT."

I'm glad you brought up the Patriot Act, because it's a good example of how the government is always able to expand its power during times of crisis. Our country's under attack! (Please let us eavesdrop on phone calls . . .) Johnstown is flooded! (Please let us tax alcohol to help the victims . . .) Our financial system will collapse! (Please let us nationalize a few banks . . .) And on and on and on.

Despite all of the calls for "more regulation" (which is really just code language for bigger government), we should remember that, once put on the books, regulations are virtually impossible to get rid of. You've heard of archaic "blue laws" before (it's still illegal for anyone 16 or older to yell at an official at a sporting event in Massachusetts) but those same kinds of outdated regulations also apply to business.

In 2003, a dairy farmer named Hein Hettinga had a craaaaaaaaazy idea: he wanted to undercut his competitors' prices. Now, I know what you're thinking, "Glenn, that's not crazy . . . businesses lower their prices all the time!" Not in dairy farming they don't. See, dairy farming is still governed by a system of regulations set up in the 1930s to protect the thousands of small farmers who ran small dairies and made their living by selling raw milk.

But look around—is that really still how the industry operates? Dairy farms now often have thousands of cows and major corporations (Dean Foods is the largest with $12.5 billion in annual revenues) are involved in every step of the process. Despite that, regulations that guarantee a set price to farmers who participate in federally operated regional pools remain on the books.

Those regulations meant trouble for our friend Mr. Hettinga. His competition hated that he had driven down prices by twenty cents a gallon at Costco (which, according to a Costco senior vice president, was creating a snowball effect as compet-

> "I think we had quite enough capitalism in the last eight years and I think we need some regulation now."
>
> —Howard Dean

CELEBRITY GUEST IDEEOT

GOVERNMENT IS GREAT!

It's pretty bad when the government says that one of their own programs isn't really working, yet nothing changes. A recent USDA report found that "while producers are, as a whole, better off with dairy programs, these programs do raise consumer costs (modestly) and increase government expenditures." The watchdog group Citizens Against Government Waste was a little more specific; they estimated that dairy programs cost U.S. consumers over $1.5 billion a year.

itors were also forced to slash prices). So those competitors set out to shut Hettinga down.

With lobbyists being paid millions by Big Milk, politicians were more than happy to scratch each other's backs and crack down on Hettinga's tyrannous plan to save consumers money. Congress passed a bill forcing Hettinga to pay into a regional "pool", run by the federal government—the Senate voted via unanimous consent (which means there was no roll-call vote) and the House passed the bill by 13 votes. Representatives who voted against the measure found an email in their inbox the next morning expressing "disappointment on behalf of the members of the International Dairy Foods Association for your vote." It added a thinly veiled threat: "We will be letting our member companies and their employees know of the outcome."

ADVENTURES in CAPITALISM
JULY 2ND
BY BEN GLECK

LEMONADE 10¢ * 2 ice cube maximum

JIMMY'S JUICE

REALIZING THAT PEOPLE LIKE COLD DRINKS ON HOT DAYS, STEVIE'S NEIGHBOR JIMMY OPENS A LEMONADE STAND OF HIS OWN.

A.D.D. MOMENT

How much of a chance do you think Hettinga had when the two main politicians against him were Sen. Jon Kyl (who, ironically, is from Arizona, one of the states where consumers could've been saving money) and Devin Nunes, a congressman from California (another state where Hettinga was lowering milk prices)? Kyl received thousands of dollars in contributions from the chairman of Shamrock Farms, an Arizona dairy producer that competes against Hettinga, and nearly $15,000 from other Shamrock executives just a few weeks before the Senate took up the case. Nunes, meanwhile, was second only to President Bush in contributions received from dairy interests. Definitely seems like a fair fight, right?

Hettinga estimates that he has to pay up to $400,000 a month into an Arizona dairy-farming pool—a sum that, ironically, will go to help his competitors. In late 2006 he filed a lawsuit against the government, claiming that the new law was unconstitutional because it was a Bill of Attainder (see our Constitution chapter for more on that). The case was dismissed, but, in April 2009, a U.S. Court of Appeals reversed that decision, meaning that Hettinga still has a fighting chance.

"I had an awakening," Hettinga, who was born in the Netherlands, told the *Washington Post*. "It's not totally free enterprise in the United States." Unfortunately, he's right—and allowing our government to rush through more regulations now (that will likely still be on the books 70 years from now) will only make that lack of free enterprise across all industries even worse.

"POLITICIANS CAN LEARN TO RUN GOVERNMENT MORE LIKE A BUSINESS."

There are a lot of people who believe that our politicians can be trained to run government more efficiently. Those people are wrong. Politicians step into office with preconceived ideas about the purpose of government and those ideas are not easily changed. Convincing people who care about [insert favorite issues/programs/pet projects here] that their primary focus should be on *not* spending money is like trying to convince John Goodman to fill up on salad at the buffet—it's against everything they stand for.

One way to clearly see that is by looking at how multiple generations of politicians do with managing taxpayer money. We all know about the debacle in Washington, but those numbers are so big they don't even seem real anymore. Instead, consider my home state of Connecticut (the Constitution State—oh the irony!), where politicians have done a legendary job of running the "wealthiest state in union" right into the ground.

In 1991, Connecticut was facing a revenue shortfall of about $2.7 billion. Using that crisis (a crisis, of course, that *they created* by being fiscally irresponsible), Connecticut's governor pushed hard for a state income tax. After a long stalemate with the General Assembly, the bill eventually passed.

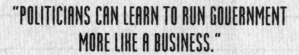

WHO SAID IT?

"We are interested in a new financial system based on justice. A real economic system."

- ❏ A. Hugo Chavez
- ❏ B. Timothy Geithner
- ❏ C. Dmitry Medvedev
- ❏ D. Mahmoud Ahmadinejad
- ❏ E. Dennis Kucinich

Answer: D. Mahmoud Ahmadinejad, April 6, 2009.

At the signing ceremony, Governor Lowell Weicker sounded optimistic. "When I sign this budget, Connecticut will be closing the book on its past and it'll be facing toward the future."

Now, 17 years later, we have a pretty good idea of what that future looks like: The income tax that was passed to close a $2.7 billion deficit has been raised several times and now brings in over $7.5 billion a year. Add in the $350 million a year that the state currently receives from Indian casinos, and Connecticut now collects nearly $8 billion more in revenue than it did in 1991.

Give any rational businessperson that kind of money

ADVENTURES in CAPITALISM
SEPTEMBER 3RD   BY BEN GLECK

THE END

UNABLE TO RENEGOTIATE HIS COLLECTIVE BARGAINING AGREEMENT WITH LOCAL 104, STEVIE CLOSED HIS STAND AND DECLARED BANKRUPTCY. DESPITE A FAILING BUSINESS AND NUMEROUS PERSONAL INCOME TAX ISSUES, STEVIE WAS QUICKLY CONFIRMED AS THE NEW U.S. TREASURY SECRETARY WHERE HE ENJOYS TELLING OTHER PEOPLE HOW BEST TO OPERATE THEIR BUSINESSES.

and profits would be a given . . . but the same rules don't apply to the government. Despite all of those extra billions, Connecticut is *still* facing massive deficits: $1.2 billion this year and *another* $6 billion to $8 billion over the next two years.

How could that possibly happen? Simple: the government *cannot be restrained.* Even if their intentions back in 1991 were good, things change. New politicians get voted in, old politicians find new donors—and "good intentions" get run through the shredder.

In Connecticut's case, out-of-control spending (surprise, surprise) was the culprit. In 1991, when the so-called crisis was happening, the state's total spending was about $7.6 billion. In 2008, total spending is projected to be $18.8 billion—an increase of 147 percent. To be fair, the $7.6 billion in 1991 dollars would translate to $11.4 billion today, but that still means the brainiacs in Hartford are spending 65 percent more than they were in 1991.

The point is that, like Oprah, government only knows how to get bigger. (Oops, guess an Oprah bookclub selection is out . . . and I was so close, too.) Try as they might to slim down, the natural order of things will always take over and ensure they grow larger than anyone ever thought possible. The only way to stop that, or at least slow it down, is by taking away their source of food: money and power.

A.D.D. MOMENT

As someone who lived in Connecticut in the '90s and again today, I can assure you that there hasn't been anywhere close to a 65-percent improvement in their schools, roads, or hospitals.

A TALE OF TWO COUNTRIES

In 1939, Finland and its neighbor to the south, Estonia, were identical in many ways. But in 1940, everything changed. The U.S.S.R. occupied Estonia and kept the small country under communist rule for the next fifty years. Finland, meanwhile, remained free.

Mart Laar, Estonia's former prime minister, described what communism did to his country:

"Look at what happened in this context during these fifty years and then you can understand how terrible the communist system really is. And it's not only in the economy. This is in all fields of life—the social structure, cultural standards, education, health care, or whatever. When you compare those two countries . . . then you will find what communism really means, and how bad it is. Our economy, our nature, and our environment were destroyed."

After the Soviets left in 1991, Estonia embraced capitalism, turning itself into a "Baltic Tiger" that experienced massive economic growth. They also did something that most so-called capitalist countries haven't done: They instituted a flat tax. Not right off the bat—they tried the whole "progressive" thing first, but they eventually realized that creating class warfare was not a way to leave the Soviet era in the past.

Estonians now pay a flat tax rate of 22 percent and, even better, it's scheduled to drop to 18 percent within a few years. It takes Estonians an average of just 10–15 minutes to file their returns online.

By 1994, just a few years free from communist rule, Estonia's life expectancy at birth was 72.6 years. Finland, just fifty miles away—but also fifty years ahead in medical advancements—had a life expectancy at birth of 75.9. But, once free and able to invest in their own health-care system, Estonia began to quickly pick up speed. In the 14 years from 1994 to 2008, Estonia gained 2.6 years in life expectancy, a rate of growth virtually identical to Finland's.

Another great measure of how communism thwarts improvements in almost all areas is the infant-mortality rate. By 1994, Estonia was experiencing 19.1 infant deaths for every thousand live births, compared to Finland's rate of 5.3. But now? Estonia has cut their number of infant deaths to 7.5 per thousand, a remarkable drop of 60 percent in just fourteen years.

Estonia has experienced other, non-health-care-related improvements as well:

★ In 1990, 20 percent of Estonia's workforce was clustered in the agriculture and forestry industries—not exactly the hallmark of a high-growth, first-world country. By 1999, they had diversified employment and cut the number of workers in agriculture and forestry almost in half.

★ In 1993, Estonia's GDP per capita was just $5,480—compared to $16,100 in Finland. By 2007, Estonia's GDP per capita had grown to $21,100, an annual compound growth rate of over 10 percent, far higher than Finland's annual growth rate of 5.8 percent over the same time period.

★ In 1993, Estonia had 25 telephones per 100 people, compared to 62 in Finland. By 2006 the numbers had shifted dramatically. Estonia had 41.4 main lines and 127 cellular phones for every hundred people. Both of those numbers surpassed Finland, and this is one reason why *The New York Times* called Estonia "a sort of Silicon Valley on the Baltic Sea."

Pretty remarkable accomplishments for a country that had Soviet tanks patrolling its streets just a decade earlier—and it all happened because markets became *less* regulated.

MY PAPA IS A SOCIALIST

My papa is a Socialist, my mamma, too, and I,
And if you'll wait a minute now, I'll tell the reason why;
I'm sure that when you understand, you certainly will see,
You'd better all be Socialists, and vote with pa and me.

You see this earth is long and wide, good things above, below,
And there are lots of people, too, who want to make things go;
Besides, we're all just quite alike, need food and clothes and rest,
And if we all were Socialists, we all would share earth's best.

But now John D. owns all the oil, most banks, and railroads, too,
And then a few own all the land, so what can poor folks do
But tramp and starve and beg for jobs, and work and work and work?
And all the wealth we make, but scraps, we give the wealthy shirk.

Now isn't every papa, most, the very biggest goose,
To give away most all he makes to men who don't produce?
So that a few rich families may all be living fine,
While all we weary working folks must suffer, want, and pine.

And then they do such foolish things, I often wonder why
They "strike" and lose their jobs, and let us freeze and starve and cry;
When, if all joined the Socialists, in four years more or five
We'd all be wealthy partners in the world's greatest working hive.

For if they'd stop to think, they'd see how easy 'twas to make,
Together, all we'd want to have, and what we'd make, we'd take;
So that the children, all alike, our papas, mammas, too,
Would all enjoy earth's happiness, as Socialists want all to.

So papa is a Socialist, mamma, we children, too;
We want to make all children rich and happy, too, don't you?
Good food and homes, nice shoes and clothes, we children want, don't you?
So all of us are Socialists; please, won't you be one too?

—From "Songs of Socialism" by Harvey P. Moyer, Co-operative Printing Co. (1906).

YOU HAVE TO LOVE HOW THE AUTHOR CONTINUALLY BASHES "THE RICH" WHILE ALSO PROMISING THE KIDS THAT SOCIALISM CAN MAKE THEM "WEALTHY" AND "RICH" AND HELP THEM BUY ALL SORTS OF NICE THINGS. BUT INSTEAD OF COMPLAINING ABOUT HOW THEY TARGET KIDS WITH THIS NONSENSE, MAYBE IT'S TIME WE JOIN THEM. HERE'S MY UPDATED VERSION OF THEIR LITTLE POEM . . .

My Papa Is a Capitalist

My papa is a Capitalist, my mamma, too, and I,
And if you'll wait a minute now, I'll tell the reason why;
I'm sure that when you understand, you certainly will see,
You'd better be a Capitalist, and vote with pa and me.

You see, we're very lucky to be living in a nation,
That knows rewarding hard work will encourage innovation.
For there are many people who, when offered an incentive,
Will use their brains and brawn to be amazingly inventive.

Our country's prospered like no other, based on a single notion,
That caused millions of people to board ships and cross the ocean.
What made so many immigrate and cross the churning sea?
The answer's really simple. Just one word: It's "Liberty."

The chance to live in freedom, where their dreams are not restrained,
The chance to pursue goals and know they can be obtained.
The promise of a better life drew, like moths to flame,
Millions upon millions who sought freedom, fortune, fame.

Look around the world and see the countries that have failed,
And you will find the reason is that hope had been curtailed.
If your future's been decided and your dreams have been ignored,
You've got no motive to succeed—because there's no reward.

But if you are enabled, placed in charge of your own fate,
The world can be your oyster. That's what makes this country great.
It's the nature of humanity to always improve our lot,
To have a bigger chicken in an even bigger pot.

So papa is a Capitalist, mamma and children too;
We're in control of our own lives. And happier, as are you.
The things we want we work hard for, so the things we lack are few.
So all of us are Capitalists; please, won't you be one too?

—From *Arguing with Idiots* by Glenn Beck (2009).

"THERE'S NO PROBLEM WITH GOVERNMENT GETTING BIGGER, WE JUST NEED TO EMBRACE IT. SURE, SOCIALISM MAY NOT HAVE THE GREATEST TRACK RECORD, BUT THAT'S ONLY BECAUSE IT'S NEVER IMPLEMENTED THE RIGHT WAY!"

Saying that socialism doesn't work is like saying that Blagojevich did a bad job as Illinois' governor—it's vastly understating just how dismal the results really are. In Venezuela, where socialist "reforms" have been under way for quite some time, the percentage of people living below the poverty line is still over 40 percent. That's some success story! In Laos, another socialist country, the rate is over 30 percent.

The people who would be least surprised by those statistics are our Founding Fathers. They knew that government *could* be good, but that, in practice, almost none of them ever were. Even governments that started out with good intentions eventually became too powerful and corrupt. They also knew that *people* were exactly the opposite—over time they usually did the right thing and made the right decisions. The result was a system of checks and balances that put significant limits on the size and power of government while simultaneously unleashing the power of the individual.

Ask a political-science nerd about what type of government Venezuela, Cuba, Laos, North Korea, China, or Vietnam have and you're likely to get a dissertation on the differences between countries with Marxist-Leninist ideologies and ones without. Whatever. The point is that this group of countries is, in practice, either socialist or communist—at least the way normal people think of it. And, no, I don't put myself in that group.

A.D.D. Moment

Unfortunately, we are now shredding that system faster than Enron employees shredded spreadsheets the day they were raided. When you confront a big-government advocate

LET'S MAKE A DEAL . . .

I take the state of Montana, and Senator Bernie Sanders, or some other avowed socialist, takes Massachusetts (sorry, you get Barney Frank and the Kennedys as well—that's non-negotiable). I institute the smallest possible government, minimal taxes, and let my people be creative and free. The socialists institute a huge government, tons of welfare programs, safety nets, unions, and publicly funded infrastructure projects—along with obscenely high taxes to pay for it all. Then we meet back in ten years and see which state is healthier, wealthier, better educated, and has less poverty and crime. If anyone wants to bet on the socialists, I am open for business.

about the consistent failure of socialism over and over and over again, what you'll usually hear back is something about how none of those countries ever did it right. In other words, their claim isn't that socialism failed, it's that the *implementation* of socialism failed.

That's a convenient little rebuttal, but it's also pretty ridiculous. The theory of "perfect socialism" is just that . . . a theory. To compare a theoretical, textbook version of a political system with a practical system that has proven itself for hundreds of years is completely unfair.

Yet "theory" is how supporters of these systems continually justify their losing positions. If only every person who makes over $1 million a year would give $50,000 to those who live in poverty . . . there would be no poverty. If only every coal plant were forced to shut down . . . there would be no global warming. If only . . .

Yeah, we get it—there's a perfect world in your head just waiting to bust out. Maybe you should go buy an island and start your own utopian Marxist micro-nation where songbirds chirp and lollipops dance. Oops—I almost forgot! . . . you can't buy an island because YOU HAVE NO MONEY. And *why* do you have no money? Because YOU SIT AT HOME THINKING ABOUT THIS CRAP.

My point is that if the perfect economic system worked just as well in the real world as it does in the textbooks, then we'd all be using it. We'd also all be very wealthy, very thin, have no need for an army, an education, or currency of any kind.

TEXTBOOK IDIOCY

Comparing "textbook" socialism to capitalism is unfair for another reason as well: The system of capitalism we're currently operating under is far removed from the way it was drawn up. I mentioned the housing market earlier as a great example of that, but so is the size of government.

In 1950, government spending was responsible for just 24 percent of our GDP. By 2008, that number had rocketed to over 37 percent and—hope you're sitting down—Goldman Sachs projects it to hit a catastrophic 83 percent by the end of the decade.

Consider this illustration, which is based on a sketch from *The 5,000 Year Leap* (a must-read book for anyone who cares about what our Founders really believed). It's a three-headed eagle, and it represents how our Founders originally set up our system of government.

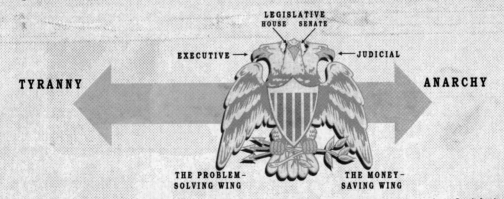

Each of the heads symbolizes a different branch of government: executive, legislative (which has two eyes—one for the House and one for the Senate), and judicial. The eagle also has two wings: a "problem-solving" wing and a "money-saving" wing. The problem-solving wing represents our compassion. We have to help the poor, the elderly, the sick, the victims of disasters, the repressed around the world, etc. The money-saving wing represents conservation. It understands that while we have to solve problems, we also have to conserve our resources for the future. It's important that those two ideals are represented by equal-sized wings, as they provide the balance necessary for the eagle to fly.

The entire eagle was also placed as close to anarchy as possible to underscore that while our Founders understood that government was necessary, they wanted it as limited as possible.

Now, here's an updated version of the Founders' Eagle:

You'll notice a few important changes.

First, both the executive and judicial heads have grown quite large and they're also trying to eat each other. The legislative branch, meanwhile, has shrunk and, just for good measure, is also now blindfolded—illustrating their inability to see how grotesque the system has become.

The problem-solving wing is now enormous, representing our desire to solve every problem, domestic and foreign, regardless of the cost. Conversely, the money-saving wing is now on fire since conserving for the future is the last thing on any politician's mind. You'll also notice that the entire eagle has also shifted on the scale—we are no longer bordering on anarchy, we're bordering on tyranny.

I would ask anyone who wants to argue that small-government, free-market capitalism has failed to take a good look at these two eagles first. Has the system our Founders set up for us really failed . . . or have we failed it?

"THEY MAY NOT BE PERFECT, BUT FRANCE IS DOING SOCIALISM RIGHT—WE SHOULD BE MORE LIKE THEM."

I can (and will) give you all sorts of stats and stories to prove that the French have created an unsustainable society, but the best evidence of all comes from an opinion column. Along with what this writer actually says, it's *where he says it* that's shocking: *The New York Times*.

> *"I lived for about a decade, on and off, in France and later moved to the United States. Nobody in their right mind would give up the manifold sensual, aesthetic and gastronomic pleasures offered by French* savoir-vivre *for the unrelenting battlefield of American ambition were it not for one thing: possibility.*
>
> *You know possibility when you breathe it. For an immigrant, it lies in the ease of American identity and the boundlessness of American horizons after the narrower confines of European nationhood and the stifling attentions of the European nanny state, which has often made it more attractive not to work than to work."*

The key word he used was "possibility" because it really sums up everything that capitalism is about. You stay at work an extra hour because of the *possibility* that your boss might notice and eventually promote you. You put your home on the line to start your own business because of the *possibility* that you might become the next Microsoft or Google. You spend your life savings to send your children to college because of the *possibility* that they will be presented with a life full of endless *possibilities*.

As the *Times* columnist said, France has lost that—and it's not hard to understand why. Archaic laws, senseless social programs, poor (but free) education, enclaves filled with disenfranchised immigrants and unemployed youths, and massive public debt have combined to make France a nice place to visit, but a pretty depressing place to live.

If anyone from France takes offense at this, I'm sorry—but sometimes the truth hurts. At least take solace in the fact that while your beloved country may already be too far gone to save, you could still stop us from suffering the same fate. Think of it as a down payment on your balance from World War II.

I talk a lot about how our government—to borrow a term from the great economist Thomas Sowell—can't think "beyond stage one." They try to solve problems with obvious solutions without thinking about the consequences of those solutions. But we didn't invent that kind of narrow, short-term thinking . . . France did.

France decided that the best way to keep their citizens working was to create all kinds of laws and regulations for employers to follow. Most of us know about their 35-hour work week and long summer vacations, but that's only the start. The number of rules that French companies have to follow in order to hire or fire someone would put the New York City Teachers' Union to shame.

But what France forgot was that for every action there is an equal *and opposite* reaction. The consequence of all those laws to prevent unemployment was massive unemployment, especially among the young. It's really just common sense—if you can hire and fire at will, you are much more likely to take a chance on new employees, especially young ones without much experience. But when "at will" instead turns into ironclad, virtually lifelong commitments, you're much more careful about whom you hire.

The best quote I've read in a while came from an *Economist* article about how the French seem to only embrace capitalism when it suits them:

> "(France has) . . . an archaic socialism that fails to understand, or at least to explain, that wealth needs to be created before it can be shared."

I hate to say it, but that simple lesson may also need to be explained to some Americans.

The numbers show that this is exactly what's happened as 23 percent of young people in France are unemployed. To fight that trend, France's former prime minister created *another* set of regulations, called the "first job contract." It gives employers the ability to hire anyone under 26 years old for what is essentially a two-year trial period. During that time the draconian state employment rules are loosened, enabling companies to take more chances.

Now, 64 percent of all French youths aged 15–24 take part in the temporary work program within a year of completing their education—but many of them hate the idea. Having grown up in a country where a job was always viewed as a right, they believe the "first job contract" program victimizes them and, as they say in their protests, "institutionalizes insecurity."

Maybe one reason why they say that is that—pardon my French—*they're not that smart.* After all, most students in France go to schools that are virtually free and have no restrictions on entry (including no minimum test scores or grade point average). In addition, teachers are government employees, which makes sense, considering that over 25 percent of all jobs in France are in the public sector.

The result of this wonderfully non-discriminatory, sunshine–and-lollipops approach to education is a drop-out rate of 40 percent, lecture halls that are bursting at the seams, universities without any interest in research, and the distinction of not even placing one school in the top 40 of the most recent worldwide rankings. France has only three schools in the top hundred.

Combining terrible educations with a government that acts like a countrywide HR department from hell does not set the French up for economic success. And it shows. While the government takes 44 percent of GDP in taxes every year (the euro-zone average is closer to 40 percent), it's not nearly enough. Someone has to pay for all the free education, health care, and short work weeks—and, right now, it's France's lenders. A government-commissioned report pointed out that, without drastic action, France's debt load will go from 66 percent of GDP today to 80 percent by 2010 to a catastrophic 100 percent in 2014.

Is America destined for the same fate? If we keep going the way we are, absolutely. For proof, just listen to the way a recent *Economist* article described the general attitude there:

"[In France] there is a lingering culture of suspicion of profit, and a demonisation of business leaders, encouraged by a mainstream left that still equates efficiency with injustice."

Now ask yourself: Is America moving toward that way of thinking, with all of its laws and feel-good regulations, or away from it?

While the top school in France (University of Paris) checks in at number 42 on the list, the greedy, discriminatory, selfish capitalists here in the U.S. have managed to place 17 different schools in the top 20. Sure, Harvard and Yale are there, but schools like Rockefeller University (#32) and the publicly funded University of Maryland (#37) also beat out the Frenchie-frenchmen.

THE SECOND AMENDMENT

Ammunition to Defend Your Rights

"A well regulated Militia, being necessary to the security of a free State, the right of the people to keep and bear Arms, shall not be infringed."

NOTHING illustrates the battle between the good forces of individual liberty and the destructive, idiotic forces of collectivism better than the ongoing battle over the meaning of those 27 little words.

Normal people understand the natural existence of the right to bear arms, the plain language guaranteeing us that right, and the clearly documented history that led to its enshrinement in the Bill of Rights. But those who distrust individual freedoms in favor of an all-powerful government are horrified by the idea that one person can possess enough power to lawfully resist, with force, unacceptable intrusions into his or her life.

Perhaps some of those opposed to the individual right to bear arms understand that, as King George once discovered, an armed populace is a populace that will not be pushed around. Perhaps they even understand Thomas Jefferson's famous observation (or was it a warning?):

"When governments fear the people, there is liberty. When the people fear the government, there is tyranny."

Whatever the reason, these people seem to appreciate, if not respect, the role of the Second Amendment in protecting our way of life. Successfully weaken it, and it's only a matter of time before all of our other rights begin to fall away, like dominoes.

That's why so many of the debates over the Second Amendment aren't really about guns at all; they're about big versus small government, rights versus responsibilities, and, ultimately, about where the balance of power in America should reside: with politicians or with the people. That's also why it's so imperative that all Americans, gun lovers or not, understand their Second Amendment right well enough to fight for it against idiots who say things like . . .

"IT'S CLEAR THAT THE RIGHT TO BEAR ARMS ONLY EXISTS BECAUSE 'A WELL-REGULATED MILITIA [IS] NECESSARY TO THE SECURITY OF A FREE STATE.' THIS RIGHT WAS ABOUT MILITIAS, NOT INDIVIDUALS."

They sure don't write laws the way they used to. Back in the eighteenth century, preambles like the one we see in the Second Amendment's militia clause were actually quite common. Who knows, maybe the politicians were a little more modest back then and believed they had to offer explanations for the laws being handed down—but, whatever the reason, the rules of English grammar haven't changed.

A.D.D. MOMENT

The argument that the militia clause somehow defines, narrows, or transforms the operative part of the right-securing language ("the right of the people to keep and bear arms shall not be infringed") proves only the sad state of modern education in America.

Just because the Second Amendment happens to have a preamble doesn't diminish the fact that the granting of this right *to the people* is perfectly clear. When our Founders intended to specifically refer to the militia or the states, guess what—*they used those words*. Look at the Tenth Amendment, for instance: "The powers not delegated to the United States by the Constitution, nor prohibited by it to the States, are *reserved to the States* respectively, or to the people." Pretty clear, right?

It becomes even more clear when you look at other instances where the Founders used the language "the right of the people." Like in the First Amendment, for example: "*the right of the people* peaceably to assemble." Or, in the Fourth Amendment: "*the right of the people* to be secure . . . against unreasonable searches and seizures."

The first clause of the Second Amendment, which discusses the necessity of a well-

Who's Making This Argument?

"In a radical break from 70 years of Supreme Court precedent, Justice Antonin Scalia, writing for the majority, declared that the Second Amendment guarantees individuals the right to bear arms for nonmilitary uses, even though the amendment clearly links the right to service in a 'militia.'"

—The New York Times Editorial Board, June 27, 2008

regulated militia, is a reason *why* the people have the right to arms. It's a perfectly good and sufficient reason, but it's not the *only* reason, and it doesn't change who has the right.

Consider this sentence:

"Being a fisherman, Joe needs to buy a boat."

Does that mean that Joe should buy a boat *only* if he fishes for a living? What if Joe also likes to water ski?

Being a fisherman is a great reason for getting a boat, but it isn't the only reason and, in fact, it doesn't even have to be true. What if Joe is actually allergic to fish? What if Joe is an accountant who happens to enjoy sailing on the weekends? What if Joe is a strict vegan, but loves to scuba dive? Would the above sentence preclude Joe from buying a boat in any of those situations?

Likewise, the militia clause of the Second Amendment doesn't *have* to be true for the rest of the statement to stand. What if a well-regulated militia is *not* necessary to the security of a free state? We are pretty secure and still (kind of) free these days, but we don't have a functioning state-militia system. Perhaps the Framers were wrong—maybe the only thing necessary to security is a nuclear-defensive umbrella, a strong navy, and just plain good luck.

"No free man shall ever be debarred the use of arms."

—Thomas Jefferson

Does a constitutional right go away simply because one of its perceived benefits no longer exists? Of course not—no individual right depends on the government's actions. That's why the Declaration of Independence made clear that the rights we were fighting for were those we were "endowed [with] by our creator" instead of some elected bureaucrat.

Judges and lawyers have understood that the flowery, explanatory language of the sort we see at the outset of the Second Amendment is of little real value. That's why, for hundreds of years, such language has been widely ignored by courts—unless absolutely necessary to explain the operative text.

In announcing one influential English decision in 1716 (remember, they still used common sense back then), the judge called the idea that a preamble can limit or redefine the operative text "a ridiculous notion." The reporter noting the decision even wrote that "his Lordship" rendered his decision "with some heat."

A.D.D. MOMENT

I wonder if any of our current reporters have used the term "his Lordship" lately?

Over a hundred years later, the interpretations were still the same. A mid-nineteenth-century legal treatise explained, "When the words of the enacting clause are clear and positive, recourse must not be had to the preamble." And, in this century, modern authorities declared

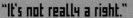

CELEBRITY Guest Ideeot

that "the preamble can neither limit nor extend the meaning of a statute which is clear. Similarly, it cannot be used to create doubt or uncertainty."

If you're still not convinced, consider that the first Congress, which approved the Second Amendment, also reenacted the Northwest Ordinance, which laid out the settlement and exploration of what then passed for the frontier west. That law declared:

"Religion, morality, and knowledge, being necessary to good government and the happiness of mankind, schools and the means of education shall forever be encouraged."

Many gun-grabbing idiots would disagree that religion, morality, and knowledge are necessary for good government, so does that mean that we can now do away with all public schools in the states of the old Northwest Territory (Ohio, Michigan, Illinois, Indiana, and Wisconsin)?

Even our original Constitution contains a Second Amendment–style preamble. Congress has the power "to promote the Progress of Science and the useful Arts," by enacting copyright and patent laws. Does that mean that every copyrighted work or patented invention *must* promote scientific progress and useful arts? Suppose Al Gore's next book advocates a radical back-to-nature lifestyle that abandons the use of cars, planes, and electric power—things that would all be against scientific progress. Would Gore still be entitled to copyright it? Of course he would. Why? Because courts don't limit copyright and patent protection only to things that might "promote the Progress of Science and the Useful Arts."

In a very similar way, "the right of the people" as stated in the Second Amendment doesn't depend on, and is not defined by, those who take advantage of it *only* in the context of a militia.

A.D.D. MOMENT

Hang on a second . . . no public schools? Maybe they're onto something with this whole "preamble" thing after all.

WHO NEEDS A GUN?

STICK™   **Price: $7.95**

Keep criminals at bay the way nature intended . . . with Stick™! Made of all-natural wood. Easily gripped with right or left hand. Best used in a threatening manner while making threatening remarks.

Caution: Do not use if opponent is armed with anything.

"BUT I'VE HEARD LINGUISTS SAY THAT THE PLACEMENT OF COMMAS IN THE SECOND AMENDMENT CHANGES WHAT IT MEANS. ARE YOU REALLY SAYING THAT WE SHOULDN'T LISTEN TO HIGHLY EDUCATED AND TRAINED LINGUISTS?"

The science of linguistics had not yet been invented by Noam Chomsky at the time the Second Amendment was written, but the rules of interpreting legal language were well understood anyway.

Gun-grabbers are not the only people who make bizarre arguments about the punctuation, capitalization, or format of a constitutional amendment they dislike. So do tax protestors, many of whom believe the Sixteenth Amendment, which permits Congress to levy an income tax, wasn't legally ratified because of alleged errors and inconsistencies in the typography of the text. People who advance those kinds of arguments generally end up being able to have a lively debate over their insanity in the same place: federal prison.

Relying on gobbledygook from the faculty lounge to contradict the plain meaning of the Second Amendment defeats a key purpose of having a Bill of Rights in the first place. As St. George Tucker, perhaps the leading legal scholar of the Second Amendment's day, said, "A bill of rights may be considered, not only as intended to give law, and assign limits to government . . . but as giving information to the people [so that] every man of the meanest capacity and understanding may learn his own rights, and know when they are violated . . ."

Sadly, Tucker apparently grossly overestimated the intelligence and "meanest capacity" of some people.

"BUT THERE HAS TO BE SOME LOGICAL REASON WHY THE SECOND AMENDMENT MENTIONS A MILITIA! I THINK IT MEANS THAT PEOPLE CAN ONLY HAVE GUNS WHEN THEY'RE ACTING AS SOLDIERS."

The gun-grabbers like to fantasize that the Founders used "militia" to mean a government-organized military unit—but, as usual, they couldn't be more wrong.

A.D.D. Moment

We've really changed what the definition of a "militia" is. Back in the 1700s, it meant all able-bodied men. But now? A militia member seems to be anyone who's not perfectly in the mainstream. According to a report done by the Missouri Information Analysis Center, people who endorse third-party candidates, are pro-life activists, enjoy the film "America: From Freedom to Fascism," or, most ironically, fly the Gadsden "Don't Tread on Me" flag, might just be in a militia. Of course, that's not all bad news—if we use their definition then everyone who voted for Ron Paul or is against *Roe v. Wade* has the right to bear arms no matter how you interpret the Second Amendment.

The Constitution gave Congress the power both to raise and support a national army and also to organize "the Militia." The army had to be "raised" because it didn't naturally exist in society, but "the Militia," on the other hand, only had to be organized. Why? Because it was a pre-existing concept.

In debating the Constitution, George Mason famously asked, "Who are the Militia?" Surprisingly, his answer didn't include camo-clothed, beer-drinking rednecks, talk-radio listeners, or Bob Barr supporters. In fact, Mason was asking a rhetorical question. The Militia, he said, "consist now of the whole people."

They still do.

Hundreds of years ago, people feared the idea of a permanent, standing army because their experience had been that, in times of peace, standing armies would occupy themselves by repressing the citizenry. Modern police departments didn't develop until the nineteenth century, so, with no army and no cops, peace and order were maintained by "the militia"—a group of ordinary civilians who were expected to use their own arms to defend the community.

As the Supreme Court long ago explained, the "militia system . . . implied the general obligation of all adult male inhabitants to possess arms, and, with certain exceptions, to cooperate in the work of defence." It went on to say that the militia are not troops or standing armies but civilians primarily: "all males physically capable of acting in concert for the common defense."

James Madison, the author of the Second Amendment, plainly understood that "the militia" meant able-bodied civilians. Dismissing fears that a federal army might become as oppressive as the English Redcoats, Madison noted that America had "a militia amounting to near half a million of citizens with arms in their hands." And, according to Madison, this broadly defined militia held "the advantage of being armed, which the Americans possess over the people of almost every other nation" with "governments [that] are afraid to trust the people with arms."

It might be difficult to imagine this today, but during the Revolution, cities like Boston and New York had accurate, quality newspapers. The *Boston Evening Post* once reported that "the total number of the Militia, in the large province of New-England, is upwards of 150,000 men, who all have and can use arms," while the *New York Packet* once declared, "Whoever asserts that 10 or 12,000 soldiers would be sufficient to control the militia of this Continent, consisting of 500,000 brave men, pays but a despicable compliment to the spirit and ability of Americans."

The colonies, then the states, and now the federal government have long declared exactly which part of the population might be

A.D.D. MOMENT

James Madison may have been a brilliant man with extraordinary foresight, but even he apparently couldn't fathom a time when our government wouldn't trust their own citizens to bear arms. If he *had* fathomed it, he might have written the Second Amendment a little differently . . . like: "All citizens have the right to keep and bear arms."

organized as "militia." Today, federal law defines "the militia of the United States" to include all able-bodied males from 17 to 45 and members of the National Guard up to age 64, but excluding those who have no intention of becoming citizens and active military personnel.

To translate, that means that every able-bodied guy of a certain age who's not in the military is in the militia. Once we understand that, it's easy to see the relationship between the Second Amendment's militia purpose and its rights-securing language. If "the people" cannot have guns, they cannot function as "militia" when needed. After all, people who are called to perform militia duties are "expected to appear bearing arms supplied by themselves and of the kind in common use at the time." No guns, no militia.

While George Mason may not have fully understood just how complex the debate over his desired protection for the right to arms would eventually become, he did realize the threats this system might one day have to endure. He explained, "The militia may be here destroyed by that method which has been practised in other parts of the world before; that is, by rendering them useless—by disarming them."

"AHA! SO IT IS ABOUT PEOPLE ACTING AS MILITIA IN DEFENSE OF THE COUNTRY. THAT'S WHY THE SECOND AMENDMENT DOESN'T SAY ANYTHING ABOUT *SELF*-DEFENSE!"

Because it doesn't have to! The militia purpose was *one* purpose that folks who had just overthrown a tyrannical king thought would be important for future generations to remember. But *everyone* understood that "the right of the people to keep and bear arms" referred to an individual right to use guns in self-defense. It was so obvious that it didn't even need to be said.

Unlike America, England had no militia system to speak of. Yet, in the 1689 Declaration of Rights, the king agreed "that the Subjects which are Protestants may have Arms for their Defence suitable to their Conditions and as allowed by Law." By 1744, English law had already "settled and determined" that "a man may keep a gun for the defence of his house and family."

John Adams, in defending the Redcoats at the Boston Massacre trial, declared, "Here every private person is authorized to arm himself, and on the strength of this

WHO NEEDS A GUN?

PLEASE, NO!

POLITE "NO!" SIGN Price: $9.95
Fight back—with manners! Big black letters on a bright yellow background make sure you get your message across. Simply hold in front of you and direct toward any intruder; they'll get the message! Rigid cardboard construction guarantees it can be used multiple times.

authority, I do not deny the inhabitants had a right to arm themselves at that time, for their defence, not for offence . . ." The disarmament of the people of Boston provoked outrage from the Continental Congress.

In 1791, the realization of the need to band together as militia was fresh in people's minds, so we'd expect the Second Amendment to highlight that function of the right to arms. But that doesn't exclude other functions, especially one like the right to self-defense that was already so widely understood.

YOU CAN TAKE MY GUN WHEN YOU PRY IT FROM MY COLD, DEAD HANDS . . . OR YOU CAN JUST PHOTOSHOP IT AWAY

In the 20th anniversary rerelease of the classic film *E.T.: The Extra Terrestrial* some things were added, and others things quietly disappeared.

Like the guns.

Fearing that shotgun-wielding federal agents were too threatening, director Steven Spielberg used the magic of digital technology to turn their weapons into harmless walkie-talkies.

That got me to thinking how interesting other famous film scenes could be if we went back and de-gunned them!

Dirty Harry—Renegade cop Harry Callahan waves a potentially filthy toilet plunger in a hoodlum's face, "Do you feel lucky, punk?"

Scarface—Tony Montana meets a violent end after a rival drug cartel's thugs storm his palatial home and kick him to death with really hard boots.

Heat—After a bank heist goes wrong, the bad guys run through the streets of Los Angeles and pin down hundreds of cops with foul language and terribly offensive gestures.

Reservoir Dogs—In this Tarantino classic, tension builds during a Mexican standoff as Eddie, Mister White, and boss Joe Cabot point soup spoons at one another.

The Matrix—In the famous "lobby scene" Neo and his colleague fearlessly take on and destroy an army of security agents with an arsenal of tremendously powerful water balloons.

"OH, BUT EVEN IF THE MILITIA REFERS TO ORDINARY CITIZENS, THE SECOND AMENDMENT SAYS THE MILITIA SHOULD BE 'WELL-REGULATED,' SO OBVIOUSLY THEY WERE TALKING ABOUT GUN CONTROL!"

I know this is hard to believe, but in 1791, America was a much more free country than it is today. Missing from the landscape were the endless numbers of alphabet soup agencies and two-bit bureaucrats that now seem to infect every aspect of our lives. Only a true idiot would envision our Bill of Rights as a celebration of *regulation*!

The term "well-regulated" meant something very different to our ancestors than it now does to some pencil pusher at the Federal Bureau of Regulation's Administration of Government Initiatives. As noted by the *Oxford English Dictionary*, "well-regulated" meant "well-functioning": i.e., "well-regulated appetites" (1709), "well-regulated clock" (1812), and "well-regulated mind" (1862). When speaking specifically of troops, regulated means "properly disciplined." "Discipline," in turn, means "training in the practice of arms."

The Patriots who formed militia groups to resist British rule, including George Washington, described their groups as "well-regulated militia." Knowing the definitions, what do you think makes more sense, that Washington's neighborhood militia was granted the Royal Seal of Approval by some kingly regulator, or that his militia was "properly trained in the practice of arms"?

"EVEN IF THE FOUNDERS WEREN'T TALKING ABOUT REGULATION THEN, THEY'D BE FOR IT NOW BECAUSE THEY DIDN'T FACE THE SAME KIND OF VIOLENCE AND CRIME THAT WE DO!"

Some people believe that people are now sooooo much smarter than those dead old guys who liked to dress up in wigs, got rid of the king, and wrote our Bill of Rights. In their world, gun violence is not only a problem that didn't exist in the 1700s, it's also a problem that the Framers could never have even foreseen because they were living in a quaint, peaceful time, and their ideas, while imaginative for three hundred years ago, aren't so hot today.

Not so much. Whatever else has changed over the years, it's not human nature. People alive in the 1700s were just as violent and crazy as they were in the 1800s, 1900s, and today. All of the modern arguments we hear about gun control today were made back then, considered, and rejected.

NO INTERPRETATION NECESSARY

"Arms discourage and keep the invader and plunderer in awe, and preserve order in the world as well as property."

—Thomas Paine

43

On July 7, 1775, the Newburn (North Carolina) *Gazette* reported that "a Demoniac" shot three people and wounded a fourth with a sword, before being shot by others. (Note the fact that sane, law-abiding people with guns handy kept the lunatic from racking up a greater body count.)

It's not as though there was no gun crime back then, or that nobody thought about whether disarming the population would result in less violence. It's just that, after thinking about it, they realized it would never work.

Nothing makes people call for gun bans more than a terrible tragedy. But if we gave in to temptation and banned guns every time one is used in a mass murder, then we'd never even have the Second Amendment because the "Demoniac" would have convinced everyone that guns are evil. Unfortunately, Great Britain didn't have the same resolve. After the 1996 "Dunblane Massacre," in which a man shot and killed 16 children and their teacher at a primary school, Great Britain instituted a handgun ban. More on how that worked out later in the chapter.

In 1764, Italian Marquis Cesare Beccaria published *On Crimes and Punishments*, a book credited with founding the science behind modern criminology. Our Founders were quite familiar with Beccaria's work— John Adams confidently quoted from it to the jury during the Boston Massacre trial and Thomas Jefferson was also a fan. In his own "Commonplace Book," Jefferson copied Beccaria's passage denouncing gun control and even called gun control an example of "false utility"—a backwards and irrational approach to crime prevention that will only make the problem of criminal violence worse.

According to Beccaria and Jefferson, gun-control laws "disarm those only who are neither inclined nor determined to commit crimes. Can it be supposed that those who have the courage to violate the most sacred laws of humanity, the most important of the code . . . will respect the less important and arbitrary ones, which can be violated with ease and impunity, and which, if strictly obeyed, would put an end to personal liberty . . . Such laws make things worse for the assaulted and better for the assailants . . . [These] laws [are] not preventive but fearful of crimes, produced by the tumultuous impression of a few isolated facts, and not by thoughtful consideration."

Gun laws don't deter criminals, but they do disarm the law-abiding, making them easier to attack, and eventually leading to the end of individual freedom. These laws are produced by panicked reaction to individual incidents and not, as the authors of our Declaration of Independence once said, by "thoughtful consideration."

The "Demoniac" of 1775 went on his shooting spree three months after the Revolution's bloody opening at the Battle of Lexington and Concord and less than a year before the Declaration of Independence was signed. Given that environment, it's not surprising that the *Gazette* also carried this clear message from the Continental Congress: "It is the Right of every English Subject to be prepared with Weapons for his Defense."

"OK, THERE HAVE ALWAYS BEEN VIOLENT CRIMINALS, BUT THE SECOND AMENDMENT IS OUTDATED . . . WE HAVE A MODERN POLICE FORCE SO CITIZENS DON'T NEED GUNS ANYMORE."

So, in other words, we can just ignore the parts of the Constitution that we feel no longer make sense because they're "outdated"? Sweetness! Why stop with the Second Amendment? What if some unelected, crazy judge somewhere thinks it would be good to bring slavery back? Or eliminate the right to privacy? Or stop having free and fair elections—after all, we keep voting for Bushes, Clintons, and Kennedys anyway. Why not just set up some sort of rotating monarchy?

If the intent is really to reduce crime and violence, the Second Amendment is an odd place to start. After all, Saudi Arabia and North Korea seem pretty peaceful and orderly, so why not mimic them and eliminate our Fourth Amendment so that police can search wherever and however they want and arrest people who just don't look right? What have you got to hide if you haven't done anything wrong?

We can get rid of the Fifth Amendment, too. Due process? Waste of time! If we can make you confess to a crime, all the more efficient. The Sixth Amendment—give me a break! Jury trials? Why, so we can have O.J. fool a bunch of morons? Do you really need a lawyer to explain your actions if you're innocent?

But the real culprit here, the part of the Bill of Rights that kills the most Americans, by far, is the Eighth Amendment. You know, the one that says fines can't be "excessive" and that people shouldn't be subjected to "cruel and unusual punishment."

Why? We're talking about *guilty* people here! Criminals! A few public beheadings or Taliban-style floggings, broadcast in prime time right between *Cops* and *America's Most Wanted* and crime rates will plummet!

If we're really worried about public safety there are lots of other things in the Constitution to target that would be far more effective. But idiots don't target those things because they know they'll lose— so they start with the Second Amendment and hope, as I said before, that destroying it will lead to a domino effect.

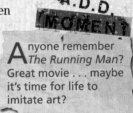

A.D.D. MOMENT

Anyone remember *The Running Man*? Great movie . . . maybe it's time for life to imitate art?

"I'M SAYING IT'S OUTDATED BECAUSE THE GUNS THEY HAD IN 1791 WERE MUSKETS, NOT MODERN WEAPONS. THOSE AREN'T PROTECTED. AND STOP CALLING ME AN IDIOT."

Does the First Amendment protect *only* the sort of speech that existed in 1791? If you're struggling with the answer to that rhetorical question then I'm not sure I actually want you to be able to own a gun.

Back in the 1700s, Al Gore hadn't yet invented the internet and, with no radio or television, Keith Olbermann hadn't yet invented hypocrisy. Yet the First Amendment protects both of those people, along with the millions of others who use new mediums to broadcast things that other people might find outrageous (and yes, that fortunately includes yours truly).

Al Gore could pole-dance topless in an internet broadcast that is then turned into a Larry Flint Blu-Ray Disc . . . and it would all be constitutionally protected. Anyone trying to stop it would likely find a militia of ACLU lawyers trying to bury them under the courthouse.

A.D.D. MOMENT It would be an interesting case on whether that ACLU "militia" could bear arms.

In 1791, we had very few practitioners of Wahhabist Islam on these shores. Mormons? Zero—Joseph Smith wouldn't be born for decades. Chicken-sacrificing voodoo preachers? Scientologists? Nope, not on the *Mayflower*. Yet, today, all of those religions, along with hundreds of others, are protected by the First Amendment's guarantee of religious freedom.

How about our Fourth Amendment rights against "unreasonable" searches? Back in 1791, there were no telephones to tap—yet the police now generally need to get a warrant before they can spy on your telephone conversations. Back then there were no helicopters to hover over your house with special thermal-imaging cameras that could peek through your roof to detect drug-making equipment—but that, too, is now considered a violation of your Fourth Amendment rights.

All of our other rights protected by the Bill of Rights have expanded based on evolving technology—so why should the right to bear arms of all kinds *not* evolve with technology? Again, if that question is hard for you to answer, then you might have a bigger problem with our Constitution than just its Second Amendment.

If Guns Kill People, Then So Do . . .

If we want to get rid of anything that can be used to kill people, we can't stop at firearms.

. . . **Toasters** In 2002, Mariela Karbowski of Victoria, Texas, was charged with beating her estranged husband to death with a two-slice toaster.

. . . **Coffins** In 2008, a Brazilian widow on the way to her husband's funeral died after the hearse she was traveling in was hit from behind in an accident. The force of the collision pushed the coffin forward into her head, killing her.

. . . **Video Games** In 2005, A South Korean boiler repairman collapsed and died after playing the video game StarCraft online for almost 50 consecutive hours.

. . . **Weird Combinations of Harmless Things** In 2006, British comedian Mark Cassidy was killed after accidentally overdosing on nitrous oxide (laughing gas) while watching pornography on his laptop computer.

"OH, FINE, THE SECOND AMENDMENT PROTECTS ALL *NORMAL* GUNS, BUT NOT ASSAULT WEAPONS!"

What's an assault weapon?

"YOU KNOW, WEAPONS OF WAR, THINGS THAT BELONG ON A BATTLEFIELD, NOT IN YOUR HOUSE."

So should the law ban only "things that belong on a battlefield"?

"NO, THE LAW SHOULD BAN 'ASSAULT WEAPONS.'"

Oh, okay, thanks for clearing that up.

Few rational people dispute that there are some weapons that should be banned from private ownership. Ted Turner may own half of Montana, but he can't defend it with nukes.

I'm not singling Turner out just because he's cozy with the United Nations, has a tendency to marry Viet Cong agents, and is prone to saying stupid things—i.e., "We'll be eight degrees hotter in ten—not ten, but in 30 or 40 years. And basically none of the crops will grow. Most of the people will have died, and the rest of us will be cannibals." Seriously, he really said that.

The Supreme Court tells us that the Second Amendment protects the possession only of weapons that can be carried on one's person and are of the type that would be in common use for lawful purposes.

But where do "assault weapons" fit into that? It depends. The word "assault" doesn't tell us anything, because any object used to harm another person can be designated as an "assault" weapon. If a mugger uses a kitchen knife, baseball bat, or fireplace poker to prey on his victims, should Congress label those items as "assault weapons" and ban them from private homes?

It seems logical that if a gun is going to be banned for being an "assault weapon," there should be something about it that makes it particularly useful for criminals, but use*less* for lawful applications. Unfortunately, there is nothing logical about the agenda of gun-grabbers. They're focused on banning as many guns as they can, as fast as possible—common sense be damned.

"BUT AREN'T 'ASSAULT WEAPONS' THE SAME KINDS OF MACHINE GUNS THAT RAMBO AND CHUCK NORRIS USE IN THE MOVIES? THEY KILLED A LOT OF PEOPLE WITH THOSE GUNS!"

No. The sort of "assault weapons" that might be used in the military or the movies are machine guns (i.e., guns that spray bullets everywhere). They are called "fully automatic" weapons because the gun automatically loads and then fires bullets for as long as

A.D.D. MOMENT

These bans have very little to do with what the guns actually do, and a whole lot more with their cosmetic appearance. Maybe a more accurate term for an assault weapons ban would be a "scary-looking weapons ban" or "cool-looking weapons ban," depending on your view.

They May Have to Give You a Permit...
but They Don't Have to Make It Easy

The following is one Glenn Beck staff member's experience in trying to obtain a residence permit for a handgun... in Manhattan.

Pick up an application at Police HQ or print it out from their website.

Wait, you want a conceal carry permit? Better get an attorney to help unless you have political connections.

Attempt to translate questions like: "Res Pct." without the help of any instructions.

Did you show up after 3:30? Come back another day.

Get everything notarized.

Show up at Police HQ to submit application. Miss a day from work and pay a week's salary to park.

Go to the room listed on form: 110A. Find out it's the wrong room.

Find right room, wait in line. Submit application.

Go back to room 110A and pay $340 filing fee and $94.25 fingerprint fee.

Go back to original room. Wait. Get fingerprinted.

Wait four to six weeks for a letter in the mail.

Letter arrives, complete with spelling errors and a new list of instructions.

Now get two notarized reference letters from friends, along with a report from the DMV showing any tickets you've received. (Aren't they the police department?)

Call your "Investigator" within 10 days of receiving letter to set up a personal interview. Wait, an interview? Yes, an interview.

Realize that it's hard to set up an interview when your Investigator never answers his phone or returns your messages.

After finally setting up appointment, call the night before interview to confirm. Told, "Oh he's out all week, sorry."

Call following week, set up new appointment.

Show up for new appointment. Told Investigator is "out today." Assigned new Investigator.

Did you say once a week? Oops, wrong answer, you can only go twice a month.

Interview consists of trick questions, like "What do you want to use the gun for?" Answer: To practice at the range. "Oh, the range, great...how often do you want to go?"

Wait two to three more months for another letter.

You have 30 days to go back to HQ to get your purchase voucher. Miss the deadline and you start over.

Approved? Congratulations!

Purchase a gun within 10 days.

Miss the window? Sorry, now you've got an illegal gun. Application denied... and prepare to be arrested.

Bring your gun back to HQ within 72 hours to get your permit.

Application denied? You can appeal... or, better yet, just move to a city with some sanity.

Bring your gun home and put on its mandatory trigger lock.

Total time wasted: 6–12 months. Total money spent: $500–$1,000. Having a handgun in spite of the New York City elitists... priceless.

the shooter keeps pressing on the trigger. These types of guns have been heavily restricted in the United States since the mid-1930s and are *not covered* by the "assault weapons" ban laws.

"WAIT A MINUTE . . . YOU'RE TELLING ME THAT THE 'ASSAULT WEAPONS' BAN DOESN'T COVER MILITARY-ISSUE WEAPONS?"

That's right. But don't take it from me. In a 1988 report laying out their strategy for banning so-called assault weapons, the Violence Policy Center declared public confusion to be a key aspect of their strategy. "The weapons' menacing looks," they wrote, "coupled with the public's confusion over fully automatic machine guns versus semi-automatic assault weapons—anything that looks like a machine gun is assumed to be a machine gun—can only increase the chance of public support for restrictions on these weapons."

In case you're not familiar with them (i.e., "you're a 'normal person'"), the Violence Policy Center isn't exactly some right-wing think tank funded by the gun lobby. In fact, they're just the opposite: They believe that guns are actually a public health issue and should be subject to government health and safety regulations. So, when they talk about the public's being "confused" by the terminology, they mean that in a *good* way.

The gun-grabbers' amazing dishonesty is right there, in plain view. They know that by inciting confusion they prevent people from asking logical questions—questions that gun prohibitionists can't answer.

Let's take a look at what these "assault weapon" bans actually prohibit. First, these laws pertain only to "semi-automatic" guns. The term "semi-automatic" may seem exotic to those unfamiliar with guns, but most guns made in the last hundred years fall into this category. It just means that one bullet will be fired each time the trigger is pulled. Keep your finger down on the trigger and you'll get a whole lot of . . . nothing. Semi-automatic guns will not "spray" bullets, but you do not need to manually reload each bullet into the chamber, a distraction that usually makes most target shooting—and self-defense uses—far less effective. "Excuse me, Mr. Serial Killer, I missed. Please sit still while I get another bullet ready to go."

A.D.D. MOMENT

Manual reloading of guns does, however, provide much better drama for the scene in the movies where the hero has to struggle to get another round in the chamber as the madman defies all laws of medicine by rising from the floor after taking a shot to the chest.

"SO WHAT TURNS A NORMAL, GARDEN-VARIETY SEMI-AUTOMATIC GUN, USED FOR PLINKING AT EMPTY BOTTLES AND RAPISTS, INTO AN EVIL 'ASSAULT WEAPON'?"

Good question. Here's what the guns-are-a-public-health-issue Violence Policy Center says:

"Defining an assault weapon—in legal terms—is not easy. It's not merely a matter of going after guns that are 'black and wicked looking.' Although those involved in the debate know the weapons being discussed, it's extremely difficult to develop a legal definition that restricts the availability of assault weapons without affecting legitimate semi-automatic guns . . . although legislation could be passed that would ban specific weapons, the world's arms manufacturers are expert at producing weapons that follow the letter, but not the intent, of the law. This often results in products that are virtually identical to the restricted weapon, yet different enough to remain on the market."

NO INTERPRETATION NECESSARY

"That the People have a right to keep and bear Arms; that a well regulated Militia, composed of the Body of the People, trained to arms, is the proper, natural, and safe Defence of a free state."

—George Mason

So the gun-grabbers' way around the fuzzy definition of "assault weapons" is to ban *specific* rifles and handguns, as well as all guns that have certain features. The now-expired federal "assault weapons" ban, enacted in the early Clinton days, put that kind of philosophy into practice. First, a laundry list of specific guns, by make and model, were deemed to be "assault weapons," and second, any gun that had some combination of "evil features" was banned.

But there's a big problem with that approach. Looking at the "evil" features targeted by assault weapon bans makes the cosmetic nature of this game completely obvious. For example, despite the almost complete lack of criminal bayoneting in this country, a mount that could accommodate a bayonet counted as a strike against a gun. Pistol grips and folding stocks—features designed to make guns easier to aim and shoot accurately and comfortably—were also deemed evil and counted as another strike. But shouldn't the government *want* people to be more accurate shooters? Cumbersome guns probably lead to more stray bullets.

But don't expect the gun-grabbers to understand what they're banning. New York's Carolyn McCarthy, who's arguably the loudest anti-gun voice in Congress, was campaigning for renewal of the federal assault weapons ban when she was asked why she wanted to ban guns that had barrel shrouds. Now, McCarthy knew she *wanted* to ban barrel shrouds, but didn't know why.

So what *is* a "barrel shroud"? Well, because gun barrels can become too hot to hold when they're in use, a barrel shroud is a piece of vented metal or plastic that surrounds the gun barrel thereby allowing the user to hold it steady while shooting. In other words, barrel shrouds make guns safer and easier to shoot.

Of course, like most gun-grabbers, Congresswoman McCarthy didn't seem to know any of those details. When asked, "Do you know what a barrel shroud is?" her answer was as stunningly honest as it was scary: "I actually don't know what a barrel shroud is . . . I believe it is a shoulder thing that goes up."

A.D.D. MOMENT

Barrel shrouds unfortunately violate the "cool-looking" test, which is why we apparently can't have them.

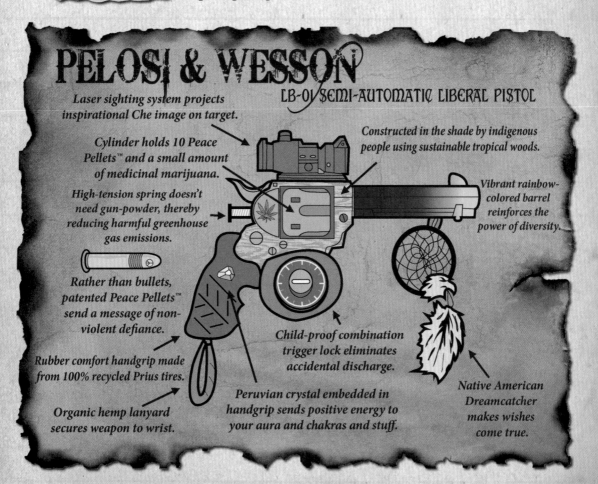

PELOSI & WESSON

LB-01 SEMI-AUTOMATIC LIBERAL PISTOL

Laser sighting system projects inspirational Che image on target.

Cylinder holds 10 Peace Pellets™ and a small amount of medicinal marijuana.

Constructed in the shade by indigenous people using sustainable tropical woods.

High-tension spring doesn't need gun-powder, thereby reducing harmful greenhouse gas emissions.

Vibrant rainbow-colored barrel reinforces the power of diversity.

Rather than bullets, patented Peace Pellets™ send a message of non-violent defiance.

Rubber comfort handgrip made from 100% recycled Prius tires.

Child-proof combination trigger lock eliminates accidental discharge.

Native American Dreamcatcher makes wishes come true.

Organic hemp lanyard secures weapon to wrist.

Peruvian crystal embedded in handgrip sends positive energy to your aura and chakras and stuff.

CLOSE ENCOUNTERS

Gun rights is one of those issues where a personal experience can really change your mind . . . either way. Carolyn McCarthy ran for Congress on a strict antigun platform after her husband was killed and son injured by an avowed racist on a New York commuter train.

Conversely, Ohio State Rep. Michael DeBose, who was solidly antigun, changed his mind after an encounter with two armed thugs near his home. "I was wrong," he said. "I'm going to get a permit and so is my wife. I've changed my mind. You need a way to protect yourself and your family. I don't want to hurt anyone, but I never again want to be in the position where I'm approached by someone with a gun and I don't have one."

Two politicians, two encounters with violent criminals, two very different reactions.

"WELL, IF WE CAN HAVE MODERN GUNS, THEN WE SHOULD ALSO BE ABLE TO HAVE MODERN RESTRICTIONS, AND GUN CONTROL IS ONE OF THEM . . ."

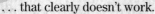

. . . that clearly doesn't work.

The statistical games played by gun prohibitionists are more creative than Charlie Rangel's excuses for why he didn't follow the tax laws he was in charge of writing. For some people, believing that guns are harmful is, like global warming, an article of faith—science be damned. But more rational people who are willing to consider neutral sources (like those wild-eyed gun nuts at the National Academy of Sciences and the Centers for Disease Control) soon realize that the evidence points in a completely different direction.

In 2003, the Centers for Disease Control and Prevention published a study investigating whether gun control actually works. They examined all sorts of gun laws, from bans on different firearms and types of ammunition, to licensing and registration mandates, waiting periods, laws designed to keep guns away from kids, and harsh enforcement regimes for different gun violations.

Their conclusion? Nothing seemed to work very well.

A year later, the National Academy of Sciences published a comprehensive review of 253 journal articles, 99 books, and 43 government publications evaluating 80 gun-control schemes. The total number of gun laws found to reduce violent crime, suicide, or accidents?

Zero.

Good Gun News . . . from the Mainstream Media?

"Recent polls show shrinking support for new gun-control measures and strong public sentiment for enforcing existing laws instead . . . Frank Newport, editor in chief of the Gallup Poll, [said], 'Every bit of data is showing us that Americans are getting more conservative about gun control.'"

—The Houston Chronicle

"THEN WHY DOES GUN CONTROL WORK SO WELL IN OTHER COUNTRIES?"

It doesn't.

Remember the English Declaration of Rights with its right to arms? Like the rest of that Declaration, it restrains only the *queen*—Parliament can do whatever they want and, being that they are idiots, they wanted to take guns away. So, in 1997, they did.

Over a decade later, the results are in: the ban is a disaster. From 1998 through 2005, the number of deaths and injuries from handguns sky-rocketed 340 percent.

But that statistic shouldn't be surprising. One European study of 21 countries recently found "no significant correlations" be-tween the number of guns in society and the corresponding sui-cide or homicide rates. Another study, comparing suicide and homicide data for 36 countries, including the U.S., between 1990 and 1995, reached the same conclusion. A third study, done in 2007, compared gun ownership and murder rates in almost every Euro-pean country. It found that countries with *more* widespread gun ownership had *fewer* murders while countries with *less* gun ownership had, say it with me: *more murders.*

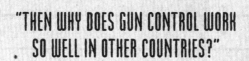

Don't forget, England is an island, meaning it's presumably *easier* to restrict what goes in and out than it would be in a country like the U.S.

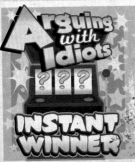

Handgun bans reduce gun violence!

Over the two years following England's ban, the use of handguns in crimes rose by 40 percent. Why? The study's authors found that "existing laws are targeting legitimate users . . . rather than criminals."

"GUN OWNERSHIP PROMOTES VIGILANTISM. WHY NOT JUST CALL 911?"

There are many heroic police officers who rapidly and professionally respond to any threat—blowing away the villain or arresting the criminal and saving otherwise helpless citizens from harm.

In the movies.

In real life, as the saying goes, when sec-onds count, the police are only minutes away. Let me illustrate what I mean by picking just one crime-riddled, tough-on-guns city: Washington, D.C.

In 2002, almost thirty years into a gun ban (which was overturned by 2008's landmark Supreme Court case *District of Columbia v. Heller*), the D.C. police force's response time to a "Priority 1" call was 8 minutes, 25 seconds. That's almost eight and a half minutes from the time the dispatcher has spoken with you and determined that there's an intruder in your home to the time the first squad car arrives.

Of course, that response time assumes that (1) you actually get a chance to make the call, and (2) once you make the call, someone will answer. In 1998, a newspaper investigation discovered that nearly 90,000 callers to 911 had to wait at least 90 seconds for an answer. Another 32,000 callers either couldn't connect at all, or got so tired of waiting that they gave up.

As the hysterically antigun *Washington Post* opined a few years ago, "The 911 system is a joke." Four years later, antigun Councilman Jack Evans exclaimed, "People constantly say they call 911 and an officer either doesn't respond or an officer responds late. Somewhere the system is still not working even after all the money we've put into this."

The 911 problem isn't unique to Washington, D.C. Call 911 in Nassau County, New York, and you might get a recording with some calming music. The police response time to 911 calls in New York City: 7.2 minutes; Los Angeles, 10.5 minutes; Atlanta and three neighboring counties, 11.1 minutes; Philadelphia, almost 7 minutes; St. Petersburg, Florida, just over 7 minutes. While on hold would you rather be holding a loaded handgun—or a wooden spoon?

It's not as though there aren't enough cops in Washington to respond. The city has the highest police officer to citizen ratio of any city in America—yet, year in and year out, it's also the nation's murder capital. More cops, more crime?

The city's police force might be more effective if it had a competent leader, but former Washington, D.C., Police Chief Charles Ramsey subscribes to the "set the bar low and you'll never be disappointed" theory of governance. In 2002, he cut his target for closing homicide cases from 65 percent down to a lowly 50.9 percent, explaining, "It's more encouraging . . . You get these stretch goals, and when you don't even come near it, you get hammered for it."

But even with those laughable goals, the numbers are still fudged. If a murder occurred in a prior year and isn't solved, it

> "The Supreme Court . . . all but ensured that even more Americans will die senselessly with its wrongheaded and dangerous ruling striking down key parts of the District of Columbia's gun-control law . . . This is a decision that will cost innocent lives, cause immeasurable pain and suffering and turn America into a more dangerous country. It will also diminish our standing in the world, sending yet another message that the United States values gun rights over human life."
>
> —*The New York Times* Editorial Board
> June 27, 2008

CELEBRITY GUEST IDEEOT

The *NYT* Editorial Board is right about one thing: A Supreme Court decision *did* send a message to the world that we value rights over human life . . . but it wasn't this one.

doesn't count against them, even though it's still very possible to find the killer. But, if by some stroke of luck, a murder that occurred in a prior year is suddenly *solved*, it counts toward the department's success. They can't lose!

What's amazing is that, even with the fudging of prior-year numbers, the rate at which D.C. solves murders is *still* barely over 50 percent. And since that rate includes solved murders from prior years, the real odds of someone finding your killer the year you are murdered is very, very low.

The truth is that it's often harder to open a business or find a parking spot in Washington, D.C., than it is to get away with murder—which is probably one big reason why there are so many of them.

The Less You Know

A 2001 audit of D.C.'s numbers by the Office of the Inspector General revealed that the *real* murder-clearance rate isn't 50 percent . . . it's 6 percent. I'm just thinking out loud here, but maybe the reason why there is so much gun violence in D.C. is that *the criminals know they'll never get caught.*

"BUT AREN'T THE POLICE REQUIRED TO TRY THEIR BEST? DON'T THEY TAKE AN OATH OR SOMETHING?"

In America, you have the right to own a gun, the right to defend yourself with it, and the right to ask your assailant to sing "Kumbaya," explore his feelings, and understand how the lack of social justice and oppressive capitalist culture forced him into bludgeoning your forehead with an axe. But the right you don't have is the one where you ask Kevin Costner to get all "Bodyguard" with you.

Despite what you may think, you do not have a right to police protection. And, once you're dead, nobody can sue the police for failing to protect you, no matter how incompetent they may have been.

The idea that police aren't responsible to crime victims is well entrenched in our legal system. One of the leading cases on this point comes to us—surprise, surprise—from our nation's capital. In March 1975, just as city officials were gearing up to ban guns, two Washington, D.C., women were awakened by the sound of their back door being broken down. Moments later, they heard their roommate's screams downstairs as she was being raped by two thugs. They quickly called 911, who advised them to remain quiet until the police arrived.

The dispatcher called police, but didn't tell them that the call was very important. It rated only a "code 2"—a lower priority than a crime in progress.

Four police cars responded to the call and three of them actually went to the victims' home. The two roommates who had called the cops managed to sneak out onto the roof, where they witnessed one police car drive slowly past their house. Another officer actually got out of his car, went to the front door, and knocked. When the rapists didn't answer the door and offer them fresh-made lemonade, the police left—they'd been there a whole five minutes.

The two women crawled back into the house. With their friend still screaming, they called the police again and were again told that help was on the way. But this time the dispatcher recorded the call only as "investigate the trouble"—and nobody ever did.

Believing that the police were on the scene, the two roommates called out to their friend. Big mistake. The rapists kidnapped all three women and brutalized them for another fourteen hours.

Given that the rapists were armed with only a knife, would it have made a difference if the women had a gun? We'll never know.

It's hard to imagine how this could have turned out much worse. . . . until the women sued the police department, and lost. As horrible as all of this was, the police owed these victims nothing under the law—another reminder that the person most incentivized to keep you safe . . . is you.

"THAT'S TERRIBLE, BUT AREN'T THERE SOME SITUATIONS WHERE THE POLICE ARE ORDERED TO PROTECT PEOPLE?"

It doesn't matter if a judge has ordered the police to protect you, they still can't be held legally responsible for failing to do so.

Jessica Gonzales suffered a rough divorce from her violent husband and obtained a nice piece of paper from the court commanding him to stay 100 yards away from the family home at all times, unless he was coming to pick up the couple's three young daughters for a prearranged visit. The nice piece of paper also commanded the local constabulary: "You shall use every reasonable means to enforce this restraining order." It even said they could arrest the bad guy, or seek a warrant for his arrest, if he violated or tried to violate the order.

 Which piece of paper would you rather have: A piece of paper that tells violent psychos to leave you alone, or a piece of paper that lets you have a gun?

You can probably guess why this story is included in this chapter. The jerk kidnapped the children as they played outside the house. About two hours later, Jessica called the police. Two officers showed up, but told her they weren't going to do anything and suggested she call back if the kids weren't back by 10 PM. At 8:30 PM, Jessica called her ex-husband, who claimed

"A militia when properly formed are in fact the people themselves . . . and include all men capable of bearing arms . . . To preserve liberty it is essential that the whole body of people always possess arms, and be taught alike, especially when young, how to use them . . ."
—Richard Henry Lee

to have the kids at an amusement park. She called the police back, but was again told to wait until 10 PM.

At 10:10 PM Jessica called again, but was told to wait until midnight. At 12:10 AM she was told to wait for an officer to arrive. When nobody showed up by 12:50 AM, Jessica went to the police station herself. The nice officer took a report and then went to get something to eat.

The police got one thing right: they had no need to exert themselves to find Jessica's ex-husband. He showed up at the police station himself at 3:20 AM. Shooting. The police gunned him down, but the three little girls—Rebecca, Kathryn, and Leslie, ages 10, 9 and 7—were already dead.

It's hard to know if a gun in Jessica Gonzales's hands would have made matters better, but it's hard to argue that they could have made things any worse. The police's guns proved useful to resolve the issue with her ex-husband, if regrettably too late. But, as a legal case against the police department, the outcome was never in doubt. The Supreme Court held that Jessica had no constitutional interest in having the nice piece of paper enforced.

WHO NEEDS A GUN?

M-60 CUT OUT

Price: $11.95 2 for $21.95

You'll go "faux-tomatic" when you wield this sturdy plywood M-60 in front of intruders. They're sure to turn the other way once they imagine what all those 7.62mm rounds could do to them if the gun were real. Use two simultaneously for the Rambo effect.

"AT LEAST THE POLICE ARE SPECIALLY TRAINED TO KILL BAD GUYS. FOR ALL THE MACHO TALK OF GUN NUTS, I BET MOST OF THEM WOULD FREEZE UP IF THEY FACED A REAL THREAT."

The great thing about guns is that almost all defensive uses of them involve an actual shooting. Most criminals aren't looking to risk getting shot, they're looking for an easy victim. If a potential victim is armed, that's cool with the crooks—they'll find some other poor sucker who isn't. It's a lot like installing an alarm in your home—sure, a criminal can still break in, but why bother when there are so many other homes without them?

Actual reports of successful defensive non-shootings are low (and you won't find them in the news—nothing could bore the media more than "no shots fired"), but that doesn't mean they aren't out there. Social scientists studying the phenomenon disagree widely about the actual numbers, but one set of thirteen different surveys

A.D.D. MOMENT

A few grassroots efforts are under way to do the job the media won't and track defensive gun uses. You can find updates on two of them here:

★ www.keepandbeararms.com/opsd
★ www.claytoncramer.com/gundefenseblog/blogger.html

yielded results ranging from 760,000 to over 3 million defensive gun uses per year. According to another particularly well-respected survey, no shots were ever fired in over three-fourths of such defensive gun uses.

If you're one of those statistics, I bet you probably have a pretty healthy respect for your Second Amendment rights.

"BUT ISN'T IT MORE LIKELY THAT THE BAD GUY WILL JUST TAKE YOUR GUN AWAY AND USE IT AGAINST YOU?"

Sure, if you're attacked by Obi-Wan Kenobi and he uses some sort of Jedi mind trick to make you give up the gun, you're in trouble. But to the folks involved in the hundreds of thousands of successful defensive gun uses each year, the Jedi mind tricks proved useless.

The science here is a little more realistic. The National Crime Victimization Survey data shows that Jedi weapon-take-away rates are, at most, one percent. And it's not like resisting a criminal attack will somehow make the aggressor *more* angry. One criminological survey even concluded that the use of a gun by the victim significantly reduced the chance of being injured.

"BUT HAVING A GUN AROUND THE HOUSE IS DANGEROUS. WHAT IF THERE'S AN ACCIDENT, OR A CHILD FINDS THE GUN?"

Yes, it is hard to have a gun accident without guns. It's also hard to have a car accident in the absence of cars. And if we banned all the airplanes, they'd stop crashing, too.

The gun-hating media sensationalizes every gun accident, leading some to believe that such accidents are common. Or maybe gun accidents are heavily covered in the press because, like plane crashes, they *are* so exceedingly rare.

In 2005, there were 789 accidental deaths from firearms in the United States. Given our population, that means the risk of having a fatal gun accident in America was 0.30 per 100,000 people—approximately the same as the risk of dying in a plane crash or from bronchitis.

Of course, most people don't fly or contract respiratory illnesses every day, but they *do* usually bathe, and that's *super-dangerous* for children relative to having guns in the home. In 2003, children 14 and under suffered 56 fatal gun accidents. But that same year, 86 children drowned in bathtubs and 285 children drowned in pools in 2003.

NO INTERPRETATION NECESSARY

"The most foolish mistake we could possibly make would be to allow the subject races to possess arms. History shows that all conquerors who have allowed their subject races to carry arms have prepared their own downfall by so doing."

—Adolf Hitler

For kids under 10 years old, the numbers are even more dramatic. As noted by economists Steven Levitt and Stephen Dubner, "The likelihood of death by pool (1 in 11,000) versus death by gun (1 in 1 million-plus) isn't even close."

"I MIGHT KILL MYSELF, OR MY KID COULD KILL HIMSELF IF HE HAD A BAD DAY."

That is complete nonsense. The causes of suicide are complex, but one aspect of this tragic phenomenon is clear: people do not take the decision to kill themselves lightly. As the World Health Organization long ago noted, "Removing an easy and favored method of suicide was not likely to affect substantially the overall suicide rate because other methods would be chosen." Shooting is an effective method of suicide, but it is not significantly more effective than hanging, asphyxiation by car exhaust, or overdosing on pills.

If guns cause suicide then Americans should be killing themselves at much higher rates than do people in other countries. But they're not. For an industrialized nation, America has an average rate of suicide. Obviously, the more guns there are, the more suicide-by-gun incidents there will be—but that doesn't mean that guns *increase* the suicide rate. In countries where guns are less available, people simply kill themselves in other ways, often at far greater rates than we see here in the "gun-filled" U.S.A.

The Japanese experience debunks the notion that more guns lead to more suicide. Gun-grabbers point to Japan as an example of a more-peaceful, relatively gun-free nation, where gun-related homicide is almost unknown. But while the Japanese may not be shooting each other, they're spending plenty of time harming *themselves*. Japan's suicide rate is more than double America's. In fact, the Japanese suicide rate actually *exceeds* the rates of suicide and homicide in gun-crazy America, *combined*.

Of course, none of that means that guns are safe in the hands of suicidal people. They're not. And neither are pills, razors, booze bottles, ropes, hibachi grills, or the collected works of Nancy Pelosi. Yet, in a free country, we don't ban things simply because they might help you to kill yourself. And remember, despite all of the arguments continually recited by all of your Idiot Friends, we *are* still a free country.

WHO NEEDS A GUN?

STREISAND MASK Price: $18.95

When the going gets tough . . . the tough get their Barbra Streisand mask on! Easily stored under your pillow for rapid deployment. Imagine what a thief will think when he sees Babs herself coming down the stairs! Stops criminals dead in their tracks, or your money back. Allergy-free latex.

A.D.D. MOMENT

Given all of those suicides, Japan must be a pretty terrible place to live, right? What makes it that way? I don't know, but it's not all of the guns they don't have.

EDUCATION

Readin', Writin', and Futility

THOSE of us with kids (whether on the lawn or on the horizon) have a vested interest in education. In fact, next to parenting itself, education is the largest part of the foundation upon which a child will build his or her life. Shortchange them early on and they'll be paying the price for years: getting pregnant at 17, taking out an absurd mortgage at 25, tacking on fifty extra pounds by 35, and, by 45, torching the house they can't afford while deep-frying a turkey for their dozen children.

Most of us don't want that for our kids. But we also innately know that the difference between our darling son decorating the front lawn with rusted-out pick-up trucks on cinder blocks and presiding over a Fortune 500 company pretty much comes down to two major influential factors in his childhood: parenting and education.

Parenting—well, that's up to us. We raise our sons and daughters the way we think they should be raised, we instill our values and we provide the security and nurturing environment for them to flourish. But, most of all, we cross our fingers and hope we're doing the right thing.

But education is different. For most of us, it's out of our hands. When the time comes, we usher our kids out from under our wings and shoo them onto a bus. We think of them learning to conjugate verbs, use correct pronouns, and assemble decent-sized sentences. We have faith that they'll be able to spell "Wednesday" without looking it up and give the name of the continent they live on without having to mull it over. We hope they'll be able to locate the state of Florida on a map, divide nine by three and know which countries made up the Axis and the Allies in World War II. We want these things for our children because we know that learning history, science, math, and geography can help them avoid wearing a sandwich board or dressing up as a banana. Even morons know that education is a key to success—that's how freaking obvious it is.

Fact: We now throw *four* times more money at public schools than we did forty years ago—back when the government decided to increase its role in teaching our children. You'd think that kind of capital infusion would have given us some pretty solid returns, like playgrounds buzzing with budding Einsteins computing the trajectories of their dodge balls. But, like lots of things the government gets involved with, return on investment was never really their goal.

A.D.D. Moment

Our schools are so bad that people who can barely afford their rent are willing to spend tens of thousands of dollars to put their kids into private schools. Can you imagine forking over thousands in school taxes every year and then another $30,000 to send your child to a private kindergarten? People in New York City can—and they fight tooth and nail for the privilege! If that's not damning evidence that public education is rotten, I don't know what is.

With very few exceptions, our public schools are costly disasters based on an antiquated tenure system and unmotivated teachers using overstuffed classrooms inside decaying buildings to pass on much of what they don't know to their undisciplined, uninterested students. (Many teachers wouldn't even know that that was a run-on sentence.) Those students then enter the workforce or college with a subpar education that is slowly but steadily costing America her standing in the world.

Nationwide, over one million incoming college students require remedial courses just to catch up. That's shameful. And the price tag for teaching those kids what our billions in tax dollars should have already taught them? It's $2.5 billion a year. That's infuriating.

Is it any wonder that no one knows when an apostrophe is called for (including me), or that plenty of people couldn't tell you the difference between *they're, there,* and *their*? Why? Because their not interested in learning that kind of stuff. There more interested in actress/singer/whatever Jessica Simpson declaring that she thought Chicken of the Sea was chicken or Miss North Carolina answering a simple question by referencing "U.S. Americans."

We all laugh at that kind of seemingly innocuous ignorance—but is it really that funny? After all, we're the most powerful, technologically advanced nation on earth. *So why are there 32 million Americans who can't read or write?*

In a recent poll conducted by *National Geographic*, 63 percent of 18 to 24-year-olds could not locate Iraq on a map, 70 percent shrugged their shoulders when asked where Iran and Israel were, and 90 percent had no clue where Afghanistan was. If you're inclined to cut them some slack for not knowing their Middle East geography, chew on this: 50 percent couldn't even locate New York State.

Americans don't seem to agree on much anymore, but most of us, regardless of faith, economic status, or party affiliation, agree that public schools are lousy. So why can't we make the commonsense decisions needed to do something about it? Simple—because there are still lots of idiots who say things like . . .

A.D.D. MOMENT

I might be willing to forgive the ignorance over Iraq/Afghanistan geography (I'm not exactly Magellan myself) except for the fact that those aren't just *any* countries, they're places where our fathers, mothers, sisters, and brothers have been fighting and dying for years to preserve the very system that these kids seem so uninterested in taking advantage of.

"OH COME ON, GLENN, WHAT'S WRONG WITH HAVING A LITTLE GOVERNMENT OVERSIGHT OF SOMETHING AS IMPORTANT AS EDUCATION?"

Oh, I don't know, maybe just the fact that *the government has no constitutional authority to be in the education business.* How does that work for you?

Education is not a federal issue, it's a local and state one—which is exactly how it was treated for over two hundred years. Then, Jimmy Carter came along and, by the slimmest of margins (we're talking about four votes in the House), won approval to create a new ginormous government bureaucracy: the Department of Education (DOE).

The creation of the DOE effectively took control from local and state governments (and Mom and Dad) and dragged it, kicking and screaming, to Washington. It also made the jobs of teachers' union lobbyists and special-interest groups much, much easier since they now needed to influence only one all-powerful entity rather than each individual school system. If you got your way with the DOE, you got your way with every public school in America.

The only threat to the Department of Education's existence came early on when President Ronald Reagan actively lobbied to dismantle it. But politics played its part and eventually weakened the resolve of the Reaganites. While the DOE didn't grow in any great strides under Reagan, it was far from dismantled.

MY SON IS STUDENT OF THE MONTH AT A MEDIOCRE PUBLIC ELEMENTARY

UNITED STATES
MINISTRY OF EDUCATION

JANUARY 27, 2016

Dear BECK, RAPHE:

We regret to inform you that your preferred choice for
college education:

HARVARD UNIVERSITY

did not have any openings. Therefore, your educational
needs will instead be served by:

GREATER LEXINGTON FUTURE TEXTILE WORKERS
ACADEMY LEXINGTON, MASSACHUSETTS

Congratulations on your admittance and future
TEXTILE career! You will receive course materials
under separate cover.

Your major will be FIBERS, NATURAL.
Your minor will be ZIPPERS.

Congratulations on your matriculation!

In pushing for his "America 2000" plan (think No Child Left Behind *Lite*), George H. W. Bush changed course from his predecessor, choosing to embrace the department rather than kill it. Though he didn't get too far (many Republicans at the time surprisingly still behaved like Republicans and strongly objected to expanding federal influence), he certainly contributed to the DOE's increasing growth.

Bush the Elder's early departure changed nothing. Bill Clinton simply picked up the baton, tweaking "America 2000" and creatively renaming it "Goals 2000." By that time, federal involvement in the school system was taken for granted—so much so that by the time George W. Bush signed No Child Left Behind (which not only fed the beast, it pumped it full of growth hormone and steroids) most Americans were completely anesthetized to the idea of national politicians being in charge of their kids' education.

Early on, many politicians knew that government would be bad for education and were opposed to a larger federal role. But, as soon as it actually happened, the old "if you can't beat 'em, join 'em" mentality took over, and politicians abandoned common sense in favor of trying to figure out how to get a piece of the action. Remember the economic-stimulus bill? Plenty of politicians were vehemently opposed to it, but as soon as it became a certainty they stopped fighting it and started figuring out how to parlay its billions into reelection.

A.D.D. Moment

Remember Frank Serpico? He was a New York cop who stood up to institutional corruption in the NYPD. He was ostracized and shot in the face for it—but he stood his ground. In the end, he won, and NYPD corruption was dealt a death blow. Serpico wound up being portrayed by Al Pacino in a great movie that bore his name. We could really use some Serpicos on Capitol Hill.

But aside from thinking that centralized planning (which didn't work so well for the Soviet Union) could fix our schools, there's another reason to keep education out of the hands of elected officials: power . . . or, more accurately, abuse of it.

GOVERNMENT IS GREAT!

You've heard the expression *too many chefs in the kitchen*? Well, when we're talking about government involvement in education, we're talking about *too many all-powerful chefs* cooking in a kitchen they shouldn't even be allowed in. Think Gordon Ramsay, except none of them know how to cook so they just get in each other's way, swear, and start grease fires.

SUGGESTED LESSON PLANS

"An Inoffensive History of the World"

"Where Texas Is"

"Columbus: Portrait of Evil"

"Grammer"

"No Child Left Behind: Answer Key Edition"

"Those Poor Indians!"

"Ché Was Awesome"

"Why Mr. Leering Can't Be Fired"

"The Evils of Capitalism"

Schools are a direct conduit to the developing brains of our children (radical Islamists know this, which is why they use textbooks to demonize Jews and Western values). Is there any better way to indoctrinate a generation than by starting on them when they're young and vulnerable?

It should come as no surprise that a "revolutionary" like President Obama's pal William Ayers is a professor. In a speech he gave alongside Venezuelan dictator Hugo Chavez in 2006, Ayers declared that "education is the motor-force of revolution." He makes no apologies for the fact that he sees his classroom as the perfect environment to indoctrinate students with his anti-American, anti-capitalist worldview. If you're trying to foment a revolution from the inside, there's no better place to do it than from in front of the blackboard.

Having the government plugged in to the *compulsory* education of our children is a bad idea because it opens the door for them to promote an agenda (i.e., the Founding Fathers were evil, old white men; Christopher Columbus was a genocidal brute; Fidel Castro is a visionary; corporations bad! government good!; Mexico was just minding its own business until America came along; and the Soviet Union was simply misunderstood), embrace certain viewpoints while censoring others, and adopt standards dictated by desk jockeys in Washington, D.C.

It also gives a single entity the power to determine what our children learn and by what methods they learn it. Then again, that's exactly what supporters of federally controlled education want. After all, how can progressive education creep its way into the school system on a national scale without national control of the school system?

"WAIT! WHAT'S WRONG WITH PROGRESSIVE EDUCATION? PROGRESS IS GOOD!"

Education is about learning. Learning, like weight loss, is sometimes hard. You have to stay committed and push yourself day after day to see results. Don't ever say this in front of a progressive (don't worry, none of them are reading this book), but some people are better learners than others because some people are *smarter* than others.

PUPIL'S REPORT CARD

Last Name	First Name	Age	Grade	School
Jolsen	James	12	7	BARACK OBAMA MIDDLE SCHOOL

Subject	Grade			Teacher's Notes
Reading	(A+)	A	A-	Jimmy really seems eager to read words so I wish our books had more than just pictures in them. Maybe 8th grade does.
Writing	A+	(A)	A-	jimmy good with letters and he do all the work and he good but i don't do him an A+ because he brings Skittles to class and you cant do that no more because of sugar
Math	(A+)	A	A-	JIMMY. HE IS GOOD AT THE MATH! I TELL HIM YOU KNOW, TO MAKE PLUS WITH THE ONE AND ONE AND HE TELL ME TWO IS WHICH IS THE CORRECT!

Grade Explanation	Promoted to the _Eighth_ grade
A+: Really Very Excellent	
A: Very Excellent	Homeroom Teacher _Mrs. Sally Muckenfutch_
A-: Excellent	

IF YOU CAN READ THIS, THANK A TEACHER. IF YOU CAN'T, THANK A TEACHERS' UNION

Of course, the progressive education movement doesn't like that. It's biased or unfair or something, I forget the actual claim. So they want to make education warmer, friendlier, happier. They believe the educational environment should be nurturing and comforting—not discouraging. That's why using red pens to correct tests is out (red is harsh!) and purple (ahh, soothing) is in.

Progressive education also attempts to "level the playing field," which, if I may translate from progressivian to common sense, means: "lowering the standards." In this feel-good, sunshine and lollipops world, everyone's work goes up on the walls because *it's all sooooo wonderful!* You see, it's not fair to *judge* a child's work because there are no wrong answers, only life experiences.

Progressive education began with the goal of providing a nurturing environment that aimed at kids' hearts rather than their heads. The movement's leader, John Dewey, was a champion of education reform and believed the whole "teachers teach students facts" concept was so nineteenth-century. He saw the role of the teacher as more of a coach and the role of the state as necessary to "bring about the improvements progressives sought."

What does that mean as far as how our kids are actually taught in the classroom? Dewey didn't try to hide his beliefs:

> *"Existing life is so complex that the child cannot be brought into contact with it without either confusion or distraction; he is either overwhelmed*

BETTER DEAD THAN RED! PART 1

Believe it or not, these are real quotes from real educators who instruct real children. And we wonder why so many kids can't handle failure?

"If you see a whole paper of red, it looks pretty frightening. Purple stands out, but it doesn't look as scary as red."
—Sharon Carlson, health and physical education teacher at John F. Kennedy Middle School in Northampton, Massachusetts.

"I do not use red. Red has a negative connotation, and we want to promote self-confidence. I like purple. I use purple a lot."
—Robin Slipakoff, second- and third-grade teacher at Mirror Lake Elementary School in Plantation, Florida.

"I never use red to grade papers because it stands out like, 'Oh, here's what you did wrong.' Purple is a more approachable color."
—Melanie Irvine, a (former) third-grade teacher at Pacific Rim Elementary in Carlsbad, California.

by a multiplicity of activities which are going on, so that he loses his own power of orderly reaction, or he is so stimulated by these various activities that his powers are permanently called into play and he becomes either unduly specialized or else disintegrated."

It gets even better:

"I believe that the teacher's place and work in school is to be interpreted from this same basis. The teacher is not in the school to impose certain ideas or to form certain habits in the child, but is there as a member of the community to select the influences which shall affect the child and to assist him in properly responding to these influences."

In other words, teachers aren't there to tell a child if he or she is "right or wrong" (especially not in red ink), they're there to help the child through a touchy-feely period of self-awareness and discovery.

The progressive methodology also emphasizes empathy over narrative. Rather than learning the cold, hard facts about historical events, it's more important how those events make you *feel*. Competition is viewed as unhealthy. Grades are hurtful.

BETTER DEAD THAN RED! PART 2

"My generation was brought up on right or wrong with no in-between, and red was always in your face. It's abrasive to me. Purple is just a little bit more gentle. Part of my job is to be attuned to what kids respond to, and red is not one of those colors."
—Justin Kazmark, teacher at Public School 188 in Manhattan.

"We try to be as gentle as we can and not slice children's thoughts to pieces with a red pen. The red mark is associated with 'This is wrong,' and as you're trying to guide students in the revision process, it doesn't mean this is wrong. It's just here's what you can do better."
—Laurie Francis, (former) principal of Del Mar Hills Academy in California.

"I tell teachers to use more neutral colors— blues and greens, and lavender because it's a calming color. And, of course, kids also like purple because it's the color of Barney."
—Stephen Ahle, (former) principal of Pacific Rim Elementary in Carlsbad, California.

Freedom is valued over structure, which means students get to do what they want rather than have to suffer through boring lessons like "how to add two numbers together." And while it no doubt makes school more "fun," you have to wonder if it bears any responsibility for the fact that there are students who can look at a map of the United States and go, "What's that?"

The progressive movement has infiltrated both public and private schools in varying degrees—and not just here. One education secretary in the United Kingdom decried progressive education as a "misplaced ideology [that] has let down generations of children."

He's right, but plenty of schools, nevertheless, pride themselves on their progressive

KIDS KNOW BEST

Dewey wasn't the only progressive to understand education's role in carrying forward their agenda. Before becoming president of the United States, Woodrow Wilson was president of Princeton University—a role that gave him ample opportunity to say idiotic, though telling, things like, "Our problem is not merely to help the students to adjust themselves to world life. Our problem is to make them as unlike their fathers as we can."

Influencing kids to be "unlike their parents" is a time-tested progressive strategy that is still being used today. Al Gore, for instance, spoke to a group of high school students in early 2009 about global warming and told them, "There are some things about our world that you know that older people don't know. Why would that be? Well, in a period of rapid change, the old assumptions sometimes just don't work anymore because they're out of date. New knowledge, new understandings are much more widely available sometimes to young people who are in school who aren't weighed down with the old flawed assumptions of the past."

Gosh I hate those old flawed assumptions, don't you? I mean, "Hard work and good grades increase your chance of success in life" is soooo outdated. Of course, the reason why progressives target kids is that they are much more receptive to the message that "America is broken and the only way to fix it is through the government." And when those kids grow up, they turn into people who have the power to turn progressive theory into actual policy, like . . . well . . . Barack Obama.

credentials. In their printed marketing materials, Manhattan's Little Red School House says its program "continues to reflect and build upon this tradition of progressive education . . . [that] emphasizes individual achievement and collective responsibility." Likewise, the Teddy McArdle Free School in New Jersey describes itself as "learner-centered"—which is a nice way of saying that the students act as teachers. Even if they're seven years old. The school has no classes, no curriculum, no homework, and presumably no future rocket scientists graduating from there, either.

The Left's influence on education also continues well beyond high school. In the least-shocking revelation included in this book, one study concluded that right-leaning college professors are majorly out-gunned on college campuses and have to work harder to get the same jobs as their liberal peers. But the prevalence of activist and politically ori-

HIGHER EDUCATION

Actual college classes that exist, or existed before someone got smart:

"Star Trek & Religion" (Indiana Bloomington University)

"The American Vacation" (U. Iowa)

"Learning from YouTube" (Pitzer)

"Feminist Critique of Christianity" (UPenn)

"Blackness" (Occidental)

"Queer Musicology" (UCLA)

Would You Send Your Child Here?

"(Our) experience nurtures social consciousness and ethical awareness . . . Drawing on the rich legacy of the progressive tradition, we believe that education is an organic, developmental and interactive process of growth encompassing all aspects of the child's nature."

—The Little Red Schoolhouse, Manhattan

ented professors has another side effect: course offerings like "The Phallus" and "Native American Feminisms." And we wonder why our college grads don't seem to know so much.

"IF WE ONLY PUT AS MUCH MONEY INTO THIS COUNTRY'S SCHOOLS AS WE DO ITS DEFENSE, EVERYTHING WOULD BE FINE."

We are all familiar with the bumper stickers pining for the day that the defense budget goes to the schools and the Pentagon has to hold a bake sale, but comparing educational spending with national defense isn't particularly fair, clever, or logical.

First of all, we *have* to spend money on defense because if we don't defend our country—well, the schools won't matter much. Take the Republic of Georgia, for instance. Do you really think citizens there are worried about standardized test scores or drunk Russian soldiers driving tanks down their streets?

Giving money to the school system is like giving money to a bum on the street: It might briefly feel rewarding, but deep down you know they're not going to spend it wisely because they *never have*. In the case of the bum, your dollar is likely going to support some global distillery, while, in the case of our schools, your dollar is going to support some politician's agenda.

Schools now enjoy four times more money per student than they did in the 1960s. Have they gotten four times better? No, they have not. Have math and reading skills improved? No, they have not. Have graduation rates improved? No, they have not. Do you think throwing even more money at the problem will improve all of that? No, it will not—though the teachers' union will probably send you a Christmas card.

The U.S. Census Bureau reports that we spent an average of $9,138 per public school student in 2005–2006. Other estimates claim the real number is actually at least *double* that amount. Either way, that's some serious money and we should demand some serious results. But we're not getting them.

The Less You Know

"The percentages of 17-year-olds at different levels (of reading) have not changed significantly in comparison to 2004 or 1971."

"The average score for 17-year-olds in 2008 was not significantly different from the scores in 2004 and 1973."

—The Nation's Report Card, 2008 Assessment

IF YOU THINK EDUCATION IS EXPENSIVE, TRY IGNANCE!

Consider two states: New York, which spends the most per student of any state in the country ($14,884), and Utah, which spends the least ($5,437). Take a look at some key test scores for each of those states:

	NY	UT	U.S. Avg.
Grade 4 Math	238	239	237
Grade 4 Reading	223	221	217
Grade 8 Math	280	279	278
Grade 8 Reading	265	262	260

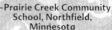

Would You Send Your Child Here?

Yes, New York slightly beats Utah in three out of four categories, but Utah, despite spending nearly $9,500 less per student, still *scores above the U.S. average* in all four categories.

If it was about the money, then places like New York and New Jersey (the two highest-spending states) should have test scores well above those of students in Utah and Idaho (the two lowest-spending states). But they don't. Why? Because it's not that schools don't have enough money, it's that they're forced by politicians, lobbyists, and special interests to spend it in ways that don't further their primary goals.

I wonder how many of our illustrious political figures have their darling progeny in *gasp* private schools. And, if they do, I would love to know why. Maybe banning the children of politicians from attending private school would be a good first step toward making sure the *public* ones get a teeny bit more attention.

> "Assessment is authentic and holistic. Children are well known by their teachers and peers. There are no tests or letter grades. Instead, narrative reports are written about children that cover all aspects of their development: social, emotional, personal, physical, and intellectual."
>
> —Prairie Creek Community School, Northfield, Minnesota

It's worth mentioning that our Constitution makes absolutely no reference to schools or education because *the federal government was never supposed to be in the education business in the first place.* The Tenth Amendment ("The powers not delegated to the United States by the Constitution, nor prohibited by it to the States, are reserved to the States respectively, or to the people") makes that pretty clear. Of course, we don't really let a little thing like "constitutionality" stand in the way of expanding the central government's powers anymore.

"SO WHAT'S YOUR SOLUTION, VOUCHERS? THAT WILL TAKE MONEY AWAY FROM PUBLIC SCHOOLS!"

I assume you mean that vouchers will take money away from the schools *that parents don't want to send their kids to.* If a parent doesn't want his or her child to go to a school, it's usually because that school is bad. Or dangerous. Or possibly both. Do you blame that parent for wanting a better education for his or her child—or isn't that exactly the kind of parents we want more of?

The best argument the antivoucher crowd can ever come up with is that vouchers will make parents want to send their children to a better school. Well . . . uh . . . yeah. And what's wrong with that?

In "normal" life we patronize businesses we like and we avoid the ones we don't. If we prefer Harry's Burger Joint to Tina's Diner, we go to Harry's—even if it's not as close or convenient as Tina's. Maybe Tina starts to realize that she's losing business because her diner is dirty or overcrowded so she changes her menu, improves the quality of her food, fires the bad waiters, and lowers her prices.

The point is that you vote with your wallet, and businesses compete for that vote. That's how this whole free-market capitalism thing is supposed to work: the best succeed; the worst fail.

But the educational system does not operate in that "normal" world. It's a government monopoly that lives in a bizarro world where fair and free choice is forbidden. If you live in Zone X (which, ironically, you presumably chose to live in because that house had a better mix of features, location, and price than its competitors) then your child must attend the Zone X school, even if it's terrible (or "up and coming" which means not as terrible as it was, but still terrible).

Imagine if we used that same system for things other than schools . . . like food (as you may know, I enjoy food analogies quite a bit): What if the government forcibly took a chunk of your money in the form of a "Dining Out" tax, but then dictated that you could eat only at Lucky Fang Chinese Restaurant—because that's the restaurant you're zoned for? I assume you'd be pretty unhappy about that, right? Well, too bad—if you don't like Chinese food, move.

But vouchers change the whole equation. They attach dollars to your child and make your child valuable to a school, instead of the other way around. With vouchers, the

A.D.D. MOMENT

35 percent of Democrats in Congress send their kids to private school. Anyone want to bet that at least some members of that group also oppose vouchers?

A.D.D. MOMENT

"In case anyone didn't notice, one of our dads was elected president of the United States on November 4, 2008. This has been an incredible beginning to a year that most of us will never forget."

—The Director of the University of Chicago Lab School, a progressive grade school founded by John Dewey himself. Yep, that's right, in the second least-shocking revelation of this book, Obama sent his kids to a private progressive school in Chicago.

A recent Department of Education study revealed that students who used vouchers were reading half a grade ahead of their public school peers. Why didn't you hear about that study? Because, according to *The Wall Street Journal*, it was buried and Obama administration officials were forbidden from discussing it. Then, just for good measure, Congress shut down funding for the D.C. voucher program. But, sure, politicians definitely just want what's best for kids.

tax dollars you're coughing up can be spent on a school you're actually excited about. What a novel idea!

When parents are given the option to move their kids from public schools to charter schools, they line up in droves. Why? Because they know that charter schools have accountability for their results. Take the Thurgood Marshall Academy (TMA), a charter school located in Washington, D.C.'s infamous Ward 8. Why is it "infamous"? Because Ward 8 is home to 30 percent of the city's homicides. Because Ward 8 is home to the lowest average income in the city ($14,000 a year). And because Ward 8 has the lowest high-school-graduation rate in a city full of breathtakingly low graduation rates.

But the Thurgood Marshall Academy is an oasis. Despite everything working against them, students there have managed to post 95 percent attendance rates, along with the third-highest test scores of any D.C. high school with open enrollment. But the most impressive stat of all is that *every single member* of the school's first four classes (it opened in 2002) went on to college.

As schools like TMA prosper, public schools will bear the consequences for their years of futility. So what happens to the schools that aren't chosen by many parents? Really bad ones might die. (*Oh my gosh, the f-word*: Failure! I hope we at least write their eviction order in purple ink.) Others might lose students, but parents will eventually recognize that smaller class sizes are a positive, perhaps leading to a resurgence.

But there's an even bigger benefit that would play out over time: Because schools would no longer be monopolies, they'd find themselves competing for dollars with other schools. That means they would actually have to try to earn your business and attract students with incentives like having better teachers, more extracurricular options and cleaner, higher-tech classrooms. Competition is good—imagine that!

Maybe the best reason of all to support school choice is that those entrenched firmly on the side of the status quo—like the teachers' unions, government bureaucrats, and politicians—are so strongly against it.

"WHY ARE YOU PICKING ON THE TEACHERS' UNIONS? OUR TEACHERS ARE PUBLIC SERVANTS WHO DEVOTE THEIR CAREERS TO HELPING KIDS!"

We have no argument there—but a classic idiots' technique is to confuse the debate. *Teachers* are completely different from teachers' *unions*, just as auto assembly line *workers* are completely different from the *United Auto Workers union*. People are people, but unions, generally speaking, are about power and control.

Unions may have been founded with a grand purpose but most are now big, bloated, self-serving bureaucracies with huge budgets and largely left-wing agendas fueled more by politics than a sense of duty to their members. Teachers' unions are no different, but instead of making bad cars more expensive, creating mounds of needless paperwork, or shutting down the subway system in a strike, they work hard to damage our children's futures. Maybe the children themselves should have a union.

In his book, *The War Against Hope*, former education secretary Rod Paige accuses teachers' unions of having maximum power over the schools with minimal accountability for their failure. He believes they're resistant to change and willing to fight tooth and nail to retain the status quo and enforce policies that are detrimental to students.

If Al Gore had any idea how much paper is wasted in keeping our students from learning, he'd cry us a new ocean. In 2005, the New York City teachers' contract was 204 pages long, with another 105-page "Memorandum of Understanding" tacked on for good measure. What could possibly be contained in so many sheets of pulped tree? Rules. Primarily, rules that protect union members in almost any circumstance you can imagine, and lots that you can't.

Trying to fire a bad teacher is, in many districts, like trying to get a cow to walk down stairs: It's just not going to happen. (See our flowchart on page 130 for proof.) In fact, school administrators know it's such an

> ### "We are not a unionized monopoly."
>
> —Randi Weingarten, president, American Federation of Teachers and United Federation of Teachers, apparently being serious.

NON-CELEBRITY, CELEBRITY GUEST IDEEOT

Would You Send Your Child Here?

"Wingra parents have to develop confidence in a system that's different from how they were taught. We don't give grades here. We don't give tests and we deliberately de-emphasize assessments that compare one student's progress with that of another."

—Wingra School, Madison, Wisconsin

UNITED STATES
MINISTRY OF EDUCATION

U.S.S.A. NIGHTMARE SCENARIO # 441

To: Mr. Glenn Beck
REALID#: 392011039100229RW-441

DEAR Mr. Beck:

On behalf of the United States government, we would like to welcome you to your new home in DISTRICT 7, ZONE 3!

Pursuant to the Zoning Act of 2012, your children have been assigned to:

Elementary: Barack Obama Elementary School

Middle: Michelle Obama Middle School

High: Bo Obama High School

Hospital: St. Barack's, 1402 Main Street

Laundromat: Yes We Clean!, 223 West Orange Street

Bank: GeithnerBank, 201 West Orange Street

Restaurant: Cantina del Mundo, 17 Abbotsford Road

Gas Station: MaliaMart, 322 Capitol Avenue

Church: Our Lady of Michelle, 384 Eastgate Drive

This is an incomplete list. You will receive other zoning assignment information shortly. WELCOME TO THE NEIGHBORHOOD!

uphill battle that they're often not inclined to even try. The L.A. Unified School District currently has 30,000 tenured teachers, yet they manage to fire just 21 a year. The ones who are eventually terminated were the worst of the worst, because the ones who *didn't* get fired include a teacher who kept pornography, cocaine vials, and marijuana at school and one who was so unable to teach or control her class that students were actually getting injured in it. Bad teachers, like bad priests, are simply shuffled throughout the system so that the damage they do is spread out.

But aside from being unable to get rid of the worst teachers, unions also prevent the best teachers from being rewarded. Salaries aren't based on merit, but on longevity. Good and bad teachers are paid the same—another remnant of that tiresome *we're all equal* mentality from the progressive era.

> **A.D.D. MOMENT**
>
> I wish I could have seen the faces of the teachers' union lobbyists when they heard Obama say, "I reject a system that rewards failure and protects a person from its consequences." Oops. I wonder if they all want their money back now.

"PRIVATE SCHOOLS AREN'T BEHOLDEN TO UNIONS, BUT THEY SHOULD BE CLOSED BECAUSE THEY'RE ONLY FOR THE RICH."

I will never agree with the premise that just because someone can't afford something, it's not good or fair. Frankly that sounds a little socialist. A lot of people can't afford a Mercedes S Class sedan—but does that mean Mercedes should be forced to stop making them? No—people generally accept the fact that in order to buy a car like that, they will need to have more money. That gives them a little something that we capitalists like to call "incentive."

Second, most schools offer financial aid to students who qualify for it. That defeats the "only for the rich" argument—as would a voucher program. Do families still have to make sacrifices? Absolutely—but what better way to have parents invested in the success of their children than to have parents literally *invested* in the success of their children?

"I SUPPOSE YOU'RE GOING TO SAY THAT THE BEST WAY TO HAVE PARENTS INVESTED IS TO HOME-SCHOOL THEIR KIDS. BUT HOME-SCHOOLED KIDS DON'T LEARN AS MUCH AND THEY ALSO SUFFER SOCIALLY."

Opponents of home-schooling spend a lot of time trying to convince people that those who take education into their own hands create ignorant social misfits. In their opinion, there's nothing worse than a child spending several hours a day learning at the hands of—shudder—*his or her own parents*! They also assume that, at the conclusion of the school day, the child is confined to a small, windowless space before being sent off to bed. The end result is ob-

A.D.D. MOMENT

If home-schooling is such a terrible idea, then why has the national home-schooling rate increased 74 percent in just eight years? Well, here are the top reasons given by parents . . . do any of these resonate with you?

★ Concern over the school environment

★ Desire to provide moral or religious instruction

★ Dissatisfaction with academic instruction at schools

viously a socially maladjusted freak who winds up living in his mom's basement or shuffling around the neighborhood in fuzzy pajamas.

Of course, the reality is that home-schooled children are like any other children. The only difference is that they get focused instruction in a more comfortable environment from an individual who knows, understands, and loves them. *Perish the thought!* There is nothing that prevents home-schooled kids from socializing with peers, playing in Little League or herdball (otherwise known as "soccer"), going to the movies, hanging out at the park, enrolling in summer camp, etc., etc.

But even if home-schooled kids don't go drink warm beer in the alley with the public schoolers, they still develop fine. In a 2000 study, home-schooled and public/private-schooled children played among themselves under direct supervision. If you expected the home-schooled kids to have spent their time hidden under the table crying for their mommies, you're going to be disappointed. All of the kids played together. Or, in the words of the report, "There is no basis to question the social development of home-schooled children."

If home-schooled kids develop just fine socially, then the only plausible argument left against home-schooling is that they aren't getting a proper education. Given the disaster in our public schools, that's a pretty dumb argument, but let's look at the data anyway.

An independent study of over 5,000 home-schooled students showed that they outperformed public school students by 30 to 37 percentile points in all subjects. Another study of over 5,000 home-schooled children showed that they scored 18 to 28 percentile points above public school averages on the Stanford Achievement Test, one of the leading standardized tests used by schools.

I'm not saying that all parents would make great teachers, or that home schooling is for everyone, but I am saying that the stigma of socially awkward kids with a below-average education is a complete fabrication. Besides, just as with school vouchers, whenever the entrenched powers-that-be are so wildly against something, I tend to think it probably deserves another look.

Some Home-Schooled Kids You May Have Heard Of . . .

Agatha Christie, Thomas Edison, Alexander Graham Bell, Ansel Adams, Woodrow Wilson (I'm not sure he helps the cause), Robert Frost, Louisa May Alcott, Venus & Serena Williams

"AT LEAST WE HAVE THE NO CHILD LEFT BEHIND ACT TO LEVEL THE PLAYING FIELD AND NARROW CLASS AND RACIAL PERFORMANCE GAPS."

As with many well-intentioned government programs, No Child Left Behind (NCLB) ultimately fails because it doesn't level the playing field, it lowers the bar—and lowering the bar is one reason why people can't spell words anymore. Let's call it a *Don't Ask, Don't Tell* policy for the stupid.

Here's a quick history lesson (especially for you home-schooled kids, since I know you never learned this stuff): Prisoners in Stalin's forced labor camps were assigned production quotas. Instead of trying to meet them, which was basically impossible, they lied, cheated, and manipulated (it turns out that fear of death is a pretty good motivator).

Authorities all the way up the chain of command turned a blind eye because, in the end, what was more important than tangible results was simply reporting to Stalin that results had been achieved. It was better to *claim* you cleared an acre of forest than to have *actually cleared* an acre of forest. Of course, that was one of the reasons why forced labor in the Soviet Union failed, leading to the failure of the Soviet Union itself.

No Child Left Behind works in very much the same way. By setting a timetable with unattainable goals and threatening schools and teachers if they fail to achieve them, they're incentivizing everyone to game the system. And they do!

One of the main criticisms of NCLB is that it motivates schools to deny children a broad education and instead focus their entire curriculum on "teaching to the test." In other words, they don't worry about teaching kids useful things (like, for example, what a "progressive" really stands for) because they're never asked that question on a standardized test.

Another way to game the system is by outright cheating. NCLB has the dubious distinction of actually turning the *teacher* into the cheater in the classroom. To improve overall scores, teachers have been caught asking weak students to

---

ALTERNATE NAMES FOR NO CHILD LEFT BEHIND

No Standards Left Unlowered

All Dummies, Move On Up!

No One Can Fail Because It Looks Bad

The George W. Bush Panders to Ted Kennedy Act

Federal Bad Idea #18728

HIGH SCHOOL GRADUATE WITH THE IQ OF A BABY ON BOARD

stay home on test days, offering "help" in solving problems, fixing wrong answers after the test is over, and allowing extra time to finish.

Cheating is so prevalent that economist Steven D. Levitt (author of *Freakonomics*) developed an algorithm with a colleague to spot it. The result? They discovered even more cheating than they originally thought. But often times you don't even need an algorithm, you just need common sense: If one year a school has a pitiful ranking and the next year it's a miraculous success—something fishy is probably going on. It's like steroids in baseball. A guy doesn't go from hitting twelve home runs in one year to forty the next without a little outside help. Yet, because the powers-that-be feel that the ends justify the means, no one cracks down before it's too late. And with our schools, it's already way too late.

Unfortunately, NCLB scams aren't just confined to individual schools. States, eager to report to Uncle Stalin just how great things are going, happily carry it on. In 2004, the number of "failing" schools in Michigan went from 1,500 to 216. A remarkable achievement—until you discover that all the state did was *lower the passing score* from 75 to 42.

Who is the big loser in this scam? Our kids, of course. And who is the biggest winner? The politicians and unions that can cash faux test scores in for heaps of federal cash. What a great system!

No Child Left Behind's national test standards are dramatically lower than the standards set by many states. Why? So that states with lower standards (and dumber kids, as a result) will be able to keep up.

"THE REAL PROBLEM ISN'T WITH NCLB, IT'S WITH TEACHER PAY. YOU GET WHAT YOU PAY FOR."

It's true, being a teacher does not pay as well as being a CEO who runs his company into the ground before bailing out of the corporate jet in a golden parachute. But being a teacher doesn't pay that poorly, either. The 2008 Bureau of Labor Statistics study puts the average middle-school teacher's annual salary at $52,570. Compare that to policemen at $52,480 or short-order cooks at $20,230. Then remember that teachers have a shorter workday, longer vacations, and public-sector health and retirement benefits that are often better than those of workers in the private sector.

The problem is not that teachers don't get paid well (although you will never hear me arguing against higher pay for teachers who deserve it), it's that their pay is based on longevity, not performance. When you don't reward someone for being good at his or her job, the incentive to be extraordinary is diminished. In fact, the incentive to be mediocre is increased because teachers who stand out are liable to rock the boat.

Textbooks 101: Why they don't teach you anything

The U.S. public school system is, by far, the largest buyer of textbooks. Since textbook publishers want to sell as much of their product as they can, they tailor their books in a way that makes them more appealing. That means pandering to book buyers who want to see diverse, politically correct, nonoffensive drivel. The result is a sterile, boring, non-educational, nonoffensive book. But at least they sell lots of them.

But good teachers aren't penalized with antiquated concepts like tenure, because "the man" is trying to keep our kids dumb; they're not paid more because of the unions. By trying to protect all jobs unions are actually helping their worst-performing members while hurting their best.

Tenure was originally introduced for college professors in 1910 as a way to protect their academic pursuits and research. And, when you think about it in those terms, it kind of makes sense. You want professors to be able to speak their mind, conduct research, and creatively teach controversial subjects without fear of losing their job. In the 1920s, as women fought for the right to vote, tenure was extended to K–12 teachers, even as the requirements for obtaining it were becoming far easier to achieve. College professors still needed to publish papers and were subject to up to a decade of probation. But grade-school teachers? Not so much.

In California it now takes just as little as *two years* for a teacher to get tenure. Two years, and then you can basically sit back, relax, and not worry about being fired . . . for the rest of your life. Can you think of any good reason why a K–12 teacher should have tenure? I can't, but the teachers' unions sure can. Governor Schwarzenegger's efforts to try and make tenure rules even slightly more reasonable were met with such fierce resistance that you'd have thought he was asking everyone to give up their Priuses.

"WELL, IT DOESN'T MATTER WHAT CHANGES YOU MAKE BECAUSE THE SYSTEM WILL ALWAYS FAVOR UPSCALE WHITE FOLKS."

If the system favors upscale white folks, it's because of the changes that *aren't* being made. It's because the schools fail our children time and again and nothing is ever done. It's because voucher programs that would take poor kids out of lousy, dangerous schools are being denied.

The system shouldn't favor *anyone*—and doesn't have to, but instead it's *failing* everyone.

Would You Send Your Child Here?

"We believe that children should develop balance in body and mind through intensive classroom study, quiet time, vigorous play, experiences of the natural world, and reflection on our role as its stewards."

—The School in Rose Valley, Rose Valley, Pennsylvania

I BRAKE FOR TENURE

The big, A+ answer (assuming, of course, that you're at a school that still allows tests) is to break the cycle of poverty with a cycle of achievement. But we'll never do that with tenure, unions, politicians, bureaucrats, and special-interest groups all standing in the way.

And blaming "The Man" for those failings is a cop-out. Suggesting that minorities from traditionally poorer socioeconomic backgrounds can't be on par with white peers is nonsense. Asian immigrants hailing from backgrounds equally as poor as their Hispanic and black counterparts routinely pummel white students in the SATs. How can that be? Shouldn't they be horribly stifled and at a tremendous disadvantage because of the fact that they're minorities and, for many of them, English isn't even spoken at home?

Absolutely—which just goes to show that scores, stats, and studies tell only part of the story. People can twist data to lead you to whatever conclusion is in their best interest, but one thing can't be twisted because it is indisputable: Our selfish unwillingness to put aside our ideological differences and stop playing politics with education will unquestionably lead not only to the failing of our children, but, ultimately, to the failing of America as well.

AMERICA'S ENERGY FUTURE

Cars, Corn, Carbon, and Controversy

IS THERE anything that makes the case for curbing government influence better than the energy issue? The decades pass, the presidents come and go, but one thing remains the same: America's appetite for oil is far bigger than her stomach.

Our energy crisis is stealthy, like termites slowly destroying a house from the inside. Unfortunately, we're about to step through one of the decaying floorboards. 2008's skyrocketing oil prices showed us just how vulnerable we are, but lost in the shock over four-dollar gas was what caused the crisis . . .

Nothing.

There was no Arab oil embargo, no Middle East war, no massive destruction of refineries from hurricanes or earthquakes—just a marketplace realizing that demand was increasing dramatically while supply was slowly, but inevitably, running out.

We've been told for years that the answer to our problems lies in green energy. Unfortunately, the facts tell a different story.

In 1981, renewable energy was responsible for about seven percent of America's total energy use. After 27 years of broken promises and billions of dollars poured into developing alternative technologies, renewable energy now accounts for a whopping 6.7 percent of our total. That's quite an achievement!

If green energy is as good, cheap, and clean as its supporters say it is, then market forces should automatically be making it a growing part of the equation. Instead, the opposite is happening.

Why?

One reason might be that many of the green lobby's leaders are not as interested in promoting new sources of energy as they are in getting rid of the old ones. While this movement may have started with good intentions, it's now been hijacked by those who see it as a vehicle to drive us back to the Stone Age or, at a minimum, to move us closer to government ownership and control of our energy supply.

The effort by those who use green energy to further their real agenda is sometimes called "the Watermelon Effect." It's a green rind of "pro-environment" policies hiding a core of wealth-redistribution policies that are as red as Marx's blood. This charade only prolongs America's oil addiction and keeps us slaves to nasty foreign governments. (We imported just over a third of our oil in 1981 . . . we import 70 percent now.)

I'M SAYING NO...
But Only Because I Care Too Much

"[It is] a $2 billion project that depends on significant taxpayer subsidies while potentially doubling power costs for the region."

—Congressman Bill Delahunt (D-MA), denouncing Massachusetts' Cape Wind project, which could reduce carbon emissions by 734,000 tons every year.

Unfortunately, that seems to be exactly what some people want. After all, the less control we have over our own energy supply, the more control others have over us. So, instead of constructively looking for solutions, you'll often hear those people launch now-familiar attacks, using idiotic arguments like . . .

"BIG OIL INTENTIONALLY DRIVES OIL PRICES HIGHER SO THEY CAN LINE THE POCKETS OF THEIR GREEDY EXECUTIVES."

kay, first, let's acknowledge the obvious: Big Oil made *a lot* of money in 2008.

Exxon made a $45.2 billion profit, shattering the record for profit by a U.S. company (a record they set themselves just a year earlier). Go, capitalism! Chevron also set a company record with a $23.9 billion profit.

Saying that the oil industry had a good year in 2008 is like saying that Babe Ruth was a decent hitter. It wasn't a good year, it was a *historic* year. So why are people so angry?

On the surface, sure, those profits sound big. Okay, they sound *massive*. Okay, they *are* massive. But so what? Are we really a country that no longer celebrates legitimate success stories or admires profits won on the battlefield of the free market?

Not surprisingly, the green lobby has been quick to latch on to this red herring. They paint the oil industry as an evil cabal that meets in shadowy, cigar-smoke-filled back rooms, scheming ways to jack up gas prices and hoodwink the average American family.

But when you look deeper into the issue and examine pesky things like numbers, facts, and economic principles, it becomes much less nefarious: From 1986 to 2006, the average price of crude was $25.95 per barrel. In 2007, the average price skyrocketed to $72.30 and, in July 2008, oil hit an all-time high of $147.27 per barrel.

Higher oil prices result in higher oil profits. If that's sinister, then so is every other principle taught in Economics 101.

Now, maybe you still believe that the oil companies are evil because they drove the price up to line their own pockets. Maybe some Oil Council of Doom, consisting of mustachioed tycoons, sat in a smoky boardroom and spun a wheel that landed on "$150/barrel." If that's what you think, I probably can't help you. But, if you're rational, you probably already understand what really happened: Prices rose because of a rise in global demand.

China, India, and other developing nations are emerging as huge economies that require massive amounts of oil to operate. Brazil's oil consumption increased seven percent from 2006 to 2007; China's consumption increased by 12 percent; and India's appetite for oil has increased 27 straight years—from 643,000 barrels per day in 1980 to 2.72 million a day in 2007.

As the global demand for oil spiked like never before, prices also spiked like never before. So unless you're against the world *developing*, it's hard to be against the rise in oil prices.

Once prices are high (and, let's be careful, "high" is a relative term . . . we may look back at $150/barrel as a bargain), oil companies—which have a responsibility to their shareholders—naturally want to sell more of their product. Why would they restrict supply in times when demand is highest? That would be like shutting down your ice-cream shop for the summer.

From 1986 to 2006, the average global output of oil was about 72.4 million barrels per day. The most recent numbers show that global average increased to 84.8 million barrels per day in 2007—an increase of over 17 percent. When profit potential is higher, businesses produce more—that's the way a free market works.

> "Climate change is the greatest threat facing mankind . . . We must act now. Future generations are depending on it."
>
> —Prince Charles recently used a luxury airliner to transport himself, his wife, and a 14-person entourage on a 16,400-mile "environmental tour" of Chile, Brazil, and Ecuador. The plane was a 134-seat Airbus A319 retrofitted into a private jet seating just 29. In total, 322 tons of CO_2 were emitted.

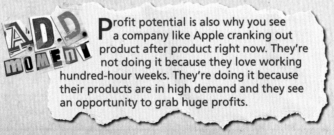

A.D.D. MOMENT

Profit potential is also why you see a company like Apple cranking out product after product right now. They're not doing it because they love working hundred-hour weeks. They're doing it because their products are in high demand and they see an opportunity to grab huge profits.

"NO, THE WAY A FREE MARKET WORKS IS THAT BIG OIL IS ABLE TO MAKE OBSCENE PROFITS OFF THE BACKS OF HARDWORKING AMERICANS."

Even after my stirring defense of supply and demand, you *still* want to focus on that giant profit number, don't you? Fine, but those profits are meaningless unless you compare them to profit rates of other big companies.

Exxon and Chevron each have a profit margin of roughly nine percent. That's less than Microsoft, Apple, Google, Johnson & Johnson, Coca-Cola, Nike, and many other beloved American corporations. Crazy, but you never hear outrage directed at those evil no-tears-shampoo-peddling tyrants from Johnson & Johnson or those nefarious techno-hippies at Apple.

Here's another way to look at it: In 2007, the oil industry made just nine cents in profit for every dollar of revenue. The average for companies in the S&P 500 index was 13 cents, meaning oil companies made *less money* per dollar of revenue than the average large U.S. public company.

I understand that an evil, greedy conservative defending the profits of the evil, greedy oil companies isn't all that compelling . . . so let me try a different angle. Not only is Big Oil *not* trying to screw over average American families, they are actively *helping* them— and not just because they do the work that allows us all to *get to work.*

Take Exxon Mobil, for instance. It's easy to drag their executives in front of Congress for their annual tongue-lashing— but those guys own less than one percent of the company. The vast majority of Exxon Mobil is owned by people like you and me.

Mutual funds, 401(k)s, and pension funds account for about 52 percent of Exxon's shares. The rest is owned by about two million individual investors—regular Americans looking to better their lives by investing in growing companies. If Exxon is evil, then I guess that means all of the senior citizens who pay for their prescription drugs and utility bills with profits from Exxon-invested pensions are evil, too.

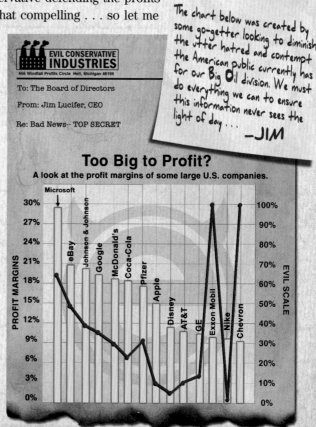

EVIL CONSERVATIVE INDUSTRIES
666 Windfall Profits Circle Hell, Michigan 48169

To: The Board of Directors

From: Jim Lucifer, CEO

Re: Bad News-- TOP SECRET

The chart below was created by some go-getter looking to diminish the utter hatred and contempt the American public currently has for our Big Oil division. We must do everything we can to ensure this information never sees the light of day . . .
—JIM

Too Big to Profit?
A look at the profit margins of some large U.S. companies.

IF OIL IS EVIL . . .

It's funny how much Big Oil is vilified in the media when you look at where the industry actually ranks in terms of net profit margin.

As of this writing, Evil Big Oil comes in ranked in 56th place with a 9.5-percent margin. That puts them behind such industries as Evil Mutual Funds, Evil Publishers, Evil Long-Distance Carriers, Evil Software, Evil Shipping, Evil Silver, Evil Copper, Evil Gold, Evil Drug Manufacturers, Evil Regional Banks, Evil Railroads, Evil Medical Supplies, Evil General Entertainment, Evil Footwear, Evil Resorts and Casinos, and Evil Education Services.

But oil profits don't just enrich investors, they enrich our government also. While giant corporations free-fall, only to be saved by billion-dollar taxpayer parachutes, Big Oil is paying the government hundreds of billions in taxes. In other words, Big Oil is giving money directly back to the people (instead of stealing it from them, which other corporations find so trendy these days).

In 2006, the oil industry paid $81 billion in income taxes. If you look at Exxon alone, you find that, from 2003 to 2007, their earnings increased by 89 percent while their income taxes skyrocketed 170 percent. Over the three-year period from 2006 to 2008, Exxon paid a total of $94.2 billion—an amount approximately equal to the annual GDP of Ecuador and Guatemala . . . *combined.*

But that's just their income tax. Exxon Mobil's *total* taxes in 2008 reached $116.2 billion—more than *twice* its net profit. That's about $318 million in taxes per day. If *anyone* is benefiting from these so-called windfall profits, it's our government.

A.D.D. MOMENT

Exxon's taxes over those three years would also be enough to pay for about half of the government's AIG bailout.

CONGRESSIONAL CIRCUS

Behold the amazing Chest-Puffing Congressman! Sightings are rare, they come out only when oil prices are high or executives receive large bonuses. In the presence of oil chiefs, the Chest-Puffing Congressman spews hellishly hot air as a defense mechanism—only to later return to hibernation for months or years at a time.

"On April Fool's Day, the biggest joke of all is being played on American families by Big Oil."
—Rep. Edward Markey (D-MA)

"Gentlemen, to all of you, I hope I can give you a bit of a reality check. Working people struggle with high gas prices and your sacrifice, gentlemen, appears to be nothing."
—Sen. Barbara Boxer (D-CA)

"Americans are now concerned whether they should be paying so much more for energy when our energy companies are recording record profits."
—Sen. Ted Stevens (R-AK)

"I think Mr. Hill wants to know how all of you can justify such exorbitant profits on the backs of the middle class and hard-working families."
—Sen. Patrick Leahy (D-VT)

"GOOD! IT'S THEIR PATRIOTIC DUTY TO PAY MORE TAXES SO THE GOVERNMENT CAN HELP THOSE WHO ARE LESS FORTUNATE."

Treasury Secretary Tim Geithner once said that additional taxes on oil companies could "be absorbed" because they are so small compared to their large revenues. Last year, Senator Dick Durbin, an Illinois Democrat, went a step further, saying, "Oil companies need to know that there is a limit on how much profit they can take in this economy."

Using the tax code as a weapon? Caps on profits? Karl Marx would be proud.

President Obama has backed off his promise to institute a windfall-profits tax, but it's not like he's suddenly turned into a Texas oilman. He still intends to rake in an additional $31.5 billion from the oil sector by raising royalty rates and implementing new taxes. The budget he proposed in early 2009 would levy a 13-percent tax on oil and gas from the Gulf of Mexico, raising about $5 billion over the next decade. He would also institute a fee on energy leases in the Gulf that are "nonproducing"—also known as "exploratory." That fee would raise another $1.2 billion over the coming decade.

While all of that may sound appetizing to those of us who don't go oil drilling on weekends, two things happen when you raise taxes on oil companies—neither of them good. First, capital moves to more favorable tax environments, meaning that U.S. companies will flock to foreign sources of oil to get cheaper prices. Second, taxing an activity discourages people from doing it. (Of course, the inverse is also true, which is why so many states have occasional "tax holidays" to promote spending.)

The tax on Gulf oil is essentially an oil sin tax that will lead companies to produce less oil from that region. That, in turn, will reduce supply, which will inevitably cause prices to rise, thereby bringing the incredible chest-puffing politicians out of hibernation once again.

Obama has also proposed raising revenue through a carbon-emission cap-and-trade system that would force companies

I'M SAYING NO...
But Only Because I Care Too Much

"It seems kind of silly to have a solar project [there]."

—Jeff Morgan, chairman of the Sierra Club group in the Coachella Valley, on a proposed solar farm in Blythe, California

"It would be all about socializing—uh, uh, would be about [awkward pause as colleagues laugh] basically taking over and the government running all of your companies."

—Rep. Maxine Waters (D-CA) to the president of Shell Oil, May 22, 2008.

CELEBRITY GUEST IDEEOT

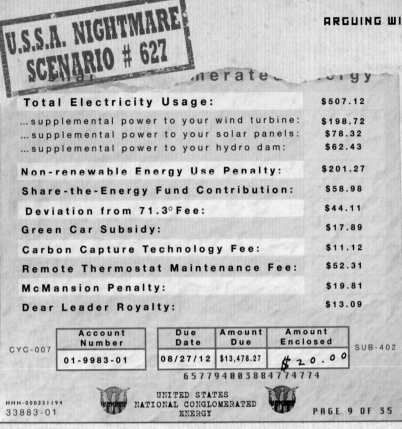

U.S.A. NIGHTMARE SCENARIO # 627

...erate...ergy

Total Electricity Usage:	$507.12
...supplemental power to your wind turbine:	$198.72
...supplemental power to your solar panels:	$78.32
...supplemental power to your hydro dam:	$62.43
Non-renewable Energy Use Penalty:	$201.27
Share-the-Energy Fund Contribution:	$58.98
Deviation from 71.3° Fee:	$44.11
Green Car Subsidy:	$17.89
Carbon Capture Technology Fee:	$11.12
Remote Thermostat Maintenance Fee:	$52.31
McMansion Penalty:	$19.81
Dear Leader Royalty:	$13.09

CYC-007

Account Number	Due Date	Amount Due	Amount Enclosed
01-9983-01	08/27/12	$13,478.27	$20.00

SUB-402

6577940038847 74774

HHH-000331194
33883-01

UNITED STATES
NATIONAL CONGLOMERATED
ENERGY

PAGE 9 OF 35

to buy permits allowing them to pollute. This program would pull in an estimated $112 billion by 2012 and would generate $50–300 billion per year by 2020. As a side "benefit," it would also essentially redistribute the wealth of our most productive companies to the least productive bureaucracy in the world—our government (and eventually to governments of developing countries around the globe).

It doesn't take a degree in economics to understand that hundreds of billions of new tax dollars have to come from somewhere. In this case, they'll come from higher prices on all kinds of products and services—something that will be terrible for the economy (not to mention those "working families" we always hear about in the stump speeches). The real reason this program is called "cap and trade" is that it puts a cap on success and trades prosperity for poverty. By penalizing companies for simply operating and

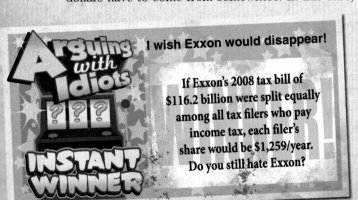

I wish Exxon would disappear!

If Exxon's 2008 tax bill of $116.2 billion were split equally among all tax filers who pay income tax, each filer's share would be $1,259/year. Do you still hate Exxon?

producing, cap-and-trade schemes will reduce manufacturing output (pro: fewer emissions; con: fewer jobs), and that, in turn, will reduce America's GDP (pro: lower carbon output; con: a lower standard of living).

"SO NOT ONLY DO YOU NOT WANT TO PENALIZE OIL COMPANIES, YOU ACTUALLY WANT TO HELP THEM MAKE EVEN MORE MONEY BY LETTING THEM SLAUGHTER INNOCENT POLAR BEARS AND ARCTIC SEALS."

It's a paradox that those who want to keep Alaska off-limits will never admit to, but the more we're prevented from tapping our own oil resources, the more the environment is put at risk. When we can't produce enough oil, we import it. The countries we import it from have to explore and drill to meet our needs. Countries like Venezuela, Russia, Saudi Arabia, and Iran. Those are countries that barely care about people . . . so how much do you really think they worry about hurting green alligators and long-necked geese, some humpty-backed camels or some chimpanzees?

Most people think about green energy as a replacement for oil. While that may very well be, it's a loooooong way off. Instead of thinking about solar, wind, and hydro replacing oil, start thinking about those alternative sources *supplementing* oil. If we can gradually increase our reliance on clean sources of energy that are both economical and efficient, then, believe me, the free markets will do the rest. Our reliance on oil will fall on its own, with absolutely no need for government subsidies or taxes that attempt to "influence" the right decision but inevitably usher in the wrong one. Corn ethanol, anyone? (More on that later.)

In 1988, President Reagan ended a windfall-profits tax on oil companies instituted by Jimmy Carter that was expected to net the government $390 billion from 1980 to 1990. In its first eight years it actually generated just over 20 percent of that, or $80 billion. Anyone think the current "cap-and-trade" revenue estimates might be just as inflated?

A.D.D. MOMENT

If you realized that that list of animals is actually from a popular Irish drinking song, then you're either (a) an alcoholic, (b) a recovering alcoholic, or (c) friendless. Considering that I actually used those lyrics in this book (from memory) I'd say that I'm both (b) and (c).

I'M SAYING NO... But Only Because I Care Too Much

"Our position is that none of this is needed."

—Jim Harvey, cofounder of Alliance for Responsible Energy Policy, on solar farms proposed for the California desert.

REALITY CHECK ARENA

Madison Square Garden has 19,763 seats. Here is how a sold-out crowd would be broken down if everyone sat based on the kind of energy they consume.

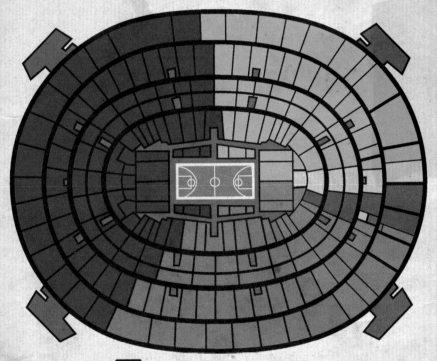

39.2% petroleum = 7,750 seats

23.3% natural gas = 4,605 seats

22.4% coal = 4,431 seats

8.3% nuclear = 1,640 seats

3.6% biomass = 711 seats

2.4% hydroelectric = 475 seats

0.35% geothermal = 70 seats

0.31% wind = 61 seats

0.08% solar = 16 seats

Yes, I understand that relying on the "free markets" to make the right choice in the future is dangerous. Not because the markets might be wrong—they almost never are over the long term—but because they might not exist.

In the meantime, our green energy prospects depend on our ability to use more of our own oil—and the most obvious place to get it is from the Arctic National Wildlife Refuge (ANWR) in Alaska.

Estimates of the amount of recoverable oil in ANWR range from 2 billion to 16 billion barrels, meaning that one small area could produce anywhere from 500,000 to 1.5 million barrels per day, thereby saving us $135 billion to $327 billion in oil imports.

In addition to creating an estimated 60,000 to 130,000 jobs, ANWR drilling would also allow the government to stuff its own coffers. Companies must bid for the right to explore for energy on federal land, such as ANWR, and the revenue from those "bonus bids" goes straight to the federal government. Think of it as eBay for Uncle Sam.

The government also collects 12.5 percent in royalties when federal land is used for energy production. If ANWR were producing oil, our government could rake in an additional $38 billion, while the Alaskan government would pull in at least $700 million a year in royalties.

"But all to the detriment of the cuddly polar bears!" you scream from your parents' basement. Not so much. ANWR technically encompasses 19 million acres, but, thanks to a congressional amendment, drilling would disturb only 2,000 of them—about the size of the University of Florida campus. Plus, wildlife has already been shown to be largely unaffected by oil development elsewhere in Alaska. The caribou herd that migrates through the Prudhoe Bay oil fields has grown from 3,000 to 32,000. Brown bear, fox, and bird populations are just as healthy as those in surrounding areas.

It's illegal to pump your own gas in New Jersey and Oregon; a law hailed by lazy people and petroleum transfer engineers.

"DRILLING IN ANWR OR OFFSHORE IS POINTLESS ANYWAY; IT'LL TAKE 10 YEARS BEFORE WE GET THE OIL!"

In 1996, we had a chance to drill in ANWR, but President Clinton vetoed it. If he hadn't, we'd be swimming in that oil now instead of still talking about how it's a decade away. It's kind of like dieting. Instead of saying, "But it'll take a year to lose 25 pounds!" and continuing to eat your way through the Waffle House menu, you could actually start on the diet.

The same idea holds true for offshore drilling. President Bush planned to open hundreds of millions of acres off the U.S. coasts to oil and gas drilling, but President Obama has put that idea on hold for further review. The Interior Department estimates 18 billion barrels of oil (even more than ANWR's estimated capacity) and 76 trillion cubic feet of natural gas would have been tapped under the plan.

"SURE WE'D GET LOTS OF OIL . . . ALONG WITH LOTS OF DEAD MARINE LIFE."

What the environmentalists don't tell you is that a whopping 47 percent of total petroleum leaked into marine environments is actually from *natural* seepage, meaning that Mother Nature has some seriously overactive pores. Only four percent of total petroleum seepage comes from offshore oil and gas development.

Guess where a big chunk of the remaining oil leakage comes from? Tankers and barges. There's a reason that when you hear "oil spill" you think of giant tanker disasters like the *Exxon Valdez* and not offshore rigs. Between 1971 and 2000, tankers and barges were responsible for 61 percent of all oil spilled in U.S. waters.

Hmm, now let me think out loud for a second here. How could we possibly reduce the amount of oil spilling from tankers and barges into U.S. waters? Oh, I know! We could drill for our own and transport it through pipelines, which accounted for a mere two percent of the total oil spillage in U.S. waters during that same timeframe.

In other words, if we stop relying on drunk tanker captains to get our oil from across the globe, both the environmentalists *and* consumers would win.

"Crude-oil seeps are natural phenomena over which humankind has little direct control, although oil production probably has reduced oil-seepage rates."
—U.S. Geological Survey, 2003.

In other words, because man safely extracts oil offshore, Mother Nature has less to pollute herself with.

"I DON'T CARE ABOUT THE NUMBERS. OIL IS YESTERDAY'S ENERGY SOURCE. TIME TO GET ON THE RENEWABLE ENERGY BANDWAGON OR GET LEFT IN THE DUST."

I'm trying, but some of the biggest opponents of alternative energy happen to be members of the green movement. Maybe they should get their house in order before they start inviting guests over for dinner.

The latest trend is for environmentalists to whine about the very wind and solar energy they supposedly support. Yes, they still drool over these sources like a 12-year-old boy walking past Victoria's Secret—but only when they're developed, installed, and used *exactly* the way they suggest.

The private sector is jumping at the opportunity to expand alternative energy—just as the greenies seem to be turning away from it. Former oil man T. Boone Pickens has mounted a $58 million campaign to promote his wind-farm idea—something that you'd have to be a hermit to not know about at this point. Similarly, Cape Wind is preparing to build America's first offshore wind farm in the waters off Cape Cod, Massachusetts, but their plans are being slowed by— wait for it—green-energy supporters.

Cape Wind's farm would occupy 25 square miles of water in Nantucket Sound—a plan that would make America only the sixth country in the world to harness offshore wind power. Supporters estimate the farm would reduce green-house gas emissions at a level equivalent to taking 175,000 cars off the road per year. Cape Wind says its 130 towers would meet 75 percent of the region's electricity needs and reduce carbon emissions by about 734,000 tons annually.

I'M SAYING NO...
But Only Because I Care Too Much

"Cape Wind . . . would adversely impact well over 1,000 historic sites around Nantucket Sound . . . [including] desecrating ancient American Native burial sites."

—Glenn Wattley, president and chief executive of the Alliance to Protect Nantucket Sound

So, what's the problem? Well, it turns out that Senator Ted Kennedy, one of the original crusaders for action on global warming, was opposed to the project. Why? Presumably because it would've ruined the view from his Hyannis Port vacation home. Yes, that's right, NIMBY ("Not in My Backyard") has, at least for the rich and famous, turned into NIMOV ("Not in My Ocean View").

In 2006, Kennedy inserted an undebated amendment into a Coast Guard bill that would have killed Cape Wind. Thankfully, the public caught wind of it (thanks, I'll be here all week, try the veal) and the backlash forced him to do a one-eighty.

But the eyesore argument isn't the only reason why the green lobby is turning against both onshore and offshore wind farms. They also claim that the turbines harm property values, they're dangerous, their output is spotty (turns out, you need the wind to be blowing—who knew?), they could harm birds, and they're expensive.

Solar farms are facing similar opposition from so-called environmentalists. A mini gold rush is happening with solar projects in the California desert due to the plentiful sunshine, high altitude, level ground, and, well, the general lack of any other possible way to use a ridiculously hot, sand-covered barren desert for anything productive.

A.D.D. MOMENT

I don't know if these green lobbyists have noticed, but you know what else is dangerous and expensive? Foreign oil.

Pacific Gas and Electric is buying enough solar-generated electricity to power 239,000 California homes. That may not sound like much, but this deal would nearly double the nation's total solar capacity. I say "would" because, once again, a plan to actually turn blueprints into green energy is facing resistance from the very people who should be supporting it.

It turns out that the locations of most proposed solar farms are also home to the Mojave ground squirrel, the desert tortoise, and the burrowing owl. Apparently none of those animals would be able to live with some mirrors scattered along the ground—so environmentalists want the solar project stopped.

California Governor Arnold Schwarzenegger and I may not agree on everything, but he echoed my thoughts on this story perfectly when he said: "If we cannot put solar power plants in the Mojave Desert, I don't know where the hell we can put it."

DO AS I SAY
(NOT AS I DO)

"[Global warming] is a very valid issue . . . I'm wondering if we need to think about other planets and dome cities."

—John Travolta, who owns a fleet of five private jets, as well as his very own runway. In one year alone he logged more than 30,000 miles—producing an estimated 800 tons of carbon emissions.

One big problem that environmentalists have with solar and wind farms is that they require transmission lines to get the energy from the source all the way back to power plants and homes. For instance, California approved the Sunrise Powerlink to connect San Diego to solar, wind, and geothermal energy being harnessed in the Imperial Valley. The transmission line has very tight environmental standards—it would circumvent a state park, an Indian reservation, and a forest, and builders are not allowed to disturb burrowing owls and rattlesnakes—but, of course, none of that is good enough for groups like the Sierra Club, which is opposing the project and taking its case to the state Supreme Court.

I guess the bottom line is that clean energy *might* be all right so long as it doesn't have to be transferred to places where it can actually be used.

I'M SAYING NO...
But Only Because I Care Too Much

"Why would you want to sail in a forest of windmills?"

—Bill Koch, a Cape Cod resident who spent $1.5 million of his own money fighting the Cape Wind project. The ironic part is that Koch only has a beautiful ocean view that could be affected by the turbines because he was formerly the founder of the Oxbow Group. According to *Forbes*, Oxbow "once made a mint off eco-friendly power plants by using laws that required power companies to buy Koch's power for above-market rates. He sold [Oxbow] for $660 million in 2000."

A.D.D. MOMENT

What about the elusive hippy drifters squatting in the desert? Are we truly willing to disturb their pristine habitat brimming with empty beer cans, discarded joints, and rusty VW vans?

"THAT'S WHY WE NEED TO GET THE GOVERNMENT MORE INVOLVED. IF THEY DON'T PASS NEW LAWS AND REGULATIONS AMERICANS WILL NEVER CHANGE THEIR ENERGY HABITS."

In March 2008, when going to the gas station was becoming cruel and unusual punishment, Americans drove 11 billion miles less than the previous March. It was the steepest decrease in driving since they began keeping records during World War II. Gas consumption was also down from the previous year, and public transportation ridership was at a 50-year high. There was no government decree mandating those changes; people altered their behavior because of two things we're now trying very hard to eliminate: market forces and common sense.

When the government actually does try to influence energy behavior, it's usually with disastrous results. Take corn ethanol, for example. Completely smitten with the stuff (gee, could the $5.5 million the corn lobby gave to politicians from 2005 to 2008 have anything to do with that?), the government subsidized corn for ethanol production to the tune of $56.1 billion from 1995 to 2006. What did we get in return? In short, really expensive corn flakes.

Here's what was *supposed* to happen: Subsidies would lower the cost of corn, which would in turn be used to create cheap fuel. Everyone would then love their cheap fuel so much

A.D.D. Moment

Where's that flying car I've been promised since I was a kid? Are you telling me that we have the capability to clone animals, spray cheese out of a can, and airbrush Susan Sarandon into something resembling a human being, but we can't make a freaking car hover? Something doesn't add up here. Who killed the flying car?

ETHANOL PR

Maybe what ethanol really needs is a public relations boost. After all, plenty of crappy products have been successful simply because of good marketing or PR. And for that, what better place to turn than General Electric, a company that seems to slowly be turning into an official government agency anyway.

I don't know this for sure, but I bet that if the government throws a little stimulus money their way, GE would be more than happy to ask their PR wing (aka "MSNBC") to do a few pro-ethanol segments. Maybe they could even convince NBC and MSNBC to turn their logos green for a week to get everyone thinking about how cool it is to "go green." Wait, what'd you say? They already do that?

GOVERNMENT ELECTRIC

U.S.S.A. NIGHTMARE SCENARIO # 832

UNITED STATES
MINISTRY OF ENERGY

To: Mr. Glenn Beck

REALID#: 392011039100229RW-832

Dear Mr. Beck,

Great News! ExxonGettyMobilShell and ChevronGulf are joining forces to bring you ONE company: PETROGOV.

No more confusing choices. PETROGOV is the choice!

Enjoy the convenience of gas prices set by Congress.

No long lines at the pump . . . you'll be assigned "pumping times" when you can drop by.

Fuel quotas mean every working family is sure to get the share they deserve.

No more pumping yourself; let our professionals fill your tank in 45 minutes or less!

We hope you're as excited about these changes as we are!

See you at the pump,

Maxine Waters

Maxine Waters
Chief Director, PETROGOV

that they'd demand more cars be built to utilize it. Carmakers would take advantage of the opportunity and, in a few years, we'd all be driving around in cars powered by a crop grown right here in America.

Here's what *actually* happened: Subsidies incentivized farmers to chase the money and use their crops for ethanol production instead of food production. That led to a full one-quarter of America's corn crop being used for ethanol, which meant there wasn't enough corn left over for food. That led to increased prices on a slew of things that rely on corn (like beef, which comes from cows that eat, yes, corn feed). It drove the price of other crops higher as well because farmers began to plant as much corn as possible, at the expense of soybeans, wheat, and other grains.

But all of those problems cover only the subsidy side of corn ethanol—the functionality of it is what really makes this experiment a historic debacle.

DO AS I SAY
(NOT AS I DO)

> "This issue of global warming is going to impact every single person.
> It's not a political issue, it's a moral issue . . . Global warming is
> happening right now, and . . . we are causing it. We are impacting the
> climate. Humans have become a force of nature themselves, and the
> impacts are going to be horrific if we don't do something about it."

—Laurie David, global-warming activist and producer of *An Inconvenient Truth*, flew on
a private jet to Texas A&M campus in order to give a speech focusing on the importance of
changing individual behavior to fight global warming. She also flies privately between her home in Los Angeles
and her 25,000-square-foot home in Martha's Vineyard, a home in which she was issued a "notice of apparent
violations" for building a 26-foot-long barbecue station, stone-and-concrete bonfire pit, and outdoor
theater on an environmentally sensitive patch of property . . . without the proper permits.

Corn ethanol is 30 percent less efficient than gasoline and far less efficient than its sugar-based ethanol cousin. Translation: It takes more energy to make corn ethanol than other fuels. Looking at it another way, one hectare (2.471 acres) of sugarcane yields 7,500 liters of ethanol, while the same acreage of corn yields about half as much fuel.

> "If it was made clear to people that we could win the war on terrorism by driving a hybrid car, that we could stop global warming by driving a hybrid, I think people would do it. But people haven't made those kind of connections."
>
> —Rob Reiner

But forget about hectares and efficiency, the worst thing about corn-based ethanol is that it's not even clean. A recent University of Minnesota study found that corn ethanol is actually *worse* for the environment than regular gas.

So corn ethanol is not only inefficient and expensive, but it also makes the problem we're trying to solve even worse. Genius! I can see why Washington threw $3 billion at it in 2007, an amount that represented 76 percent of all renewable-energy tax credits.

"WHO CARES, CORN ETHANOL IS YESTERDAY'S NEWS. NOW WE REALIZE THAT WE COULD SOLVE A LOT OF OUR ENERGY PROBLEMS IF WE'D EACH JUST MAKE SMART CHOICES LIKE BUYING HYBRID CARS."

Let's play a game. Behind one curtain is $3,000. Behind the other curtain is absolutely nothing. To make it easy, I'll even tell you in advance which curtain has the cash behind it. You can't lose! Do you want to play?

If so, you're in the minority. This game, which is called "Buy a Hybrid and Get a Tax Credit of Up to $3,400," is being offered by our government to all Americans—yet only two percent of car buyers are

CELEBRITY
GUEST IDEEOT

signing up to play. Imagine that—after all of the media attention, celebrity harassment, and expensive government incentives—hybrids *still* make up only about two percent of the market.

Still, the dedication to the hybrid doctrine is at a near-religious level. For example, take a look at the government's "cash for clunkers" program, which is meant to encourage you to turn in your old "clunker" of a car and replace it with a more fuel-efficient one, thereby alleg-edly saving the environment. Sounds great, except for one small problem: as much as 28 percent of a vehicle's carbon dioxide emissions come from manufacturing it and transport-ing it to a dealer. Even environmentalists admit that, unless you're trading in a tank for a solar scooter, the best thing you can do for the environment is run your current car into the ground.

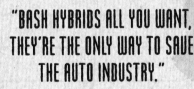

Despite the evidence that they're not particularly helpful (either for the environment, or for sales), cash incentives for hybrids continue to flow from the government to consumers who, by and large, don't need the money.

Consider this: The purchase of a new hybrid is a better indicator of household wealth than a doctorate degree. The average hybrid-buying household earns $113,400 a year—more than twice the median household income in America.

Isn't that exactly the sort of thing liberals are supposed to be infuriated by? We're giving hundreds of millions of dollars in tax credits to households that earn more than six times the poverty line! Yet, instead of outrage, the silence is deafening. Apparently the environment has leapfrogged the poor on the liberal food chain of victimhood.

A.D.D. MOMENT

I don't mean the current cafeteria-catholic "church only on Christmas" kind of religion, I mean the old school, 1400s, burn-everyone-at-the-stake-who-doesn't-agree-with-you kind.

"BASH HYBRIDS ALL YOU WANT, THEY'RE THE ONLY WAY TO SAVE THE AUTO INDUSTRY."

As Barack Obama was defining his new job as car company CEO, he said, "If the Japanese can design an affordable, well-designed hybrid, then, doggone it, the American people should be able to do the same . . . So my job is to ask the auto industry: Why is it you guys can't do this?"

A.D.D. MOMENT

I remember everyone making fun of Sarah Palin for saying things like "doggone it" during the campaign. I must have missed the same treatment for President Obama. I should watch the news more.

But, do the Japanese really even do what the president suggested? Is *anyone* really doing it? And is going green really the best way to bring in the green, as so many people seem to think?

The Toyota Prius is far and away the most successful hybrid of all time. Yet, even after a decade and over a million cars sold, the Prius is, according to the *Washington Post*, "still widely believed by analysts to be losing money on each one sold."

But even if the Prius is slightly profitable for Toyota, it's the exception, not the rule. Consider what other automakers have said about the world of hybrids. Nissan admitted: "Hybrids today are not a very viable economic proposition." Ford is finally hoping to see the light at the end of the tunnel after years of having to "subsidize the price of the hybrid technology." Despite having more hybrid models than any other manufacturer, GM reportedly still has "years of bleeding red ink ahead." And the outlook on GM's next-generation all-electric Chevy Volt? "We won't make a dime on this car for years."

In fact, of all carmakers, Honda is probably the most optimistic: "If we were making money on the Civic hybrid," a Honda spokesman said, "we weren't making a lot."

But even with nearly nonexistent profits, car companies still have a tough time moving hybrids that aren't named "Prius." For example, the Toyota Camry and Honda Civic were the second and third best-selling hybrids in 2008, yet their *combined* sales were less than half those of the Prius. The Prius sold at more than eight times the rate of the Toyota Highlander and Ford Escape/Mercury Mariner SUV hybrids and it outsold the Nissan Altima hybrid 18 to 1.

So, how has the Prius bucked the hybrid sales trend? By becoming a rolling status symbol. The number-one reason people give for buying a Toyota Prius isn't higher fuel economy, lower emissions, or love of new technology, it's that it "makes a statement about me."

The point is that the Prius was like catching lightning in a bottle, you don't just come up with another one easily, doggone it. Yet that's exactly what the president's strategy is. He is essentially telling American

Conservative columnist George Will was attacked by left-leaning blogs for saying the Prius is "affordable because Toyota sells it at a loss, and it can afford to sell it at a loss because it is selling twice as many gas-guzzling pickup trucks of the sort our president detests." As evidence against Will, these blogs point to the fact that Toyota has said the Prius is finally profitable . . . which I believe may be the first time liberal bloggers have ever actually believed a company about anything.

A.D.D. Moment

In other words, solve your problems by finding a way to stroke people's greego. (That's a new term I'm testing: Green + Ego = Greego.) It's a tough task for automakers, especially considering that it's mostly rich (probably white!) people buying hybrids anyway. Ahhhh, the greego of a gringo.

Of all the reasons why people buy a Prius, "lower emissions" finished second to last, actually coming in *behind* "distinctive styling." Ouch.

THE WORST CAR REVIEW IN HISTORY?

Honda makes a lot of good cars but, according to Jeremy Clarkson of *The Times of London*, the Honda Insight hybrid is not one of them.

> "It's terrible. Biblically terrible. Possibly the worst new car money can buy. It's the first car I've ever considered crashing into a tree, on purpose, so I didn't have to drive it anymore. . . . [it] makes a noise worse than someone else's crying baby on an airliner. It's worse than the sound of your parachute failing to open. Really, to get an idea of how awful it is, you'd have to sit a dog on a ham slicer.
>
> "So you're sitting there with the engine screaming its head off, and your ears bleeding, and you're doing only 23 mph because that's about the top speed . . . [it] feels as if it's been made from steel so thin, you could read through it. And the seats . . . are designed specifically, it seems, to ruin your skeleton . . . the idiotic dashboard, which shows leaves growing on a tree when you ease off the throttle . . . built out of rice paper . . . poor ride, the woeful performance, the awful noise and the spine-bending seats.
>
> "Acceleration 0–62 mph: 12.5 seconds. One star (out of five) . . . Good only for parting the smug from their money."

automakers to solve their problems by simply inventing the next "ultra-trendy-low-profit-highly-subsidized-status-symbol-for-the-rich." Sounds like a reliable business strategy.

"WELL, THEY BETTER FIGURE OUT A WAY TO MAKE IT A RELIABLE BUSINESS STRATEGY, BECAUSE AMERICANS ARE DEMANDING MORE FUEL-EFFICIENT CARS!"

Yes, we want fuel efficiency. We just don't want it at the expense of almost anything else. We like to fancy ourselves driving fuel-efficient cars, but, like dropping those last twenty pounds, "saying" and "doing" are two entirely different things.

Despite all of the green hype, the best-selling vehicles of 2008 were the Ford F-150 and the Chevrolet Silverado. Neither one is powered with celery, eco-juice, or environmental magic powder. They're big trucks with big engines that haul big things.

A.D.D. MOMENT

Americans can be so rude sometimes—it's like they don't even consider Al Gore's feelings when making what is generally their second-biggest purchase in life.

One car you *won't* find on the 2008 automotive best-seller list is the vaunted Toyota Prius. Even with gas at record levels and the media and politicians never more pretentious and persistent, the Prius didn't even make the top ten. The Ford Focus, a serviceable car for sure—but far from a worldwide celebrity and media phenomenon—finished tenth, and still outsold the Prius by 16 percent.

Sure, there were plenty of car buyers who wanted sensibly priced sedans that get decent gas mileage and cost around $20,000. And an awful lot of those buyers even walked into a Toyota dealership to buy a car. But that's when the rubber hit the road. Faced with the choice between the hybrid Prius and the gas-powered Toyota Camry, 71 percent of those buyers drove off the lot in the Camry.

"But Glenn! Maybe their vision stopped them from buying a Prius because of its hideous styling!" Ooh . . . sorry, try again. The Camry also has a hybrid version that looks *exactly the same* as its evil earth-killing counterpart, yet 89 of every 100 people who bought a Camry chose the gas-powered planet murderer. They must all have been bribed by Big Oil.

The Honda Civic attracts a similar customer and also has a hybrid that looks exactly the same as the gas-powered version. Only 9 percent of buyers chose the hybrid.

The worst news of all for hybrid zombies is that even the Prius may finally be losing its luster. Sales actually fell by 12 percent from 2007 to 2008 and, through the first five months of 2009, they're down 45 percent compared to the same period in the previous year.

Those drops are, of course, partially due to the well-publicized rough patch for automakers, but, as the crisis worsened, hybrid sales actually plummeted *faster* than their gas-powered competition.

Meanwhile, as hybrid sales were crashing, Ford announced the addition of a third shift to its Dearborn, Michigan, plant. Why? To make more F-150s. That extra shift, by the way, will employ 1,000 people, and annoy 1,000,000 environmentalists.

A.D.D. MOMENT

Half of the top ten cars sold in 2008, including the top two spots on the list, were American vehicles. I'm sorry, but haven't we been told that the Big Three were making vehicles that no one wanted to buy?

I'M SAYING NO... But Only Because I Care Too Much

"I'm a strong supporter of renewable energy and clean technology—but it is critical that these projects are built on suitable lands."

—Sen. Dianne Feinstein (D-CA) on her campaign to block hundreds of thousands of acres of California desert from being used for solar farms by designating the land a "national monument."

"IF PEOPLE AREN'T EXACTLY IN LOVE WITH HYBRIDS YET IT'S ONLY BECAUSE THEY DON'T KNOW HOW MUCH MONEY THEY CAN SAVE ON GAS!"

Why haven't Americans rushed to dealer showrooms to fully embrace hybrids? Well, because, unlike many of our politicians, they find that the potential glory of their peers lauding them as "green" doesn't shut down the math part of their brains.

In 2007, the Department of Health and Human Services sent out a newsletter that instructed its 67,000 employees to make fuel efficiency their top priority when buying new cars. It specifically mentioned the Camry hybrid and the Nissan Altima hybrid as two options. Unfortunately for our government, people don't just blindly listen to them. Yes, the Altima hybrid is more fuel efficient than the gas version, but it also costs a lot more.

This A.D.D. moment is really for you. I know you need time to sit back and consider how incredibly stupid it is for our own government to be encouraging its employees to buy foreign cars and then later beg for billions of taxpayer dollars to bail out American carmakers. Are you ready to continue reading yet? I'll wait . . .

With gas prices just under two dollars a gallon, you would have to drive the Altima hybrid over 350,000 miles just to make your money back. Even with gas at its peak of $4.11 a gallon, you'd still have to drive the hybrid 159,000 miles to break even.

But it gets even worse. As the Associated Press noted, "Driving 15,000 miles a year with a commute that keeps you on the freeway, you'd have to drive the car until 2057 to save enough gas to make the hybrid cost-effective, even at . . . record gas prices." I hate to say it, but even that analysis is optimistic because they don't include the extra money you'd spend on financing the car, or the interest you'd make on your money by investing the cash you would've saved by sticking with that evil gasoline.

In other words, our government is stupid. Surprise, surprise.

The Al Gore Hypocrisy Calendar

NOVEMBER 29 2006

On November 29, 2006, the United Nations released a report which found eating meat worse for the climate than the entire transportation sector. Years later, Al Gore is still NOT a vegetarian.

"WHO CARES IF PEOPLE *WANT* GAS-GUZZLERS? DRIVING MORE FUEL-EFFICIENT CARS IS SIMPLY WHAT WE MUST DO TO SAVE THE PLANET!"

DO AS I SAY
(NOT AS I DO)

I understand the argument: I'd like a fountain of cheddar cheese in my office to be the answer to my double-chin epidemic, but that doesn't mean it would be. Likewise, the fact that so many people *want* hybrids to be a simple answer to lowering carbon-dioxide emissions doesn't mean they are. And if you're going to tell me what I can and cannot drive, you'd better be solving a lot of big problems. Instead, they're creating new ones.

The National Highway Traffic Safety Administration ran the numbers on what an increased focus on fuel efficiency would mean for the climate. In a 939-page report (which, by the way, generally supported such a move, claiming that it "addressed climate change") they found that, if successful, new regulations would shave one part per million from the carbon dioxide in the atmosphere by the year 2100. To give that some perspective, the doomsday scenario from the U.N. Intergovernmental Panel on Climate Change (IPCC) that is constantly recited by the media is *970* parts per million.

But that's just scientific jargon to most people. Global warming is about temperature, right? Well, the new regulations would result in an estimated total decrease of 0.004 degrees Celsius (0.0072 degrees Fahr-

1 There are so many A.D.D. thoughts in my head right now, I don't even know where to start. First, remember that these completely insignificant decreases aren't the result of one town making changes in fuel efficiency, it's our entire country, aka "the largest economy in the world."

2 All of those wonderful benefits are depending on the science of global warming being correctly "settled." We went into much more detail on that science in my #1 *New York Times* bestseller *An Inconvenient Book.* The consensus is that you should read it. Or at least buy it.

3 Ever notice how the only time that conservatives ever blindly trust *The New York Times* is when their names appear at the top of their bestseller list?

A.D.D. MOMENT

"We must make concrete changes in our lifestyles to help solve this energy crisis and now is the time to do it . . . [turn your thermostats up to] 78 degrees when you're home and 85 degrees when you're out . . . and try to line-dry [your clothes] as much as possible."

—Barbra Streisand's seaside estate includes five homes and a 12,000-square-foot air-conditioned barn, as well as a lawn sprinkling system that uses $22,000 a year in water. Her most recent tour rider included the following demands:

"Please arrange parking for the following vehicles . . . • Thirteen (13) 53-foot semi-tractor trailers (plus one for merchandising) • Four (4) rental vans • Fourteen (14) crew and band buses • One (1) limousine (artist)"

When asked about her apparent hypocrisy, Streisand's spokesman said, "She never meant that [those concrete changes in our lifestyles] necessarily applied to her."

enheit) by 2100. In other words, it would save us 1/1,600th of the doomsday-level global warming we're constantly told to be so petrified of. In fact, the potential decrease is so insignificant that it's equal to only 1/45th of the *margin of error* in the past century's temperature change.

Want a way to make this even easier to relate to? Try this: Put your thumb and finger about one centimeter apart. For those of you who understand the superiority of the good old English system, that's about 40 percent of an inch. Now, cut that distance in half. Now, cut it in half again. Now, again. Again. One more time. The remaining space between your thumb and finger is about how much the proposed efficiency standards would decrease the allegedly forthcoming sea-level rise. The grand total is 0.04 centimeters by 2100, which is equivalent to 1/15,240th of the sea-level rise Al Gore warned about in *An Inconvenient Truth*.

Focusing on increasing fuel efficiency might be worthwhile to keep America from having to bow before slimy dictators, but government mandates aren't the way to accomplish that. And if your goal is combating global warming, you're completely wasting your time.

A study for the journal *Energy Policy* by experts at Monash University in Australia laid out what changes would really be necessary if the politicians of the green revolution get their way. "Our calculations show that not even the best combination of fuel efficiency, hybrid and electric cars, alternative fuels and car pooling could provide the reductions needed to meet the 2050 targets for avoiding dangerous climatic change." These changes would require a "near-total shift from the private car to public transport."

Their bottom line on the automobile is of particular significance as our government claims to be able to save the planet and the auto industry simultaneously: "The car," they said, "is doomed."

With predictions like that, it's hard to figure out whether to laugh or asphyxiate yourself with a fossil-fuel-created plastic bag and a little exhaled CO_2.

"FINE. IT MIGHT NOT SAVE THE WORLD, BUT THERE'S ONLY UPSIDE TO THE GOVERNMENT RAISING FUEL-EFFICIENCY STANDARDS."

If there is an upside, it's very difficult to find. But that's not going to stop our government from trying anyway. After all, they have political points to win, and they're not going to allow a few pesky facts to get in the way of collecting them.

So, in addition to putting pressure on the consumer side with massive incentives and tax credits, they pressure the automaker side as well. No, they don't tell the companies what cars they can make; they'd *never* do something like that. But they do have a tool that's not nearly as obvious and just as effective: CAFE standards.

CAFE stands for "Corporate Average Fuel Economy" and the standards were implemented in reaction to the Arab oil embargo of 1973–74. Without boring you with the details, CAFE forces each car company to hit a minimum average fuel economy across their entire fleet, with differing standards for cars and light trucks. Politicians love the standards and, depending on the poll, between 78 and 92 percent of Americans are in favor of CAFE standards being raised because, really, who doesn't support higher gas mileage?

As Christmas 2007 approached, President George W. Bush saw an opportunity to appear bipartisan, so he signed the first major hike of CAFE standards since 1975 into law. (I'm sure the polling data didn't have *anything* to do with it.) As a result of the new legislation, automakers would be forced to raise their overall fuel efficiency by about 40 percent by 2020 to a fleet-wide average of 35 miles per gallon. Environmentalists cheered, politicians posed, and logic wept in the corner.

A.D.D. MOMENT

We should know by now that instituting new standards, regulations, or legislation in *reaction* to anything is usually a pretty bad idea.

As you may have noticed, one thing that the auto industry did not need was an expensive new mandate forcing them to create more unprofitable cars that buyers don't want. The changes were so disliked by automakers that they were even fought by Toyota, the enviro-angels from the land of the rising sun.

At the time the new CAFE standards were announced, the EPA had rated 1,153 different vehicle models for gas mileage. Guess how many hit the newly proposed efficiency standards in both the city and highway categories. Half? Maybe 100? How about 20? Nope.

A.D.D. MOMENT

By the way, that's the same "rising sun" that has nothing to do with global warming.

Two.

The Toyota Prius and the Honda Civic hybrid. That's it.

A few other models hit 35 mpg on the highway or in the city—but not both, and all of those were compacts or subcompacts. Exactly *zero* SUVs qualified, including the hybrid models. In other words, these new standards would cost automakers around the world *a lot* of money to meet.

But new leadership and new circumstances bring new ideas. After all, elections have consequences! So, under President Obama, and with auto companies in a slow-motion, very public collapse, these new onerous restrictions would surely be loosened, delayed, or canceled . . . right?

Of course not. As a matter of policy, the Obama administration is seemingly dismantling everything the Bush administration

I'M SAYING NO...
But Only Because I Care Too Much

"The idea that we're going to sacrifice critical pieces of our environment to protect other pieces of our environment seems a little ironic...That's an irony I cannot accept. We have to find a way to do both."

—Elizabeth Goldstein, president of the California Parks Foundation, on her apparent "no compromise" policy toward environmentalism.

did well and doubling down on everything they did terribly. Within a few months of taking office, not only did Obama show unwavering support for the new CAFE standards, he also presented a plan to force the auto companies to meet even tougher standards four years *earlier*.

The new CAFE standards increase will add about $1,300 to the price of every new car, according to that extreme right-wing organization . . . the Obama administration. You won't be surprised to learn that some outside observers find that estimate to be optimistic. For example, Bob Lutz, former vice chairman of General Motors, estimated the additional cost of the less restrictive Bush standards at $6,000 per vehicle.

The higher CAFE standards have other consequences as well, like eliminating thousands of auto industry jobs that the government claims to care so much about. The Bush plan would have cost over 11,000 jobs by 2015, while the plan most similar to Obama's ups that number to almost 49,000 lost jobs.

I guess Obama isn't doubling down on Bush's bad ideas; he's more like *quadrupling down*.

"EVERYTHING IS ALWAYS ABOUT MONEY WITH YOU CONSERVATIVES! SOME THINGS ARE MORE IMPORTANT!"

Hmm, you mean like safety?

Killing auto companies is one thing. Killing people is another. When car companies get hit with higher mileage standards they have to try their best to make cars that people still want to buy, while also complying with the government. They typically don't do that by inventing magical new super-fuels, especially when the timeline is tight and the standards are so difficult to reach. They do it by making their cars lighter because, to state the obvious, lighter cars get better gas mileage.

A.D.D. MOMENT

Between 97,000 and 195,000? Could they have been a tad more specific? Why not say "We estimate CAFE caused between . . . like . . . 1,000 . . . and 3,000,000,000,000 additional injuries. Somewhere in there."?

Unfortunately, when lighter cars get into accidents, more people die. The National Academy of Sciences estimated that CAFE standards kill about 2,000 people every year, along with between 13,000 and 26,000 additional incapacitating injuries and 97,000 to 195,000 additional overall injuries.

An analysis done by *USA Today* found that CAFE killed an additional 46,000 people (and that was only through 1999.) That is approximately the combined death toll of 9/11 and Hurricane Katrina . . . times ten.

Another study, by economists Robert Crandall of the Brookings Institution and John

Graham also said, "To the best of my knowledge, these findings have never been disputed in the peer-reviewed scientific literature." I'll have to check my Al Gore playbook, but does that mean we should end this section now because the debate is over?

Graham of the Harvard School of Public Health, also found that CAFE was likely responsible for tens of thousands of deaths. They reported: "The negative relationship between weight and occupant fatality risk is one of the most secure findings in the safety literature."

"WEIGHT IS JUST AN EXCUSE. QUALITY AND ENGINEERING ARE FAR MORE IMPORTANT TO SAFETY."

Let's think this out for a second: When you add $1,300 in pointless regulation to the cost of a car, what do you think the consumer can afford less of? Things like quality and engineering.

The supposed evidence behind this claim is a clumsy reference to a 2007 study from the Insurance Institute for Highway Safety that found the Mini Cooper is safer than the Ford Excursion. While the Mini Cooper does perform slightly better than the average automobile, it's the only small, two-door car that did. The study showed that that category has a fatality rate about two and a half times as high as large/very large SUVs. Additionally, it showed that you have about three times the chance of dying in a light car than you do in a heavy one. And this is the study they *want* you to look at?

Could we continue talking about tragedy and death on the roadways like we're a 1960s classroom driving-safety video? Sure. But let's leave our road trip through the infuriating intersection of environmentalists, government, and automobiles on a positive note.

Remember those incredibly ugly station wagons with wood paneling on their sides? Most people believed they went away because they were incredibly ugly and had wood paneling on the sides. But, actually, CAFE standards killed them off. (Okay, CAFE and the fact that they were unbelievably ugly with wood paneling on the sides.) The station wagons weren't fuel-efficient enough to hit the new standards and car companies had little choice but to make them extinct (which probably would have happened anyway because they had, well, incredibly ugly wood paneling on the sides).

But people still had families. They still had to go to the store and pick up furniture or groceries. They still needed a way to carry

I'M SAYING NO... But Only Because I Care Too Much

"Remote solar arrays destroy all native resources on site, and have indirect and irreversible impacts on surrounding wildernesses."

—Terry Frewin, chairman of the Sierra Club's California/Nevada desert committee.

around half of the Little League team and all of its equipment. So automakers shifted their focus and worked toward creating a vehicle to meet this demand in the "light truck" category with a less-restrictive efficiency standard. What was their most successful solution?

The "sport-utility vehicle."

Anyone who says that environmentalists have never brought us anything good isn't being fair, because we can all thank the green movement for the creation of the SUV. I'll make sure to think of that the next time my giant Escalade is crushing a Smart Car like a monster truck.

UNIONS

When Is America Finished Paying Her Dues?

WHEN unions first gained power in the United States, they gave mistreated and beleaguered workers the right to collectively bargain in the face of tremendous disadvantages and hardships. Brave men and women stood up and stared down politicians, special interests, monopolies, and robber barons and fought for fairness and a slice of the American dream. They didn't demand special rights, they demanded *equal* rights.

Boy, have times changed.

We've gone from a world where labor unions sacrificed for the right of all American workers to collect a fair wage to a world where Big Labor sacrifices their workers in exchange for more power and influence.

These days, unions have become powerful political machines that work against individual rights in favor of special interests. They look down on fundamental American ideals like competition, capitalism, and freedom of choice and instead embrace monopolies and bureaucracy—the very things they once fought against.

Fortunately, most Americans aren't fooled. A recent Rasmussen survey, mirroring many other polls, found that 81 percent of nonunion workers do not want anything to do with union representation. Overall, only a measly nine percent said they would actually *like* to join a union. Like a roach motel (or is it an Eagles' song?), you can check in anytime you like, but you can never leave.

A.D.D. MOMENT

Maybe the nine percent of people who'd like to join a union aren't smart enough to understand this, but no one is stopping them. It's like telling a pollster that you'd "like to wear a blue shirt tomorrow." Why not stop talking about it and just do it?

Even those who find themselves in danger of losing their jobs, a group of people you'd expect to be wildly interested in the "security" of a union, aren't pining for representation. Among those companies that are laying workers off, just nine percent of employees are interested in joining a union—the exact same pro-union percentage as the general population.

Survey results like that are probably why union membership has been in a freefall. In the late 1950s, one-third of all private-sector workers belonged to a union. By the mid-'70s, that number had dropped significantly, but a quarter of all private-sector jobs were still unionized. (Of course, the mid-'70s also brought us Jimmy Carter and the Bee Gees, so something was clearly off.) But now? Unions are basically an afterthought—only 7.6 percent of nongovernment workers belong to one.

Given how great unions supposedly are and how much influence they now wield, you'd think people would be running to them in droves.

So why is the complete opposite happening?

From 1997 to 2004, private-sector employment grew from 66.1 to 103.6 million. But over those same years, union membership *declined* from 14.3 to 8.2 million. Either something is seriously wrong with the unions' product, or they have the worst marketing department of all time. I'm going with the former.

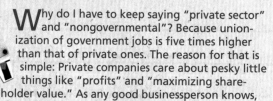

Why do I have to keep saying "private sector" and "nongovernmental"? Because unionization of government jobs is five times higher than that of private ones. The reason for that is simple: Private companies care about pesky little things like "profits" and "maximizing shareholder value." As any good businessperson knows, unions result in higher labor costs and more red tape, two things that hurt a company's ability to compete—but two things that a government monopoly could not care less about.

Over time, it's become obvious that workers who get to choose between job security and success almost always bet on their own success. And with the multitude of laws that now protect workers from management abuse, along with a diverse job market created by free enterprise, most people have realized that the red tape of unions does nothing but hold them back. The ones who haven't? Well, they're idiots who usually say things like . . .

"OH, COME ON, GLENN, UNIONS ARE ONLY TRYING TO LEVEL THE PLAYING FIELD FOR THE WORKING MAN!"

Have you noticed how union groups talk like it's still 1930 and their members are headed down into the coal mine without any water or flashlights? Guess what? It's not 1930. These days, workers have rights, protections, and benefits that those from the early twentieth century couldn't even fathom.

So, why are unions still around? Good question, easy answer: they've got lots of friends in very high places.

During the 2008 election, candidate Obama promised that he would offer a more union-friendly administration, saying,

"This election is our chance to finally have a president who doesn't choke saying the word 'union.'" Unsurprisingly, unions responded to that sentiment—big-time. They worked as if their lives depended on electing Obama and other Democratic candidates across the country—and, in some ways, maybe they did. With dwindling membership, a growing irrelevance, and the marquee companies they "bargain" with disappearing faster than Obama's campaign promises, it was only a matter of time before unions would be fighting for their very existence.

To prevent that from happening, unions long ago decided to start paying a lot more attention to political campaigns. According to Open Secrets, a website that tracks political fundraising, Big Labor made up twelve of the twenty top donors from 1989 to 2008. Here are those twelve, along with a mystery percentage for each . . . see if you can figure out what it is.

Arguing with Idiots

INSTANT WINNER

Unions aren't political organizations!

"We spent a fortune to elect Barack Obama—$60.7 million, to be exact—and we're proud of it."

—SEIU President Andy Stern. 94% of the SEIU's 2008 contributions went to Democrats.

Big Labor, Big Donors

2. American Federation of State, County & Municipal Employees 1%
6. International Brotherhood of Electrical Workers 2%
7. National Education Association 6%
8. Laborers Union 7%
9. Service Employees International Union 3%
10. Carpenters & Joiners Union 9%
11. Teamsters Union 6%
12. Communications Workers of America 0%
14. American Federation of Teachers . . . 0%
16. United Auto Workers 0%
17. Machinists & Aerospace Workers Union 0%
20. United Food & Commercial Workers Union 1%

The percentage next to each union is . . . drum roll, please . . . the amount of money each group has given to *Republicans* over the last decade. Yep, of the twelve big unions that made the top twenty list, every single one of them leaned "strongly" toward the donkey with their contributions. In other words, for ten straight years, the communication workers, teachers, auto workers and aerospace workers unions have given a combined zero dollars to Republicans. That's some balance! I guess we should be thanking the carpenters for stepping up to the plate with nine percent.

The truth is that most unions are no longer worker-rights groups, they're political action committees. They don't work to enact changes in their own companies or industries as much as they work to enact changes in laws that will help them claim more power and influence—something that's about as far away from their original mission as you can possibly get.

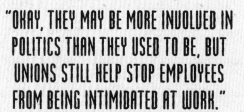

"OKAY, THEY MAY BE MORE INVOLVED IN POLITICS THAN THEY USED TO BE, BUT UNIONS STILL HELP STOP EMPLOYEES FROM BEING INTIMIDATED AT WORK."

If management intimidation is really as bad as many claim, then why do 60 percent of all private-ballot elections (in which workers decide whether or not to form a union) actually *succeed*? Isn't big, bad management supposed to be pulling the fire alarm or calling in fake bomb threats any time a few workers sit down together in the lunchroom?

Many people who are forced to join unions don't appreciate that their dues are used as political donations to elect a candidate the member doesn't even like. But what many members don't know, because the unions don't exactly advertise this, is that they have something called "Beck Rights." (Seriously, that's really the name.) Based on a 1988 Supreme Court decision, workers cannot be forced to pay any dues other than the amount specifically needed to fund their collective bargaining. Hmmm, that gives me an idea: How about we unionize all union workers with the intent of collectively bargaining with their leaders to reduce membership dues?

When management intimidation does undermine union efforts to organize (and, whom are we kidding, that certainly does happen), there are about a trillion laws on the books (give or take) to make sure that someone pays. The National Labor Relations Board gets plenty of complaints about unfair labor practices—but those complaints are levied against both sides: employers and unions.

RIDDLE ME THIS. . .

1. Labor unions fight for more jobs and higher wages by overwhelmingly supporting Democratic politicians.
2. Democratic politicians overwhelmingly support lax immigration policies.
3. Lax immigration policies clearly result in more illegal workers.
4. More illegal workers inevitably result in *fewer* available jobs and *lower* wages.

Unions claim to only want a level playing field, but what they really want is special treatment. Despite winning 60 percent of workplace elections, union leaders are still dragging out the intimidation myth and using it to argue that secret ballots are no longer fair. Their proposed remedy is something called the Employee "Free" Choice Act (EFCA) . . . aka "card check," and it's an idea that's been around for a long, looooong time. The difference now? Big Labor savior President Obama.

According to the National Labor Relations Board, there were 22,497 unfair-labor-practices charges filed in fiscal year 2008. 16,179 were filed against employers and 6,210 were filed against unions—83 percent of which were for "alleged illegal restraint and coercion of employees." It just goes to show that when you lend your power to someone else there's nothing to stop them from using it against you.

A.D.D. Moment

Since there are no limits to the idiotic names politicians attach to things, why not go on a retroactive renaming campaign?

Let's call the internment of Japanese Americans "The Involuntary Vacation Act." The American Recovery & Reinvestment Act can be renamed "The Socializing of America Act." And the War on Terror can be turned into the much-friendlier-sounding "Overseas Contingency Operation." (Oh, wait . . .)

The National Labor Relations Board (NLRB) currently oversees anonymous, secret ballot workplace elections supervised by impartial federal regulators. Unions want to trash that system because, they say, management has too many opportunities to scare their workers out of voting "yes."

Holy Hypocrisy!

It's funny how people can view an issue entirely differently once they're directly affected by it (i.e., the story in the Second Amendment chapter about the gun-control advocate who changed his mind after being mugged). But *The New York Times* takes this to a whole new level. Their editorial board is unabashedly pro-union, recently writing, "There is little doubt that American workers need unions . . . A bill that would have made it easier for unions to organize workers died in the Senate last June. Congress should take up this issue again to stop companies from using threats and other aggressive tactics to keep organized labor out, and to help win workers their rightful share of the economic pie."

There's only one problem with that: The New York Times Company, which owns the *Times*, along with other newspapers around the country, was engaged in a major stand-off with *their* unions, demanding millions in wage concessions and threatening to shut down operations and lay off workers if they didn't comply.

In response to this apparent hypocrisy, the company's spokeswoman said, "Each of our 18 daily newspapers has independent editorial control, and the business side has no say in the positions taken by our editorial boards." In other words, populist issues like fighting for a "rightful share of the economic pie" are easy to talk about in the abstract, but when the rubber meets the road and real jobs and profits are on the line, things become much more complicated.

And that's where card check comes in. It eliminates secret-ballot elections in favor of public ones. *Very* public ones. In fact, under card check, there are no elections at all; the "voting" can be done via a piece of paper passed around the office. If a majority of employees sign that paper—poof!—you have yourself a union.

Think about it—you're minding your business on the welding machine when a few guys approach you. They hand you a clipboard and a pen and give you a little "talk" about the benefits of union membership, along with the possible consequences of not playing nice. Are you going to sign?

Of course you are . . . and a few signatures are all it takes for a union to be recognized. "Card check" moves the election from a private voting booth to a private meeting between you and the enforc—sorry, I mean organizers.

> ### NAME THAT LIBERAL ICON!
>
> *"I believe in the secret ballot as a very important part of our democracy. When we elect a president, sheriff or member of Congress, we walk into the voting booth and pull the curtain free of anyone trying to twist our arm . . . it is in the interest of labor and management to have a secret ballot."*
>
> —Former Democratic presidential candidate George McGovern, talking about card check.

REDEEM THIS COUPON FOR A FREE STEAK DINNER. JUST SIGN BELOW!

DO YOU LOVE YOUR CHILDREN? SIGNING = YES!

GIRLS! GIRLS! GIRLS! ... REALLY. JUST SIGN, ALREADY.

✓ _____
SIGN HERE!

SIGN THIS CARD IF YOU LOVE PUPPIES!

WORKER AUTHORIZES LOCAL 199 TO COLLECTIVELY BARGAIN FOR THEM.

Workers of the World Demand Card Check!

Peter Hurtgen, a former member of the NLRB, explained exactly who is pushing for these so-called free elections: "In my experience, neutrality/card check agreements are almost always the product of external leverage by unions, rather than an internal groundswell from unrepresented employees."

That's a fancy way of saying that the only people who are demanding a change in voting systems are the people at the top who are just looking for more power.

If the idea that merely getting a majority of employees to sign a card can result in an official union scares the bat crap out of you, then buckle up, because it gets much worse. The EFCA has no regulations or safeguards that mandate what "voting" cards must look like or say—not the size of the card or font, or even the language. In fact, the only requirement seems to be that the card has to contain a single, vague line somewhere mentioning that the card authorizes a union to represent the worker.

Believe it or not, despite all of the yelling about "card check," it isn't even the most economically destructive demand in the EFCA. Another provision, far less talked about, is one that would impose *binding government arbitration* if the employer and union fail to reach agreement within 90 days of a new union's being certified.

Imagine how this would play out in a private business: You are haggling with a prospective boss about your salary. A few months have gone by and you haven't yet reached an agreement, but you're getting closer. Suddenly, there are some uninvited visitors in your waiting room. It's the Feds. They're there to inform you of your new salary, along with what your benefits will be and what your raises will be for the next five years.

Senator Arlen Specter, who holds a pivotal vote on the card-check issue, announced in March that he wouldn't support the EFCA because the recession makes it "a particularly bad time." That in itself is an amusing line since, if we are to believe the unions, card check *creates* jobs—but what's not amusing is how Specter qualified his decision. He might reconsider, he said, "when the economy returns to normalcy."

In retrospect, when Specter said that, he was just one month away from seeking political asylum with the Democrats, so what Specter probably *meant* to say was that he might reconsider "if Big Labor helps him get reelected."

In another era, that was called "communism."

Given this provision, unions would have exactly zero incentive to bargain in good faith. After all, why bargain when you can get exactly what you want (if not more—don't forget those political contributions) simply by waiting a few months for the government to ride in on their white horse and save the day?

Three major corporations that have resisted unions, Starbucks, Whole Foods, and Costco, proposed a compromise that would have left most of the EFCA intact if these two poisonous components (the elimination of secret ballots and the use of government arbitration) were shelved. They were immediately rejected. Compromise is not in the unions' vocabulary.

The bottom line is that unions believe that a 60-percent win rate is for losers. They dream of the day when every American worker is in a union (and, more important, paying their dues), whether they want to be or not.

Fortunately, even with Obama in the White House and a Democratic majority in Congress that unions helped to put there, card check is such a terrible idea that it *still* might not pass.

"YOU MAKE IT SOUND AS IF UNIONS DON'T CARE ABOUT THEIR OWN WORKERS. THAT'S RIDICULOUS!"

Do you ever wonder what kind of positive changes organized labor could make if they didn't spend hundreds of millions of dollars trying to buy elections? How much good do you think that kind of money could do in the private sector? Or a charity? How many jobs could unions actually create or save? How much better could the benefits be?

History is littered with examples of groups that began with the best of intentions, but were eventually hijacked by people who cared only about accumulating as much money and power as possible. As a result, these groups lose sight of their original mission and instead waste money on things (like lobbyists) when it would be far better spent on their own constituents.

In the middle of the EFCA campaign, the Service Employees International Union (SEIU), the fastest-growing union in the country, fired 75 of its 220 employees. Despite spending a holy fortune electing Barack Obama, they couldn't scrape together a few thousand bucks to salvage the jobs of some poor schlubs in their own organization? That should prove pretty definitively where their priorities really lie.

In the irony of ironies, the laid-off workers filed unfair labor practices charges against the SEIU with the National Labor Relations Board. I'll pause here so you can let that soak in . . .

If you can believe it, there is actually an organization called the "Union of Union Representatives" that represented the aggrieved union workers. Dumb question, but if unions are so fair and magnificent and necessary to workers, then why would union employees need unions to protect them from a union?

A.D.D. MOMENT

Pleaaaaaaaaaaaase, tell me there is a "Union of Union of Union of Representatives" that worked on behalf of the Union of Union Representatives that worked on behalf of the fired union members. That would make my year.

So why did the SEIU fire those poor "hardworking" souls that have the right to a job, a fair wage, fair benefits, fair blah, blah, blah? Here's the explanation, straight from the top: "This is not a financial issue," explained SEIU president Andy Stern. "We need to respond to the once-in-a-lifetime opportunity our members created by helping elect President Obama."

Huh? I guess with that kind of nonsensical double-talk it's not a surprise that Andy Stern heads a union.

The SEIU spent $80 million during the 2008 election cycle to get their candidates elected

> ### If You Made This Up, No One Would Believe You . . .
>
> "The staff union, the Union of Union Representatives, has complained to the National Labor Relations Board, asserting that the S.E.I.U. has failed to bargain about the impact of the layoffs and has sought to dissolve the staff union by reducing its membership."
>
> —The New York Times

A MORE PERFECT UNION: OBAMA & THE SEIU

ANNA BURGER

THE SECRETARY-TREASURER OF THE SEIU IS CURRENTLY A MEMBER OF PRESIDENT OBAMA'S ECONOMIC RECOVERY ADVISORY BOARD.

JOHN J. SULLIVAN

SEIU'S ASSOCIATE GENERAL COUNSEL; NOMINATED BY PRESIDENT OBAMA TO THE FEDERAL ELECTION COMMISSION. .

CRAIG BECKER

ASSOCIATE GENERAL COUNSEL, SEIU; MEMBER OF OBAMA TRANSITION TEAM; APPOINTED BY OBAMA TO THE FIVE-MEMBER NATIONAL LABOR RELATIONS BOARD, WHICH OVERSEES UNION ELECTIONS.

PATRICK GASPARD

FORMER EXECUTIVE VICE PRESIDENT OF POLITICS AND LEGISLATION FOR LOCAL 1199 SEIU. LED SEIU'S FEDERAL LOBBYING EFFORTS FOR THE STATE CHILDREN'S HEALTH INSURANCE PROGRAM (SCHIP) AND SERVED AS SEIU'S ACTING POLITICAL DIRECTOR. NOW WHITE HOUSE POLITICAL DIRECTOR (THE SAME POSITION HELD BY KARL ROVE DURING PRESIDENT BUSH'S FIRST TERM).

SCOTT WHITE

TECHNOLOGY PROJECT DIRECTOR, LOCAL 1199 SEIU. APPOINTED BY THE GAO TO THE NEWLY CREATED "HEALTH INFORMATION TECHNOLOGY POLICY COMMITTEE" — A NEW HEALTH-CARE ADVISORY BODY ESTABLISHED BY THE STIMULUS BILL.

T. MICHAEL KERR

ASSISTANT TO SECRETARY-TREASURER ANNA BURGER AT THE SEIU, IN CHARGE OF FINANCE AND ADMINISTRATION; NOMINATED BY PRESIDENT OBAMA TO BECOME THE ASSISTANT SECRETARY FOR ADMINISTRATION AND MANAGEMENT IN THE DEPARTMENT OF LABOR.

and was planning to spend tens of millions more to advocate on behalf of universal-health-care and card-check legislation. In other words, they spent money on politicians instead of payroll. If that's not a "financial issue," I'm not sure what it is.

Remember when the SEIU branch in Nevada gave a key endorsement to Obama that put him over the top there? That, along with their millions in campaign contributions, apparently bought a lot of goodwill in Washington, goodwill that they are all too happy to cash in:

CELEBRITY
Guest Ideeot

★ You may have heard that California has had some budget issues (i.e., they were about $42 billion short). As programs were cut and taxes were raised, it became clear that sacrifices would have to be made by everyone—everyone except the SEIU. After losing their battle over cuts in wages of home health-care workers in Sacramento, they went to Washington instead. Officials there lent a sympathetic ear and California was threatened with the loss of $6.8 billion in federal Medicaid money unless they reconsidered their cuts.

A.D.D. Moment

Want to know exactly what $33 million in campaign contributions buys you? Well, it turns out that the SEIU was given "unprecedented access" to a conference call between Washington officials and state officials who were talking about the proposed wage cuts for home-health-care workers. "This is an unusual situation," said a spokeswoman for the California Department of Health and Human Services. "It is incredibly unusual in our experience to have stakeholders on a call like this."

★ In Illinois, Hartmarx, a men's suitmaker, filed for Chapter 11 bankruptcy protection after being unable to pay back $141 million in loans from its bank, Wells Fargo. Seems pretty cut-and-dried, except for the fact that Hartmarx plant employees are represented by the SEIU. The union turned to the state government (and we all know how ethical those Illinois politicians are), which then publicly threatened Wells Fargo—not with violence, but with something much worse: loss of business.

It turns out that Wells Fargo is the custodian for the Illinois State Portfolio and, as the Illinois state treasurer put it: "Unless the company remains open, [Wells Fargo] will not be doing business with the State of Illinois any longer."

Is it just me, or does the word "extortion" come to mind?

Friends in High Places . . .

"Words are cheap, everybody, there is not a presidential candidate, a gubernatorial candidate, a congressional candidate, who won't tell you that they're pro-union when they're looking for an endorsement. I've been working with SEIU before I was elected to anything."

—Barack Obama, preaching to the choir at a post-debate party hosted by the SEIU.

"OKAY, SO UNIONS THROW THEIR WEIGHT AROUND, BUT WHEN COMPANIES FAIL, UNIONS SUFFER JUST AS MUCH AS MANAGEMENT."

Not quite. Unions, especially ones that helped to elect our politicians, often seem to be "exempt" from sharing in the necessary sacrifices.

One of the best examples of this is the failure of Chrysler. After the company declared bankruptcy, the unions walked away with a better deal than virtually anyone else. Due to the arm-twisting from the government (they're called "Uncle Sam" because they're really good at getting people to say "uncle"), companies and investors that had lent Chrysler the capital they needed to stay afloat were forced to take it on the chin—but not the unions.

For example, consider "The International Union, United Automobile, Aerospace and Agricultural Implement Workers of America," better known as the UAW. Their sacrifice was to make unspecified cuts to wages and benefits, alter some work rules, and waive Chrysler's $8 billion payment to their retiree health-care fund. *Okay, that sounds fair*, you're probably thinking—but that's only because you haven't heard what they got in return: a $4.6 billion government loan to a new retiree health-care fund, $600 million for their pension fund and—the icing on the cake—a whopping *55 percent* equity stake in the newly reorganized Chrysler.

In other words, the unions now own more than half of Chrysler, all for a measly $3 billion.

Other parties didn't fare quite so well. Before the bankruptcy, Daimler held $2 billion in secured loans to Chrysler and owned a 19 percent stake in the company. After the deal, in a disappearing act that would make Houdini jealous, Daimler *waived* the $2 billion they were owed and *also* gave up their entire stake in Chrysler. What did they get in return? The privilege of putting an *additional* $600 million into the UAW pension fund.

Cerberus, a private-equity firm that was basically the life preserver to Chrysler's flailing, splashing, drowning business, was also strong-armed into giving up everything for nothing in return. Prior to the government-led agreement, Cerberus held $500 million in secured loans,

NEW AMERICAN MATH

"Special Interests"
+
"Corporations"
+
"Government"
= Fascism

BUT

"UAW"
+
"Chrysler/GM"
+
"The Obama Administration"
= Capitalism?

A.D.D. MOMENT

The UAW gave 99 percent of their 2008 election-cycle donations to Democrats. I'm sure that didn't have *aaaaaaaanything* to do with how the Chrysler negotiations went down. Right?

U.S.S.A. NIGHTMARE SCENARIO # 988

GENERAL MOTORS DEBUTS EXCITING NEW CAR AT DETROIT AUTO SHOW

New Collabora is brainchild of elite team of union and government automakers.

FOR IMMEDIATE RELEASE -- The Collabora was unveiled Thursday at the Detroit Auto Show in a lavish ceremony hosted by hilarious comedienne Wanda Sykes.

"I hope Rush Limbaugh dies violently," announced Sykes. "I hope he really, really suffers."

The Collabora is the first car produced since General Motors was fully acquired by the U.S. Government and the United Autoworkers Union (UAW) in a landmark deal. It is the end result of 54 months of cooperation between the unions and politicians. "This car is the future," declared UAW president Gary Williams. "We have somehow managed to please every single special interest group that called with a request. It wasn't easy, but our call-center agents did a tremendous job with the mechanical engineering."

The Collabora features a 1.1 liter, 2 cylinder corn-ethanol engine. The three gallon capacity tank is conveniently located under the driver's seat for easy access. It can hold up to one small adult with only minimal discomfort and the absence of front airbags allows for a steering column and small glove compartment. Glass allows occupant to look outside. The car's aluminum frame makes the car lightweight so that it can easily be pushed once the fuel runs out. With manual pushing averaged in, the Collabora gets approximately 41 mpg, exceeding federal standards.

The Collabora is highly customizable for those who wish to add a rear-view mirror or license plates and it comes standard with roll-down windows, guaranteed to work whether the car is in automatic or manual-push mode. It is expected to retail at a base price of $78,000. Contact your Congressman for purchasing information.

an 80-percent stake in Chrysler, and full ownership of Chrysler's headquarters. After the arrangement? The firm gave up all of its assets and received *absolutely nothing* in return. Who was negotiating this deal for them, Gerald Levin?

And, of course, let's not forget the taxpayer. Remember when the government loaned Chrysler $4 billion in TARP funds and another $3.2 billion in bankruptcy financing? Hope you weren't too attached to it (and it's not like we really need the money anyway) . . . because it's all gone. But here's the best news of all: We're lending the company *another* $4.7 billion. Isn't the definition of insanity doing the same thing over and over and expecting a different result?

> **OBSCURE REFERENCE TRANSLATOR**
>
> Gerald Levin = Former Time Warner CEO who decided to merge with AOL, a deal that cost shareholders over $200 billion. He was recently named one of the "20 Worst CEOs Ever."

In return for the new $4.7 billion loan, taxpayers got an eight-percent equity stake in Chrysler. But don't worry! That we now officially own a big piece of Chrysler doesn't mean the government is going to be involved in their turnaround. Remember, the president doesn't "want to run auto companies . . . (he's) got more than enough to do." Like running our banks.

Even Canadian taxpayers got screwed over by this disaster. The Canadian government handed over $3 billion in loans, which, and you have to admire their honesty, they assume Chrysler won't ever be repaying. Talk aboot a raw deal, eh?

"GOOD FOR THEM! LOOK AT THE RESULTS UNIONS HAVE ACHIEVED FOR THEIR WORKERS. ISN'T IT IMPORTANT FOR WORKING PEOPLE TO MAKE AS MUCH MONEY AS POSSIBLE? AREN'T YOU A CAPITALIST?"

I sure am. When Americans make money from the fruits of their free-market labor, it's the greatest thing in the world. But when they make it based on blackmail, monopolies, and taxpayer funds . . . not so much.

Big Labor will constantly—and I mean *constantly*—tell you about how their workers make more money than a corresponding nonunion employee. And they're absolutely right. But there is an old saying that while statistics don't lie, liars use statistics, and this so-called union triumph is a great example of that. Yes, union workers make an average of $195 more per week than nonunion workers, but is that really the whole story? After all, in-

These Kinds of Deals Happen All the Time!

When St. John's University labor-law professor David Gregory (no known relation to the Bush-hating NBC "journalist" by the same name) was asked to name other unions that have done as well as the UAW did in the Chrysler deal, he replied: "Nobody's even close."

mates in state prisons pay far less in health-care benefits than their nonjailed counterparts. Does that mean that we should all strive to do twenty to life?

Of course not—because being in a union, like being in prison, has consequences.

Unions are able to attain higher pay and unheard-of retirement goodies for their workers because they can hold companies and taxpayers hostage. (It doesn't hurt their case that most of them operate in government-backed cartels, either.) But even if you're okay with that, the data itself is still skewed. Union workers typically have automatic raises built into their contracts. In times when the economy is in a downturn and most workers are taking cuts, union workers stick to their guns and demand their contractual raises.

Higher pay is a great benefit of unions—but there is a major downside: your salary doesn't really matter if you no longer have a job. So while unions trumpet the wages they secure for their members, they bury statistics that reveal how their heavy-handed policies cost jobs.

Unions and prisons, not as different as you might think:

★ Neither offer you the option to decline membership.
★ Once inside, you are completely ruled by the decisions of others.
★ The benefits are fantastic (smoke breaks, afternoon naps).
★ "Newbies" have to watch their backs.
★ You spend most of your time lying down with nothing to do.

This graph shows private-sector job growth from 2003 to 2008 in three types of states: those with heavy unionization (above 9.1 percent of private employees in unions), those with low unionization (5 percent to 9 percent in unions), and those with very low unionization (under 5 percent).

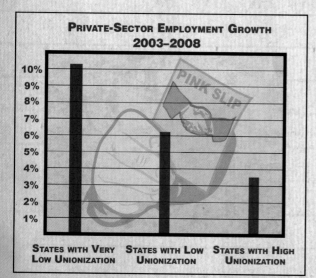

PRIVATE-SECTOR EMPLOYMENT GROWTH 2003–2008

States with Very Low Unionization · States with Low Unionization · States with High Unionization

The results are straightforward and striking: The more unionization, the less job growth. Heavily unionized states had about *two-thirds less* total private-sector job growth than states with very low unionization. That represents tens of thousands of missing jobs, which forces workers to rely on social safety nets like unemployment or welfare, putting an even heavier burden on state budgets.

But there are other consequences to unionization as well, because when unions "win," consumers lose. The costs of unrealistic contracts aren't borne by greedy

A.D.D. MOMENT

President Obama fired General Motors Chairman and CEO Rick Wagoner—a man selected by a private board of directors and approved by private shareholders. But what about Ron Gettelfinger, head of the United Autoworkers Union? He was the man on the other side of every labor contract Wagoner had to sign. Doesn't he bear *any* responsibility in saddling GM with labor and benefit costs that proved completely unsustainable?

Apparently not.

Why? Well, as evidence of how much the unions had given back in trying to keep GM solvent, UAW president Ron Gettelfinger told the Senate Banking, Housing and Urban Affairs Committee that they'd agree to slash wages in half for new workers and exclude them from the legacy health and pension plans that were saddling the company.

Sounds great, except for one little problem: Since 2000, the number of hourly workers at GM is down 50 percent. In other words, there are no new workers.

executives, they're borne by customers (many of whom are also "hardworking" men and women).

By not basing labor costs on a free-market system of supply and demand, expenses quickly become out of whack with reality. Over time, those expenses (high salaries, unheard-of pensions, low-cost health care, etc.) inevitably increase the cost of products, thereby destroying industries (cars, airlines, etc.) and costing thousands of people their jobs.

Mark J. Perry, a professor of economics and finance at the University of Michigan (and an expert on the car industry), calculated the average compensation for employees of the Big Three auto companies, including benefits, at $73 an hour. At the same time, U.S.-based employees (who are apparently *not* "working men and women") of Japanese automakers earn $48 an hour—52 percent less.

In 2007, the legacy costs (things like pensions and health-care costs) of every car produced by the Detroit Big Three amounted to $1,800. These days, because production is down and early retirement is up, legacy costs now account for around $3,000 per car.

Think about what those costs do to a business trying to compete in a global free market against other companies that don't have that same albatross around their necks. A car that costs an automaker $20,000 to make jumps to $23,000 before a profit is even considered. That puts U.S. automakers at a severe disadvantage to their counterparts, a disadvantage that has finally proven too much to overcome.

But it's not only the legacy costs. If you really want to see how deeply inefficiency, waste, and plain stupidity are embedded into the union mind-set, look no further than "job banks"—an idea that only a combination of government and organized labor could possibly dream up.

In the 1980s, some Detroit automakers (like GM and Chrysler) placated the auto unions by creating the Job Opportunity Bank

> "It's a human rights issue. It's just bottom-line fair that workers should be paid for their labor fairly."
> —Martin Sheen, who is apparently unaware that we have a national minimum-wage law.

CELEBRITY **GUEST IDEEOT**

Security System, or job banks for short. Despite their name, those banks weren't about creating jobs, they were about keeping people without them busy. Union employees who were laid off were put into these "banks" and paid nearly their full salary to just hang out and improve themselves watching movies and taking enrichment classes.

After the auto bailouts, many Americans were so disgusted by job banks that the pressure finally became too much and unions officially began to close them. Participants (who had already been laid off once) were all laid off again. Sort of. This time they went home and began collecting over *72 percent* of their full-time pay.

That, my friends, is what they call union sacrifice.

"OKAY, UNIONS MIGHT NOT WORK IN THE AUTO INDUSTRY, BUT THEY WORK WELL FOR THE PUBLIC SECTOR."

One of the major reasons that unions first came into existence was to provide a balance against the power of monopolies. Monopolies made it nearly impossible for workers to get a fair shake because they had nearly complete power over their respective industries. That's why it's ironic that unions now rely on the biggest and most powerful monopoly in the world to acquire and maintain their power: the government.

While most of us rely on competition and a sense of personal achievement to bring out our best, public union employees are protected regardless of their talents or accomplishments. And that goes to the very core of what is wrong with unions: they celebrate mediocrity. What is the point in exerting yourself when the reward doesn't change? What is the point of coming in early, staying late, or putting any extra effort into your job when your status and pay are defined by 500-page collective-bargaining agreements?

If you think this is an overly harsh critique, just look at one of the most prevalent and powerful examples of this in the country: teachers' unions.

A.D.D. MOMENT I mentioned earlier that public-sector workers are five times more likely to be in a union than private-sector workers, but what's kind of ironic is that even union members who *thought* they were working in the private sector, like those in the UAW, are now essentially working for the government anyway. I guess a pretty good marketing strategy for the unions would be to convince the government to nationalize everything. Oh, wait a second . . .

First, the requisite disclaimers: There are a ton of great teachers in America, many of whom have decided to forgo far more lucrative careers because of their love of education. And it's often a thankless job—anyone who has kids knows how tough it can be. But the unions only make the task even harder. They virtually guarantee that mediocre teachers stick around, while high-performing ones get so frustrated that they leave.

Let's imagine for a moment a world without teachers' unions. (Cue dream-sequence music and wavy lines.) All employment would be "at will." Teachers would work at a school because they *want* to and, conversely, schools would employ only teachers that are doing a good job. Like employees at most businesses, teachers would strive to do their best in order to get promoted or receive a year-end bonus and bad or dangerous teachers would be immediately dismissed—no questions asked.

In other words, let's imagine a world where teachers earn their salaries through hard work and talent, and where, as a result, American children lead the world in academic achievement.

Okay, the crazy dream sequence is now over. Back to reality.

Unions invest far more heavily in controlling school boards and stocking state houses and city councils with friendly supporters than they do in actual education. And that is where a government-union partnership is at its most destructive.

Out of 43,000 tenured teachers in the entire Los Angeles school district (which has a less than 50-percent graduation rate), only 112 were terminated for the entire decade of 1995–2005. That's 0.26 percent of teachers. Talk about job security.

A Los Angeles public school union representative explained why there are so few firings: "If I'm representing them, it's impossible to get them out. It's impossible. Unless they commit a lewd act."

But that rep may have spoken too soon because, in some districts, even a lewd act may not be enough.

When *20/20* anchor and best-selling author John Stossel confronted New York City public-school chancellor Joel Klein about a teacher who sent a sexually explicit email to one of his 16-year-old students, he got a taste of how hard it is to get rid of a teacher.

"He admits [to it]," Klein told Stossel. "We had the e-mail."

"You can't fire him?" Stossel asked.

"It's almost impossible."

Why? According to Stossel it's because "of the rules detailed in the New York school system's 200-page contract with their teachers. There are so many rules that principals rarely even try to jump through all the hoops required to fire a bad teacher. It took six years of expensive litigation before the teacher was fired. During those six years, he received more than $300,000 in salary."

Do we want our private industry to be run like the school systems of major urban areas? If unions have their way, that's exactly what is going to happen.

HOW TO FIRE A TENURED

STEP ONE:
EVALUATE AND DOCUMENT INCOMPETENCE BY PLACING NOTES IN THE TEACHER'S FILE.

A. THE TEACHER MUST SIGN EVERY NOTE AND CAN ADD A RESPONSE.

B. NOTES MAY NOT BE ADDED MORE THAN THREE MONTHS AFTER AN INCIDENT.

C. LETTERS THAT DON'T RESULT IN DISCIPLINARY CHARGES MUST BE REMOVED AFTER THREE YEARS.

STEP TWO:
AFTER ACCUMULATING ENOUGH DOCUMENTATION, YOU SUBMIT AN UNSATISFACTORY RATING.

A. THE COMMITTEE OVERTURNS THE RATING. RETURN TO STEP ONE.

B. THE COMMITTEE UPHOLDS THE RATING. CONTINUE TO STEP FIVE.

STEP THREE:
THE TEACHER APPEALS TO A COMMITTEE DESIGNATED BY THE CHANCELLOR.

A. AT THE HEARING, THE TEACHER MAY BE ADVISED BY AN EMPLOYEE OF THE CITY SCHOOL DISTRICT OR A UNION REPRESENTATIVE

B. WITNESSES AND EVIDENCE ARE INTRODUCED.

STEP FOUR:
THE COMMITTEE RENDERS A DECISION.

STEP FIVE:
THE DECISION IS FORWARDED TO THE CHANCELLOR FOR A "FINAL" DECISION.

A. THE CHANCELLOR OVERTURNS THE RATING. RETURN TO STEP ONE.

B. THE CHANCELLOR UPHOLDS THE RATING. CONTINUE TO STEP SIX.

STEP SIX:
THE TEACHER NOW HAS THREE OPTIONS.

OPTION A- APPEAL TO THE STATE COMMISSIONER OF EDUCATION.

I. THE TEACHER HAS 30 DAYS TO APPEAL.
II. THE COMMISSIONER TRIES TO ISSUE A DECISION WITHIN SIX TO EIGHT MONTHS— BUT CASE LOADS ARE HIGH AND DATES AREN'T GUARANTEED.

III. COMMISSIONER OVERTURNS, BACK TO STEP ONE.

IV. COMMISSIONER UPHOLDS DECISION.

OPTION B- FILE IN STATE COURT TO HAVE THE CHANCELLOR'S DECISION OVERTURNED.

I. TO THE COURT-ROOM YOU GO!

OPTION C— DO NOT APPEAL

I. EVEN IF THE TEACHER DOES NOT FILE ANOTHER APPEAL, THEY CANNOT BE FIRED YET. TERMINATION CAN ONLY RESULT FROM A HEARING UNDER s.3020-A.

V. PROCEED TO THE TERMINATION HEARINGS UNDER s.3020-A OF THE EDUCATION LAW.

Teacher in New York City

A. The hearing officer must give a written decision within 30 days after the hearing.
B. Copies go to the commissioner of education.
C. The commissioner forwards copies to the teacher and to the clerk or secretary of the board.

D. In determining the penalty, the hearing officer must consider whether the school board first made efforts toward remediation, peer intervention, or an employee assistance plan.

I. YES

1. Congratulations! You have succeeded in firing one inept teacher.
2. EXCEPT that the teacher can appeal.
3. Within ten days of the decision, either the teacher or school board can appeal to the New York State Supreme Court.
4. You are now involved in a lawsuit. Please consult your school attorneys.

II. NO

1. The hearing officer can order efforts to correct the employee's behavior, instead of dismissal.

STEP ELEVEN:
Hearing decision

STEP TEN:
Hearing procedures

A. The teacher has the right, but not the obligation, to testify.

B. Each party has the right to have lawyers and to subpoena and cross-examine witnesses.

STEP NINE:
Pre-hearing conference. Occurs 10 to 15 days after panel is in place.

A. At the conference, the hearing officer can:
i. Issue subpoenas.
ii. Hear and decide all motions, including motions to dismiss the charges.
iii. Decide any discovery disputes about materials either side wants to have before the hearing.
iv. Set the timetable for the hearing.

A. Both sides exchange witness lists, statements and physical evidence.

STEP EIGHT:
Prepare for formal hearing.

C. The teacher only has to give the school board documents that the board can prove are relevant.

B. The school board must provide the teacher with copies of investigatory statements, notes, exculpatory evidence and relevant student records.

1. The school board must issue a statement of the charges and maximum possible penalty and send a notice outlining the teacher's rights.

2. Within ten days, the teacher can request a hearing and elect to appear before either a single hearing officer or a panel of arbitrators.

3. Pending the outcome of the hearing, a teacher can be suspended without pay if:.
A. The teacher is convicted of, or is pleading guilty to, a felony.
B. The teacher has been charged with an act constituting sexual misconduct.
C. An arbitrator finds there is probable cause that the charges involve felony drug use or possession, physical or sexual abuse of a minor or student, a felony on school property, or a felony involving a firearm.

3A. Over 700 NYC teachers are currently in "rubber rooms"—offsite space where they are waiting months or years for their hearings. Each teacher collects their full salary, costing taxpayers $65 million/year.

STEP SEVEN:
File charges to terminate the teacher.

A. The board will vote on whether the charges are valid.

II. Potentially valid? Continue.

I. Not valid? Obtain further documentation. GAME OVER.

ILLEGAL IMMIGRATION

The Chapter Americans Just Won't Write

U.S. Code Title 8, Section 1325

Any alien who (1) enters or attempts to enter the United States at any time or place other than as designated by immigration officers, or (2) eludes examination or inspection by immigration officers . . . shall, for the first commission of any such offense, be fined under title 18 or imprisoned not more than 6 months, or both, and, for a subsequent commission of any such offense, be fined under title 18, or imprisoned not more than 2 years, or both.

APPROXIMATELY two thousand people willfully ignore that statute every day, making illegal immigration a national crisis that you're apparently not supposed to notice. Official estimates of our illegal population range from 10 to 20 million, and, at least if we're to believe the politicians and activists, not a single one of those people is anything other than a hardworking, down-on-their-luck foreigner trying to provide for their family.

Americans are begging Congress, mayors, governors—anyone who will listen—to simply enforce our laws. But they're not listening. In fact, it seems like the only people who *are* being heard are the activists who viciously attack anyone who dares to suggest that illegal immigration might be, well, *illegal*. For example . . .

"They are hiding under the American flag claiming to be good patriots but they are actually promoting racial hatred."
> —LULAC Chapter President Paul Martinez, on Minuteman patrols.

"He is, without question, a racist."
> —Protestor at San Diego Campus of University of California speaking about Lou Dobbs.

"Nothing short of base racism."
> —Nativo V. Lopez, president of the Mexican-American Political Association, after Governor Schwarzenegger called for closed borders.

"The message they are trying to send is that white people can take the law into their own hands and do whatever they want to people of color, and in 21st-century America, that's just not going to fly."
> —Ray Ybarra, ACLU worker who organized against the Minutemen Project.

"This announcement blatantly promotes baseless persecution of Latinos. Is it KMBC's new policy to turn Kansas City into a police state? Will Kansas citizens start turning anyone who has brown skin over to immigration officials? Most people find turning their fellow human beings over to persecution and destruction rather distasteful. It was distasteful when the Europeans turned in Jews to the Nazis; it was distasteful when the Japanese were interred . . . People should not be punished—or destroyed—for existing."
> —Clara Reyes, editor of *Dos Mundos*, after Kansas City TV station KBMC aired a public service announcement asking citizens to report illegal aliens to authorities.

"Wrongheaded and bigoted . . . [Its intention] is to scare Latinos out of the state."
—Bill Chandler, of the Mississippi Immigrant Rights Alliance, speaking of the Mississippi Employment Protection Act, designed to crack down on illegal hiring practices.

We are a nation of immigrants. Not only do I understand that, I also cherish it. But that has nothing to do with the issue we're talking about—and spinning an argument about the rule of law into one about hatred for immigrants is unfair to what should otherwise be a legitimate debate.

Hatemonger Quote of the Day

"In proportion to their number, [foreigners] will share with us the legislation. They will infuse into it their spirit, warp and bias its direction, and render it a heterogeneous, incoherent, distracted mass."

—Thomas Jefferson, 1782

Bipartisan Idiocy

"An American is an idea. No group owns being an American. Nobody owns this. We are not going to run people down. We are not going to scapegoat people. We are going to tell the bigots to shut up."

—Senator Lindsey Graham (R-SC), after accepting a leadership award from the National Council of La Raza, the largest Hispanic civil rights and advocacy organization in the United States.

But Glenn, we have to help the less fortunate! I agree—but it's not that cut-and-dried. Illegal immigration activists know that if they can get people to rely on their own compassion instead of the law, they win . . . but that doesn't make it a logical argument.

The truth is that over three billion people in the world live on less than $2.50 a day. The real question isn't whether we should be compassionate—absolutely we should . . . but to whom? Who's the most deserving of our charity—those who break our laws or those who have done everything by the book and still can't make ends meet? It's easy to look at a family of struggling illegal aliens and feel your heart break—but should they have priority over the family of Americans who've paid taxes for decades and are now facing job loss, homelessness, or massive health-care bills? If the latest economic crisis taught us anything, it's that we can't help *everyone*.

We are a charitable country, which is why we've allowed so many people to sneak in here for so long with virtually no repercussions. But there's nothing charitable or compassionate about looking the other way while employers pay illegal wages and force workers to endure grueling hours in unsafe conditions. In fact, that's the opposite of compassion—it's economic slavery.

Senator Bill Frist once said, "A nation that can't secure its borders can't secure its destiny or administer its laws." As long as our borders are as secure as a job at GM, I have to agree. So, how do we change our fate? By using some common sense against idiotic arguments, like . . .

A.D.D. MOMENT

A former U.S. attorney once told me the story of an illegal worker who was severely hurt on the job. The employee called his supervisor for help, but, instead of calling 911, the supervisor, who was obviously aware of the employee's immigration status, called the government. I guess compassion ends where the threat of a federal investigation begins.

A few years ago some research was done to figure out how the Bush administration successfully connected the war in Iraq to 9/11. They figured out that it all had to do with the words that were chosen, and their findings supported that theory: "Those who control the language control the argument, and those who control the argument are more likely to successfully translate belief into policy."

The exact same thing is happening with the immigration debate. They're not "illegal immigrants or illegal aliens," they're "migrant workers" or "economic refugees." What's next, "unlicensed entrepreneurs"? Stop falling for the language tricks!

FUN WITH WORDS!

The meaning of words can change over time. Case in point: Having a "gay old time" means something totally different today than it did forty years ago. But, in some cases, words change for political expediency, because people want to make themselves feel better, or, in some cases, for reasons no one will ever understand . . . Does anyone know why "stewardess" was so bad?

In the immigration debate, an illegal immigrant or illegal alien suddenly became an "undocumented worker." It doesn't change the fact that he or she is here illegally, but it sure sounds better. With that in mind, here are a few ideas on how we can label other lawbreakers so that no one's feelings are hurt.

OLD TERM	SUNSHINE & LOLLIPOPS TERM
Fugitive	Itinerant Federal Guest
Drunk Driver	Mobile Beverage Quaffer
Tax Evader	Dedicated Tariff Dissenter
Prostitute	Non-Platonic Contractor
Suicide Bomber	Device-bearing Courier
Pirate	Impromptu Crew Member
Osama bin Laden	Special Event Coordinator
Rapist	Unilateral Involuntary Boyfriend

"ILLEGAL ALIENS DO THE JOBS AMERICANS WON'T DO!"

Americans build bridges, work in coal mines, collect garbage, slaughter chickens, clean sewers, and much worse. (Have you ever seen *Dirty Jobs*?) I'm not exactly sure what job it is that Americans won't do—I guess it would help if those who make this stupid argument were a little more specific.

A more accurate argument would be that illegal aliens take the jobs that Americans *can't* do because employers won't pay minimum wage or provide reasonable benefits or safe working conditions.

I realize I'm not as well versed in economics as Ben Bernanke, but I am a thinker. It seems to me that if you

Black janitors in the hotel industry in Los Angeles once earned $12 an hour with benefits. Then illegal labor flooded the market. Wages dropped to $3.35 an hour, displacing almost all legal employees.

flood the market with lots of cheap labor, wages go down. Supply and demand, right? If you *supply* businesses with millions of workers willing to take $3 an hour, then *demand* for higher-priced minimum-wage workers goes down.

Data on illegal jobs is inconclusive (it turns out that employers aren't real big on telling the government about all of the laws they're breaking). However, studies have shown that minorities and the poor are hit the hardest by illegal labor entering the market. Again, I bring you back to the word "compassion"—people may think they're helping one family by looking the other way as they cross the Rio Grande, but they're hurting three other families in the process.

Relying on cheap labor also has another impact—one that often goes unseen: It makes businesses lazy. Those who have fallen into the dreamy bliss of illegal labor don't have to upgrade equipment, streamline processes, or deal with human-resource issues because they're virtually guaranteed high profits due to their unfairly low labor costs.

A.D.D. Moment

Bear Stearns reported that between four and six million jobs have moved to the underground economy since 1990. Those aren't the "jobs Americans won't do," but rather the jobs they *used to do* before illegal labor became much more attractive to employers. If the president is really serious about "creating or saving 600,000 jobs" he could do it a lot faster by cracking down on the companies that hire illegal workers rather than by funneling billions into subsidizing solar panels and windmills.

A.D.D. Moment

The Roman empire based its economy on slave labor, which reduced exports and hindered technological innovation. We all know how that worked out.

If every illegal alien left the country tomorrow, we'd still build new homes and grow fruit and (reluctantly) vegetables. How? By leveling the playing field. When Immigration and Customs Enforcement (ICE) conducted raids on cheating employers who got ahead by hiring illegal workers and paying them illegal wages, some amazing things started to happen . . .

★ Swift & Company meat-processing plants lost about nine percent of their workforce when they were raided in six states. After the raids, Swift raised their pay by almost two dollars an hour and hundreds of residents lined up the next day to take the jobs illegal aliens used to have.

Illegal immigrants often live in such squalor that law enforcement officials conducting raids on their living quarters find "moving walls"—a term that describes the phenomenon of flipping a light switch and seeing thousands of bugs scurry all over the wall, creating the illusion that it is moving.

137

★ Howard Industries, an electronics maker in Laurel, Mississippi, was raided in the fall of 2008. Hundreds of citizens soon lined up to apply for the new job opportunities, including one woman who drove 40 miles.

★ Crider Inc., a chicken-processing company in Stillmore, Georgia, suddenly raised their pay to more than a dollar an hour over what they were paying illegal aliens. About 400 unemployed people showed up for interviews, half of whom were subsequently hired.

Those are only three examples out of hundreds of raids, but you can't tell me that Americans are unwilling to work. When fair jobs become available, Americans line up to do them. And if a company goes under because of illegal labor violations, then they obviously weren't meant to survive anyway. (Shh, don't tell Tim Geithner.)

"GREAT, SO WE CRACK DOWN ON EMPLOYERS AND THEN OUR ECONOMY COLLAPSES! LIKE IT OR NOT, ILLEGAL WORKERS ARE VITAL TO KEEPING THINGS CHEAP!"

Don't be fooled by those who say that illegal aliens contribute billions to our economy and take little from it. They're wrong. Many work off the books, earn low wages, pay little to no taxes, send millions of dollars in remittances to their home country, and use social services at a higher rate than American citizens. The truth is that, yes, illegal aliens *are* important to our economy— but only if you're talking about the destruction of it.

Illegal immigrants tend to be less skilled and less educated than those who got off the ships at Ellis Island. While new immigrants used to earn just 14 percent less than native-born Americans, that gap had widened to an average of 34 percent less by 1998.

Before the New Deal, if you came to America and couldn't make it, you went home. Now, our growing welfare state is feeding off those who fall short of the educa-

EVERYBODY FREAK OUT!

EMPLOYERS DON'T HAVE THE RESOURCES TO VERIFY CITIZENSHIP STATUS

In 1997, the federal government implemented a system to help companies assess the citizenship status of new hires. It's called "E-Verify" and it's free, web-based, 99.5 percent accurate, and takes less than five seconds to get results. Unfortunately, it's also voluntary.

While I understand that, to our politicians, using the internet for something other than porn is confusing, that doesn't excuse the fact that the Senate recently voted to extend the use of E-Verify for only six months instead of the requested five *years*. Given our shaky economy and constant lobbying by business groups that claim it's too much of a "burden" to use, the future of this commonsense program is uncertain.

tion and skills necessary to achieve the American Dream. Illegal immigrants are 50 percent more likely to use welfare than citizens. They get free education, Medicaid, cash assistance for kids (WIC), and sometimes food stamps. While children of illegal immigrants make up only six percent of the population, they account for almost twelve percent of our nation's poor.

The progressive magazine *Mother Jones* reported, "We can be virtually certain that illegal immigrants earned less than $24,000 per year, on average, probably much less. Workers who earn so little pay very little income tax. A majority of illegal immigrants fall below the income threshold at which income taxes become significantly positive."

Yes, illegal aliens pay some taxes because they buy things. You can't live in this country and avoid paying sales tax or, in some cases, even Social Security tax (if you were lucky enough to steal someone's Social Security number . . . or buy one on a street corner in California for about $150).

We're being taken advantage of worse than Lindsay Lohan at a frat party. Our nation spends more than $4.7 billion a year on health care for illegal aliens and California has been forced to close over 70 hospitals over the last ten years alone. About 17 percent of all those in federal prison are illegal aliens—an astonishing number when you consider that they represent only three percent of the population. Of course, free room and board in prison isn't free—we're paying for them to be there as well. We're also spending about $30 billion each year to educate illegal aliens in our schools—money that we could probably use to figure out how to educate our own children since we're doing such a miserable job at it right now.

The Statue of Liberty was originally meant to be a symbol of "liberty enlightening the world," a gift from the French to celebrate America's hard-fought independence. However, the vision of Liberty in the harbor as European immigrants arrived on boats caused the press to begin reporting on her significance. A plaque was placed inside Liberty's pedestal with a snippet of the poem "The New Colossus" by Emma Lazarus and voilà—a symbol was born for those seeking freedoms here in the United States that they could not find elsewhere.

EVERYBODY FREAK OUT!

CRACKING DOWN ON ILLEGAL IMMIGRATION WILL MAKE THE COST OF LETTUCE SKYROCKET!

Labor makes up only about six percent of the cost of fresh produce. Eliminating all illegal labor would likely increase the cost of your produce by about $8 a year. Since the average household spends more on alcoholic beverages than on fresh fruits and vegetables, I doubt anyone would notice.

BALANCING THE BUDGET: STEP ONE

The Federation for American Immigration Reform estimates that there are more than 425,000 "anchor babies" (children born to illegal immigrants that are immediately granted U.S. citizenship) born in the U.S. each year. In 2006, 70 percent of women who gave birth at Parkland Memorial Hospital in Dallas were illegal aliens. Those births cost Medicaid $34.5 million, the federal government $9.5 million, and Dallas taxpayers another $31.3 million. That's over $75 million spent in one hospital, in one city, in one border state.

"GLENN, YOU'RE LOOKING AT THIS ALL WRONG. LEGAL VS. ILLEGAL IS IRRELEVANT BECAUSE BORDERS AREN'T NECESSARY ANYMORE."

Despite what you may read in liberal blogs, nobody believes that all illegal aliens are terrorists—but the problem is that those who come here to work and those who come here to kill are all using the same door.

Law enforcement will readily admit that they have no idea exactly how many people are slipping into the country undetected—they know only how many get caught. As one U.S. terrorism official reported to the House Committee on Homeland Security in 2006, "We don't even know what we don't know."

The most obvious problem, and the one that will get you labeled an intolerant xenophobe the fastest, is the 2,000-mile border we share with Mexico. Almost 70 percent of illegal aliens are Mexican—and our border agents simply can't keep up.

A typical day on the border means sorting through the latest crop of crossers to determine

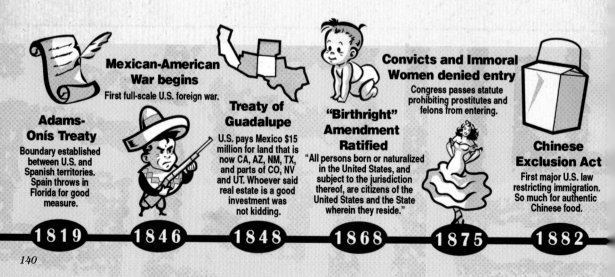

Adams-Onís Treaty
Boundary established between U.S. and Spanish territories. Spain throws in Florida for good measure.
1819

Mexican-American War begins
First full-scale U.S. foreign war.
1846

Treaty of Guadalupe
U.S. pays Mexico $15 million for land that is now CA, AZ, NM, TX, and parts of CO, NV and UT. Whoever said real estate is a good investment was not kidding.
1848

"Birthright" Amendment Ratified
"All persons born or naturalized in the United States, and subject to the jurisdiction thereof, are citizens of the United States and the State wherein they reside."
1868

Convicts and Immoral Women denied entry
Congress passes statute prohibiting prostitutes and felons from entering.
1875

Chinese Exclusion Act
First major U.S. law restricting immigration. So much for authentic Chinese food.
1882

their nationality. If they're Mexican, and it appears they aren't wanted in the U.S. for a crime, we send them back to Mexico. If they're Other Than Mexican (OTM)—even if they are from one of the "special-interest" countries that make us nervous—they are usually released right onto our streets. Why? Because we can't send them to Mexico and, since our detention centers are usually full, we can't lock them up. Therefore, we politely ask them if they wouldn't mind hanging out in the United States while they wait for their immigration hearing. You can probably guess how that works out: 85 percent of "catch-and-release" aliens are never seen again.

We need illegal aliens to do the jobs Americans won't.

There are over 13 million unemployed Americans.

Releasing lawbreakers into society is incredibly frustrating for border-patrol agents who thought they signed on to uphold the law and instead find out that they are professional babysitters. T. J. Bonner, president of the National Border Patrol Council, says that "it's more than a little demoralizing. [Agents] feel like social workers. They are not enforcing the law; they are simply enabling people to break it—and that goes against the grain of any law enforcement officer."

On February 18, 2009, Catherine Herridge of Fox News reported that there are currently 554,000 illegal-alien fugitives on the loose in the U.S. If only .001 percent of them want to do any harm to the country, that means we're looking for five or six needles in a haystack made of needles. I don't know about you, but I don't really feel like "playing the odds" when it comes to terrorism.

It's ironic that if you bring up the idea that a few of the millions of people who've come here illegally might be terrorists you're called a fearmonger or a racist—as if you're trying to

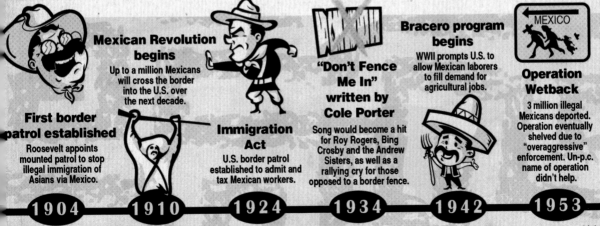

First border patrol established — 1904 — Roosevelt appoints mounted patrol to stop illegal immigration of Asians via Mexico.

Mexican Revolution begins — 1910 — Up to a million Mexicans will cross the border into the U.S. over the next decade.

Immigration Act — 1924 — U.S. border patrol established to admit and tax Mexican workers.

"Don't Fence Me In" written by Cole Porter — 1934 — Song would become a hit for Roy Rogers, Bing Crosby and the Andrew Sisters, as well as a rallying cry for those opposed to a border fence.

Bracero program begins — 1942 — WWII prompts U.S. to allow Mexican laborers to fill demand for agricultural jobs.

Operation Wetback — 1953 — 3 million illegal Mexicans deported. Operation eventually shelved due to "overaggressive" enforcement. Un-p.c. name of operation didn't help.

ARREST WARRANT
UNITED STATES DISTRICT COURT

Instructions: Type or legibly print. After execution of warrant use to make confetti.

Name	District	Court Docket No.
MONTOYA, INIGO	EL PASO	N/A

Reason for Warrant: **Immigration Violation**

Brief Description of Violation

Unauthorized entry into the United States via Mexico border. Suspect approached agent because he had to use bathroom.

Court Date: ☐ _____ Or ☒ first available date june 6, 2013

Date	Issuing official	Signature
27 August 2009	Deputy Clerk	S. Crockett

☐ You are hereby commanded to arrest the above-named person and bring this individual forth with before the nearest available United States Magistrate or District Court Judge to answer the above stated charges in the complaint.

☒ You are hereby commanded to arrest the above-named person briefly and then, because our hands are tied, just kind of let him go and hope he returns home.

Feed This End into Shredder

First Maquiladoras established
U.S. companies begin building factories in Mexican border towns to take advantage of cheap Mexican labor.

Immigration and Naturalization Act
Law intending to place limits on immigrant ethnicities accidentally opens floodgates to millions of Hispanics.

Illegal immigrant population tops 1-million mark

Carter calls for amnesty of "undocumented" aliens
President Carter admits problem of "undocumented workers" is out of hand. Doesn't want to hurt their feelings by calling them "illegal."

Genesis releases "(It's No Fun Being an) Illegal Alien"
Song reaches #44 on *Billboard* charts, then reaches #13 on *Blender* magazine's Top 50 Worst Songs Ever.

North American Free Trade Agreement (NAFTA) ratified
"Giant sucking sound" Ross Perot predicted turns out to be sound of millions of Mexicans crossing U.S. border in search of work.

1964   1965   1972   1977   1983   1984

SOMETIMES CRIME DOES PAY

Arizona ranchers Roger and Barbara Barnett were sued by a group of illegal aliens who were crossing their property on their way into the U.S. Mr. Barnett held them at gunpoint and waited on the authorities, which the aliens said traumatized them and violated their civil rights. Barnett lost in court and had to pay $78,000 in damages to the aliens. That might be considered a bargain, considering they'd sued him for $32 million.

scare people into sealing our borders. I say it's ironic because apparently the only time you're allowed to make the case that something terrible might happen is *after* something terrible *does* happen. It's as though people will only be convinced that our open borders are a security threat if we happen to catch Osama bin Laden himself trying to paddle across the Rio Grande.

Why, for once in our history, can't we be *proactive* about something? Rapes, kidnappings, murders, and unspeakable violence are happening almost daily in our border cities: Phoenix, Arizona, now has the second-highest number of kidnappings *in the world*, and according to a report from the U.S. Joint Forces Command, Mexico is at risk of a "rapid and sudden collapse"—yet we still don't think it's time to take practical precautions?

Actual terrorists must look at our open borders with a mix of anticipation and bewilderment. Al Qaeda gets most of the public's attention, but Hezbollah (which an FBI official says "makes al Qaeda look like Sunday-schoolers") has already taken note of our messy southern border. The 9/11 Commission Report said that Lebanese nationals sympathetic to Hezbollah and Hamas entered the U.S. with the help of "corrupt Mexican officials" and, in March 2006, FBI Director Mueller reported that his agency busted a Hezbollah smuggling ring that was using the Mexican border to get operatives into the United States. A former DEA agent reported in March 2009 that Hezbollah relies on "the same criminal-weapons smugglers,

Launch of Taco Bell ad campaign "Make a Run for the Border."

Customers subsequently conceive slogan: "Make a run for the bathroom."

Operation Gatekeeper

Bill Clinton directs a 40-mile long, double-high, 14-foot fence to be erected in San Diego area, leaving only 1,960 miles wide open.

Bush calls for "Virtual Fence"

Bush announces plans for "virtual fence," calling the $6.7 billion Arizona pilot project "the most technologically advanced border security initiative in American history."

First Taco Bell opens in Mexico

Critics in Mexico protest, calling it "like bringing ice to the Artic."

Virtual Fence plan shelved

After spending $600 million, project scrapped after inspectors discover that "virtual fence" does "virtually nothing" to stop flow of illegal immigrants.

Obama to jump start Virtual Fence

Homeland security announces plan to use economic stimulus package to accelerate plan to begin work again on virtual fence. You can't make this stuff up.

Millions of Illegal Immigrants — 15, 10, 5, 0

1988   1996   2006   2007   2008   2009

document traffickers and transportation experts as the drug cartels."

In March 2005, FBI Director Robert Mueller told the House Appropriations Subcommittee, "There are individuals from countries with known al Qaeda connections who are changing their Islamic surnames to Hispanic-sounding names and obtaining false Hispanic identities, learning to speak Spanish and pretending to be Hispanic immigrants." Maybe they are all going to move to Mexico and live happily ever after, or maybe they are going to come here and blow up buildings—the point is that there are too many "maybes" involved for my liking.

Another incident involving terrorists and our borders happened in early 2009 when al Qaeda recruiter Abdullah al-Nafisi was seen on video talking about how they could exploit our southern border. "Four pounds of anthrax—in a suitcase this big—carried by a fighter through tunnels from Mexico into the U.S. are guaranteed to kill 330,000 Americans within a single hour if it is properly spread in population centers there," al-Nafisi said. "What a horrifying idea; 9/11 will be small change in comparison. Am I right? There is no need for airplanes, conspiracies, timings and so on. One person, with the courage to carry four pounds of anthrax, will go to the White House lawn, and will

The postal service can't get your birthday card to Grandma on time, but the government is apparently capable of sending illegal gang members back home for Christmas. According to a Federal investigator, an MS-13 gang member who was in the U.S. illegally wanted to get a free trip home for Christmas so he turned himself in to the authorities. Did it work? Yep. They sent him home on the taxpayers' dime, where he spent the holidays with his family and then returned to the U.S. by illegally crossing the southwest border. In fact, the ploy worked so well that he did it over and over again.

> "It's very easy to blame immigrants for the disastrous state of our economy, the failure of the health-care system, the educational crisis, the disappearing middle class and just about every ill that makes this country unwelcoming to the immigrants. That is a smoke screen to distract us from the real sources of these problems. I stand with the founders of this country and the sentiment written on the Statue of Liberty."
>
> —Susan Sarandon

CELEBRITY GUEST IDEEOT

❮ Maybe someone needs to clue Ms. Sarandon in to two facts: (1) No one is blaming *immigrants* for anything; and (2) That the "sentiment" written on the Statue of Liberty ends with this line:

I lift my lamp beside the golden door!

Why would our door be "golden" if, as Sarandon seems to suggest, anyone and everyone should be allowed through it? Wouldn't that be more like a "brass" door?

SOMETIMES CRIME DOES PAY

In April 2005, Texas Deputy Sheriff Gilmer Hernandez stopped a van at midnight in his small town. When he approached the vehicle he noticed a group of people lying on the floor. The driver took off and tried to run Hernandez over. Hernandez shot at the tires and everyone ran away, except for one woman whose teeth were damaged by shrapnel. The U.S. government, aided by Mexican officials, prosecuted Hernandez for violating the civil rights of the illegal aliens in the van and for using excessive force. Hernandez spent almost a year in jail and was fined $5,000. The illegal aliens also sued Hernandez for damages including medical expenses, pain and suffering, and mental anguish. They sought $1.5 million, but settled for a mere $100,000.

spread this 'confetti' all over them, and then we'll do these cries of joy. It will turn into a real celebration."

Is that just propaganda to convince new recruits that al Qaeda is still relevant? Perhaps . . . but considering that the tunnels he mentions actually exist, we would be smart to take him at his word.

While the crisis down south gets all of the headlines, the open Canadian border is just as dangerous. It's twice the size of the Mexican border and we have only about one fifth of the border patrol agents stationed there. Up until late 2007, Canadian border agents had no access to firearms and had to call in the Canadian police to handle dangerous individuals. Canada expects to train and arm all of their guards by 2017 but, as of now, some have only pepper spray, a baton, and the ability to yell "Eh!" very loudly. You do the math.

While all of the stats and studies are nice, the winning response to the border argument really revolves around common sense. I defy you to name just one nation that has prospered without defending its borders. You won't be able to, and the reason is simple: Open borders not only invite violence and national security concerns, they also inevitably result in a country importing poverty while exporting high-paying jobs and wealthy, educated citizens. Keep that up for as long as we have and soon you will have a country with massive deficits, growing rates of unemployment, and fewer and fewer wealthy people able to support them all.

Oh, wait a second . . . .

You're Just a Fearmonger!

"First, our cities will not be flooded with a million immigrants annually. Under the proposed bill, the present level of immigration remains substantially the same."

—Ted Kennedy, speaking in favor of the Hart-Seller immigration bill of 1965, which changed immigration into a civil-rights cause and resulted in an increase in illegal immigrants coming to this country. In retrospect, Kennedy was right, our cities weren't flooded with a million immigrants a year . . . they were flooded with 800,000 *illegal* immigrants a year.

"SO THAT MEANS YOU WANT A FENCE, EH?"

kay, stop with the Canadian accent. I don't want "a" fence, I want *two* of them. And I want them double-layered and really, really high.

Some people will point out that we've already tried to build a fence, but it's proposed to be only 670 miles long and government incompetence has plagued it the whole way. Critics say that the cost is too expensive—but that argument doesn't hold up when you start comparing the costs to what we've spent recently. Costs vary by mile, depending on the specifications and what kind of terrain the fence covers, but estimates range from $2 to $10 million per mile. A fence running the entire length of the U.S.-Mexican border—twice—at the highest estimate of $10 million/mile, would cost us roughly $40 billion.

That's expensive, right? Sure is, but it's also equal to the amount of money the stimulus bill set aside to increase and extend unemployment benefits. That's an ironic comparison, given that we likely wouldn't *need* those benefits extended if illegal laborers were prevented from taking American jobs.

Only $5.99

NEW

From the geniuses who brought you the "Virtual Fence"...

Virtual Condoms

Works just as well as the virtual fence... not at all!

America's #1 Choice for Virtual Birth Control!

The government, along with environmentalists, has other ideas. A real fence is so old-school, they say, we need to progress in our thinking and consider a "virtual fence" instead. I will spare you the question of why the White House, Fort Knox, and Rikers Island all use "real" fences and instead ask this: If a virtual fence is such a no-brainer, then why has it taken three years to even *start* construction on just 23 miles of cameras and sensors?

In typical government fashion, even when the $6.4 billion project is complete, it won't be complete. According to *The New York Times*, "Within five years . . . the [virtual] fence is expected to extend along the entire 2,000-mile border except for some 200 miles in the area of Big Bend National Park in Texas, a stretch that is to be addressed later." Isn't that kind of like installing a home-security system but putting a note on the front door saying that the back door doesn't have a sensor yet?

"THAT'S JUST A SMOKESCREEN, THE REAL REASON YOU WANT A FENCE IS THAT YOU'RE A CONSPIRACY NUT WHO THINKS WE'RE MERGING WITH CANADA AND MEXICO."

I might be crazy, but lots of stuff going on in our government doesn't add up—or, it adds up, but not in a good way. Yes, I believe there is an effort under way by a few well-connected groups to establish something akin to a North American Union. But the difference between me and the black-helicopter crowd is that I don't believe it's a *conspiracy*—I think it's happening right out in the open and it's all being championed by profit-minded global corporations.

If you are interested in the names of the people and the companies behind this effort you can read the illegal-immigration chapter in *An Inconvenient Book*—I'll spare you the details here—but one key point I made is that the idea of a more "cohesive hemisphere" is nonpartisan. Presidents and business leaders from both sides of the aisle are becoming convinced that the economic and security benefits of uniting, like the European Union, outweigh the risks. That doesn't necessarily mean that "America" goes away—it just means that instead of answering only to our Constitution, we'd be answering to a whole set of additional

WHO SAID IT?

"I frankly don't understand all the brouhaha lately from Congress and even from some of my colleagues about referring to foreign law. Why shouldn't we look to the wisdom of a judge from abroad with at least as much ease as we would read a law-review article written by a professor?"

Who said that . . . maybe some nut-job conspiracy theorist? I guess that depends on what you think of Supreme Court Justice Ginsburg—because the quote is from her.

I understand that the idea of a North American Union sounds insane, but is it really any crazier than a Supreme Court justice suggesting that we take legal guidance from foreign countries? The point is that the traditional way of thinking about borders is, unfortunately, "progressing"—and that means the traditional way of thinking about sovereignty will soon be progressing as well.

147

international laws (as we do now after ratifying an international treaty).

Is President Obama a fan of this idea? Who knows—though his nomination of Harold Koh (an avowed transnationalist who believes that we must respect the "opinions of mankind") to an important State Department position would lead me to believe that he's more open to blurring borders than strengthening them. There is also the matter of Obama's odd, misleading reply to a question about the NAU—which I know is circumstantial evidence (hmm, maybe it could be admissible in a *foreign* court?) but is suspicious nonetheless.

At a 2008 Town Hall meeting in Lancaster, Pennsylvania, Obama was asked about his relationship to the Council on Foreign Relations (CFR), one of the groups that allegedly supports increased globalization and a decreased focus on the sovereignty of individual countries. "I don't know if I'm an official member," Obama responded. "I've spoken there before. It's basically just a forum where a bunch of people talk about foreign policy. There's no official membership. I don't have a card or a special handshake or anything like that." (Audience laughs.)

He went on to discount the idea that a European Union-style entity may be on its way here by saying, "I see no evidence of this actually taking place."

I have two issues with what he said. First, his hilarious joke about secret handshakes notwithstanding, the CFR most definitely does have an "official membership" list. In fact, the CFR's own website spends over 1,500 words describing the specific steps that one must take to become a member ("Complete application and submit curriculum vitae," "Obtain a letter of nomination from an existing member," "Submit three letters of recommenda-

EVERYBODY FREAK OUT!

THE RESTAURANT INDUSTRY WILL COLLAPSE IF WE ABOLISH ILLEGAL LABOR!

Labor makes up about 30 percent of a restaurant's operating costs. If illegal labor were eliminated and wages raised to accommodate legal workers, the cost of your meal would likely increase between three to six percent. That means a $100 steak dinner might cost you around $104 instead—hardly enough of an increase to put restaurants out of business.

> "To be so repressive isn't democratic or free . . . to be putting up fences, chasing Mexicans, that isn't right. The U.S. needs better answers than repression, weapons and violence."
>
> —Vincente Fox

CELEBRITY Guest Ideeot

❮ Former Mexican president Vicente Fox certainly knows a little something about repression, weapons, and violence.

A.D.D. MOMENT

Obama claims the CFR is just a little forum for chatting about foreign policy—but listen to the words of David Rockefeller, former CFR chairman of the board and now their honorary chairman:

"Some even believe we are part of a secret cabal working against the best interests of the United States, characterizing my family and me as 'internationalists' and of conspiring with others around the world to build a more integrated global political and economic structure—one world, if you will. If that's the charge, I stand guilty, and I am proud of it."

Wow—that's a pretty big vision for a little weekend discussion club, isn't it?

tion," etc.). In other words, President Obama knows very well whether he's a member and people deserve an honest answer from him rather than a comedic dismissal.

Second, regardless of whether President Obama is a CFR member, many of his advisors and cabinet members, like George Mitchell (special envoy to the Middle East), Richard Holbrooke (special envoy to Pakistan and Afghanistan), and Treasury Secretary Timothy Geithner reportedly are. Even Obama's wife, Michelle, was reportedly on the board of directors of the Chicago branch of the CFR.

Given those connections, you'd think that the president would be a little more familiar with what the CFR has been working on—most notably their 2005 task force report entitled "Building a North American Community." (Sample of their findings: "To that end, the Task Force proposes the creation by 2010 of a North American community to enhance security, prosperity, and opportunity . . . Its boundaries will be defined by a common external tariff and an outer security perimeter . . . ")

Of course, none of this means that President Obama supports further integration between the U.S., Mexico, and Canada—but, as I said in *An Inconvenient Book*, one sure way for him (or *any* leader) to prove he doesn't support it is by *strongly* supporting a double-layered fence along both of our borders, along with crippling fines on businesses that hire illegal workers.

"GREAT, SO AFTER WE BUILD YOUR PRECIOUS FENCE, THEN WHAT? DO WE DEPORT EVERYONE WHO'S ALREADY HERE? THAT'D BE IMPOSSIBLE!"

The media loves to trot out stories about immigrants living in fear of deportation. For example, an *ABC News* story from 2008 (innocently titled "Immigration Raids Cripple Small Towns") contained a section labeled "Immigrant Mother Describes Terror" about a raid at a Mississippi plant. Only once you started to read the article did you find out that the "immigrant" mother was

"It's insulting that the law would call an immigrant a criminal . . . it's horrible."

—Actor John Leguizamo. I know what you're thinking, because it's the same thing I am: "Who?"

We have a deportation program going known as "ICE Air" that sounds better than any commercial flight I've ever taken. At a cost to taxpayers of about $680 per one-way ticket, illegal aliens are flown home and provided with sandwiches, chips, fruit, bottled water, juice, civilian clothing, checked baggage, and a private nurse.

That apparently wasn't enough for Ismael Martinez, a recent passenger being deported for domestic battery. "People tell you about all the opportunities in the United States, but they don't reveal the bad things like this, where they treat us like animals," he said. If Martinez thought that was bad, I wonder what he'd think about flying on Continental.

actually an "undocumented Mexican" and that her "terror" came from the fact that federal agents had the audacity to show up at the place where she was working illegally and ask her for proof of her status. Oh, the inhumanity!

Latino groups also love to denounce the government's (usually feeble) attempts at enforcement. After Homeland Security Secretary Janet Napolitano conducted deportation raids in early 2009, some groups complained that they "destroyed families" and "spread terror." What is rarely mentioned—or quickly glossed over—is that these raids are usually triggered by suspicion of identity theft and it's *that* crime that is usually prosecuted. But that angle doesn't seem as sexy as "Big Bad U.S. Government Terrorizes Helpless Immigrants," so it's generally ignored.

I know this will come as a shock to some people, but I'm actually not in favor of destroying families *or* spreading terror. I think it's terrible that we could potentially be taking a mother or father away from their children (although, to be fair, it's not like anyone is requiring that they leave their children behind). That is why I am open to doing something that so many others aren't: *compromising*.

I am more than willing to talk about a program for people who want to come out of the shadows, admit they are guilty of a crime, and pay an appropriate penalty. But, and this is where I lose most people, I'm willing to talk

Giving amnesty will end the problem once and for all!

In 1986, the illegal alien population was about 5 million.

Various forms of amnesty were granted in 1986, 1994, 1997, 1998, and 2000.

In 2009, the illegal alien population is 2 to 4 times larger than what it was in 1986.

about that only *after* we have secured both borders to my satisfaction. After all, if we learned anything from Ronald Reagan's amnesty program, it should be that amnesty without security only incentivizes more people to break the law.

A.D.D. MOMENT

In 2004, word began to get out about President Bush's plan to offer something-akin-to-amnesty-but-definitely-not-amnesty to illegal aliens. Shortly afterward the border patrol began to ask those they captured why they were trying to get into the country. In some districts as many as 90 percent reported they were coming now in order to be grandfathered in for the amnesty program.

The truth is that "comprehensive" immigration reform should be "comprehensive" only in that it deals with how we will comprehensively shut down the border and turn off the job magnet first. Once that happens, it will be much easier to have a logical discussion about what to do with those who are left (many of whom, at that point, will likely be trying to figure out how to get over the fence and back into Mexico on their own because of the lack of illegal jobs available here).

If that doesn't work, we can always pack up our stuff and leave this country to the politicians and activists who seem to be so intent on dismantling it.

Besides, I hear Mexico is nice—especially this time of year.

THE NANNY STATE

Saving You from Yourself,
One Right at a Time

IF THERE'S ONE THING that liberals, conservatives, communists, capitalists, vegetarians, teetotalers, pet lovers, bureaucrats, Republicans, and Democrats can all agree on, it's telling you how you should live your life.

From punitive "sin" taxes and laws dictating your house's paint color to rules and regulations aimed at smoking, drinking, dancing, eating, washing your car in the driveway, keeping a cat in your store, smiling for your driver's license, or playing tag, you can rest assured that local, state, and federal governments are more ready, willing, and able than ever to make decisions for you. Laws and taxes are passed in the name of improving community standards, keeping you safe and healthy, maintaining order, spreading morality, or because somebody somewhere complained, died, or had their feelings hurt.

Even if a seemingly trivial ban on the sale of cheap cigars doesn't affect you directly, eventually one of these mini-tyrannies will. Before you know it you'll find yourself breaking the law because your pants are too baggy, you didn't wear a helmet for soccer, you went trick-or-treating when you were 12 or—perish the thought!—you sat on a milk crate.

Where's all this madness coming from?

Good intentions. A great deal of the plague of the Nanny State stems from the desire of various individuals to make the world a better place for everyone—the proverbial "greater good" argument that progressives so often recite. Of course, "a better place" means different

LIVE FREE, OR . . .

★ . . . live in Concord, New Hampshire, where a manicurist received a 30-day suspended sentence for not having a license to give a manicure.

★ . . . live in Farmers Branch, Texas, where some residents have asked the city to forbid "bold" colors on houses.

★ . . . live in Washington, where state officials banned washing your car in the driveway.

★ . . . live in Arizona, where a restaurant was harassed by officials because it allowed patrons to dance.

★ . . . live in some poor areas of Los Angeles, where fast-food restaurants are off-limits.

★ . . . live in Belmont, California, where you can no longer smoke in your own apartment.

★ . . . live in New York City, where officials want corner-store owners to get rid of their cats.

★ . . . live in Texas, where admitting what a vibrator is for is illegal.

★ . . . live in Indiana, where you're not allowed to smile for your driver's license.

★ . . . live in Virginia, where some students can no longer play tag.

★ . . . live in Philadelphia, where the sale of individual "blunt" cigars is banned.

★ . . . live in small-town Louisiana, where baggy, sagging pants are banned.

things to different people—and that's a big part of the problem. Fidel Castro thinks he made Cuba "better" but there are a few folks who might disagree.

Nanny State-ism often starts with a universally accepted, noble idea that on its own seems quite hard to argue with. For example: *We must stop drunk drivers.* They're a menace. They kill thousands of people a year and put innocent families at risk. So you say, *Heck yeah! We need to get rid of drunk drivers.*

But how?

In the Nanny State, the answer is "By law, of course!" Using legislation to "solve" an issue at the expense of some of your personal liberty. And laws, as we all know, are always subject to "mission creep."

First they came for the cigarettes, and I didn't speak up because I'm not a smoker.

Then they came for the trans fats and I didn't speak up because I'm a healthy eater.

Then they came for the foie gras and I didn't speak up because it's French.

Then they came for the ice cream and I didn't speak up because I'm lactose intolerant.

And then they came for the rib eye. And by that time there was no one left to speak up because all of the restaurants were already out of business.

The United States was founded on a few simple principles, life, liberty, and the pursuit of happiness being some of my favorites. I'll leave life and happiness for another time, but for now I want to deal with liberty since that's something the Nanny State movement isn't quite able to fully comprehend.

The principle of "liberty" puts each of us in control of making the decisions that will affect our lives, for better or for worse. Thomas Jefferson put it like this:

> *"It does me no injury for my neighbor to say there are twenty gods or no God. It neither picks my pocket nor breaks my leg."*

In other words, you and I are free to think as we like and do as we like—as long as doing so doesn't harm anyone else. Live and let live. Simple, right? Not anymore. Not with the State involved.

Back to drunk driving. The Nanny State approach is to use the police department to set up roadblocks and spot-checks (which, as a fun side benefit, helps to concentrate law enforcement personnel in one area, thereby creating traffic jams and penalizing innocent people who are merely trying to get home from work). Then, the ideas become more intrusive and inane: banning the sale of cold beer, banning the sale of fruity adult drinks, dictating the exact composition of a martini, watering down beer, making establishments and their workers liable for *your* getting drunk, demanding "Happy Hour" be renamed and, the Grand Prize: requiring ignition-locking breathalyzers in all cars—an idea promoted by Nanny Statist New York assemblyman Felix Ortiz.

Does it matter if you don't drink *at all* or that you'd never, ever consider driving under the influence? Nope. It'll be a round of breathalyzers for everyone.

For Every Action

Nanny State laws aim for "positive impact" but there's always a catch . . .

★ Punitive **taxes on cigarettes** resulted in smuggling and a thriving black market that harmed local, legitimate businesses.

★ The **banning of alcohol** from legitimate sources meant criminals like Al Capone made millions and millions from the bootlegging and sale of it during Prohibition.

★ The number of DUIs increased after **smoking was banned** in bars because smokers drove to jurisdictions that did not have smoking ordinances.

★ **Food-handling legislation** in Indiana effectively rendered the average potluck dinner illegal.

★ A law **punishing legislators** for passing stupid laws resulted in better politicians being elected. (Just kidding, that'll never happen.)

A.D.D. Moment

Some hospitals collected DNA samples from newborns so they could be screened for genetic predispositions to diseases. Sounds like a good idea . . . until mission creep kicked in and suddenly the government was saying, "Hey, why don't we hold on to those samples for . . . like, forever?"

Unrelated A.D.D Moment: I wonder if scientists will ever discover a gene that makes people prone to revolutionary thought. If so, I wonder if that will show up in DNA samples. And, if so, I wonder if those babies will ever live life outside a prison cell?

Completely unrelated A.D.D. Moment: **A.D.D. Moment** I should call Steven Spielberg and tell him I have the premise for *Minority Report II*.

155

Now, if you make the really, really terrible decision to get liquored up and hit the road, you deserve to be *severely* punished. Choosing to call a friend or a cab is your personal responsibility, and, until recently, each of us used to be personally responsible for it. But not anymore. Now the government, assisted by a wide assortment of legislation-happy enablers, has decided that it knows what's best for you.

And that's the problem: In their effort to make the world better, Nannies enact nuisance laws that undermine our liberty, punish *everyone* equally—and make our world worse.

Candy Lightner founded Mothers Against Drunk Driving in 1980 after her daughter was killed by a drunk driver, but she ended up leaving her own organization. Why? Mission creep. Here's what she said:

> "[MADD has] become far more neo-prohibitionist than I had ever wanted or envisioned . . . I didn't start MADD to deal with alcohol. I started MADD to deal with the issue of drunk driving."

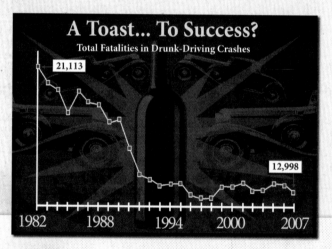

A Toast... To Success?
Total Fatalities in Drunk-Driving Crashes

21,113

12,998

1982   1988   1994   2000   2007

Here's a good illustration of the way most well-intentioned Nanny State ideas progress. MADD started out by bringing awareness about drunk driving to the masses and, from 1982 to 1992, the results were spectacular. Since then, despite increasingly draconian proposals that are taking away freedoms from law-abiding Americans, progress has been dismal.

Nanny State programs are a lot like weight loss—you can drop a lot of pounds quickly by doing some basic, commonsense things, but soon you hit a plateau where every successive pound becomes harder to lose, and you end up doing increasingly crazy things to eke out small wins. No one is saying that MADD doesn't serve a great purpose—but there does come a point where the benefit to society no longer justifies the ever-increasing costs.

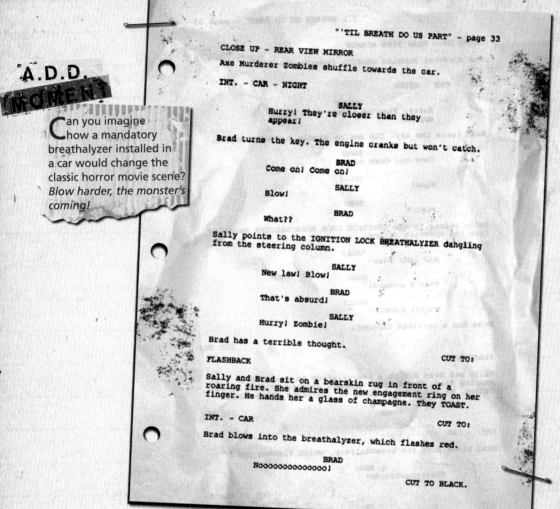

Can you imagine how a mandatory breathalyzer installed in a car would change the classic horror movie scene? *Blow harder, the monster's coming!*

"'TIL BREATH DO US PART" - page 33

CLOSE UP - REAR VIEW MIRROR

Axe Murderer Zombies shuffle towards the car.

INT. - CAR - NIGHT

                    SALLY
            Hurry! They're closer than they
            appear!

Brad turns the key. The engine cranks but won't catch.

                    BRAD
            Come on! Come on!

                    SALLY
            Blow!

                    BRAD
            What??

Sally points to the IGNITION LOCK BREATHALYZER dangling
from the steering column.

                    SALLY
            New law! Blow!

                    BRAD
            That's absurd!

                    SALLY
            Hurry! Zombie!

Brad has a terrible thought.

FLASHBACK   CUT TO:

Sally and Brad sit on a bearskin rug in front of a
roaring fire. She admires the new engagement ring on her
finger. He hands her a glass of champagne. They TOAST.

INT. - CAR   CUT TO:

Brad blows into the breathalyzer, which flashes red.

                    BRAD
            Noooooooooooooooo!

                                CUT TO BLACK.

She started an organization for a noble purpose but was incapable of stopping it from expanding its mission far beyond her intentions. As MADD transitioned from fighting drunk driving to more of a zero-tolerance stance on alcohol, she became disenchanted.

MADD is now one of the staunchest supporters of ignition-interlock (aka *Prohignition*) legislation in the country. They've helped pass laws requiring installation of the technology in the cars of first-time DUI offenders—but that was just the beginning. An article in *USA Today* said the group doesn't *currently* support installing the technology in all cars. Not because they don't agree with the concept, but because they don't believe in the technology. Yet. In other words, baby steps.

'TIL BREATH
DO US PART
DYING FOR A DRINK
NOW IN
DRAMAVISION!!!
A MICHAEL BLOOMBERG PICTURE

Here's something that Nanny Staters don't like to talk about: The largest percentage of vehicular deaths related to alcohol are from *repeat offenders*. Therefore, the commonsense solution is that you lose your license after a second DUI. Forever. Problem solved.

Deter bad behavior by targeting every *offender*, not every *person*. But ideas like ignition-interlock reverse that. They target *everyone* with the hope of catching the proverbial drunk needle in the haystack.

Drunk drivers? Let's make cars more expensive and force everyone to blow into their dashboard to go to the bank.

Millions of law-abiding citizens wind up penalized for the irresponsibility of a relative few. And, of course, the tiny percentage of repeat offenders the technology is actually meant for will find a way to get around it anyway.

IGNITION INTERLOCK? NO PROBLEM!!

IF YOU'RE NOT AT LIBERTY TO DRIVE WHEN IT PLEASES YOU, THEN AIR FARCE™ INTERLOCK-BLOCK BALLOONS ARE A BREATH OF FRESH AIR. JUST PLUG IN, SQUEEZE AND DRIVE OFF!

COLLECTED FROM 100% ALCOHOL-FREE MORMON EXHALE — AN ECOLOGICALLY SOUND, SUSTAINABLE RESOURCE!

ONLY $2.95 EACH, OR GET A "BREATHER'S DOZEN" FOR $29.95!

AirFarce™

Nanny State legislation unrealistically assumes that 100 percent of human behavior can be corrected. Even in a scary totalitarian state like China, a place that has over 60 crimes punishable by death, you will still find people who will break the law. Why is that? If their uncontested, all-powerful government can create any law they want to outlaw any behavior they deem undesirable, then why does China have a need for prisons or their terrifying mobile execution vans?

The answer is simple: No matter what we do, no matter what laws we enact or what creative punishments we invent, there

A.D.D. MOMENT

Never underestimate an alcoholic's resourcefulness. Believe me, I know. One man with the interlock installed on his car simply rented a car that didn't have it. Another repeat offender figured out that the best way around it was to use a balloon filled with (someone else's) alcohol-free breath.

will *always* be people who will make bad decisions. It's human nature, but, more important, it's the price we pay for liberty.

What's truly alarming is that as those liberties are quietly being chipped away at by federal laws, overzealous city councils, school boards, lobbyists, activist groups, and power-hungry politicians, we do nothing about it. We shrug our shoulders as officials frighten us with scary (often manipulated) statistics and we applaud draconian legislation because we're told it saves lives, protects the children, keeps other people from being annoyed, or any of the myriad excuses the Nanny Staters give. They've learned that it's easier to slowly whittle down your rights rather than seize them *en masse*—which tends to cause people to notice.

Nannies are truly a bipartisan, eclectic, cross-cultural group. From the pale-faced vegans of PETA working to keep live lobsters out of supermarkets, to the God-fearing folks of Alabama who can't stay out of your bedroom, to concerned college administrators devising Orwellian speech-and-conduct codes for students, and bored bureaucrats who simply need to justify their paychecks—it's nearly impossible to pick a Nanny Stater out of a lineup.

Of course, they do all have one thing in common: They're all idiots. Here's what you might face if you ever have the opportunity to argue with one of them . . .

THE NANNIES
WINNER

MOST POINTLESS
The Boston City Council wants to ban dog rental because it's "disrespectful to the dog."

"LOTS OF PEOPLE NEED GUIDANCE IN THEIR LIVES AND THAT'S WHAT THESE LAWS OFFER."

So let me get this straight . . . The government can't efficiently run the post office, the school system, or the DMV. It can't police our borders properly, it failed to prevent the S&L crisis, 9/11, the dot-com bubble, the housing collapse, and the credit crisis. Its IRS created a fully incomprehensible 78,000-page tax code and its Congress writes bills so long that no one has time to read them—but I should still trust it to make personal decisions for me against my will?

I think I'll pass.

The fatty-fat-fatsos of America are a good example of how this works in practice. We can all agree that, in most cases, saying "It's glandular!" just doesn't cut it anymore. Obesity is, by and large, caused by someone making bad decisions like eating too many unhealthy foods, sucking down sodas, and using their Nintendo Wii for exercise.

But the government ignores those commonsense explanations and instead assumes that you're a moron. They believe that you must have no idea that a 64-ounce fountain soda contains an unhealthy amount of sugar or that a Hardee's Monster Thickburger with bacon,

A.D.D. MOMENT

Kudos to David Harsanyi's great book *Nanny State* for letting us know that the Hardees Monster Thickburger not only exists, but has . . .

1420 calories, 108g fat, 43g saturated fat, 230mg cholesterol, 2770mg sodium, 46g carbohydrates and 100 percent deliciousness.

cheese, burger patty, more bacon, more cheese, another patty, more cheese, more bacon and mayonnaise isn't healthy. And you can't possibly be expected to instinctively know that coffee is hot or that a venti-triple-caff-mega-lard-mocha-choco-rama has lots of calories.

After unilaterally deciding that you're an idiot, the government then decides that it must act to protect you from yourself. The result is warning labels, calorie counts, bans on advertising, purging chips and soda from schools, restrictions on portion sizes, sin taxes, suspending honor students who dare bring candy to school—you name it. Of course, the easiest and least intrusive thing to do would be to simply say: *Hey, buddy, if you eat too much junk food, you'll get fat*—but the very first thing the Nanny State ever outlawed was common sense.

A.D.D. MoMent

I've been turning more and more libertarian lately and that side of me would really like to know why people can't just get as fat as they want. Sure, it may not be good for you, and, yes, I don't want to see you in a Speedo on the beach, but it is still YOUR life, isn't it?

Look, if you decide that 45 great years eating nothing but pizza and ice cream, watching movies, and making fun of joggers is better than 85 mediocre years eating salads on the treadmill, who am I to second-guess you? Like Thomas Jefferson said, *it neither picks my pocket nor breaks my leg* . . . though I will grant you that Jefferson didn't have to deal with the Speedo thing. Or the weight limits on elevators. Or the middle seat on an airplane. Or TLC documentaries with names like *The Half-Ton Man*.

But, most importantly, Jefferson didn't have to deal with the imminent adoption of government-run health care. Nowadays, when your irresponsibility means your fat has grown into the fabric of your couch, resulting in emergency crews having to knock down your wall, load you on a flatbed, and get you to a hospital to staple your stomach at taxpayer expense—guess who pays? We all do. And that picks *my* pocket . . . and makes me want to break *your* leg.

Our Founding Fathers never intended for government to start micromanaging our lives. That's why the Constitution is a four-page document that primarily lays out what the government *can't do* to individuals, rather than what it can do. But Nanny Staters act as though it's the complete opposite by trying to get legislation passed that prohibits individual rights instead while expanding governmental authority.

THE NANNIES
WINNER

MOST LIKELY TO BE BROKEN

St. Charles, Missouri, officials proposed banning swearing in bars.

Ask your server about our weekly specials!

TREAT YOURSELF TO OUR...

Only $8.95 [1]

FREAKIN' ONION

FREAKIN' ONION

PRICE: $8.95 *plus tax*

An Appleday's original! We take an imported Gigantor™ onion, hand slice it into perfect bite-size morsels and then deep fry it until it's golden brown and super-delicious![2] The Freakin' Onion! is served with one ounce[3] of our world famous[4] spicy dipping sauce, three napkins[5] and unlimited amounts of yum![6]

Calories	Total Fat	Trans Fat	Fiber Level	CDC Rating	CSPI Rating	PETA Rating	Allergy Alert(s)	Carbon Factor
1,733	29g	9g	Dangerously Low	F	Avoid	Cruelty Free	Onions	6.2

If you'd like to order the Freakin' Onion! please ask your waiter to recite the Federal Freakin' Onion! Fun Facts Disclosure and then sign the Intent to Consume Fatty Foods (Form DHHS 427-1) as required by City Council regulation NS-1028.

Please Note: City ordinance 112-D requires the purchase of two accompanying steamed vegetables with your Freakin' Onion! County ordinance H3909 forbids the Freakin' Onion! from being taken to-go. State statute 876-098 requires that a minimum of two (and maximum of four) people consent to equally consume the Freakin' Onion!

In accordance with Massachusetts law, the Freakin' Onion! is called the Happy Onion!

Sorry, the Freakin' Onion! is not for sale in Chicago.

SURGEON GENERAL'S WARNING:

FRIED FOODS KILL

[1] Pursuant to the Fair Disclosure in Pricing Act the total cost of this item, including federal, state and local taxes, along with service charge, is $11.19. Using your credit card may result in interest charges that could significantly increase the final amount you pay for the Freakin' Onion!

[2] The adjective "super-delicious" is for descriptive purposes only and does not guarantee that you will agree that the Freakin' Onion! contains a superior level of deliciousness.

[3] Health regulations forbid us from providing more than one ounce of spicy‡ dipping sauce per table.

[4] Although the Freakin' Onion! is highly popular, we are required by law to disclose that no attempt has been made to certify it as "world famous" and it has not been deemed "world famous" by any official source.

[5] Pursuant to EPA Statute 212-354, we may provide only three napkins per appetizer. For additional paper products, please visit our restrooms.

[6] Total "yum" per table may be limited by local regulations.

‡ The use of the adjective "spicy" was approved in accordance with U.S. Department of Descriptors directive 002B. In our double-blind taste test, 83 of the 100 participants agreed that our sauce could be reasonably defined as "spicy." Individual experiences may vary.

THE U.S. DEPARTMENT OF HEALTH FORBIDS THE SALE OF THE FREAKIN' ONION! TO CHILDREN 16 AND UNDER, ADULTS 72 AND OVER, OR ANYONE WHOSE FEDERAL HEALTH RECORDS INDICATE A HISTORY OF, OR POTENTIAL FOR, HEART DISEASE OR IRRITABLE BOWEL SYNDROME.

NO SMOKING • NO MORE THAN 4 PEOPLE PER TABLE
CUSTOMERS MUST WASH HANDS BEFORE EATING
NO CELL PHONE USE NEAR PREGNANT WOMEN
SEATBELTS SAVE LIVES • DRIVE 55

WARNING: THIS ITEM IS FRIED AND THEREFORE IS INTENDED TO ARRIVE AT YOUR TABLE IN A STATE OF ELEVATED TEMPERATURE. PLEASE WAIT 4-6 MINUTES BEFORE ATTEMPTING TO TOUCH OR EAT THE FREAKIN ONION! TO AVOID SERIOUS BODILY INJURY.

WE PROUDLY ADHERE TO ALL FEDERAL AMBIENT TEMPERATURE LAWS.
BAGGY PANTS ARE ILLEGAL - PLEASE DRESS ACCORDINGLY.

APPLEDAY'S NEIGHBORHOOD GRILL & BAR

A GREAT PLACE TO RELAX

433

"OKAY, BUT YOU HAVE TO ADMIT THAT WE HAVE A RESPONSIBILITY TO PROTECT OUR CHILDREN."

Y ou're right, we do have that responsibility—but most Nanny State laws aimed at protecting our children do a lousy job of it. We have children who can't play tag or dodgeball for fear they might get hurt. We have teachers who can't correct with red ink because it might hurt kids' feelings. We have soda machines stocked with water because soda might make kids fat. We have spanking bans, playgrounds without slides or swings, and a whole host of other laws eager to protect our children. So our kids are much safer now, right? Of course not. In fact, it's just the opposite.

Psychologists have been telling us that our over-protected, over-coddled children are unprepared to deal with the realities of life *because they've never experienced them.* They are more prone to feeling angry and confused when faced with problems because they've never failed. They're technically "safer" from bruises and scrapes than any generation in history, but they're also more likely to be anxious and unhappy.

NAME THAT FOUNDING FATHER!

N ame the founding father who said:

"Though liberty is a blessing, it must be managed closely, for only the collective can truly know what is best for the individual."

Answer: Seriously? You actually thought a Founding Father said that? Time to reread the Constitution.

30 Years of Progress?

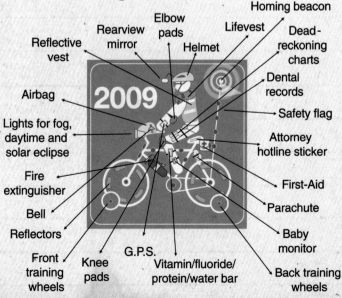

It seems as though we love our kids so much that we're protecting them to death. Remember: Bad things happen all the time—and we learn from them . . . or at least we would if we were allowed to.

A.D.D. MOMENT

One of the most frequent questions when it comes to people's faith is: *Why do bad things happen to good people?* Well, the simple answer is because our Creator isn't a Nanny. I believe that our Creator allows violence, death, and destruction to happen because He knows that the implications of *stopping* those things are far worse. I only wish the State would heed His advice. Unfortunately, most of our politicians believe they're smarter than He is.

"I DON'T HAVE A PROBLEM WITH A LAW IF IT CONTRIBUTES TO THE GREATER GOOD."

Oh, well, if it's for the greater good then by all means, seize my freedom and strip me of my rights! Big round of applause for The Greater Good, everybody—it'll be here all week, tip your waiters!

The truth is that there are lots of things we could do for the greater good . . . but we don't. Sterilizing Paris Hilton before she has a chance to make babies with some goateed moron in a wool hat would *definitely* be for the greater good. Stopping young kids from playing violent video games so they would instead read a book would be for the greater good. Forcing you to eat broccoli with every meal would be for the greater good. Ceding control of Berkeley, California, to Europe would be for the greater good.

EVERYBODY **FREAK OUT!**

News headlines that compelled us to take (pointless) action.

"400,000 die from obesity every year!"
Actually, no. The 400,000 included those who may have been fat, but died of other diseases. Like old age. Actual toll: 25,000.

"Saccharin causes cancer!"
Yes: If you're a male rat that is force-fed pounds of it, beware.

"MSG causes headaches!"
No study was ever able to back that up, but the damage was done nonetheless.

"Baby bath seats can lead to drowning!"
If you are stupid enough to leave a child unattended in a tub full of water, then yes, lots of bad things could happen.

But we don't do any of that because, among other things, they would all result in a severe violation of our rights as American citizens. Like it or not, Paris Hilton has the *right* to reproduce, no matter how awful the concept. You have the *right* to let your kid play *Grand Theft Auto IV* instead of improving their brain. You have a *right* to eat all the good stuff and leave the broccoli untouched. And, unfortunately, the people of Berkeley have a *right* to be American (or anti-American) citizens.

A lot of Nanny State legislation that stems from the "greater good" argument relies on scary statistics. Remember saccharin? A laboratory test conducted in 1977 tied the artificial sweetener to bladder cancer in rats. People freaked out. Politicians demanded action. Labels were made. Warnings were given. Saccharin was maligned.

But there was just one small problem: The test was conducted on *rats* under conditions that no human would ever experience unless they drank 800 diet sodas . . . a day. *A day.* Not even I could pull that off—and I love my fake sugar.

As always, unwarranted hysteria was quickly followed by unnecessary laws. If it's not saccharin, it's trans fats, bacon, milk, salt, nonpasteurized cheese, red wine, Tylenol, or eggs. Different day, different boogeyman, same predictable reaction.

THE NANNIES
WINNER
"MOST IDIOTIC"
Los Angeles county officials attempted to symbolically ban homicide for 40 hours, but after much ridicule they opted to "promote peace" instead.

Did you know there's a silent killer in your house that claims the lives of around 75 children a year? Terrible, I know. We need to do something about it for the greater good. We need legislation. That's why I'm proposing we immediately eliminate all bathtubs. They're far more dangerous than saccharin. Or lawn darts.

The Prohibition Amendment was a progressive reform, passed by the teetotalers—for, of course, the greater good. After all, alcohol was a vice. People got drunk and did bad things. Some even ruined their lives—a concept that, as a recovering alcoholic, I can definitely relate to. Banning it would be for the greater good, right?

Right?

The problem—and you'll find this happens a lot with idealistic Nanny State legislation—is that the 18th Amendment ignored one very important fact: *Lots of people liked alcohol.* Yeah, it's true! And lots of other people *REALLY* liked alcohol. They still do! In fact, December 5, 2008, was the 75th anniversary of "Repeal Day" and it was widely celebrated by bar owners and patrons alike. You can be pretty sure a law was bad when, three-quarters of a century later, people are still toasting its demise.

The progressives' attempt at prohibition failed. Instead of creating a sober utopia where everything was sunshine and lollipops, it drove the entire industry, along with all of its customers, underground. Legitimate businesses closed or became speakeasies. Legitimate, licensed breweries and distilleries closed and gave way to fly-by-night bathtub-hooch operations that weren't subject to any kind of regulation. In one Prohibition year in Philadelphia at least 875 people died from alcohol-related incidents—mostly connected to bad moonshine. Over 4,100 died nationwide in 1925! And all the alcohol-related tax revenue that the government used to collect? Much of it went straight into the pockets of tax-evading organized criminals like Al Capone, as well as countless opportunists, entrepreneurs, and bootleggers—possibly including Joseph Kennedy, Sr. (whose resulting political dynasty still plagues us today).

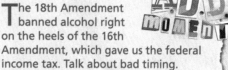

The 18th Amendment banned alcohol right on the heels of the 16th Amendment, which gave us the federal income tax. Talk about bad timing.

During the nearly 14 years of Prohibition, people who wanted to drink still did so, but legitimate business owners suffered. Organized crime flourished and the murder rate in large cities increased nearly 80 percent.

But at least it was all for the greater good.

"FINE. BUT I STILL THINK IT'S GOOD TO DISCOURAGE BAD HABITS WITH PUNITIVE TAXES."

Ahhhh, there's nothing like the good old government stepping in to punish you financially for something you like to do. Nannies cannot comprehend that people who drink *like* to drink and people who smoke *like* to smoke—that's why they spend so much of their money buying cigarettes. You can run all the commercials you want showing people talking through a hole in their trachea or doctors scraping goo out of diseased aortas—people are still going to buy their smokes.

In New York City, cigarettes are now in the vicinity of $10–$11 a pack. Is that because they're shipped to New York in private jets and limousines? Are they wrapped in velvet and gold foil? Does every pack come with a small, nearly flawless diamond?

No. It's because every pack comes with something else: a whopping $2.00 in punitive taxes. Wait, did I say $2.00? I meant $3.25. No, sorry, I meant $4.00. Actually, hang on, I was wrong—it's still going higher and now President Obama has even tacked on his own tax.

But people keep smoking anyway.

When the price of a pack of cigarettes is astronomical compared to the average price across the U.S., something crazy happens: *Smokers buy their cigarettes from somewhere cheaper.* In 2007, one in three cigarettes sold in New York had been illegally channeled, without tax, through New York's Indian reservations. That's at least $1 billion in lost state tax revenue. Bootleggers and online vendors have pulled in another $500 million.

All of that spells really bad news for the struggling guy running the legitimate corner convenience store. One told *The New York Times* that his cigarette sales were down 75 percent. "In two or three months, you

THE NANNIES
WINNER

"MOST TALIBAN-ESQUE"
Indiana forbids you from smiling for your driver's license photograph.

THE LAW OF UNINTENDED CONSEQUENCES . . .

The skyrocketing price of cigarettes turned 19-year-old Cody Knox into a bootlegger and entrepreneur. Unfortunately, his start-up venture went prematurely bust when Knox was stabbed to death on the streets of Brooklyn. Turns out he'd tried to lower the price of his smokes in an effort to attract new customers, something that his rival bootleggers didn't appreciate.

won't see me here," he said. "I should never have gotten into this business." Another said that, if not for the lottery, he'd have no morning traffic at all.

Black markets mean that local and state budgets lose out as well. And here's another bonus: At least three individuals accused of funding terrorists overseas got their funds from trafficking bootleg cigarettes here in the good ol' U.S. of A. Way to go, helpful government bureaucrats!

"FINE, LET PEOPLE SMOKE THEMSELVES TO DEATH, BUT KEEP THEM AWAY FROM MY DINNER BECAUSE SECOND-HAND SMOKE KILLS! *HACK * COUGH * SPUTTER*"

Don't get me wrong, I hate cigarettes. Nasty, stinky, smelly habit. But think about this logically for a moment. If I'm a smoker who owns a restaurant, and I want my patrons to be able to enjoy a smoke as well, I'm out of luck in most places.

Why do people who'll probably never set foot in my establishment get to tell me how to run my business? After all, I'm a businessman who is putting my own time and money on the line in the hope of making a profit by accommodating my customers. If people aren't coming to my restaurant, then let *me* make the decision to toss out the ashtrays. Or to hire mimes. Or to put an inflatable-balloon ad on my roof (except in Houston, where that's banned). If I'm a bad businessman and I ignore the demands of my customers and refuse to innovate, then I deserve to go out of business, or *at least* to get a nice interest rate on a loan from the federal government.

A.D.D. MOMENT

Smoking bans must present a terrible quandary for the government. On one hand they would love to ban all smoking because it's evil and bad for you, but on the other hand they make a ton of money from taxes and lobbyists. I really feel for them.

Attention, Morons!

Things you would never have known if not for the Nanny Staters.

- ★ There are 490 calories in a Starbucks snowman cookie.
- ★ Smoking is not good for you.
- ★ You should not leave your infant child alone in a bathtub.
- ★ You should not use a hair dryer in the bathtub.
- ★ You should not use a hair dryer on an infant child in a bathtub.

- ★ Coffee is hot.
- ★ You should not iron a plastic shower curtain.
- ★ You should not put a toilet brush in your mouth.
- ★ You should remove your child before folding up the stroller.
- ★ You should not touch a chainsaw blade if it's moving.

Our finger-wagging politicians could learn a thing or two from the Strawberry Street Café in Richmond, Virginia. They didn't get rid of their smoking section because meddling Nanny Staters told them to. They got rid of it because a poll of customers and staff revealed that over 70 percent of them wanted a smoke-free establishment. Many cited health concerns, but at least one waiter said the motivation was financial: the smoking section was never busy.

That's exactly how it *should* work. If the poll had gone the other way, there's no reason a bitter Nanny State complainocrat should deny them the right to be an all-smoking, all-cigar, all–Barry Manilow, all-the-time dining establishment. There are plenty of other places for the nonsmoking crowd to go. As the restaurant's owner told a reporter, "We did what was right for us at Strawberry Street Café. No one wants government in their business." Amen to that.

"BUT I DON'T WANT TO FOOT THE MEDICAL BILLS FOR SOME LOSER WHO SMOKES AND GETS LUNG CANCER!"

Okay, what about AIDS, then? It costs us a fortune and transmission would cease almost entirely if people abstained from sex. No more sex allowed!

Obesity costs us $93 billion a year. Fat people take more sick days off from work, weigh down their cars (which uses more gasoline), and many wind up with diabetes or heart disease. Let's ban fast food and sofas and require gym attendance.

Wait a second! Cars result in a tremendous number of accidents . . . I don't want to pay for them either. Let's ban cars!

But there is good news. Kind of. A study showed that by living longer, healthy people can accumulate more health-care costs over their life spans than a smoker. In other words, *healthy people are a drain on our health-care system*! Ban the healthy!

"GAMBLING LAWS ARE DIFFERENT—THEY LOOK OUT FOR THE FAMILIES OF PEOPLE WITH REAL PROBLEMS."

The big government Nanny Staters are always looking out for our own good— unless it's in their own best interest. Let's look to the *Live Free or Die* state of New Hampshire for an example. It's the only state left in the Union that has the common sense to let drivers exercise *their* common sense by deciding whether or not to buckle up. A round of applause for that—but don't clap for too long because, sadly, even New Hampshire isn't immune from Nanny State–itis.

Two New Hampshire men found themselves facing felony charges and jail time because they operated video poker machines at their local VFW post. The outraged authorities made sure to point out that these terrible men and their evil machines were guilty of helping irresponsible people divert money away from their loving families.

Fair enough, gambling *can* do that.

But the kicker here is that the state doesn't have a problem with gambling so long as they are involved in it. The same people who took the moral high ground on video poker are able to find the low ground when it comes to games like Megabucks, Powerball, Hot Lotto, Pick 3, Pick 4, Weekly Grand, Paycheck, and a variety of scratch tickets that range from $1 to $30 a pop. And they don't mind dog racing, horse racing, or casino ships either. In fact, gambling seems to be fine so long as the state gets its slice of the action.

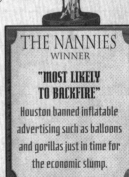

THE NANNIES
WINNER

"MOST LIKELY TO BACKFIRE"
Houston banned inflatable advertising such as balloons and gorillas just in time for the economic slump.

I guess that Nanny State laws aren't always meant to ban vices, sometimes they're also meant to protect the state's monopoly on them.

"SO YOU'RE AGAINST SEAT-BELT LAWS, TOO? THEY SAVE LIVES!"

Actually, seat-belt *laws* haven't saved anyone's life—those who wear seat belts save *their own* lives. You simply can't legislate personal responsibility and intelligence. But, just for the sake of argument, let's assume you're 100 percent right: seat-belt laws save lives. *So what?* A 5 mph speed limit would save even more lives, as would staying locked in your house all day. Banning yard work (count me as a supporter), hang-gliding, and swimming pools would save lives as well. But where do we draw the line? At what point do we decide that we want Lady Liberty to wag her finger in our face whenever we opt to do something that can cause ourselves harm?

You *should* wear a seat belt, they *do* save lives—but while you could argue that it's the government's job to inform you of that, it's *not* their job to penalize those who don't play along—like they did to a Texas mother who was stopped and arrested in front of her children because she was unbuckled. However, it *is* their job to solve murders, hunt down criminals, and protect the public—all things that get harder to do when you're cuffing renegade soccer moms.

Don't agree with me? Perhaps we need a law that will require you to see things my way.

"OH, COME ON, GLENN. GIVE ME THIS ONE. IT'S JUST A SEAT-BELT LAW."

Nope, sorry. And here's why: I mentioned mission creep earlier and the seat-belt law is a great example of it. Originally, it was a "secondary" law, meaning you couldn't be pulled over specifically for not buckling up, they had to stop you for another reason. But now, some states have made seat-belt laws "primary"—allowing the police to stop you *solely* for seat-belt infractions.

As I write this, several more states are considering the same thing. Is it because they love you so much it hurts? Not really, it's because their budgets are in the red. Ohio estimates that pulling drivers over for seat-belt infractions would bring in nearly $27 million in revenue a year.

THE NANNIES
WINNER

"MOST INVASIVE"
Officials in Los Angeles have proposed banning fireplaces in all new homes.

A.D.D. Moment

Fortunately for Ohio, that $27 million can't be touched by bankruptcy magnet (and alleged friend of the aliens) Dennis Kucinich.

Speaking of millions of dollars, The National Highway Traffic Safety Administration spent $7.5 million to tell you to "Click It or Ticket" in 2008. And that doesn't even include what individual states spend every year to "educate" you about seat-belt use. Think about that the next time your school district is forced to cut teachers or deny free treatments at the city hospital.

"YOU REALLY THINK A FEW DUMB LAWS HERE AND THERE IS THAT BIG OF A DEAL?"

On their own these Nanny State laws may seem petty, annoying, ridiculous, or unimportant. Some might even seem tolerable because they address our personal pet peeves (like teenagers who wear pants clearly meant for someone of Barney Frank's girth). But, when you bundle together these myriad intrusions into our lives, you wind up with Death By a Thousand Paper Cuts.

The Nanny State is poison to a free society, a very dangerous overextension of government that usurps our personal autonomy and undermines a wide variety of freedoms, all the while claiming that doing so is beneficial to us and our fellow citizens.

Every Nanny law chips away at our individual liberty—one of the pillars of strength that make this country great. By conditioning you to look to the State to make even the most mundane decisions, it creates the mind-set that the government is the answer to all problems. That opens the door for the powers-that-be to take further control of your financial affairs, appearance, diet, and virtually every other aspect of your life.

Land of the Free?

After all, if they're telling you what to eat or wear, shouldn't you also trust them to tell you how much money you can earn or how to spend it? Of course not, but when citizens willingly surrender the rights and privileges they don't care about, they soon realize that it's too late to stop them from taking the ones they *do* care about

Remember: *First they came for the cigarettes . . .*

OWNING A HOME

Waking Up from the American Dream

IF you want to see the American process of buying and selling a home mangled to the point of looking like a bloody victim in *The Texas Chainsaw Massacre*, then you've come to the right place.

When it comes to housing, I am the idiot.

For my entire life, I have lived in a world where home ownership was the only acceptable ideal. When I rented, I felt like I had failed. I felt truly successful only when I "owned."

While owning a home is still a great idea for many people, I think we've all become too sold on seeing the "sold" sign in our front yards. And that includes our government. For years they've done everything possible to make it easy for Americans to own a home—all the while never even bothering to figure out whether that was even a worthy cause.

> Looking at my mortgage statement, using the word "owned" is as ridiculous as using the word "married" to describe the way I look at Gisele.
>
> **A.D.D. MOMENT**

The collapse of the housing bubble has finally made people begin to question many of the pro–home ownership policies that have long been in place. But maybe the discussion shouldn't be limited to interest rates, tax breaks, or how so many seem to believe that we have the right to own property rather than the right to pursue happiness. Maybe instead we need to take a big step back and reconsider whether home ownership is something that the government should even be involved in. Should the American dream really be defined by signing a piece of paper that "indebts" you to a bank for decades?

175

That question is one big reason why I've started to rethink many of the arguments in favor of home ownership that I've always taken for granted (my latest home appraisal is another). After all, maybe it's because idiots like me relied on conventional wisdom instead of common sense that we now find ourselves on the wrong side of what was quite possibly the largest financial bubble of all time.

"These two entities—Fannie Mae and Freddie Mac—are not facing any kind of financial crisis."
—September 11, 2003

"OWNING A HOME IS UNQUESTIONABLY A GREAT INVESTMENT!"

The idea that real estate is a great investment seems to be beyond reproach. It's the Angus steak of sacred cows. (The Kobe beef of sacred cows comes later in this chapter.)

The thought that our residence doubles as a revenue stream and wealth-builder is a concept that's handed down from generation to generation. Stories of "I bought that house for $45,000 and sold it for $250,000!" litter our memories and were seemingly reinforced with real-life evidence that came in the form of fancy-looking charts and graphs.

U.S. Home Prices

YEAR

This graph suggests that you could've bought a home at any time in history and sold it at any other time for a profit. Usually a big one.

A.D.D. MOMENT

The one exception would be the recent housing bubble. Looking at that chart, you really get a sense for what an incredibly dramatic and historic event it was.

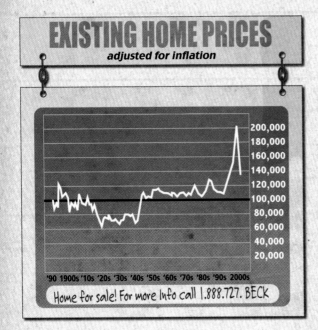

EXISTING HOME PRICES
adjusted for inflation

200,000
180,000
160,000
140,000
120,000
100,000
80,000
60,000
40,000
20,000

'90 1900s '10s '20s '30s '40s '50s '60s '70s '80s '90s 2000s

Home for sale! For more info call 1.888.727. BECK

But that chart is about as misleading as a Barack Obama budget projection. Why? Because it's not adjusted for inflation. While our perception of housing prices is one of a smooth slope upward, the truth is that it's been more like a trail of moguls than a ski jump.

A.D.D Moment

For those of you who live where it's always warm, moguls = bumpy skiing. Also, I hate you.

The chart to the left also shows the history of home prices, but this time it's been adjusted for inflation.

It's almost sacrilegious myth-busting to suggest that housing prices are actually not on an interminable upward swing, but it's true.

The American saga of real estate is one of a relatively flat history—save for one flash of irrational exuberance over the past few years. The reality is that there have been only two good ways to make real money in the housing market over the past century: time the peaks and valleys perfectly, or buy a house during the Great Depression and sell it afterward.

A.D.D. MOMENT

If you're under 100 years old, option two was probably never very practical.

Everyone knows the story of a homeowner who's been able to time the peaks. I'm one of them. I'm proud to say that I sold my house in 2006—right near the absolute peak of the housing bubble. The problem was that I then had no place to live. So I also *bought a house* near the absolute peak of the market.

Being the super-savvy financial guru that I am, the new house that I bought was larger and more expensive than the house I sold. But that's pretty common, right? As we get older, we generally get wealthier and are able to buy bigger houses. But that also locks you into a pattern: if you fail, it's likely to be on the biggest bet you've ever made in your life. Do you really know enough about the real-estate market to play those odds? I now know that I don't.

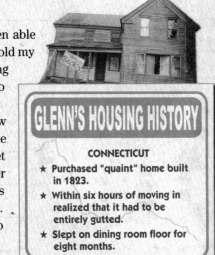

GLENN'S HOUSING HISTORY

CONNECTICUT

★ Purchased "quaint" home built in 1823.

★ Within six hours of moving in realized that it had to be entirely gutted.

★ Slept on dining room floor for eight months.

"WELL, AT LEAST I'M NOT THROWING MONEY AWAY ON RENT!"

Many people rationalize their purchase by using that argument, but renters actually spend, on average, about 26 percent less on rent than owners do on their mortgage. At the height of the bubble, the difference was even more remarkable: renters were spending an incredible 66 percent less.

If renters are disciplined enough to save or invest the difference in something safe (like guessing at the hottest upcoming Christmas novelty toy or something), they wind up way ahead of the game, especially in the short term. Plus, owners—unlike renters— have to worry about losing their life savings if they mistime the market. The recent housing bust put millions of homeowners upside down on their mortgages— and caused many people to rethink the supposedly settled science of home ownership.

A.D.D. MOMENT

I'll have to ask Al Gore if questioning this settled science makes me a Housi-cost denier.

We also tend to forget that there's more to the cost of home ownership than meets the eye. About 7 to 10 percent of the cost of buying a home goes to closing costs and other transaction fees. Upkeep on the property ranges from about 2 to 4 per-cent per year. Property taxes can approach 2 percent of the home's value each year, and, in states like New York, can exceed 8 percent of the area's median salary. And don't forget interest. When you sign on the dotted line for a 7 percent, 30-year mortgage on a $300,000 house, you've actually decided that home is worth $718,527.60, be-cause that's how much you will have paid for it by the time you stop getting monthly nastygrams from your mortgage company.

A.D.D. MOMENT

Not to mention, you have to mow the lawn, fix the pipes, and shovel the driveway (or pay/threaten neigh-borhood kids to do it).

"WELL, IF IT'S NOT SUCH A GREAT INVESTMENT THEN WHY ARE HOMEOWNERS MORE FINANCIALLY SOUND THAN RENTERS?"

That is really a question of whether the chicken owned or rented the egg. Yes, it's undoubt-edly true that homeowners are typically in much better financial shape than renters— some estimates have found that their net worths are about 35 times higher—but there are downsides to having so much of your wealth (if you're lucky) locked up in a home. As the *Economist* explained, "It sucks up disproportionately large amounts of money, falling foul of the idea that investors should diversify: in America the equity tied up in houses accounts for 45 percent of the net worth of the average householder. And it is illiquid. If you need to raise money, you cannot sell a room or two, whereas you can always sell a few shares."

But if owning a home isn't an obvious way to build wealth, then why are owners more wealthy? It's actually common sense: When people get money they buy houses with it. Homeowners are also twice as likely to be married as renters, meaning that they're also more likely to be economically stable and/or have two incomes. Plus, homeowners are generally older and have had more time to accumulate wealth than renters.

It's a boring but happy fact of life in America—the longer you live in our (somewhat) capitalist system, the more likely you are to set aside money to make a major investment that costs several hundred thousand dollars.

Our perception of homeowner stability generally comes from the fact that stable people decide to own homes. They're not made stable by their purchase.

"Fannie and Freddie are fundamentally sound, they are not in danger of going under . . . I do think their prospects going forward are very solid."
—July 14, 2008

A.D.D. Moment

Owning a home does help in one major way: If things go well it basically forces people to save. Renting, on the other hand, can be an effective stupidity tax for some people. "Look at all this extra money I have! I should ~~buy~~ lease a BMW!"

A.D.D. Moment

It's like looking at prisons and wondering why they're all full of criminals. They're in prison *because* they're criminals.

"FINE, BUT IT'S NOT ALL ABOUT THE MONEY. HOMEOWNERS ARE FAR MORE INVOLVED IN THEIR COMMUNITIES THAN RENTERS."

That may be true in some ways, but involvement doesn't necessarily mean *positive* involvement. In fact, one of the most common ways that homeowners become "involved" in their communities is by supporting restrictive zoning and environmental laws in their towns and cities.

Politicians have realized that pushing local initiatives with "green" or "clean" in the title is a nice way to give them something to do, plenty of money to do it, and a fancy photo-op to boot. So-called open space laws are virtually guaranteed to pass

GLENN'S HOUSING HISTORY

ARIZONA

★ Purchased from a bankruptcy, had been vacant for months.

★ Reached into fireplace where it had been cool, dry, and dark for months.

★ Discovered nest of black widow spiders. Somehow still lived.

★ Only later wondered why a house in Phoenix would have a fireplace.

when voted on in local elections, but there's a major downside that you won't hear in the congratulatory speeches: they create housing shortages that artificially increase prices.

A.D.D. MoMent

One thing I've learned over the last couple of years: artificially increasing home values . . . bad.

"The more people, in my judgment, exaggerate a threat of safety and soundness, the more people conjure up the possibility of serious financial losses to the Treasury, which I do not see."
—September 10, 2003

Barney's Greatest hits

For example, Houston, which has no zoning restrictions at all, also has among the most affordable housing of any major city in America. Only a few cities (all of which are much smaller than Houston) are able to beat its $700 a month average mortgage payment. That's 25 percent less than Detroit, 44 percent less than Philadelphia, 48 percent less than Barack Obama's Chicago, and, if you're moving from Nancy Pelosi's San Francisco—you've just saved yourself 82 percent.

Because Houston generally avoided the *artificial* bubble, the city was better shielded from the *very real* collapse all too familiar to other communities across the country. Their economy was resilient because it was built on a foundation that is relatively free of regulation and government interference. After all, strict zoning laws that stop businesses from building near your neighborhood also restrict those businesses and jobs from building in your city, hurting the local economy and driving up the price of property ownership.

GLENN'S HOUSING HISTORY

TEXAS

★ Tried to remodel home myself.
★ Fell out of second-story window while doing so, hurt back.
★ It seemed to heal eventually until later in life when I found myself living in Kentucky.

Yes, there are some areas of Houston that would even make the inventor of strip malls contemplate suicide, but there are also plenty of quiet areas with gorgeous housing and scenic landscapes. Instead of overreaching and broad zoning laws, Houston communities use deed restrictions to keep neighborhoods sensible without massive economic intervention.

The result of Houston's freedom is clear! People are voting with their feet and moving to Texas at about twice the rate as heavily regulated states like California. Texas created more new jobs in 2008 than every other state in the country

. . . combined. And, as the housing crisis was kicking in during 2006 and 2007, Houston had the largest population increase in the entire country. It could be that people suddenly became infatuated with the Astros, but somehow I doubt it.

"OKAY, BUT HOMEOWNERS ARE HAPPIER AND LEAD MORE SATISFYING PERSONAL LIVES."

Research shows that this perception is essentially a myth. When you figure in basic things like household income, housing quality, and health, the difference between renters and owners in perceived happiness mostly disappears. Where there is a small difference, it seems to usually favor the renter.

For example, homeowners spend more time cleaning and doing household chores and less time participating in "active leisure" than their renting counterparts. As a guy who bought a "quaint-fixer-upper" that wound up taking more of my time than working, sleeping, and raising two daughters combined, I'm particularly sensitive to the amount of work a home can require. I'm also particularly receptive to considering arson to erase such work.

"I want to roll the dice a little bit more in this situation towards subsidized housing."
—September 25, 2003

Glenn Beck Rule 892: If it's "active" it ain't "leisure."

But it's not just pure self-inflicted laziness that costs homeowners happiness—owners also spend less time with their families, partly because they spend more time commuting. While it personally benefits me to have you in your car with your radio on as much as possible, you'd probably rather spend time with your family instead of listening to me whine about Woodrow Wilson for another hour. But, because that beautiful house you bought is 27 miles away from your office, you're stuck with me instead.

While the sum of this research doesn't make me want to title my next book *Rent Your Way to Happiness*, it's far from the runaway win for homeowners that most of us would expect.

"BUT OWNING A HOME IS WHAT AMERICAN FAMILIES HAVE ASPIRED TO FOR GENERATIONS."

I'm not trying to say that home ownership is a horrible idea. It works for many people. But the perception that owning is *always* the best option for *everyone* is simply a relic from the past. It was created when our grandparents lived in the same town for 50 years, worked at the same job for 30 years, and stayed married for longer than six months.

These days over 20 million Americans change jobs every year and the typical worker changes jobs about ten times before age 40. We move from town to town, state to state, and, increasingly, from country to country. Estimates show that the average person now moves about 12 times in his or her life. Unless you're planning on living to 360 years old, how does a 30-year mortgage fit into that lifestyle?

A.D.D. MOMENT

Given how much we all move around, buying a home with a 30-year mortgage is akin to buying a new car with a five-year loan and selling it after 10 months, only to buy *another* car with *another* five-year loan. Of course, the difference is that we expect auto values to constantly fall, unlike home values, which we expect to constantly rise. Just ask one of the Lehman Brothers how infallible that plan is.

The truth is that a home may be where the heart is, but it's also where the rest of your body is stuck. Owning a home can put you in a position where the local economy dictates your personal economy. For example, think about "Allentown." Not the real Allentown in Lehigh County, Pennsylvania, that has had almost exactly the same unemployment rate as the rest of the country for the last 20 years. I mean, Billy Joel's "Allentown," that miserable place where they've *taken all the coal from the ground,* and all *the union people crawled awaaaayaaayyyaaayyyyaaayaaaayayayay.*

A.D.D. Moment

Union people crawled away? Doesn't sound *that* bad.

You see, when *you're living there in Allentown, and they're closing all the factories down,* the appropriate response is not to start *killing time, filling out forms, and standing in line.* Instead, it's a much better idea to pack up and move to Orlando. Or some other place where jobs are available.

But, when you own a home, that decision isn't really yours. It depends on convincing someone you don't know that

The Less You Know

If you've ever sung "it's getting very hard to staaaaayaaayyy-aaayyyyaaayaaaayayayay" about your town—it's time to stop staying.

the town *you want to leave* is a place *they want to live*. Then, they have to want it bad enough to buy your house at a price that doesn't put you tens of thousands of dollars in the hole.

There's no better way to understand this than to attempt a career in radio. It is a business for pseudopsychotic antisocial nomads (and I'm proud to be a part of it). Think about the radio stations you listen to in your hometown. If you like news/talk, there are probably a maximum of three stations that you can listen to. That means if you're a guy who makes a living by doing mornings on a news/talk station, there are about three possible jobs in the entire city that you want. In radio, your only chance to continue doing what you love is to uproot your family and move to an unfamiliar city halfway across the country.

So that's exactly what I did. In my career I've worked in Seattle, Houston, Tampa, Louisville, Corpus Christi, New Haven, Washington, D.C., Philadelphia, New York City, Provo, Baltimore, Phoenix, Dayton, Mount Vernon, Puyallup, and yes . . . Walla Walla, Washington.

GLENN'S HOUSING HISTORY

KENTUCKY
- ★ Wanted new light by garage.
- ★ Dug 50-foot-long trench by hand for wiring.
- ★ Didn't realize that modern digging equipment existed.
- ★ Spent several days at chiropractor.

In my chosen profession, moving around is normal (if you can use that word when talking about radio). But, in most other (sane) careers, people tend to see their current community as their sole source of opportunity. For a very basic illustration, let's go back to Allentown and assume you're a nurse who lives there and is looking for a job. As I write this, Monster.com lists 28 recently posted openings for nurses within 30 miles. But if you open up your job search nationwide, you find 2,926 openings. My calculator tells me that's 104.5 times more opportunities. It's not the nineteenth century, where it would take you three years to go state to state in a wagon train. If your dream job doesn't exist in your own backyard—move your backyard.

A.D.D. MOMENT

You may need to weigh your job opportunities against your carbon-dioxide emissions and the harm you'll be doing to the environment. Plus, if you make more money you'll consume more, which means more waste and greenhouse gases. In other words, if you move for a better job you're pretty much the BTK of the earth.

You might think you're abandoning your community by leaving your hometown, but you very well might be helping your country by making the economy more efficient. You are the supply. The supply needs to be where the demand is. But if you own a home, you limit your mobility. It could take months or years for a homeowner to up and leave, whereas, for a renter, it could take a day. That difference can be seen clearly in the statistics. As the housing crisis kicked in and the market became less forgiving, the number of Americans changing residences dropped to levels not seen since 1962, when the country had 120 million fewer people in it.

It's not just schlubs like me who have these theories. British economist Andrew Oswald found that a rise in the level of home ownership was associated with a rise in the level of unemployment. He found that when one category was high, the other usually was as well. Spain had the highest rate among industrialized nations in both unemployment and home ownership; Switzerland had the lowest rate in both.

Oswald found that not only does home ownership contribute to joblessness, it makes workers take jobs that aren't great fits for their skill sets because they base their employment decisions on where they live rather than what they do best. Sure, there are a lot of reasons other than employment to stay in a certain area (like easy access to a Sonic), but it's important to recognize what you may be giving up by staying put.

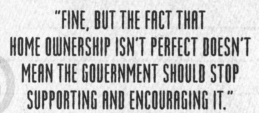

"FINE, BUT THE FACT THAT HOME OWNERSHIP ISN'T PERFECT DOESN'T MEAN THE GOVERNMENT SHOULD STOP SUPPORTING AND ENCOURAGING IT."

For decades, under both Republicans and Democrats, Washington has tried to encourage the belief that home ownership is the only way to go. Millions of Americans, including me, bought into it. We all took pride in the rise in home ownership rates, even while we crinkled our noses a bit when we considered the aftereffects. It made us feel good . . . and the government knew it. That's why tax advantages, low-interest-rate loans, perks for first-time buyers, and other benefits were offered to anyone who would take them. And while it's still the home buyer's name on the contracts, these pathways to home ownership were presented by the government and mortgage companies as no-lose propositions. A chance to be part of the party. And most of us lapped it up.

But while our government celebrated itself as the savior of the poor, who do you think is really hurt when things go bad? People with money in the bank and stable employment are not the ones who get foreclosed on. The fact that I made the biggest purchase of my life at the absolute peak of the market might tell you a little about my intelligence, but as long as I keep my job(s), I should still be able to make my mortgage payments. It's those who just barely

> "I believe there has been more alarm raised about potential unsafety and unsoundness [of Fannie Mae and Freddie Mac] than, in fact, exists."
> —September 25, 2003

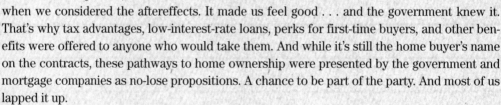

U.S. Home Ownership 1965–2008

| | 1965 | 1970 | 1975 | 1980 | 1985 | 1990 | 1995 | 2000 | 2005 | 2008 |

(y-axis: 69%, 68%, 67%, 66%, 65%, 64%, 63%)

.cleared the line, those who were artificially put into homes they couldn't afford by government policies designed to entice them to do so, who are first in line to really get burned. We're taking good, responsible citizens who would likely be good, responsible renters and turning them into homeowners-in-default, left to hope for massive government intervention to save them from bankruptcy.

The policies might have felt good at the time—like we were somehow doing the world a favor by ignoring income, credit, and stability—but, in the end, is the collapse of an economy worth that temporary warm feeling? Is the heroin high worth the heroin hangover?

GLENN'S HOUSING HISTORY

FLORIDA

★ Bought a house "on a golf course."
★ Later realized that "on a golf course" meant "on a golf course."
★ House constantly hit with stray drives on 12th hole.
★ People really need to work on their slices.

A.D.D. Moment

On the other hand, the 6,000-calorie German chocolate cake was DEFINITELY worth the inevitable pointing and laughing at my love handles. (My wife, Tania, is prohibited from commenting on the previous sentence.)

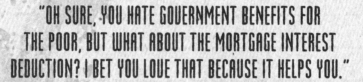

"OH SURE, YOU HATE GOVERNMENT BENEFITS FOR THE POOR, BUT WHAT ABOUT THE MORTGAGE INTEREST DEDUCTION? I BET YOU LOVE THAT BECAUSE IT HELPS YOU."

Ahhhh, we've finally gotten to the Kobe beef of sacred cows: the mortgage interest deduction. I can already feel you getting ready to light this book on fire for my even bringing the topic up.

The deduction, which allows homeowners to deduct their annual mortgage interest on their federal tax returns, certainly has its strong points: The government takes too much of our money; enough of us have problems paying our mortgage as it is; and touching the deduction is political suicide.

As we've seen over the past couple of years, owning a home isn't just about smiling kids playing on the swing set in the backyard, neighborhood barbecues, and pool parties. It's a huge and sometimes dangerous investment. Should the government really be encouraging it with such massive economic incentives?

A.D.D. MOMENT

If entitlements are the third rail of politics—the mortgage interest deduction is the giant wall in the middle of the tracks. Any politician who publicly entertains eliminating it will find his or her chance of getting reelected about the same as that of Mahmoud Ahmadinejad becoming prime minister of Israel.

If the deduction really acted as a way for people to keep more of their own money, I might understand it. But that's not typically what happens. In practice, it just allows people who would already be buying a home to buy more than they normally could have afforded.

Harvard economist Ed Glaeser put it this way: "The bulk of the benefits go to fairly rich people who aren't particularly close to the margin between owning and not owning. . . . It mainly serves to induce prosperous people to buy bigger homes and pay more for those homes."

What he didn't say is that those people must borrow more and more money and become even larger investors in a real-estate market they probably don't understand. Then, once they're in the house, they have higher utility bills, higher property taxes, and more room to fill with useless junk.

Arguing with Idiots

Your wife: "Rent? No way! I want a house and I can't believe that you'd blah blah blah..."

The average female homeowner is 12 pounds heavier than those who rent.

INSTANT WINNER

Where are liberals on this? The mortgage deduction makes billions of tax dollars disappear and is a huge gift to the mortgage and real-estate industries. All those hedge-fund billionaires buy larger and larger properties because those dastardly rich people can get the deduction too. It moves people away from renting, which means they buy houses far away from the cities they work in. That increases urban sprawl and greenhouse gas emissions, which leads to uncontrollable global warming. (You'll know it's here when temperatures cool for a decade.)

Our government has seemed to move from tax policy to attempted behavior control. Our laws make it seem more sensible to invest in a home than in almost anything else, but for what benefit? Research suggests that the main positive attribute of a neighborhood with more home-owners than renters is the number of gardens. Flowers are nice, but I'm not sure that deducting 30 years of interest on a six-figure investment is the best way to get more of them. "Give people who plant a garden a subsidy to buy mulch and leave it at that," said Glaeser.

Am I ready to dissolve the deduction? Not quite. Until the government decides their spending is going to be more responsible than Eliot Spitzer in rural Nevada—they aren't getting another path to my cash. Making the most untouchable tax break in the world disappear would have to be part of a large-scale tax-reform package.

And not President Obama's, I mean a good one.

"BUT GLENN, OWNING A HOME WITH A WHITE PICKET FENCE IS THE AMERICAN DREAM."

My point isn't that owning a home isn't the best situation for many, it's just that it's not always the best situation for everyone. The unquestionable superiority of home ownership has not only been ingrained into our societal DNA, it's also been a main priority of government—supported, urged, and pushed by policies at every level.

GLENN'S HOUSING HISTORY

CONNECTICUT (again)

★ Caught in a bidding war . . . we "won."

★ Purchased near absolute peak of housing bubble.

★ Spent a year arguing with town about building a fence in my own yard.

★ Neighbor called cops, blaming me for a plastic bag in their yard.

But perhaps it's time to start thinking about what the American dream is really supposed to represent. A full 65 percent of American homeowners say that the "dream" is one of the reasons they purchased their home. But the American dream isn't about deductions, mortgage rates, or even that racist white picket fence. In fact, it's safe to say that when our Founders were designing the American dream, a Realtor wasn't required to achieve it.

The American dream is not about owning a *home*, it's about owning your *destiny*. For many, buying a home is an important step in maximizing their chance at the *real* American dream, but it's important to recognize that it's not the only way.

Perhaps idiots like me will someday finally learn that.

ECONOMICS 101

Smaller Government, Bigger Wallet

OVER the last eight years, government programs to help the poor have been cut to the bone. At the same time, taxes on the wealthy have been slashed so that mega-yacht owners can drink champagne out of ruby slippers. In fact, life in America has become remarkably simple: If your parents were rich, you will be rich. If they were poor, you are predestined by your DNA to be poor as well.

Welcome to the victimization thesis of America. It is the transcendent new creed of those who think that government is the answer to whatever ails us. It is an ideology that tells us to toss aside our ambitions, determination, grit, and sweat, and it has swiftly replaced the old code of personal responsibility and merit—a code that took America from a bunch of disgruntled British colonists to the wealthiest country the world has ever known in less than two hundred years.

The victimization thesis says that, whatever our personal failures, shortcomings, and weaknesses, our troubles are caused by anyone and everyone *except* ourselves. It's not that people don't want to succeed; it's that they *can't* succeed. The deck is always stacked against us—and if you're poor or black or short or old or handicapped or female or gay or uncoordinated, then don't even bother trying.

Fortunately, it's all a fairy tale. That's not to say we don't stumble and fall short of our dreams—we do—but remember, Americans have never been *guaranteed* happiness, only the *pursuit* of it. There is no guarantee of equal results, only of a level field upon which the game can be played.

But now our leaders are trying to change the rules of that game. The blinding fast expansion of government is threatening to slam shut the doors of economic opportunity. The $9 trillion increase in our national debt, the $2 trillion in bailouts, the increased taxes on "the rich" (and, eventually, just about everyone who works at least 40 hours a week) are the new glass ceilings on economic advancement. Washington seems to be more preoccupied these days with making rich people poor than with making poor people rich.

Turning around our economic future requires a lot of things, but the first is a change in mind-set. Big-government, eat-the-rich policies may sound good in campaign commercials and sound bites, but history has proven that they always lead to the same disastrous place: a government that collapses under its own weight. If you learn that history and understand the signs to watch for, then you'll also know exactly what to say the next time you hear someone make an idiotic argument, like:

"THE RICH HAVE HAD IT TOO GOOD FOR TOO LONG, IT'S TIME FOR THEM TO PAY THEIR FAIR SHARE."

If you ask people how much of America's total tax burden they think is shouldered by the wealthiest one percent, most would likely say it's less than 10 percent. Some might even believe it's less than five percent. But they would all be wrong. Very wrong.

In 2006, the most recent year that comprehensive IRS data is available, the richest one percent of Americans paid *39.9 percent* of the country's total income tax bill. The top ten percent of filers paid 71 percent of the tab.

Here's an even more amazing showstopper that you'll never hear mentioned by the pro-France crowd: the bottom 50 percent of earners now make 13 percent of the country's total income yet pay *less than* **three** *percent* of the income taxes.

Pause. Take a deep breath. Now consider that stat again: Those in the top 50 percent pay 97 percent of the income tax.

Who's Making This Argument?

"By adjusting the top rates and reducing windfalls paid out to some of the wealthiest individuals in the nation, we can help restore a sense of equity and fairness that is critical to the success of our voluntary tax system."

—Charles Rangel, Chairman of the House Ways and Means Committee

A.D.D. MOMENT

I always love when politicians call our tax system "voluntary," as though people have a choice whether or not to pay them. Ask Wesley Snipes how voluntary it is to file a 1040.

One reason why that statistic probably sounds so shocking is that it runs counter to everything we read in the popular press or hear from politicians. But that obvious spin on reality should tell you everything you need to know about their agendas.

Many people have probably heard the story that billionaire Warren Buffett likes to tell about how he pays a smaller share of his income in taxes than his secretary, who makes just $60,000 a year. If that's really the case, then Buffett must be an expert at tax avoidance because the statistics show that the average tax rate (i.e., taxes paid as a share of income) rises steadily as people get wealthier.

Who Pays the Taxes?

	Share of Pre-Tax Income*	Share of Individual Income Taxes*
Top 1%	18.1%	38.8%
Top 5%	31.1	60.7
Top 10%	40.9	72.7
Top 20%	55.1	86.3
Bottom 20%	4.0	-2.9

*All statistics based on CBO study for 2005.

A.D.D. MOMENT

Maybe the part of Buffett's story we should be focusing on is why the richest man in the world is paying his secretary only $60,000 a year.

In 2005, the effective tax rate on a person in the lowest income group was 4.3 percent. The effective rate for someone in the middle class, like Mr. Buffett's secretary, was 14.2 percent. And for the super-duper rich, the top .01 percent of all earners, the effective federal tax burden was 31.5 percent.

The truth is that our tax system does not favor the wealthy, it penalizes them. As a recent Congressional Budget Office report said, "High-income households have a disproportionate share of comprehensive income and pay a disproportionate share of federal taxes." Those who argue that we need to have a progressive tax system are simply refusing to acknowledge the reality that we *already do*.

A.D.D. MOMENT

One reason why Buffett's effective tax rate is so low (aside from the team of attorneys and accountants he likely has helping him file) is that he likely makes a lot of his money through capital gains, which are taxed at a lower rate than ordinary income. *Why* is the rate on capital gains lower? Because the government knows that capital investments are proven to create jobs so they want to incentivize more of them. So, sure, Warren, we can get your tax rate a little higher just for the fun of it, but how many middle-class jobs is it worth to you?

NAME THAT OBSCURE POP-CULTURE REFERENCE!

"The difference between tax avoidance and tax evasion is (a) whatever the IRS says; (b) a smart lawyer; (c) ten years in prison; (d) all the above. Being a tax lawyer's got nothing to do with the law, it's a game. We teach the rich how to play it so they can stay rich. The IRS keeps changing the rules so we can keep getting rich teaching it. It's a game."

Answer: Gene Hackman in The Firm

"SURE, FEDERAL INCOME TAXES ARE PROGRESSIVE, BUT WHAT ABOUT THE PAYROLL TAX? THAT TAX HITS THE POOR HARDEST."

While it's true that the distribution of taxes changes once payroll taxes are accounted for, the change is much smaller than most progressives would like you to believe.

The Tax Policy Center, which is run by two liberal think tanks, the Urban Institute and the Brookings Institution, recently studied payroll and income taxes paid by each income group. They found that the richest one percent still pay 27.5 percent of the total tax burden, but the bottom twenty percent pays only 0.4 percent.

One good explanation for the low tax burden on the poorest fifth of Americans is that most of the people in that category (who earn income at a job) get reimbursed for at least a portion of their payroll tax through a tax-back payment called the "earned income tax credit" (EITC). In other words, we *already* refund taxes back to hard-working families that are struggling to make ends meet, thereby ensuring that the payroll tax, like the income tax, is progressive.

A.D.D. MOMENT One of the reasons the EITC has been around so long and generally enjoys bipartisan support is that you can claim it only if you *earn* money. In other words, it incentivizes people to actually work, unlike so many other antipoverty programs which seem to reward people for *not* working.

Distribution of All Federal Taxes by Income

Cash Income Percentile	Percent of Taxes*
Lowest Quintile	0.4%
Second Quintile	2.3%
Middle Quintile	7.7%
Fourth Quintile	17.0%
Top Quintile	72.4%
Top 10%	57.1%
Top 5%	45.1%
Top 1%	27.5%

*Income tax, corporate income tax, and payroll tax for calendar year 2007.

"WELL, OF COURSE THE RICH PAY MOST OF THE TAXES. THEY HAVE ALL OF THE INCOME!"

Not exactly.

It is true that the share of the total income earned by the rich has been rising. The richest one percent now earn about 21 percent of all income, up from about nine percent in 1980. But then—

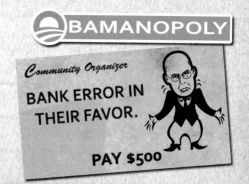

OBAMANOPOLY

Community Organizer

BANK ERROR IN THEIR FAVOR.

PAY $500

"SEE! I KNEW IT . . . THE RICH *ARE* GETTING RICHER!"

You didn't let me finish.

Yes, the super-rich now earn a larger share of total income, but every study over the last thirty years that's tracked real people has found that the rich *lose* income over time while the poor have large income *gains*. In other words, the poor don't stay poor long and the rich don't stay rich long.

A recent study by the U.S. Treasury Department found that the richest .01 percent of Americans at the time the study began experienced the largest income *declines* over the following ten years. And those declines were remarkable: an average reduction in median income of 65 percent compared with 24 percent income *gains* for the average person. Overall, only *a quarter* of the richy-rich people in the top 1/100th of one percent were still in that group a decade later.

Looking at the other end of the income spectrum, the study revealed that "roughly half of taxpayers who began in the bottom income quintile in 1996 moved up to a higher income group by 2005."

Isn't that exactly how the economy is supposed to work? Why do people keep trying to make us believe that the system is broken?

It is true that, because of huge income gains by the very wealthy over the last three decades, the gap between the jet-set crowd and the poor has widened, but even that is not as malicious as it sounds. It's actually more of a consequence of mathematics than of economics.

Let me explain with an example. Assume there are two twin brothers and the year is 1989. One brother is making $40,000 a year as an electrician and the other earns $100,000 as an executive. Now, fast-forward twenty years to 2009. The wealthier brother is now making $110,000 a year and the electrician is now making $44,000. Both brothers increased their incomes by *exactly ten percent*, but the difference in salaries has widened from $60,000 to $66,000 a year.

A.D.D. MOMENT

Reading studies about the rich losing income must be like porn for progressives.

A.D.D. MOMENT

There's even worse news for the super-rich: this study was done *before* two major sources of upper-class wealth, real estate and stocks, basically collapsed.

A.D.D. MOMENT

When the rich stumble, others are all too willing to take their place. Consider this: Of the 400 wealthiest people on the *Forbes* 400 list in 1982, only 32 of them are still there today. That means there are 368 newbies on that list . . . and yet we're supposed to believe the lie that the American dream is dead?

What's on your iPod,
BARACK OBAMA?

- *Take the Money and Run,* Steve Miller Band
- *Eat the Rich,* Aerosmith
- *All at Once,* Whitney Houston
- *Livin' on a Prayer,* Bon Jovi

Given that scenario, the headline from the media would likely be: GAP BETWEEN RICH AND POOR WIDENING! Okay, sure, that's technically true . . . but does that really tell the whole story? Both brothers increased their incomes at the same rate and, more important, both are now *richer* than they were twenty years ago.

That is how badly things have been twisted in America. No longer is it good enough for a rising tide to lift all boats, the tide must lift the smaller boats *more* than the mega-yachts for some people to be happy.

READING RAILROAD

PRICE: N/A
THIS RAILROAD WAS
NATIONALIZED, AND IS
NOT FOR SALE.

OBAMANOPOLY

A.D.D. MOMENT And for progressives to be happy, the tide has to lift all of the small boats and then turn into a massive tsunami that destroys only the mega-yachts.

The truth is that the bottom twenty percent of earners in 1996 saw their incomes rise by an average of 233 percent by 2006. That is a far higher gain than any other income group and it should tell us (if it were ever publicized) that Americans don't stay poor for long. This is still the land of opportunity!

Other studies have verified the Treasury's findings. The Congressional Budget Office confirmed that, from 1994 to 2004, Americans in the bottom twenty percent of income had higher

increases in income than any other group. A second study by the Treasury Department found the same thing. It's amazing but the richer a person is at any given point in time, the smaller their subsequent income gains generally are.

Why aren't any of these facts more widely known? Because they're buried. After all, if people understood that existing policies help the poor get richer, they wouldn't be able to make the argument for more progressive taxes and massive increases in government power under the guise of "righting the injustices" of our system.

The Poor Get Richer and the Rich Get— wait a second!

Income Change Over Time

	1996-2005	1987-1996
Poor	+109%	+81%
Middle Class	+26%	+9%
Rich	+9%	-2%
Super Rich (top 1%)	-23%	-24%
Super-Duper Rich (Top 0.01%)	-65%	n/a

"ALL YOUR STUDIES ARE GREAT, BUT THEY DON'T APPLY TO MINORITIES WHO ARE STILL FALLING BEHIND BECAUSE 'GEORGE BUSH DOESN'T CARE ABOUT BLACK PEOPLE.'"

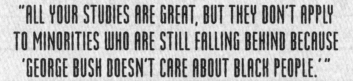

Those, of course, are the immortal words of America's favorite family entertainer, Kanye West. If you don't know (and really, how could you not?), he's the super-talented artist behind the hit song "Gold Digger." C'mon, you know the one, sing along with me . . .

If you ain't no punk holla we want Prenup—WE WANT PRENUP!
Yeah, it's something that you needs to have, Cause
when she leave yo a**, she gonna leave with half.

> **A.D.D. MOMENT**
>
> While doing media interviews for his new book, Kanye said, "I am a proud non-reader of books."

Reading those lyrics (believe me, they're going to be in your head all day now), I can't for the life of me think of one good reason why we *wouldn't* turn to Kanye for insightful political commentary—but I bet that even he couldn't guess which demographic group has made the largest income gains over the past twenty years. (Hint: It wasn't white, wealthy males.)

It was African-American women.

Their earnings rose 80 percent versus an increase of 40 percent for everyone else. Oh, and the worst-performing group? White men. Sorry, Kanye, back to the baseless-racist-accusation drawing board.

George Bush Hates Black People: Real Median Income Growth, 1980-2007	
Black Women	80%
White Women	78%
Black Men	34%
White Men	10%
All People	40%

"GO AHEAD AND DEFEND YOUR PRECIOUS FORMER PRESIDENT ALL YOU WANT BUT IT'S TIME NOW FOR THE RICH TO SACRIFICE SO WE CAN FINALLY HAVE SOME SHARED PROSPERITY."

Why not just raise the tax rate on the rich who supposedly benefited so much from the economic expansion? After all, they can *afford* to pay more. If we raise their rates to 40 or 50 percent, how much harm can it really do? The very rich will just have to stock fewer bottles of Dom Pérignon in their wine cellars.

Sounds like great logic except for one big, inconvenient problem. Before we drench the rich with taxes, there is something we need to know: about two-thirds of them are small-business owners and operators. They

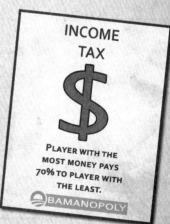

INCOME TAX

$

PLAYER WITH THE MOST MONEY PAYS 70% TO PLAYER WITH THE LEAST.

OBAMANOPOLY

are the people who create jobs and write the paychecks that keep millions of American families going. They are also the people who will be hurt most by jacking up the top tax rates.

The Tax Foundation calculated that simply restoring the top tax brackets to the rates that were in place during the Clinton years would negatively impact 45 to 55 percent of small-business income. Do you think owners will just accept that loss of net income, or do you think that perhaps they might try to cut expenses . . . like salaries?

The question I always ask people who make this argument is a simple one: *How can you create jobs by taking more money away from the people who do the hiring*? I'm still waiting to hear a good, logical answer.

THE MILLIONAIRE MYTH

There's a pervasive myth among people that we can all click our heels and pretend that taxes don't matter to the rich. When Florida resident Rush Limbaugh publicly announced that he would never broadcast from New York again because of a new millionaire's tax proposal (which Rush said is like "punishing the achievers for the mistakes and the lack of discipline on the part of a bunch of corrupt politicians"), New York governor David Paterson personally responded. Did he offer a deal, or maybe a promise that the tax would be only temporary?

Nope. He offered a snarky, elitist attack that shows just how out of touch politicians can be. "If I knew that would be the result," Paterson said, "I would've thought about the taxes earlier."

Funny stuff! So, despite a massive deficit that forced New York agencies to produce "Doomsday Budgets," the governor apparently felt like it was fine to watch a guy who makes $54 million a year publicly leave town, depriving his state and city of what could be millions of dollars a year in tax revenue.

A.D.D. Moment

If New York doesn't care about the tax revenue from Limbaugh, then someone should ask the governor why, according to Limbaugh, they've audited him for twelve straight years . . .

"WELL IF WE CAN'T RAISE TAXES ON ANYONE THEN HOW THE HECK ARE WE SUPPOSED TO BALANCE THE BUDGET?"

Finally, a good question! Unfortunately, you've fallen prey to the tax myth. The way this one goes is that, prior to President Obama riding into the White House on a white horse, all essential government "investments" were basically neglected. Hate-mongering conservatives spent years cutting taxes as an ugly plot to "starve the beast" of government, resulting in a severe decline of federal revenues that forced us to neglect important priorities, like caring for sick children. According to the myth, the only way out of this mess is to now "reinvest" in all the vital programs that were starved for funding from 2001 to 2008.

It's a great story, but it's just that, a *story*.

Federal spending *before* the Obama administration took over expanded from $1.8 trillion in 2000 to $3 trillion in 2008. That's a 66 percent increase in just eight years. Raise your hand if you saw *your* income grow by 66 percent over that time.

A.D.D. MOMENT

Now, quick, put it back down before someone from the Obama administration sees you.

The chart below compares government spending in some major areas that we are continually told need more funding. The total inflation rate over this period was 22 percent. But transportation spending was up 43 percent. Health-care spending was up 46 percent. The Department of Education budget was up more than 85 percent. Welfare spending was up 60 percent.

It looks to me like the people who have been the most greedy were the lobbyists, politicians, and Beltway bureaucrats who run these programs—most of which grew by four, five, or six times the rate of inflation! If that is neglect, I'd hate to see what happens when our politicians *really* start spending.

Remember, all of these figures are from *before* the Obama torrent of spending began. In 2009, the average federal program saw an increase of 48 percent! That's more than *30 times* the rate

What's on your iPod, TIMOTHY GEITHNER?

- *Tax Man*, Beatles
- *Been Caught Stealing*, Jane's Addiction
- *Money for Nothing*, Dire Straits
- *Money's Too Tight to Mention*, Simply Red

GOVERNMENT IS GREAT!

Have you noticed that government subsidies, giveaways, and pork projects have suddenly now become known as "investments"? Aren't you just tickled pink that your tax dollars went to pay for such vital national investments as Old Tiger Stadium Conservancy in Detroit, Pleasure Beach water-taxi service in Connecticut, and Dance Theater Etcetera in Brooklyn?

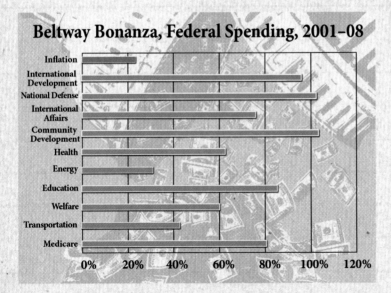

Beltway Bonanza, Federal Spending, 2001–08

Categories (top to bottom): Inflation, International Development, National Defense, International Affairs, Community Development, Health, Energy, Education, Welfare, Transportation, Medicare

Scale: 0% 20% 40% 60% 80% 100% 120%

of inflation. And while Bush deserves much of the blame (his last budget pegged 2009 spending at $3.1 trillion), President Obama has taken things to a whole new stratosphere. His latest estimates put 2009 spending at $4 trillion, an increase (of $900 billion) that is larger than the economies of Norway and Austria . . . *combined*.

Is it any wonder that we are losing jobs in manufacturing, business services, construction, wholesaling, financial services, but we are *gaining* jobs in government?

Since 2007, the only three sectors of the economy that have created jobs are (1) government, (2) education, and (3) health care. Of course, education and health care are practically adjuncts of government at this point anyway, but let me ask the obvious question: Somebody has to pay for these government jobs, right?

Of course—and they're being paid for with tax dollars. But if we aren't creating private jobs so that the overall tax base increases, then where is the money coming from? After all, we can't have everyone sitting *inside* the wagon; we still need some people available to pull it.

GOVERNMENT IS GREAT!

From April 2008 to April 2009 the private sector lost 5.4 million jobs. But the public sector? They *added* 162,000 jobs. I guess it helps to have a blank taxpayer check available to make payroll with.

"OH, GLENN, WHAT AN OLD-FASHIONED WAY OF THINKING. DON'T YOU UNDERSTAND THAT GOVERNMENT SPENDING IS AN ECONOMIC *STIMULUS*? BECAUSE OF THE 'MULTIPLIER EFFECT,' EVERY DOLLAR OF GOVERNMENT SPENDING WILL GENERATE $2, $3, OR EVEN $4 OF PRIVATE-SECTOR EXPANSION!"

Remember the mythical Tooth Fairy that we always looked forward to? Guess what . . . she really exists. Her name is Nancy Pelosi and, while she may not look like you expected, she is just as generous. Except, she doesn't hand out quarters, she hands out billion-dollar checks, courtesy of the U.S. government. Oh, and the money doesn't go to good little children, but to the good little lobbyists and union leaders that leave her favors under their pillows.

A.D.D. Moment

Remember when President Obama somehow kept a straight face and said, "That's why I've charged the Office of Management and Budget . . . with going through the budget— program by program, item by item, line by line— looking for areas where we can save taxpayer dollars"? Given their results, I'm sure glad we haven't put those guys in charge of looking for anything we were actually hoping to find.

As I flip through President Obama's budget—which is as thick as the Manhattan phone book—and I observe the 9,000 subsidy programs that give money to Harry and take more from Louise—all I really see is more and more spending for nearly every government program imaginable.

GOVERNMENT MATH

When I hear people talk about the "multiplier effect" I feel like they believe government is the elusive perpetual economic motion machine that scientists have been trying to invent for centuries. It's not. In fact, there is a lot of evidence to suggest that there is no multiplier effect at all; that every dollar in government spending results in *less than a dollar* being added to our GDP.

Noted Harvard economist Robert Barro looked at federal spending and corresponding GDP growth during World War I, World War II, Korea, and Vietnam. In each case he found the "multiplier" to be exactly the same: 0.8. In other words, for every dollar our government spent, $0.80 was added to our GDP. Even worse, Barro thinks that wartime spending probably *increases* the multiplier . . . it's likely even lower when you try to spend your way out of a recession.

A.D.D. MOMENT

I'm pretty sure I know why Robert Barro isn't on Obama's Presidential Council of Economic Advisors.

Remember the stimulus bill, with its $787 billion price tag and money for the National Education Association, unemployment insurance, windmills, new cars for federal bureaucrats, and the like? When you put that spending on top of the regular operating budget, you find that spending for the average government agency *increased* by about 50 percent. In other words, at a time when families were pulling back on their spending and suffering through a deep recession, Uncle Sam was living higher on the hog than ever before.

If you haven't figured out my point by now, it's that the answer to how we can balance the budget without burying the rich in taxes is easy: We have to *balance* the budget. In other words, we've got to bring our spending side—which I'm pretty sure I've proven is completely out of control—down to match our revenues, not the other way around.

GOVERNMENT IS GREAT!

The government had so much money to spend in 2009 that it actually contemplated allocating $5 million for the care of cats and dogs . . . in foreign countries. No one in Washington seems to care though, because $5 million is nothing but a rounding error in the $108 billion that President Obama wants to give to the International Monetary Fund (IMF) in foreign aid this year. (In fact, he wanted the IMF to have the money so bad that he was willing to compromise the security of our troops by agreeing to release torture photos in exchange for votes). Maybe those in the Capitol haven't received the memo yet, but we should be on the *receiving* end of that foreign aid.

Community Organizer

CHRYSLER

FROM SALE OF STOCK YOU GET NOTHING.

HOLY HYPOCRISY!

There's no way that the Democrats who are now *supporting* reckless, historic levels of government spending would've been hypocritical enough to *criticize* reckless Republican spending just a couple of years earlier, right? *Riiiiiiight?*

"This nation must come to grips with the repercussions of recent fiscal irresponsibility."
—Charlie Rangel, 2007

"When it comes to deficits, this president owns all the records. The three largest deficits in our nation's history have all occurred under this administration's watch."
—Harry Reid, 2006

"After years of historic deficits, this 110th Congress will commit itself to a higher standard: pay-as-you-go, no new deficit spending. Our new America will provide unlimited opportunity for future generations, not burden them with mountains of debt."
—Nancy Pelosi, 2007

In addition to her now ridiculous "pay-as-you-go" promise, Nancy Pelosi also told us that, with Democrats in charge, she would return Washington to "fiscal responsibility" and cut earmark spending in half.

After we made this wonder woman from San Francisco Speaker of the House, she got right to work . . . on spending more of our money. Our deficit went from $161 billion in 2007 to $459 billion in 2008. A year after that, the deficit went to . . . no, not zero, not $161 billion, not $459 billion . . . $1.8 *trillion.*

"I KNOW YOU'RE NOT A FAN OF SPENDING, BUT THE ONLY WAY OUT OF A DEEP RECESSION IS FOR THE GOVERNMENT TO TAKE ON MORE DEBT AND HELP TO GENERATE NEW JOBS."

We now know that a major trigger point for the recession was too much spending that we couldn't afford. Households accumulated too much credit-card and mortgage debt. Businesses took on too much leverage (think of Bear Stearns with its debt-to-asset ratio of more than 35-to-1). And the federal government took on more debt than any other institution in the history of the world.

What's on your iPod, HANK PAULSON?

- *Impulsive*, Wilson Phillips
- *Let's Go Crazy*, Prince & The Revolution
- *Shakedown*, Bob Seger
- *All I Need Is a Miracle*, Mike & The Mechanics

Shhhhhhhhhh . . .

Here's a dirty little secret you won't hear from Nancy Pelosi or Barack Obama, who in June 2009 renewed Nancy Pelosi's 2007 call for "pay-as-you-go" budgeting to be used in Congress: It applies only to *new* entitlement programs or *expansion* of current ones. In other words, programs like Medicare are exempt, along with *all discretionary spending*. But the saddest part of all is that, even with all of those exceptions, our politicians still can't stick to it.

We also know that most of this debt was used to finance absurdly wasteful spending: Individuals bought televisions, vacations, cars, and granite countertops; the government bought entitlement expansion, wars, and federal bailouts.

Maybe I need some advanced degree in economics from the People's Republic of Harvard or a Nobel Prize to understand this, but if excessive debt *caused* the economic crisis, then how is *more* debt supposed to get us out of it? Is the idea to borrow more and more money to pay off all the people we borrowed money from over the last twenty years? If so, then isn't that exactly what got Bernie Madoff thrown into prison for 150 years?

It's ironic that when individuals rob Peter to pay Paul they end up having to be careful in the shower, yet when the government runs the same kind of Ponzi scheme, we call it an "economic stimulus." No wonder Washington is called "America's only work-free drug zone."

ELECTRIC COMPANY

PRICE: $150
PLUS $500
CARBON TAX

BAMANOPOLY

"GLENN, YOU NEED TO READ HISTORY—THE NEW DEAL RESULTED IN TONS OF NEW SPENDING AND IT GOT US OUT OF THE GREAT DEPRESSION!"

Sorry, no. As Burt Folsom has proven in his book *New Deal or Raw Deal*, FDR's economic-recovery plan was an absolute bust. Federal spending as a share of GDP more than *doubled* in the 1930s, but the unemployment rate stayed high throughout the decade. Shouldn't all of that money have created lots of new (*non-government*) jobs?

Change
ADVANCE TOKEN TO THE NEAREST RAILROAD AND PAY THE GOVERNMENT TWICE THE AMOUNT TO WHICH IT IS OTHERWISE ENTITLED. DON'T EXPECT ANYTHING IN RETURN.

By 1940, eight years after the New Deal was launched, the U.S. unemployment rate was *still* hovering around 15 percent. Wow, that is some success story! To put that into perspective, it would be like the United States having a 15-percent unemployment rate in 2016 and everyone celebrating the success of Obamanomics.

Even Henry Morgenthau, FDR's own Treasury secretary, acknowledged that the blizzard of government spending didn't create new American jobs. Testifying in front of the House Ways and Means

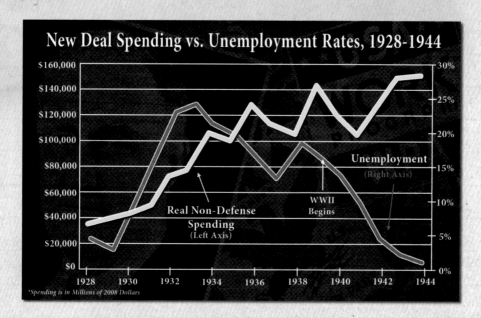

New Deal Spending vs. Unemployment Rates, 1928-1944

Spending is in Millions of 2008 Dollars

Committee in 1939, Morgenthau said, "We have tried spending money. We are spending more than we have ever spent before and it does not work. And I have just one interest, and now if I am wrong . . . somebody else can have my job. I want to see this country prosperous. I want to see people get a job. I want to see people get enough to eat. We have never made good on our promises . . . I say after eight years of this administration, we have just as much unemployment as when we started . . . And enormous debt to boot."

I guess Tim Geithner was too busy not paying his taxes to heed Morgenthau's advice.

"OKAY, WELL WHAT ABOUT JAPAN? THEIR GOVERNMENT HAD TO SPEND A LOT TO GET OUT OF THE 'LOST DECADE.'"

Japan tried eight—yes, *eight* fiscal-stimulus plans in the 1990s and early 2000s to end their nearly two-decade-long depression that began in 1991. They basically paved over the whole island with public-works programs and then started paving over the ocean (literally) to build "the world's most expensive airport" once they got done with that.

GOVERNMENT IS GREAT!

Believe it or not, during the New Deal, the federal government actually burned fields of crops in order to reduce the supply of food and keep prices high so that farmers' incomes would also stay high. (No, I'm not making this up.) Meanwhile, as the government was destroying crops, cities were filled with tens of thousands of Americans who were going to bed hungry each night thanks to a lack of jobs and cheap food.

What was the result of all that borrowing and "broken-window" (i.e., you break all of the windows in a house and then pay someone to fix them) stimulus spending? In 1991, the Japanese Nikkei stock index stood at 30,000. By 2007, after spending the equivalent of at least $1.4 trillion (in today's U.S. dollars) on stimulus packages, the Nikkei was at 12,000. After 16 years of government pump priming, sixty percent of the country's financial wealth had disappeared.

But, sure, by all means, why wouldn't we want to emulate that model?

Given the obvious failure of big-spending programs in the past, we have good reason to be worried about the current one. This chart shows the "stimulus plan" in comparison to other major spending initiatives throughout American history—adjusted for inflation. The stimulus is number one. By far. It is larger than the Marshall Plan, the Apollo plan to put a man on the moon, the Louisiana Purchase, the Civil War, Reconstruction, or World War I. In fact, we've spent more money to fight this recession than America spent to defeat the Nazis and Japanese in World War II.

A.D.D. MOMENT

The modern-day equivalent of "broken-window" stimulus is "green jobs." We invent a crisis and then spend billions on finding a way to solve it.

What's on your iPod, RAHM EMANUEL?

- *Smooth Operator*, Sade
- *F**k It*, Eamon
- *Money Changes Everything*, Cyndi Lauper
- *The Real Slim Shady*, Eminem

The Bailouts: Putting It All on Red

Over the next ten years the Obama budget chains America to a future of $15 to $16 trillion of debt. That is obviously unsustainable and will unquestionably lead to inflation and a declining U.S. dollar. No nation in history has ever devalued its way to prosperity, but U.S. policymakers are giving it their best effort. During the Bush years, the dollar fell relative to virtually every other major currency and, in late 2007, it reached a new symbolic and ignominious low, falling below the Canadian dollar in value for the first time ever.

If you think I'm exaggerating the crisis (I know, I have that reputation for some reason . . .) then look at how our government is financing all of its debt: The chart below (Solving One Crisis by Creating Another) shows the money supply over the past ten years. It was consistently stable . . . until about the summer of 2008 . . . and then all hell broke loose.

You don't have to have a Ph.D. in Obamanomics to understand what the inevitable consequence of this will be: Say hello to my little friend inflation.

After World War I, Germany's inflation got so bad because of their debt that people had to fill wheelbarrows with cash just to have enough money to buy groceries. Here's a tip: *Invest in wheelbarrows now, while they're still affordable!*

"YEAH, BUT THIS TIME IS DIFFERENT. BESIDES, WE COULDN'T JUST SIT BY AND LET THE ECONOMY COLLAPSE, WE HAD TO DO *SOMETHING!*"

No one knows for sure how much the government has spent so far to "stimulate" the economy—after all, who can count that high?—but if you add up the cost of all the bailout plans, stimulus measures, debt measures, and all the spending by the Federal Reserve Bank to buy up bad assets, the figure is near $3 trillion.

President George W. Bush and his Treasury secretary, Hank Paulson, said that if we didn't bail out the banks and big investment houses, like Bear Stearns and AIG, the economy would collapse like a house of cards. So, they asked for about $1 trillion in new spending and our Congress—frightened, confused, or both—agreed.

When Barack Obama was elected, the economy was still headed south and we

Solving One Crisis by Creating Another
The U.S. Adjusted Monetary Base

Dec-98 Dec-00 Dec-02 Dec-04 Dec-06 Dec-08

PERSPECTIVE: HOW MUCH IS A TRILLION?

A trillion is $1,000,000,000,000. That's twelve zeroes. One trillion is one million times one million. If we filled Michigan's football stadium with people (all 100,000+ seats occupied) and then gave every person there one thousand dollars, we'd have to fill the stadium every weekend for roughly the next 40,000 years before we would have passed out a trillion dollars.

Still not good enough? How about this: NBA superstar LeBron James earns about $40 million a year to play for the Cleveland Cavaliers. To earn $1 trillion, he would have to play in the NBA for the next 25,000 years.

were told that another trillion in spending and bailouts was essential. In addition, the Federal Reserve Bank—made up of unelected officials who helped usher *in* the crisis, through policies that encouraged excessive money creation—decided to intervene on their own and spend another trillion.

Saying that we had to unleash all of that debt to prevent the economy from collapsing is a little like what the barbarians used to say when they ransacked Europe: "We had to burn the cities—in order to save them!" It's a great line for another reason as well: There's no way to disprove it.

We can, however, look at specific spending programs and measure their effectiveness. The federal government has already committed over $80 billion to bailing out GM, Chrysler, and GMAC. That's $80 billion to save roughly 320,000 jobs.

To put that into perspective, we could have given every worker at these companies a $250,000 check and it would have been cheaper than all these bailouts. And that's assuming that $100 billion is the end of it—which is probably a bad assumption unless you think that Uncle Sam and the United Auto Workers are somehow going to produce profitable cars.

> "It's politically fashionable to rant against government spending and demand fiscal responsibility. But right now, increased government spending is just what the doctor ordered, and concerns about the budget deficit should be put on hold."
>
> —Paul Krugman

CELEBRITY Guest Ideeot

It Could've Been Worse!

YOU: But unemployment kept rising way past most economists' expectations, even after all the stimulus money had been approved!

THEM: Yeah, but unemployment would have been even worse.

YOU: But GM and Chrysler both went bankrupt even after you gave them billions!

THEM: Yeah, but they would have been even *more* bankrupt.

My point is that we are wasting money on such a massive scale that we've lost any sense of reality. The $787 billion we spent on the "stimulus" plan is supposed to create three and a half million jobs. Good luck, but if that does somehow happen it would mean a cost to taxpayers of about $225,000 per job. Again, I know it's a rhetorical question, but couldn't we have just given three million unemployed people that money and called it a "stimulus"?

So why hasn't the economy roared back to life in response to all of this vital spending? Simple . . . because government money doesn't appear out of thin air, it has to come from one of three places:

What's on your iPod, NANCY PELOSI?

- *Little Lies*, Fleetwood Mac
- *Out of Touch*, Hall & Oates
- *We Didn't Start the Fire*, Billy Joel
- *Burning Down the House*, Talking Heads

A.D.D. MOMENT

As part of the "stimulus" we also earmarked tens of billions of dollars for increased unemployment insurance. How, exactly, does paying people not to work create more jobs?

1. *Taxes.* The government can take the money right out of your wallet and magnanimously give it to someone else. But redistribution is not stimulus . . . the net effect on the economy is basically zero.
2. *Borrowing.* "Please, China, can we have some more?" When we borrow, we put one dollar into the economy, but we also add a dollar, plus interest, to our liabilities. That's a net *decrease* in future growth.
3. *Printing.* The government can always call up the Treasury and tell them to keep printing those $100 bills, 24/7. But when the government prints an additional dollar, every dollar that you and I have in our wallet or our savings account is worth a tiny bit less. Supply and demand, right? So printing money is just a way of taxing people without their permission and it results in no positive economic growth.

The point is that government spending as an economic stimulus is an illusion. We don't create any new wealth or jobs, we just redistribute money from people who pay taxes or hold dollars to people who helped our politicians get elected.

GOVERNMENT IS GREAT!

Among the biggest donors to the Democratic Party in the 2006 and 2008 election cycles were the unions. Guess who wound up getting most of the money from the stimulus plan? Guess who gets the Chrysler bailout money? Guess who gets all that education money that is supposed to be "for the kids"? Yep, the unions, the unions, and the unions.

Should that be called "stimulus," or "payback"?

"YOU'RE JUST THE 'PARTY OF NO.' THE WHOLE REASON WE'RE IN THIS MESS IS BECAUSE YOUR IDIOTIC REPUBLICAN ECONOMIC THEORIES WERE A DISASTER!"

First of all, there have been no real "Republican" economic policies in place for a long, long time (unless you think that massively expanding entitlement programs is right out of the Reagan playbook). Yes, President Bush cut taxes, and yes, cutting taxes is what Republicans generally want—but Bush missed a key part of the equation: cutting *spending* as well. Cutting taxes while increasing spending is not a Republican economic theory . . . because it simply doesn't work.

Second, I will never defend a party, because I don't believe in them anymore . . . but when someone tries to convince you that the answer to excessive spending and debt is obscene levels of spending and debt, I think you have a responsibility to say, "No . . . enough is enough."

But let's suspend our disbelief for a moment and accept the notion that the government had to do something. Here is an amazing but true statistic: Instead of spending $3 trillion on bailouts to homeowners, banks, insurance companies, Wall Street executives, and car companies, what if we had simply suspended the personal- and corporate-income taxes for a year until the economy got better? In 2008, the personal- and corporate-income tax raised about $1.45 trillion.

In other words, we could have told every business and every worker in America: You don't have to pay income tax this year if you work, if you invest, if you earn a profit, if you expand your business and hiring. You keep it all. Can you *imagine* how fast our economy would have grown under that scenario? We would have had more jobs than people to fill them!

So why didn't we suspend the tax . . . even for a few months as a "stimulus"? Simple, because cutting taxes for everyone doesn't allow you to do special favors or properly "redistribute" income. That's why we have rebate checks that are skewed toward the poor. They tell us it's because the poor are more likely to spend them . . . but the truth is that we do it that way because it fits the progressive Robin Hood agenda.

"In the U.S. there are over 40 million unemployed, homeless people."

—Iranian "President" Mahmoud Ahmadinejad, who apparently didn't get the memo that the number of chronically homeless in America fell to 124,000 in 2007.

CELEBRITY GUEST IDEEOT

"YOU'RE JUST BEING OVERLY DRAMATIC BECAUSE DEMOCRATS ARE NOW IN CHARGE, YOU REPUBLICAN ZOMBIE. THE GOVERNMENT REALLY HASN'T GROWN AS MUCH AS YOU SAY."

When Ronald Reagan entered the White House in 1980, his message to voters was plain and simple: Big government is the problem, not the solution.

At the time, federal spending was at just over $500 billion. Now the budget is $4 trillion—a sevenfold increase. Even after adjusting for inflation, federal outlays have increased over 250 percent since 1980.

But let me be very clear, this isn't about the donkey or the elephant, *both parties* are to blame for the situation we now find ourselves in. In fact, I think you can make a good case that the Republicans deserve your anger more than the Democrats. At least most Democrats have been fairly honest about their progressive agenda—Republicans have shredded our Constitution while smiling and pretending that they actually care about the principles our Founders stood for.

The thing that's unleashed the federal leviathan the most since our founding is the concept of entitlements. In 1933, the modern entitlement state was born in the form of the federal government's first and most expensive income transfer program: Social Security. In the 1960s, LBJ launched the Great Society, creating a whole new menu of entitlement programs, chief among them Medicare, Medicaid, food stamps, public housing, and Aid to Families with Dependent Children (AFDC).

It's not just the *federal* government that was spending like Keith Olbermann at a Shakespeare festival—state and local governments were as well. Since 1960, state and local spending is up 495 percent (after inflation)! Spending totaled about $367 billion back then (in 2008 dollars) . . . it's $2.2 *trillion* now.

Once created, these redistribution programs were virtually impossible to restrain. It wasn't long before people began to feel like they were in the minority if they weren't taking advantage of some free government program. It got so bad that, twenty years ago, author Matthew Lesko (aka "the guy who wears the question-mark suits") started writing bestselling books chronicling the thousands of federal programs and agencies that gave out "free" money.

When Medicare was created it was estimated to cost about $12 billion by 1990. The actual cost? $107 billion—proving once again that government cost estimates are about as accurate as Iranian vote counts.

A.D.D. MOMENT

There are a lot of ways you can be known in life, but it's hard to pick one worse than "the guy who wears the question-mark suits."

There is a lot of truth to the adage that a system that robs Peter to pay Paul can always count on Paul's support. Unfortunately, if Peter ever decides that he's sick of being robbed and leaves the country, the whole scam falls apart.

40 percent of American households now not only don't pay any federal income tax, but actually get money *back* from the government every year. That makes it awfully hard to pass fiscally responsibly policies. But what happens when that number gets to 50 percent? At that point, the only way you'd ever convince the country to lower taxes and cut government programs would be to convince the 50 percent of people who don't pay taxes to stay home on Election Day. Or, since we're shredding the Constitution anyway, why not just restrict voting to those who pay income tax? I'm just thinking out loud here . . .

What's on your iPod, ALAN GREENSPAN?

- *Tiny Bubbles*, Don Ho
- *Saved by Zero*, The Fixx
- *Don't Dream It's Over*, Crowded House
- *No One Is to Blame*, Howard Jones

How much of a welfare state have we become? One of every six dollars of Americans' income is now a federal or state check or voucher. In 2009, the government will spend an average of $17,000 on each U.S. household, meaning that the government is funding more of Americans' income that any time since we started keeping records in 1929.

For an even more stark illustration of government creep, consider that, in 1900, total federal, state, and local expenditures were $33 billion. Now? Americans support a nearly $3 trillion government, an increase of almost 10,000 percent!

"STATISTICS DON'T LIE, BUT LIARS LIKE YOU, MR. BECK, USE STATISTICS. SURE, SPENDING IS UP 10,000 PERCENT, BUT THAT'S BECAUSE OF INFLATION. BESIDES, OUR ECONOMY IS MUCH LARGER NOW THAN IT USED TO BE!"

Fair point! So instead of looking at it in dollar terms, let's look at the size of government relative to the size of the economy. Would that be okay with you?

★ In 1900, the federal government consumed less than 5 percent of total economic output.
★ In 1950, the federal government consumed roughly 15 percent of total output.
★ In 1999, the federal government consumed roughly 19 percent of total output.
★ In 2009, the federal government will spend 28.1 percent of total output . . . and climbing.

Happy now?

"FINE—BUT WHO CARES ABOUT THE SIZE OF GOVERNMENT ANYWAY. IF I HAVE A JOB, I COULD CARE LESS HOW MUCH THEY'RE SPENDING."

It's really pretty simple: More government means less personal freedom. As economist Walter Williams of George Mason University has noted, if the government can lay claim to half of the fruits of our labor, then we are truly at most only half-free.

But now, even after allocating $10.5 trillion on direct and indirect stimulus ideas over the last two years, we still have a $6 trillion national debt (climbing to $16 trillion with the new ten-year budget) and we face another $50 trillion in unfunded liabilities for entitlement programs like Social Security and Medicare. Are we even really "half-free" or is that just wishful thinking?

A.D.D. MOMENT!

There are only two problems with the Social Security trust fund. First, there's no trust. And second, there's no fund. In 2009, the outflow for Social Security was $675 billion and the inflow was $655 billion. That's a negative $20 billion cash flow. Oops. Thanks to the recession, payroll tax receipts are way down because fewer people are working. We've sunk into red ink almost ten years ahead of schedule.

So now, Social Security appears to be *contributing* to the massive $1.8 trillion deficit, rather than helping to reduce it. That means we now have two deficits: the operating budget and Social Security budget. Add in Medicare and we've got our third . . . though it's definitely not the charm.

In other words, the government has cost us our freedom by putting us into financial shackles. If you have a job now, that's great—but that shouldn't make you feel confident about the future. After all, it's that kind of short-term-pleasure-over-pain thinking that got us here.

We've got a lot of work to do to rebuild our economy and regain our freedom, but here are a few steps:

★ Get the government out of the way.
★ Make the dollar as good as gold again.
★ Pay your bills.

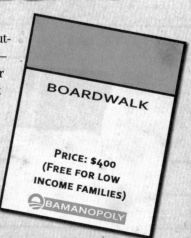

BOARDWALK

PRICE: $400
(FREE FOR LOW INCOME FAMILIES)

OBAMANOPOLY

★ Balance your budget.
★ Audit every federal agency and find all the waste that can be cut.
★ Make sure our taxes pay for only the *essentials* of government, not the frivolous and extravagant.
★ Don't allow those who are beneficiaries of the "frivolous and extravagant" to decide what the definition of "essential" is.
★ Ensure our politicians put America's future over their own by instititing term limits at all levels.

Government is, in the memorable words of President George Washington, "a fearsome master." So how have we permitted it to grow so far beyond its constitutional boundaries? Easy: We've let Congress rewrite the Constitution virtually every day it is in session without an ounce of oversight from the fourth, and most important branch of government: "We the People."

Members of Congress are sworn to uphold the Constitution, but most seem to be as familiar with its contents as they are with the thousand-page bills they vote for in the middle of the night. Shame on them for trampling the vision of our Founding Fathers for their own selfish gain.

Shame on us, for letting them.

U.S. PRESIDENTS

A Steady Progression of Progressives

IN JULY 2007, when the Democratic nomination for president was still very much up in the air, Hillary Clinton, Barack Obama, and six other candidates (remember Mike Gravel?) gathered for the CNN/YouTube debate. The world watched as millions of dollars in technology was used to ask questions that the moderator could've read off of index cards.

But one question actually managed to elicit a response that *should've* caused people to take notice. "Mrs. Clinton," Rob from California asked, "how would you define the word 'liberal'?—and would you use this word to describe yourself?"

Clinton complained for a minute about how the word "liberal" had taken on a new meaning before going on to describe exactly how she views herself politically:

"I prefer the word 'progressive,' which has a real American meaning, going back to the progressive era at the beginning of the twentieth century. I consider myself a modern progressive, someone who believes strongly in individual rights and freedoms, who believes that we are better as a society when we're working together and when we find ways to help those who may not have all the advantages in life to get the tools they need to lead a more productive life for themselves and their family.

"So I consider myself a proud modern American progressive, and I think that's the kind of philosophy and practice that we need to bring back to American politics."

It's possible that Hillary hasn't gotten the memo, but there's no need to bring progressivism *back* . . . because it never left. Sure, the ideas have evolved, and progressive politicians are a little more careful about how they advertise themselves, but the progressive agenda has been steadily chugging along for over a century.

To really understand where America is headed, you first have to understand where we've been and what motivates those who believe that our founding documents must evolve because they were written in a "different era." Here's a look back at three presidents from the "Progressive Era." As you read their thoughts and vision for America, you might recognize some stark parallels to today's crop of politicians—from both sides of the aisle.

Great Moments in Debate History

When I was combing through the transcripts of that CNN/YouTube debate, one candidate's response stuck out at me that, in retrospect, could now take on an entirely new meaning:

"I believe that on the issues that directly affect women's lives, I have the strongest, boldest ideas and can bring about the change that needs to be brought."

—JOHN EDWARDS

Just remember, no matter what progressives say or promise, they all have the same fundamental misconception: Our Founding Founders didn't set up a system that was meant to adapt to a changing world—it's the other way around.

★ TEDDY ROOSEVELT ★

"ROOSEVELT WAS A GREAT REPUBLICAN. IF CONSERVATIVES WOULD JUST BE MORE LIKE HIM WE MIGHT FINALLY GET THIS PARTY BACK ON TRACK."

Teddy Roosevelt assumed the presidency after William McKinley was assassinated in 1901, a time when large multistate corporations were first being created. Right out of the gate, Roosevelt fired off 40 lawsuits in an attempt to "trust-bust" and federally control large corporations.

Roosevelt, like other progressives, did not trust businesses or wealthy individuals because he likely didn't believe that any of them were ultimately capable of doing what was best for the collective. Only government was capable of that. (Please resume reading once you finish laughing.)

As you read this section, remember that John McCain has said that Old Teddy Bear Roosevelt is his political idol. It will not take long for you to realize just how horrible a selection the GOP really made.

A.D.D. MOMENT

In 1910, Roosevelt gave a landmark speech called "The New Nationalism" that clearly laid out his vision for America. "It has become entirely clear," he said, "that we must have government supervision of the capitalization, not only of public-service corporations, including, particularly, railways, but of all corporations doing an interstate business."

To progressives, government supervision is the answer to any problem supposedly caused by the "free market." It happened after the 1907 banking crisis, the Great Depression, and, of course, after the credit crisis, when President Obama proposed sweeping changes to the financial regulatory system.

Roosevelt continued, "I have no doubt that the ordinary man who has control of [meat, oil, coal, or other large, important companies] is much like ourselves. I have no doubt he would like to do well—but I want to have enough supervision to help him realize that desire to do well."

In other words, progressives believe that everyone innately *wanted* to do what was best for society, but, just in case they succumbed to greed or selfishness for a minute, there would be government "supervision" in place to help them see the error of their ways.

Roosevelt not only distrusted the rich, he actually seemed to *despise* them. While delivering a standard populist line about the need for justice to be administered to all equally, Roosevelt couldn't help but slip in his hatred for the upper class:

> ## Great Moments in Debate History
>
> **A**fter Mike Gravel flatly accused Barack Obama of violating his campaign promise and taking money from lobbyists, this classic exchange took place:
>
> OBAMA: And that's the kind of leadership that I've shown in the Senate. That's the kind of leadership that I showed when I was a state legislator. And that's the kind of leadership that I'll show as president of the United States.
>
> GRAVEL: Wait a minute . . .
>
>   (APPLAUSE)
>
> ANDERSON COOPER: Our next question is for Senator Biden.

*" . . . and the wealthy man, whomsoever he may be, **for whom I have the greatest contempt,** I would fight for him, and you would if you were worth your salt."*

"Greatest contempt" for the wealthy man? This was a *Republican*? Yes—but you have to understand that progressivism has nothing to do with the "R" or the "D." Progressive politicians from opposite parties may have different methods for achieving their goals, but those goals are always the same: benefiting the collective at the expense of the individual. Remember Hillary's words from the debate as she described progressivism: *"We are better as a society when we're working together."*

Seeds are based on an average of various presidential rankings done by third-parties.

(1) Theodore Roosevelt
(1) Roosevelt
(8) Zachary Taylor
(1) Roosevelt
(4) Andrew Jackson
(5) Adams
(5) John Quincy Adams
(2) Jefferson
(3) Lyndon B. Johnson
(6) Madison
(6) James Madison
(2) Jefferson
(7) Jimmy Carter
★
(2) Jefferson
(2) Thomas Jefferson

(1) Franklin D. Roosevelt
(1) Roosevelt
(8) Benjamin Harrison
(1) Roosevelt
(3) James Polk
(3) Polk
(6) Gerald Ford
★
(7) Taft
(4) James Monroe
(5) Bush
(5) George H. W. Bush
(7) Taft
(7) William H. Taft
(7) Taft
(2) John F. Kennedy

SMACKDOWN! ★

★ = Featured matchup. See recap later in chapter.

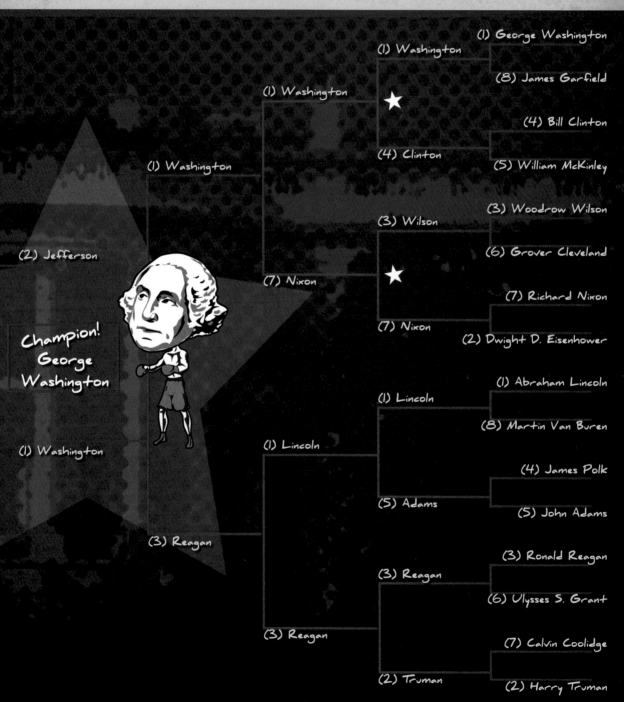

(1) Washington — (1) George Washington

(8) James Garfield

(1) Washington

★

(4) Clinton — (4) Bill Clinton

(5) William McKinley

(1) Washington

(3) Wilson — (3) Woodrow Wilson

(6) Grover Cleveland

★

(7) Nixon

(7) Nixon — (7) Richard Nixon

(2) Dwight D. Eisenhower

(2) Jefferson

(1) Washington

(7) Nixon

Champion!
George
Washington

(1) Lincoln — (1) Abraham Lincoln

(8) Martin Van Buren

(1) Lincoln

(4) James Polk

(5) Adams — (5) John Adams

(1) Washington

(1) Lincoln

(3) Reagan — (3) Ronald Reagan

(6) Ulysses S. Grant

(3) Reagan

(3) Reagan

(7) Calvin Coolidge

(2) Truman — (2) Harry Truman

AT LEAST HE WAS HONEST . . .

"I stand for the square deal. But when I say that I am for the square deal, I mean not merely that I stand for fair play under the present rules of that game, but that I stand for having those rules changed so as to work for more substantial equality of opportunity and of reward for equally good service."

—Teddy Roosevelt, in his "New Nationalism" speech

Roosevelt continued, "We grudge no man a fortune in civil life if it is honorably obtained and well used. It is not even enough that it should have been gained without doing damage to the community. We should permit it to be gained only so long as the gaining represents benefit to the community."

Progressives like Roosevelt would, on the surface, seem to defend capitalism, but there is almost always a big "IF" attached to their rhetoric. In Roosevelt's case, saying that someone can make boatloads of cash IF they obtain it honorably is one thing—you can at least make the case that he meant "lawfully"—but IF their wealth is "well used"? What does *that* mean? And who, exactly, decides the definition of "well used," some government board?

He went on, "This, I know, implies a policy of a far more active governmental interference with social and economic conditions in this country than we have yet had, but I think we have got to face the fact that such an increase in government control is now necessary."

PROGRESSIVE

PROGRESSIVE-LITE

FREE!

Of course it's "now" necessary—there's no other way to achieve the progressive agenda without a "far more active" government. After all, could a small, limited government ever help usher in a philosophy like this:

"Every man," Roosevelt said, "holds his property subject to the general right of the community to regulate its use to whatever degree the public welfare may require it."

Notice the language: *public welfare.* You can have property so long as the greater good doesn't require that the government take or regulate it. Government controls your business. Government controls your money. Government controls your property. Government controls your life.

As most conservatives understand, creating and implementing progressive government programs to solve problems only leads to more government control. For example, the Hepburn Act of 1906 gave the Interstate Commerce Commission (ICC) the power to, among other things, replace existing railroad rates with "just and reasonable" rates. Take a wild guess at who got to define what was "just and reasonable." Yep, the Roosevelt administration's ICC. When you cut through all of the noise, that is nothing more than government wage control—a big step past progressivism and right toward socialism . . . or worse.

Of course, another thing that most real conservatives understand is that whenever government tries to solve a problem, they create another one—usually much bigger than the original. Because of the caps on railway rates, the value of railroad securities plummeted (turns out investors aren't so fond of government price controls—who knew?), helping cause the bank panic of 1907. That gave progressives a *new* problem to solve. Hmm, what to do, what to do. Let me put my progressive thinking cap on for a second. Wait—I know: we need more government supervision! Roosevelt's

★ PRESIDENTIAL SMACKDOWN ★

George WASHINGTON (1) vs. **Bill CLINTON** (4)

WASHINGTON
★ Commanded Continental Army to victory over the British
★ Presided over the Philadelphia Convention and the drafting of the Constitution
★ Our first president—set the bar for all others

CLINTON
★ Cheated on wife with tubby intern
★ Lied about the affair
★ Was impeached for obstruction of justice

RECAP: Clinton got a 4 seed? Really?

WINNER: Washington

GOVERNMENT IS GREAT!

Most people didn't favor the creation of a "central bank" after the 1907 panic. So how did the government get away with setting one up anyway? Simple . . . they changed the name and called it the "Federal Reserve" instead. Control the language and you control the argument.

answer was to create the "National Monetary Commission," which, just five years later, led to the creation of the Federal Reserve system.

The banking panic of 1907 was calmed, in large part, by J. P. Morgan and his efforts to pool together funds (both public and private) and inject them into the banking system. But, given Roosevelt's distaste for corporations and wealth, Morgan's contributions must have been frowned on, right? Nope. Ironically enough, Mr. For the People, Mr. Darn These Special Interests, Mr. Trust-Buster himself Teddy Roosevelt thanked Morgan by allowing him to expand his steel empire and buy the Tennessee Coal and Iron Company for $45 million—about *five percent* of its true market value.

I guess all those values and principles that Roosevelt held so dear went right out the window once he realized that only capitalism could save America from the disasters created by progressivism.

A.D.D. MOMENT

Who would ever have foreseen a crisis being triggered by the government stepping in to determine reasonable rates? Oh wait, that's how almost *every* financial crisis is triggered. Free markets are generally pretty efficient over time . . . but free markets aren't free when progressive bureaucrats stick their dirty fingers into them under the guise of serving the "public good."

ACTIONS SPEAK LOUDER THAN WORDS

The "New Nationalism" speech included a lot of extreme-sounding sound-bites, but, unlike our weasely modern-day politicians who never intend to live up to their word, Roosevelt did. These weren't just ideas he was offering, he had detailed policies in mind to back them up:

★ Universal Health Care and Universal Health Insurance (Roosevelt was the first president to call for it).

★ Social Insurance (you probably know this now as the wildly successful "Social Security Insurance" program).

★ Created the Department of Labor, wanted it to have wide authority over "matters affecting the conditions of labor and living."

★ Sought after a "more easy and expeditious" method of amending the federal Constitution.

★ Called for a "graduated tax" on disproportionately large incomes and fortunes.

★ WOODROW WILSON ★

"WILSON WAS A MODEL DEMOCRAT AND A GREAT AMERICAN. EVEN MOST REPUBLICANS LIKE HIM!"

Wilson is routinely rated as one of the top ten presidents of all time and, truthfully, he made my list as well—but it has a slightly different title: The Top Ten Bastards of all time. Pardon the language, but Wilson's assault on the First Amendment was like nothing this country has seen before or since from anyone who's taken an oath to protect and defend our Constitution.

Wilson believed that our rights didn't come from our Creator, they came from the government, and his reasoning was influenced by one of his favorite political theorists, Edmund Burke. Burke, who was from the UK, suggested that a man should consider his rights as "an Englishman" rather than simply a "man." He opposed the abstract, arguing instead that politicians must place themselves in the here and now and base their political principles in "historical reality."

> I f you get into an argument over the pros and cons of Woodrow Wilson—you need to get some new friends ASAP.

Edmund Burke is commonly considered to be the founder of modern conservatism. With Wilson, an ardent liberal, being influenced by Burke, a conservative icon, it's not hard to see when the poisonous political crossbreeding began.

Does your head hurt yet? It only gets worse. Wilson, who was president of Princeton University before taking the White House, was apparently just waiting to make a big theoretical discovery when one fell right in his lap:

"I had been casting around in my mind for something by which to draw several parts of my political thought together when it was my good fortune to entertain a very interesting Scotsman who had been devoting himself to the philosophical thought of the seventeenth century. His talk was so engaging that it was delightful to hear him speak of anything, and presently there came out of the unexpected region of his thought the thing I had been waiting for."

This is what they call in the business, a "cliffhanger." Can't you just feel the excitement!? *What did the Scotsman tell Wilson??*

Editor's Note: *If you are currently feeling one ounce of excitement to find out what some intellectual Scotsman told Woodrow Wilson over a hundred years ago, then seriously, you really need to get a life.*

I won't leave you in suspense any longer, it's just too cruel. The thing that Wilson had been waiting for was a theory to prove that the United States Constitution is a living document.

"[The Scotsman] called my attention to the fact that in every generation all sorts of speculation and thinking tend to fall under the formula of the dominant thought of the age."

I know what you're thinking: Huh?

It's hard for us nonintellectuals to understand such deep, tweed-jacket thinking, but fortunately Wilson clarified his new understanding for us:

"The makers of our Federal Constitution . . . constructed a government as they would have constructed an orrery to display the laws of nature. Politics in their thought was a variety of mechanics. The Constitution was founded on the law of gravitation. The government was to exist and move by virtue of the efficacy of 'checks and balances.'

"The trouble with the theory is that government is not a machine, but a living thing. It falls, not under the theory of the universe, but under the theory of organic life. It is accountable to Darwin, not to Newton . . . Society is a living organism and must obey the laws of life, not of mechanics; it must develop.

"All that progressives ask or desire is permission in an era when 'development,' 'evolution,' is the scientific word to interpret the Constitution according to the Darwinian principle; all they ask is recognition of the fact that a nation is a living thing and not a machine."

A.D.D. Moment

Yes, a nation is a living thing, but our Constitution is not. Freedom of speech and the right to bear arms weren't things that our Framers threw in there and thought to themselves, *You know, in a few decades this stuff will probably all be obsolete.* They included those rights because they knew they were absolutely necessary for the Republic to survive. While progressives look at a right and say "obsolete," I look at it and say "essential."

Top Ten Bastards of All Time

10. POL POT Forced slave labor and executions resulted in the deaths of about one million Cambodians—about 26 percent of the country's entire population.

9. ROBERT MUGABE Tortured and killed white farmers in order to replace them with blacks, but forgot to pick blacks who knew how to run farms. Country no longer has a currency.

8. TEDDY ROOSEVELT First progressive U.S. president. Place on list solidified when McCain announced him as his political idol.

7. BERNIE MADOFF Scammed investors out of more than $50 billion.

6. ADOLF HITLER Killed six million Jews.

5. KEITH OLBERMANN Any human being who says, "For this relief, I give you much thanks" (Google it) automatically lands on the bastard list.

4. PONTIUS PILATE Crucified Jesus Christ.

3. FDR Four terms as president . . . is this America or Venezuela?

2. TIGER WOODS He's got a Swedish-supermodel wife, a gazillion dollars, and he plays golf for a living . . . bastard!

1. WOODROW WILSON Shredded our First Amendment by arresting thousands of people for speaking out against U.S. involvement in WWI.

First of all, could you imagine spending five minutes with this guy? I would have killed myself as soon as the word "orrery" came out. Who, besides Keith Olbermann, actually talks like that?

Given Wilson's clearly articulated views during the campaign (the above quotes were from actual campaign speeches he gave in 1912), it shouldn't be surprising that, after beating Taft, and Roosevelt, Wilson fulfilled his own constitutional rape fantasy.

 Wilson or Roosevelt . . . Obama or McCain. Different century, same choice: progressive or progressive-lite.

"YEAH, BUT WILSON WAS BRAVE ENOUGH TO SECURE AMERICA'S FUTURE BY LEADING US INTO WORLD WAR I!"

It wasn't so much leading us into the war that I care about; it's what he did after that. Wilson felt it was a priority to make sure that anything interfering with the war effort was stopped—including, unfortunately, those who disagreed with it. That's why, shortly after the war began, he pushed through the Espionage Act, a grotesque attack on free speech that made it a crime:

★ PRESIDENTIAL SMACKDOWN ★

Woodrow WILSON (2) vs. **Richard NIXON** (7)

WILSON
★ Imprisoned people for speaking against government
★ Thought the Constitution was outdated
★ Wrote in extremely boring fashion about ways to destroy all that our Founding Fathers designed

NIXON
★ Burglarized Democratic HQ
★ The only president to ever resign office
★ Most famous for saying "I'm not a crook"

RECAP: Nixon sneaks by because I'll take a crook over a dictator any day of the week and twice on Sunday.

WINNER: Nixon

"To convey false reports or false statements with intent to interfere with the operation or success of the military or naval forces of the United States or to promote the success of its enemies when the United States is at war, to cause or attempt to cause insubordination, disloyalty, mutiny, refusal of duty, in the military or naval forces of the United States, or to willfully obstruct the recruiting or enlistment service of the United States."

Clinton was the real first black president.

Violating that act was punishable by a maximum $10,000 fine (almost $170,000 in today's dollars) and 20 years in prison (almost 20 years in today's time). If it was in place during the Iraq War, every single person at *The New York Times* would probably be in jail or broke.

But Wilson didn't think that Act was restrictive enough, so he pushed through an amendment to it called The Sedition Act, which added this key clause:

A.D.D. MOMENT

Given the New York Times Company's current stock price, they might be broke anyway.

> *"And whoever, when the United States is at war, shall willfully utter, print, write, or publish any disloyal, profane, scurrilous, or abusive language about the form of government of the United States, or the military or naval forces of the United States, or the flag . . . or any language calculated to bring [any of those things] into contempt, scorn, contumely or disrepute, or shall willfully utter, print, write, or publish any language intended to incite, provoke or encourage resistance to the United States or to promote the cause of its enemies . . . shall be punished by a fine of not more than $10,000 or imprisonment of not more than twenty years, or both."*

A.D.D. MOMENT

If applied today, the Sedition Act would likely result in the lockup of every liberal blogger and commentator who ever opened his mouth during the past seven years.

Who's Making This Argument?

"Wilson's [great] reputation . . . was built on his destruction of America's cherished noninterventionist policy in his second term."

—*The Times* of London, which ranked Wilson as the 10th greatest U.S. president.

Notice the word "utter" is used several times. Wilson wasn't just concerned with the media, he was worried about private citizens "uttering" things in private conversations! I guess those of us who think that's an assault on free speech are just closed-minded idiots who don't see our nation as a "living thing." And to those modern-day progressives who are so keen to look back at Wilson with nostalgia, how do you feel knowing that if he were president in 2004 he probably would've wanted you serving 10 to 20 years in a federal prison?

Eugene Debs, who received a respectable number of votes as a Socialist candidate for president, saw firsthand that Wilson wasn't bluffing. On June 18, 1918, Debs gave a speech about the wonders of socialism. Just nine months later he was in prison—sentenced to ten years for committing "hate speech" crimes in violation of Wilson's Sedition Act.

The Sedition Act at first made it possible for the postmaster general to deny mail delivery to dissenters of government policy during wartime. How would Olbermann have survived without his monthly delivery of *Cosmogirl*?

THE COURTS WILL PROTECT OUR RIGHTS!

If your trust is in the Supreme Court to stand up for our Constitution, then it's in the wrong place. When a valid constitutional question was raised about the government's attempts to re-write law during the Chrysler/Fiat merger, they declined to hear the case. But that's not surprising, given the Court's reluctance to get involved even as our most basic rights are shredded.

In 1919, Supreme Court Justice Oliver Wendell Holmes, Jr., called all the commotion over the Court's unanimous ruling against Debs "a lot of jaw about free speech" and said, "If a man thinks that in time of war the right of free speech carries the right to impede by discourse the raising of armies [then he had] better not monkey with the buzzard."

The hate he was guilty of spewing: "Questioning America's entry into World War I."

Normal Aging   **Presidential Aging**

8 Years Later

A.D.D. MOMENT

Hey, Hillary, was this the "real American meaning" of progressivism you spoke about at the debate?

Anyone who's listened to me for more than five seconds knows that I hate almost everything socialists stand for, but who's worse: a socialist with strong principles but misguided policies, or a president who shreds our own Constitution by tossing people in jail who try to exercise the rights it grants them?

★ FRANKLIN DELANO ROOSEVELT ★

"HE WAS ELECTED FOUR TIMES, OBVIOUSLY HE WAS POPULAR!"

FDR is another president who is inexplicably ranked near the top of many "best presidents ever" polls. The fact that he is the only president to ever be elected four times is oft cited as proof of his popularity, and popularity, as we all know, always equals competence.

A.D.D. MOMENT

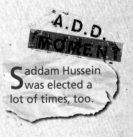

Saddam Hussein was elected a lot of times, too.

A.D.D. MoMent

Did I just use the word "oft"? Wow, I really need to stop reading history books.

The fact that FDR stayed in office for so long isn't proof of his massive popularity, it's proof of his massive ego. Worse, instead of using all of that time to change the country for the better, he used it to do more damage to the framework of America than any other president in history.

A.D.D. MOMENT

"The only thing we have to fear is fear itself . . . "

. . . and FDR serving a fifth term.

If FDR was so popular, then why did we ratify the Twenty-second Amendment, which limited future presidents to two four-year terms, so soon after finally getting FDR out of office? After all, if America had come away from FDR's terms thinking, "Man, that really worked out well!" then you'd think the country would've been in no mood for strict term limits.

I don't know this for a fact (I know, you're shocked), but President Obama's Chief of Staff Rahm Emanuel probably had a poster of FDR on his bedroom wall while growing up, because FDR was one of the first to realize that you should "never let a crisis go to waste." He used economic turmoil and war to make the case for a massive expansion of government and he used the Great Depression to make people believe that he was the *only one* who could solve America's problems when, in reality, he was only making them worse.

"THE COUNTRY WAS IN CRISIS—HE HAD TO DO SOMETHING!"

On March 4, 1933, Franklin D. Roosevelt won the election in a landslide. He took office with a lot of political capital, both houses of Congress under Democratic control, and an American public supportive of immediate action. So FDR delivered—promising a "New Deal" for Americans who couldn't stand another "four more years of the same failed Republican policies" that Harding, Coolidge, and Hoover had delivered for the last decade.

The Less You Know

A.D.D. MOMENT

Actually, that quote about failed policies is from Hillary Clinton in 2008 referring to George W. Bush . . . but really, what's the difference?

FDR ran his campaign on a familiar theme: hope, change, and blame. He blamed Hoover for the high unemployment rate (25 percent), for fostering the growth of greedy, out-of-control corporations, and for problems with regulation and oversight. He then made the case that the only solution to those problems was through a massive New Deal that would be implemented by the federal government.

Calling FDR's victory a "landslide" is like calling Karl Marx a "liberal"—it's an epic understatement. FDR won 472–59 in the Electoral College and 22.8 million to 15.7 million in the popular vote. Hoover won only five states, and you'll probably be shocked to learn which ones they were: Pennsylvania, Vermont, New Hampshire, Maine, and Connecticut. No, I'm not kidding.

HOPE & CHANGES

FDR's "mandate" resulted in the following terrific new federal agencies, administrations, authorities, and acts:

1933 – Emergency Banking Act
1933 – Economy Act
1933 – Civilian Conservation Corps (CCC)
1933 – Agriculture Adjustment Administration (AAA)
1933 – Tennessee Valley Authority (TVA)
1933 – National Industrial Recovery Act (NIRA) which created the NRA
1933 – National Recovery Administration (NRA)
1933 – Public Works Association (PWA)
1933 – Banking Act
1933 – Federal Emergency Relief Administration (FERA)
1933 – Home Owner's Loan Corporation – later Federal Housing Administration (FHA)
1933 – Civil Works Administration (CWA)
1933 – Frazier Lemke Farm Bankruptcy Act
1933 – Federal Securities Act
1933 – Glass-Steagall Act
1933 – Federal Deposit Insurance Corporation (FDIC)

1934 – National Housing Act
1934 – Securities and Exchange Act
1934 – Indian Reorganization Act of 1934
1934 – Home Owners Loan Corporation (HOLC)
1934 – Works Progress Administration (WPA)
1935 – National Youth Administration
1935 – Social Security Act (SSA)
1935 – National Labor Act (Wagner Act)
1935 – Public Utilities Holding Companies Act
1935 – Resettlement Administration Act
1935 – Rural Electrification Administration
1935 – Revenue Act
1936 – Soil Conservation and Domestic Allotment Act
1937 – Farm Security Administration (FSA)
1937 – National Housing Act
1938 – Second Agricultural Adjustment Act
1938 – Fair Labor Standards Act
1939 – Executive Reorganization Act

Oh, and it had to be done quickly.

Is any of this sounding familiar?

In his first hundred days in office, FDR created a whole bastion of new federal programs and signed at least 15 major pieces of legislation into law. Here's what all of that government spending bought us:

Unemployment during the New Deal and New Deal II:

1933: 24.9%	1935: 20.1%	1937: 14.3%
1934: 21.7%	1936: 16.9%	1938: 19.0%

AT LEAST HE WAS HONEST . . .

"Here is my principle: Taxes shall be levied according to ability to pay. That is the only American principle."

—Franklin Delano Roosevelt

It wasn't until America got thrust into war that the economy rebounded. FDR actually *prolonged* the Depression with his big government "solutions." (See our "Economics 101" chapter for a lot more on that.)

FDR was able to launch all of these hugely expensive projects despite the fact that, on the campaign trail, he had promised "a reduction in federal expenditures." It's a shame we didn't have MSNBCNNFOX back then or else that sound bite would now show up in the montages alongside "Read my lips," "I did not have sexual relations with that woman," "The British Government has learned that Saddam Hussein recently sought significant quantities of uranium from Africa," and the soon-to-be-forgotten-because-it-was-a-mistake-not-a-lie, "I can make a firm pledge: Under my plan, no family making less than $250,000 a year will see any form of tax increase."

GOVERNMENT IS GREAT!

"FDR DIDN'T WANT TO EXPAND GOVERNMENT SO MUCH, BUT THE DEPRESSION FORCED HIS HAND."

While the Depression provided a convenient excuse for FDR's actions, the truth is that he must not have been a very big fan of the Founding Fathers. What other reason could there be for all the do-overs? A "New Deal," a "Second New Deal," and then a *second* Bill of Rights? I mean, geez, why not just send another declaration to England apologizing how poorly worded the first one was?

Technically, yes, FDR was most likely an American citizen, but the stuff he proposed sounded more like entries from Karl Marx's diary. For example, in his 1944 State of the Union address he said:

> A.D.D. MOMENT
>
> How egotistical do you have to be to issue a "new" Bill of Rights? I mean, that'd be like trying to write a new version of *Common Sense*. Oh, wait a second . . .

"In our day these economic truths have become accepted as self-evident. We have accepted, so to speak, a second Bill of Rights under which a new basis of security and prosperity can be established for all—regardless of station, race, or creed. Among these are:

★ *The right to a useful and remunerative job in the industries or shops or farms or mines of the nation*

PROGRESSIVE MATCH GAME

Below is a quote from FDR's first Inaugural Address (one down, three to go!) . . . see how many progressive buzzwords and phrases you can identify.

"We now realize as we have never realized before our interdependence on each other; that we cannot merely take but we must give as well; that if we are to go forward, we must move as a trained and loyal army willing to sacrifice for the good of a common discipline, because without such discipline no progress is made, no leadership becomes effective. We are, I know, ready and willing to submit our lives and property to such discipline, because it makes possible a leadership which aims at a larger good."

Answer: Seven. ("interdependence," "must give," "willing to sacrifice," "common discipline," "progress is made," "submit our lives and property," "a larger good.")

- *The right to earn enough to provide adequate food and clothing and recreation*
- *The right of every farmer to raise and sell his products at a return which will give him and his family a decent living*
- *The right of every businessman, large and small, to trade in an atmosphere of freedom from unfair competition and domination by monopolies at home or abroad*
- *The right of every family to a decent home*
- *The right to adequate medical care and the opportunity to achieve and enjoy good health*
- *The right to adequate protection from the economic fears of old age, sickness, accident, and unemployment*
- *The right to a good education.*

While FDR was proposing all sorts of new rights for the needy, he was also making sure that he could pay for it all by taking the U.S. off of the "gold standard," thereby paving the way for trillions in debt to be racked up over the ensuing years. I guess "progress" isn't cheap.

That is typical socialist rhetoric that sounds good for the two seconds it takes before your brain starts to engage. So let's look at a few of those new "rights" a little more closely:

★ **The right to a useful job**—I thought the rights we fought for were "life, liberty, and the pursuit of happiness"? Maybe Jefferson just forgot to include "useful job" in there?

This is one of those "rights" that might feel good but that stands against everything a free-market system stands for. Is the owner of a coal mine supposed to hire every 400-pound fatty who shows up with his Second Bill of Rights in hand? Is a shop owner required to hire a person who can't communicate with customers because he or she doesn't speak English? If so, then what happens to these businesses? They suffer, profits decline, bankruptcies ensue, and more Americans are forced to go on the government dole—which is exactly what FDR was probably hoping for.

★ **The right to earn enough to provide adequate food and clothing and recreation**—If this one doesn't make you seethe inside, then you can't consider yourself a real lover of capitalism. What is the incentive to study and work hard when you know that you have a government-gifted right to not only earn enough for food and clothing, but also to pay for your entertainment?

The Only Right You Don't Have: Owning Gold

"All persons are hereby required to deliver on or before May 1, 1933, to a Federal Reserve Bank or a branch or agency thereof or to any member bank of the Federal Reserve System all gold coin, gold bullion and gold certificates now owned by them."

—Executive Order 6102, signed by FDR on April 5, 1933

Supporters of these rights will argue that as the richest nation on earth, we have a responsibility to help our poor. I couldn't agree more—and that's why we have Medicaid, Medicare, S-CHIP, welfare, food stamps, Section-8 housing, shelters, food kitchens, counseling, etc., etc. But taking the next step by making our government the grantor of rights takes America from being the land of opportunity to the land of guarantees.

★ *The right of every family to have a decent home*—We've tried really hard over the last couple of decades to make FDR's failed dream a reality, and I think we're now all seeing how that kind of thinking turns out.

Giving people something—whether it be clothing, recreation, or yes, a home—that's out of proportion with how hard they worked to get it is a recipe for disaster. While I happen to be against homelessness (I know, shocking), we have plenty of safety nets in place to help those who have fallen on truly hard times. In New York City, for example, no family who is in urgent need of shelter is denied it (unless they break a rule by being drunk or high). And while no one would ever consider a homeless shelter a "decent" home, I think it's fair to say that shelters and support services constitute fulfillment of the obligation to protect the poor and weakest.

★ PRESIDENTIAL SMACKDOWN ★

William TAFT (7) vs. **FDR** (1)

FDR
★ Raped the Constitution
★ Massive government expansion
★ Believed recreation was a "right"
★ Elected four times . . . in America

TAFT
★ Fattest president in history
★ Enjoyed doughnuts
★ Often got food stuck in his mustache

RECAP: Is there a better way to have the beloved-by-the-men-in-tweed-coats FDR get knocked out of the tournament than by the only president who actually needed an Oval office because he was so fat? Nope.

WINNER: Taft

Here's a great example of the government using tax dollars to provide an appropriate safety net. From the NYC Department of Homeless Services: "Drop-In (locations) provide hot meals, showers, laundry facilities, clothing, medical care, recreational space, employment referrals, and other social services. Staff can also help you find a safe and secure place to sleep. All Drop-Ins operate 24/7—so please come by."

A.D.D. Moment

But FDR couldn't have disagreed with that more. *"All of these rights spell security,"* he told Congress. *"And after this war is won we must be prepared to move forward, in the implementation of these rights, to new goals of human happiness and well-being. America's own rightful place in the world depends in large part upon how fully these and similar rights have been carried into practice for our citizens."*

At his 1944 inauguration (it must have been getting old by then—the fourth time is never the charm), FDR said, "People who are hungry and out of a job are the stuff of which dictatorships are made."

As usual, he was wrong. The truth is that presidents who overstay their welcome by convincing Americans that the man is more important than the office are the stuff of which dictatorships are made.

★ PROGRESSIVE ERA, ROUND TWO ★

"THE PROGRESSIVE ERA WAS JUST THAT: AN ERA. IT'S OVER. MOVE ON WITH YOUR LIFE, LOSER."

How I wish that were true. Unfortunately, if you look at the list of presidents since FDR, it would be easier to name the ones who *weren't* progressives. Let's see . . . there was Ronald Reagan and . . . well . . . uh . . . . honestly, I think Reagan was about it.

Over the years, it hasn't seemed to matter whether a Republican or Democrat was in office—the government just kept growing and growing. Very few presidents met an agency, department, or program that they didn't want to create or expand and our debates have become less about big vs. small government and more about obscenely large vs. really large government.

While it's true that some presidents embraced more progressive ideals than others, virtually all of them have relied on the infamous "greater good" argument to justify their expansions of government.

Lyndon B. Johnson's expansion of Medicare and his Head Start and Job Corps programs were all part of his "Great Society," which he described as "a place where men are more concerned with the quality of their goals than the quantity of their goods." Jimmy Carter's Department of Education was all about our collective interest in having the federal government get involved with our local schools. ("Education is our most important national investment," he wrote in the signing statement.) President Bush's Department of Home-

---

AT LEAST HE WAS HONEST . . .

"When you spread the wealth around, it's good for everybody."

—Barack Obama, responding to a question from Joe the Plumber, and sounding eerily reminiscent of FDR.

land Security was about our collective desire to be safe and secure, and his Medicare Part D (Prescription Drugs) bill was in response to our collective "obligation" to care for our seniors.

In fact, when President George W. Bush signed the bill that included Medicare Part D, a massive expansion of government that's added billions to our debt, he gave a quote that seemed to come right from the progressive handbook:

"Medicare is a great achievement of a compassionate government and it is a basic trust we honor," Bush said. "Each generation benefits from Medicare. Each generation has a duty to strengthen Medicare. And this generation is fulfilling our duty."

President Bush's expansion of government was historic, but his records won't last for long if President Obama has his way. While Bush may have been a progressive-lite, Obama is an extra-strength version: a president who seems to be willing to push the progressive agenda farther than most supporters could've ever fathomed.

Obama is rewriting America's future (and, in some cases, its Constitution as well), and he's doing it with blinding speed. Like Teddy Roosevelt, he seems to believe that wealth must

★PRESIDENTIAL SMACKDOWN★

Jimmy CARTER (7) vs. **Thomas JEFFERSON** (2)

CARTER
★ Destroyed U.S. economy
★ U.S. choppers burning in desert
★ Pummeled in reelection bid
★ Was a nice enough guy

JEFFERSON
★ Established West Point
★ Wrote the Declaration of Independence
★ Created the foundation for the greatest country in history

RECAP: Carter doesn't even belong in the top 32. It's an embarrassment to even mention Jefferson and Carter in the same set of encyclopedias, let alone the same sentence.

WINNER: Jefferson

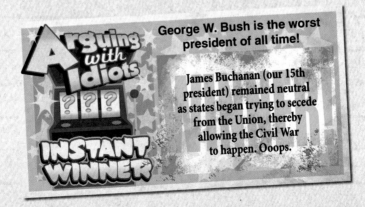

George W. Bush is the worst president of all time!

James Buchanan (our 15th president) remained neutral as states began trying to secede from the Union, thereby allowing the Civil War to happen. Ooops.

be "well used," like Woodrow Wilson he seems to believe in the idea that our Constitution is a "living" document, and, like FDR, he seems to believe in the right to health care, a good job, and a decent home. In other words, Obama is like a progressive Frankenstein—a president who's created out of the most grotesquely destructive policies of his predecessors.

There is at least one other unintended consequence to all of this. If Americans continue to embrace the New Progressive Era that President Obama seems so intent on ushering in, then likely it won't be long before we start renaming things in honor of our new national hero. That will not only take us even farther from the vision laid out by our Founders, but it will also make looking for directions a whole lot more complicated.

A.D.D. MOMENT

Any bets on how long it will be before President Obama mirrors FDR's belief that Americans have a right to adequate recreation? I'm really going to be angry if I have to start paying for someone's jet ski rental.

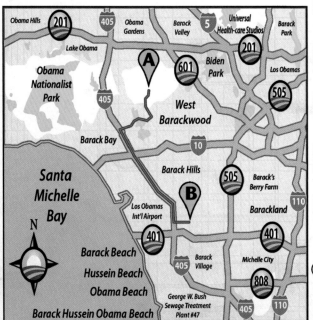

O-ogle MAPS

Directions from:
Obama Junior High
Barack Hills, OB 90210

Directions to:
Barack Hussein Obama Wax Museum
Barack Hills, OB 90250

19.3 mi - 33 mins - up to 55 mins in traffic

(A) Obama Junior High School
Barack Hills, OB 90210

1. Head **east** on **Obama Rd** toward **Obama Ct** — go 0.3 mi / total 0.3 mi

2. Turn **right** at **Obama Parkway** — go 1.0 mi / total 1.3 mi

3. Slight **right** on **Barack H. Obama Turnpike** — About 1 min — go 1.5 mi / total 2.8 mi

4. Turn **right** at **OB-2/Obama Hwy 101** — About 3 min — go 0.5 mi / total 3.3 mi

5. Slight **right** on **Barack Obama Expressway** — About 4 min — go 2.7 mi / total 6.0 mi

6. Slight **right** to merge onto **Obama 405 S** — About 2 min — go 11.2 mi / total 17.2 mi

7. Pay toll at **B.H.O. Fair Share Toll Booth** — About 2 min unless your annual income is more than $250k — go 0.2 mi / total 17.4 mi

8. Turn **left** at **Santa Michelle Blvd** — About 1 min — go 0.2 mi / total 17.6 mi

9. Turn **left** at **Barack Bay Pass** — About 3 min — go 1.1 mi / total 18.7 mi

10. Turn **right** at **OB-107/Obama Blvd** — About 1 min — go 0.3 mi / total 19.0 mi

11. Make a **U-turn** at **44th Barack Obama St** — Destination will be on your left — About 1 min — go 90 ft / total 19.1 mi

(B) Barack Hussein Obama Wax Museum
Barack Bay, OB 90250

 Carbon Tax: $35.08

These directions are for planning purposes only. Inflate tires to proper PSI. Do not drive with children 10 or under in your vehicle. Use hybrid or eco-friendly vehicles only. Pay carbon tax within 5 business days.

UNIVERSAL HEALTH CARE

Why a Paper Cut May Soon Be Fatal

PICKING UP women at a trendy South Beach nightclub and debating health care . . . two times when it's more difficult to be a conservative than a liberal.

Unless it's articulated properly, the conservative argument on health care tends to come off as though you don't care about children. When articulated poorly, it comes off like you want children to die. Either way, it isn't exactly the quickest path to popularity.

On the other hand, the liberal position on health care comes off as the best thing to be created since the Creator started creating. It heals the sick! It lifts the poor from poverty! It's like a governmental Moses parting the Red Sea . . . only without all that religion stuff.

A.D.D. Moment

As far as conservatives' luck at dance clubs goes, I've found that attractive women don't generally talk to guys whose "game" includes chit-chat about more restrictive tort reform. But that's another chapter for another book.

Even when conservatives are somehow successful and actually stop the creation of another ineffective government behemoth, the fight still isn't over. Given enough time, there's always someone else who will step up to the table and argue that we need another new and giant government something or other. It's like a game of multitrillion-dollar whack-a-mole.

To illustrate what I mean, look at this beautiful mountainside . . .

Let's say that there's agreement on both sides of the aisle that not enough people are willing to trek down an endless dirt road and hike for half an hour just to take in this spectacular view.

Conservative politicians suggest allowing a private company to come in, pave the road, add a viewing platform, and make the location more accessible to tourists. Liberals go the other way. They argue that there is a massive problem with the *mountain itself*. More people would surely come, they argue, if we just made the mountainside look like this . . .

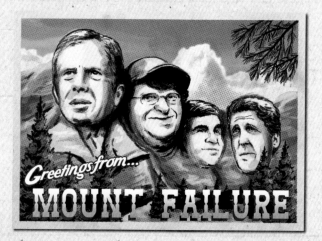

If conservatives somehow win the argument over Mount Rushmore II, the mountainside gets a few intelligent, low-cost, targeted improvements. But, in a few years, everyone forgets the logic behind those decisions and another idiot shows up and suggests yet another massive overhaul that conservatives will once again try to stop.

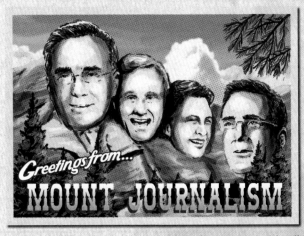

MOUNT JOURNALISM TOURIST FACT: To artistically express Keith Olbermann's ego and complete awesomeness, his head appears twice.

On the other hand, if liberals win the argument over Mount Rushmore II, the mountain gets carved, leaving Jimmy Carter or Keith Olbermann's giant skull to creepily stare down on tourists for all eternity. We wind up spending infinitely more money, and we're worse off than we were before.

Republicans in Congress need to remember one simple rule, a rule that George W. Bush forgot when pushing through Medicare Part D (aka "The Prescription Drug Plan," "The Largest New Entitlement Since the Great Society," or "The Biggest Nail in the Coffin of Bush's Fiscal Conservatism"): Once Mount Rushmore II is carved, it can never be un-carved. Put simply, it's easier to *do* something than it is to *un-do* it.

The Jimmy Carter head that's entirely made of stone in this illustration is actually more intelligent than the original.

Universal health care is the ultimate un-carvable mountain.

I know Americans generally have pretty short memories, but didn't conservatives already win this argument back in the '90s? Didn't we decide *not* to do it? Hillary Clinton? France? "You don't want the same people who run the post office cutting your chest open for an angioplasty"? Hello? Doesn't *anyone* else remember all of this?

A.D.D. MOMENT

Maybe instead of engaging in another debate we should just adopt the Al Gore philosophy of yelling "the debate is over" and see how that works out.

A little over a decade later, an issue that used to be a national embarrassment for the Democratic Party has been transformed into one that every major presidential candidate made part of their platform. In fact, the very same person who blew it with health care in the '90s came within one Barackstar of being president. Even Mitt Romney, the top choice of many conservatives in 2008, enacted a version of universal health care in Massachusetts when he was governor.

So here we stand: a new decade, a new president, same old debate over universal health care. For those who missed all of this the first time around, let's start at the beginning . . . again, by taking on idiotic arguments, like . . .

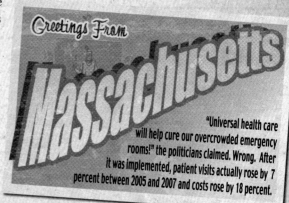

Greetings From **Massachusetts**

"Universal health care will help cure our overcrowded emergency rooms!" the politicians claimed. Wrong. After it was implemented, patient visits actually rose by 7 percent between 2005 and 2007 and costs rose by 18 percent.

"AS THE RICHEST COUNTRY IN THE WORLD, HOW CAN WE ACCEPT THAT 46 MILLION HARDWORKING AMERICANS ARE UNINSURED? IT'S A DISGRACE."

The claim that "we're the richest country in the world" is typically left unchallenged. Sure, America is relatively well off, no one is arguing that, but this claim is specifically designed to make you believe that "we're so rich, we can afford to spend a lot more." Unfortunately, that's not even remotely close to true. If your neighbor has a Porsche in the driveway of his McMansion, but can't pay any of his bills—is he really the richest guy in the neighborhood? It's not that we have *no* money as a nation—it's that we have *less than no money* as a nation—and it's only getting worse. Our balance sheet is deteriorating almost as quickly as NBC News' credibility.

Almost. **A.D.D. MOMENT**

To go back to our McMansion-Man analogy, adopting universal health care now would be like our bankrupt Porsche-owning neighbor pulling out his Capital One card and booking a monthlong excursion to Fiji. We don't have the money for a trip to Fiji. We don't even have the money for a bottle of Fiji *water*. I can promise you that we definitely don't have the money for universal health care.

**A.D.D.
Moment**

Since the economy has been just a little unstable recently, I'm hoping that Fiji water will retroactively compensate me for that very subtle mention of their product. Fiji, contact me at: me@glennbeck.com if you want to talk terms. Same address if you represent Capital One, Porsche, or Jimmy Carter.

Fortunately, it's not all bad news. Our health-care system is actually much healthier than the media and some politicians would have you believe. Their claim about the number of uninsured is about as inflated as my stomach in a hotel room when someone else is paying for room service.

The figure "46 million uninsured" is a marquee argument for those advocating more government control of our health care. But, if you know the facts, it's apparent that they are using that exaggerated, headline-grabbing number as a way to get America to spend tens of billions of dollars on a new entitlement for people who aren't entitled to anything.

To illustrate what I mean, let's break down the 46 million into a few different groups. First, about 10 million of the uninsured are illegal aliens or other noncitizens who likely wouldn't even qualify for "universal health care" if we had it.

> ## Who's Making This Argument?
>
> *"The problem keeps getting worse. Health-care costs are rising fast as the number of those who lack insurance, pegged by the Census at 46 million in 2007, is swelling."*
> —USA Today, May 31, 2009

"HI, MY DADDY MAKES SIX MILLION DOLLARS A YEAR AND YOU'RE PAYING FOR MY COUGH MEDICINE!"

That leaves us with around 36 million uninsured left— which is still a large group, but this is where the general concept of personal responsibility comes in. About 18 million people without insurance have a household income of over $50,000 per year. More than half of them have a household income of over $75,000 a year—certainly enough to afford health insurance if it were a top priority for them. (You can bet that very few of those people go without a cell phone, cable or satellite television, and/or a high-speed internet connection.) But isn't that their choice? Until the government runs our lives like we're a car company in decline, they shouldn't be able to examine our budget line by line and tell us how to spend our money.

> In their infinite wisdom, government subsidizes care even for the wealthy through various entitlement programs. In fact, they encourage the practice. Why else would states like Pennsylvania be running commercials that inform parents "No family makes too much money for low-cost CHIP [Children's Health Insurance Program], so apply today. Don't think you make too little or too much."

Most rational people will argue that they aren't looking to give their tax dollars to non-citizens and people making over $75,000 a year—they just want to help Americans who really need it. Can't the government get involved to support people like that?

Well, they sure can. And they sure do. In the supposedly free-market world of American health insurance, 83 million people already benefit from some sort of government health care. Think about that. While we were looking the other way arguing the pros and cons of government health care, close to 30 percent of our country is already living under it! In addition, another 14 million of America's "uninsured" already qualify for government insurance; they just haven't applied for it yet.

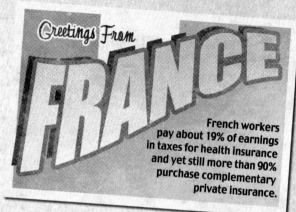

Greetings From FRANCE

French workers pay about 19% of earnings in taxes for health insurance and yet still more than 90% purchase complementary private insurance.

That brings our original group of 46 million down dramatically, although it's impossible to know exactly how far because there are overlaps between the categories and different studies measure different things. In this country, you can be sure there are at least a few illegal immigrants who make over $75,000 and still qualify for government assistance.

The real size of the group that is chronically uninsured is likely in the area of three percent of our population. Still too large? Of course, but it's vastly smaller than the number portrayed by the media, which routinely quotes "experts" who refer to the problem as "worse than an epidemic."

Our health-care system is far from perfect. But when politicians yell "46 million!" without context, they do it for only one reason: to make you think about a gigantic group of nameless, faceless Americans and ignore all of the subtleties that make their claim ridiculous. That way, you'll feel like it's not only a problem, but also one that only the government can solve.

That makes universal health care the perfect issue for those who want to grow the government. It relies on compassion, has billions of dollars at stake, and is the last great issue standing in the way of all Americans, regardless of economic status, becoming reliant on Washington. After all, once you give the government control over whether your heart is beating or not, you're destined to also become dependent on them for just about everything else.

"FINE, BUT WHETHER IT'S 46 MILLION OR JUST 46, NO ONE SHOULD BE WITHOUT HEALTH CARE FOR EVEN ONE DAY!"

I agree with you on principle, but it's hard to have an honest debate on this topic when people are so intent on manipulating the numbers for their own benefit. For example, let's assume that you have health insurance through your job. One day you hit the lottery for $300 million

THE ADVOCACY GROUP "FAMILIES USA" RELEASED A STUDY THAT PURPORTEDLY REVEALED THAT ONE OF EVERY THREE AMERICANS, ALMOST 90 MILLION PEOPLE, ARE UNINSURED. THEY ILLUSTRATED THIS ON THE COVER OF THE REPORT BY SHOWING ONE OF EVERY THREE CARTOON PEOPLE FALLING INTO A BLACK HOLE OF EMPTINESS. WHILE THE REPORT FAILED TO USHER IN THE MEDIA HYSTERIA IT PROBABLY HOPED FOR, IT DIDN'T FAIL IN SUCCESSFULLY RESHAPING THE DATA TO SUIT THEIR NEEDS. SO, HOW'D THEY DO IT? HERE'S A QUICK OVERVIEW . . .

How to Build a Headline for the Media!

VOL.CLVIV ...No.65,275   NEW YORK, SATURDAY JULY 4, 2009 $19.25

TURN 3% INTO 33% IN 4 EASY STEPS!

Step 1: Ignore! Shut off all communication between anyone pointing out problems with the standard measures of calculating the uninsured (like their income level and citizenship).

Step 2: Shorten! Instead of counting only people who were without insurance for a significant amount of time, count everyone who lost insurance for even a few weeks.

Step 3: Lengthen! Instead of looking only at one year, double it! More time—more people!

Step 4: Erase! Remove everyone 65 and older from the study as though they don't exist. Why? Well, because they're all covered already! That's no fun!

and quit. While you're waiting for the first lotto check to cash (so you can waste your money on something that will later make you the subject of a Conan O'Brien monologue), you let your insurance lapse for a month. Then, once the check clears, you buy the greatest health-insurance policy in human history. Given that scenario, how do you think you should get categorized?

Well, if it's up to the major advocacy groups (you know, the ones the media loves to quote), you're now one of the "millions of uninsured" in America.

More than half of those who are considered to be "uninsured" are in that state for less than a year as they move between jobs or deal with other temporary changes in their lives. Yes, that opens them up to a short period of risk, but the overwhelming majority of those people are lucky enough to avoid falling off a roller coaster or picking up a nasty case of the rickets over that period.

Insurance is supposed to manage risk, but different people have different ideas about how much of it they are willing to take on at any given point in time. Close to two-thirds of uninsured Americans are between the ages of 18 and 34. They're overwhelmingly young, healthy people who have consciously decided that it's worth the relatively small chance that they get very sick. Many also figure, correctly or not, that they have their parents to back them up in case the worst-case scenario becomes the real-life scenario. As you would expect, most of them are simply playing the odds—and they usually win.

"BUT THEY'RE GAMBLING BECAUSE INSURANCE IS TOO EXPENSIVE!"

Blue Cross/Blue Shield, Aetna, Humana, and many other insurers offer basic youth-oriented health-insurance plans for around $50 a month, depending on your home state. (Don't get me started on the ridiculous restrictions on buying across state lines. Eliminating those would go a long way toward ending these problems.)

You can do even better on price if you're a full-time student. Rates on those plans are often lower than the average cell-phone plan (and the difference is even more dramatic once you factor in ringtone downloads).

This is all part of the idiocy that is the idea of universal health care. When you give "free" insurance to someone who can afford it, but who instead chooses to spend their money on other things, you are in effect paying for those *other things*. I refuse to have our government

ALTERNATE BIPARTISAN PUNCH LINES

Instead of "National Endowment for the Arts," how about:

Libertarians: *See:* Everything that we've ever spent any money on.

Democrats: *See:* The war in Iraq that we were duped into voting for! He lied, they died!

Communists: All money is government money. There is no joke here.

subsidize anyone's Pussycat Dolls ringtone . . . although that wouldn't be the worst way the federal government has ever spent money. (For that see: National Endowment for the Arts.)

We all know by now that just one person who can't get access to health care is too many, but, outside of a complete government takeover, there is no way to get *everyone* covered—it's just not practical. Remember, about 15 percent of drivers have no auto insurance despite the fact that it is required in 48 states and costs less than health insurance, and despite the fact that jail time is a possible punishment.

"WE SHOULD HAVE HEALTH CARE THAT'S AT LEAST AS GOOD AS THE UK'S! THE ONLY WAY TO GET THERE IS THROUGH UNIVERSAL GOVERNMENT HEALTH CARE."

Flying in the face of all facts and evidence, some will still claim that the government is capable of doing . . . well, anything correctly. What government service are people truly happy with? Is it the never-ending road construction, the thousands of pages of tax code, the tens of trillions of dollars in debt, or the peachy demeanor of the average DMV or USPS employee? I know it's a cliché, but where does anyone get the idiotic idea that government could run health care better than anything else it already runs?

Perhaps it's the American spirit of optimism. We are the people who faced the Rocky Mountains with nothing but horses, carriages, and extra-long old-timey beards and said, "Let's see what's on the other side."

A.D.D. MOMENT

After we found out what was on the other side of the Rockies, we came back, grabbed a cable car to the top, and strapped a couple of boards to our feet so we could go back down for fun.

For better or worse, Americans believe we can accomplish anything, apparently including expecting competent surgery from a multilayered bureaucracy related to the same people who made me wade through two years of paperwork just to build a fence around my own yard.

My pessimistic side (yes, it's true, I have one!) tells me that this country, founded by people who risked sailing off the end of the earth just to have the right to hold their destiny in their own hands, has transformed itself into a nation of people who think they now need a government forklift to hold their destiny for them.

That worries me a lot, but maybe it's why so many people are willing to overlook the embarrassing failures around the world of universal government health care. The next time someone tries to claim that the grass is greener across the pond, ask them if they're ready to import any of these classics from universal health care in the UK.

Greetings From **ITALY**

Need a mammogram?
You'll be able to get plenty done in the meantime—the average wait is 70 days.

Remember, the UK isn't some poor incompetent country filled with maniacal so-cialists. While they're farther down the road than we are, they still share many of our same values, strengths, and weaknesses—and they have the fifth-largest economy on earth.

The wonderful world of "patient stacking"

Wait times in emergency rooms were so long that the government created a target mandating that patients be seen in less than *four hours.*

Close your eyes for a second and just imagine the convenience of being able to see a doctor in about the time it takes to watch the Super Bowl (including the halftime and pregame shows). Ahh, dare to dream. Of course, mandate or not, the government *still* couldn't hit those embarrassingly feeble targets. So now, tens of thousands of people who call the equivalent of 911 are held out-side the hospital in a parked ambulance, sometimes for five hours or more, before being let into the emergency room. Why? Because the government-mandated four-hour clock doesn't officially start until they actually come through the doors.

It's a clever way to cheat the system, but while ambulances sit idling (global-warming activists beware, universal health care is killing the environment!), they're unable to go pick up some other poor schlub who really needs it. Of course, since the patient would be going to a government hospital anyway, it might be better for them to roll the dice with Web MD, some vodka, and a dirty steak knife.

GOVERNMENT IS GREAT!

You have to appreciate the irony of the government artificially creating a problem and then trying to solve it through even more regulations. It'd be like them installing a single toll booth on a major highway and then, when traffic backs up, mandating that all cars must get through it in 30 minutes. Huh? Why not just get rid of the toll booth?

When hospitals resemble amusement parks

The four-hour-emergency-room target led to patients' starting to feel like they were at a really boring government version of a Six Flags amusement park. When you get in line for the newest, most-hyped roller coaster, you inevitably stand for hours in an everlasting snaking line of sweaty tourists before finally approaching what you think is the finish line. But when you walk into that room you realize that it's just *another* everlasting line snaking through even more sweaty over-weight tourists wearing spandex, fanny packs, and Crocs.

Senator Harry Reid recently complained, "In the summer-time, because [of] the high humidity and how hot it gets here, you could literally smell the tourists coming into the Capitol." While I'm sure he's right—people do stink—the stench can't possibly approach the job he's doing as Senate majority leader. Hey, Harry, how about getting your approval rating higher than the speed limit in most cul-de-sacs before complaining about the odor of the people who employ you?

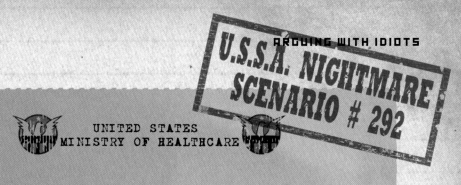

**UNITED STATES
MINISTRY OF HEALTHCARE**

To: Mr. Glenn Beck
REALID#: 392011039100229RW-223

Dear Mr. Beck:

According to the results of your last mandatory annual physical submitted to us by your Assigned Physician, you have a BMI of 28.2, total cholesterol of 214 and a suspicious looking mole on your upper back.

All of this is cause for concern. Both your BMI and cholesterol readings exceed U.S. guidelines established by the HealthFirst! Act. As such, you are placing an unnecessary burden on our nation's system of universal coverage.

These ratings must be brought to the levels indicated in the enclosed document (DUHC-Form 117) within 90 days from receipt of this letter or you may be subject to additional tax obligations, penalties, and dietary restrictions.

In addition, your mole must be biopsied. Please find your appointment information on the summons below.

Thank you for your attention to this matter. Remember, good health is patriotic!

R.Simmons
U.S. Healthcare Czar

Official Summons

You are required to appear at:

48 West 59th Street, Suite 909, on February 23, 2016

Your appointment will take place between 10am and 4pm. You may bring in lunch so long as it complies with regulation 2087.2a "Foods allowable in federal buildings."

That's basically what was happening in UK emergency rooms. To hit their targets, hospitals were waiting until just before the four-hour deadline was up before admitting patients, only to then make them suffer through another interminable wait once inside. Problem solved! The effect was the government target being hit, but without an actual improvement in quality of care, and at ten times the cost.

This scheme worked especially well in combination with another government incentive that offered hospitals close to $1,000 for every patient admitted. Hospitals smartly figured, "Why treat patients without admitting them when we can walk them a few feet down the hall and get some free government cash?"

The result was that patients who didn't even need hospital admission were admitted anyway (and usually released the same day), making wait times worse for people who really did need it. Only in the world of government could we figure out a way to actually pay people more for worse service.

Dirty laundry about dirty laundry

At Good Hope, a government-run hospital in the UK, members of the housekeeping staff were reminded that washing bedsheets would cost 0.275 pence each (about 40 cents). Their solution? Don't wash the sheets in between visitors, just turn them over! Surely, those killer bacteria could never find their way all the way through the cotton!

This policy was implemented soon after another government-run hospital found itself in trouble for sending a memo to the staff about saving $5 per day by "prescribing cheaper medicines, reducing the number of sterile packs used, cutting hospital tests and asking patients to bring drugs in from home."

A.D.D. moment

On a positive note, this marked the first time in recorded history that a government program tried to *save* money.

Like pulling teeth to get teeth pulled

How bad is dental insurance in the UK? Almost half of dentists say that they won't accept any patients using government health care. That has led to about 1 in 5 people deciding against getting *any* dental care because the cost is so high (wasn't it supposed to be free?). Six percent of patients have even resorted to "self-treatment," like pulling their own teeth and using superglue to reattach crowns.

Based on dismal scenarios like these, the government negotiated new contracts with dentists to improve dental care and make it more available. The result? Fifty-eight percent said the changes made care *worse*, and 84 percent said it didn't get any easier to find a dentist. The truth is that dental coverage in the UK is an absolute, complete disaster. You can judge that by the statistics, or by a less scientific but just as effective method: their smiles.

Waiting times for operations are "shorter than ever"!

This quote, from a self-congratulatory 2006 government press release, was unsurprisingly optimistic. It was the result of yet another grand government target promising that you would be able to get that surgery you need within—wait for it . . . just six months! It's like a big twenty-six-week hug from the government!

While this target did help some of those who were waiting *several years* for surgeries, it actually made the delays for the typical person even longer. Across the board, wait times increased by about 20 percent, with waits for certain types of care, such as orthopedics, increasing by 143 percent. Given that result, perhaps a more accurate press release from the government might have been: "We've reduced waiting times for some procedures from several years to a half a year, while making almost everyone else wait longer! And if you need a new hip—wow, are you screwed."

NICE: Not So Nice

NICE, or the National Institute for Health and Clinical Excellence, is quite possibly the most misleading acronym in world history. Why? Because it's their job to let you know if your life is worth living. I don't mean that in some ethereal "meaning of the universe" sort of way, I mean it in actual dollars and cents (i.e., How much currency is it worth to keep you alive?). The idea that our system is portrayed as brutally cold and uncaring is laughable when you look at what citizens of the UK are forced to deal with.

NICE has been around for ten years and its target mission has always been front and center: to develop what *The New York Times* calls a "standard method of rationing." That standard method has concluded that if you have breast cancer, the drug Tykerb, which has been shown in clinical tests to delay the progression of the disease, is worth more than your life.

In fact, so is the average two-bedroom apartment in Manhattan.

Newspapers in the UK are littered with similar stories of drugs and treatments deemed too pricey to extend life. Yet, somehow NICE isn't seen as an embarrassment to the UK, it's actually the envy of the world! Top health officials from around the globe closely watch the decisions and mimic the procedures of NICE.

A.D.D. MOMENT

Another candidate for the worst acronym in world history is the: Hebrew Institute of Tolerance, Learning, Excellence, and Respect.

Congratulations!
You're worth less than an apartment!

	$5K
	$4K
	$3K
	$2K
	$1K
	$0

Average monthly rent for a 2Br doorman apartment:	What your life is worth to NICE:
$5,129[1]	**$3,792**[2]

[1] Monthly Rent in Manhattan   [2] Allowable monthly treatment cost.

While all of this UK bashing might make us feel good, it's important to remember that we aren't doing much better. Take Medicare, for instance. After a New York investigator discovered millions of dollars in false state Medicare claims (for such things as pregnancy treatments for men, 450 fake eyeballs for people who didn't need them, and medicine for people who were already dead), she unleashed a quote that can be found only in the world of government-run health care:

"It just seems to me that a pharmacist should know if his patient is dead or not. There are a lot of patients in New York who are getting treated when they're dead."

Former Senate Majority Leader Tom Daschle praised many NICE-ish policies in his 2008 book *Critical: What We Can Do About the Health-Care Crisis*. He advocated the creation of a "super board" to tell doctors how they should and should not be treating you. "In choosing what it will cover and how much it will pay," Daschle wrote that this "super board" of "government experts" "could steer providers to the services that are the most clinically valuable and cost-effective, and dissuade them from wasting time and money on those that are neither." That sounds totally different from the framework that leads to rationing expensive and experimental care, doesn't it?

Greetings From GREAT BRITAIN

About 20 percent of patients with treatable colon cancer at the time of discovery are considered incurable by the time treatment is finally available.

Daschle further explained: "The federal government could exert tremendous leverage with its decisions on covered benefits and payment incentives." If you're wondering what it's like to be on the wrong side of a government version of "tremendous leverage" backed up with "payment incentives," then just ask Rick Wagoner, who, thanks to the administration, is now the *former* CEO of General Motors.

And if you think that all of these ideas from Daschle are too radical to ever work their way into our system, then just remember that Daschle was Barack Obama's first choice as secretary of Health and Human Services.

But while the antics of Obama/Daschle may not surprise you, this might: the government has already tried to implement many of NICE's policies—and it happened under a president with an "(R)" after his name.

Dr. Sean Tunis, who served as the Chief Medical Officer of the Center for Medicare and Medicaid Services under George W. Bush, said he spent a lot of his time in government "learning about NICE and trying to adopt the processes and mechanisms they used, and we just couldn't."

While we've looked at the UK for problems, it's also important to listen to those who live there for solutions. Daniel Hannan, a British politician, made a three-minute speech excoriat-

While Barack Obama says he supports a massively increased role for government in health care, he still seems to stop short of a total takeover. But if you listen to Obama's occasionally candid words (before becoming president) on what his long-term plans really are, it becomes clear that this is nothing more than a pit stop.

★ "If I were designing a system from scratch, then I'd probably set up the single-payer system [but] making that transition in a rapid way, I think would be very difficult."

★ "There was a lot of resistance to a single-payer system . . . Over time it may be that we end up transitioning to such a system. For now, I just want to make sure every American is covered . . . I don't want to wait for that perfect system."

★ "I happen to be a proponent of the single-payer universal-health-care plan . . . That's what I'd like to see. But as all of you know, we may not get there immediately because first we have to take back the White House and we have to take back the Senate and we have to take back the House."

Check. Check. Check.

ing Prime Minister Gordon Brown over the ridiculous amounts of debt that his country had acquired in their attempt to solve their spending problems with more spending. While the British press largely ignored it, the video went viral and, in just one day, became the most watched video in the country. A few days later I invited Hannan, who isn't exactly a tool of the right—he supported Barack Obama for president and opposed the Iraq War—on my radio program.

"You should learn from our mistakes," Hannan told my audience. "I mean, the single biggest area where I could see you making this mistake is on this thing of the nationalized health-care system. I mean, I hope that sanity is going to prevail. I know it's been kicked around before and it hasn't happened. I love my country even more than I love yours, you know, but God, I would love to get rid of our system and have something that puts patients in charge rather than putting doctors' unions and bureaucrats in charge. That's the single biggest thing."

Plus, he said it in an English accent. So it sounded even cooler than it reads.

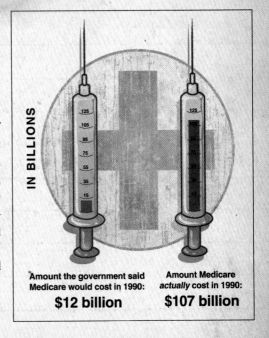

IN BILLIONS

Amount the government said Medicare would cost in 1990:

$12 billion

Amount Medicare *actually* cost in 1990:

$107 billion

"WELL, IF THE UK ISN'T THE MODEL TO FOLLOW, THEN MAYBE WE SHOULD LOOK TOWARD CUBA. MICHAEL MOORE PROVED ONCE AND FOR ALL THAT EVEN THEY OUTPERFORM US!"

O f the six biggest* documentaries of all time, one of them features Al Gore, one of them features penguins marching, and three of them feature Michael Moore.

Moore has become the largest figure in the genre* and his influence on idiots in this country cannot be understated. While his movie *Sicko* was somewhat of a disappointment commercially, it included almost every tired argument about health care that's ever been made. So let's go through a few of them one by one:

MOORE: "The United States slipped to number thirty-seven in health care around the world, just slightly ahead of Slovenia."

A s Moore says this line in the movie, a graphic pops up on the screen showing the United States just one slot ahead of the happy-fun-land of Slovenia, and two slots above the island paradise of Cuba. Seemingly damning evidence of our disastrous health-care system, right?

Wrong—because what Moore doesn't tell the audience is where those statistics come from, and, more important, how they're calculated. The truth is that Moore's prized statistics come from an all-time favorite media source: the report card of the best health-care systems in the world, dutifully delivered on a silver platter by the World Health Organization/United Nations.

You might be thinking that the U.N. isn't exactly a fair arbiter of the policies of the United States . . . and you'd be right—but it's actually much worse than that. They admit their data has been (and this is a direct quote, though I didn't see it used in the movie) "hampered by the weakness of routine information systems and insufficient attention to research." At times when good numbers weren't available, they "developed [data] through a variety of techniques."

Mostly though, they just blindly accepted what governments all around the world told them, including the always reliable Castro regime in Cuba. I guess the U.N. thinks that the best place to get good information on the likelihood of drug addiction is from a pamphlet given to you by a crack dealer.

I pray they didn't forget to stuff the crust.*

T his man should not be making movies about health care.

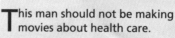

*None of these are fat jokes. All just terrible coincidences.

The WHO/U.N. study is little more than a political how-to guide on the best way to run the most U.N.-like government. For example, the U.S. gets punished in the study for not having a progressive enough tax system. What does that have to do with health care?

The most damaging category that contributes to America's overall ranking is our 54th-place finish in the oh-so-objective category of "fairness," something they define as "the smallest feasible differences among individuals and groups."

To truly understand the absurdity of that definition, consider this scenario: Let's say you have two patients (one rich and one poor) who can be cured only by an expensive or experimental treatment. By the U.N.'s standard, a country that lets both patients die is superior to one that manages to keep one alive.

> **A.D.D. MOMENT**
>
> After this, some accused Michael Moore of being a tool of Cuban propaganda (I accuse him of just being a tool in general). I'm pretty sure they're right, but doesn't that make the U.N. one also?

A.D.D. Moment

I'm sure the United Nations' opinion of what constitutes fairness is completely rational and consistent with American values. After all, any organization that gives Russia and China lifetime privileges to unilaterally veto anything they want should always be trusted.

What the U.N. sees as so undesirable and unfair actually works fairly well. In America, rich people could likely buy whatever treatment they need. Those who aren't rich still have lots of options: They can get a loan, ask family members or charities for assistance, or they can search for a doctor or company willing to work with them at a reduced rate. Those scenarios are all quite common in America.

Over time, the rich people end up subsidizing the majority of the research and development costs by paying big fees early on. Companies are then able to make profits, which brings prices down and makes that treatment more affordable for everyone (including the socialist countries that wouldn't pay for it before).

It's not perfect, nothing is—but it's a lot better than the U.N.'s way of thinking, which would result in a country like the United States ranking behind an entire nation filled with doctors who act like Jason Voorhees and murder each patient with a machete whenever they schedule an appointment. "Sure, all patients are brutally slaughtered, but at least everyone is treated equally!"

> ### Who's Making This Argument?
>
> It's not just Michael Moore who loves to cite the anti-American WHO/U.N. report. Everyone from New Jersey governor Jon Corzine, to Tom Daschle, NPR, CNN, *The New York Times*, and the *San Francisco Chronicle* has relied on that biased report to substantiate their calls for urgent action.

The report claims there are only two ways to achieve their version of "fairness":

1. "The healthy subsidize those who are sick." This is, of course, a basic tenet of health insurance.

2. "The rich subsidize those who are poor." This is, of course, a basic tenet of socialism. Thus, Michael Moore and others use a study that *requires* socialism to have a good health-care system to prove that socialists have good health-care systems. It's like citing a report done by Burger King on hamburger quality that heavily depends on such objective measures as "Prominence of Flame Broiling." My guess is that McDonald's wouldn't do that well.

How did the WHO/U.N. come up with how the "fairness" category would be figured? Simple . . . they asked *themselves*. Here's how they explain it: "To derive a set of weights for the different achievements that compose overall attainment, WHO conducted a survey of 1,006 respondents from 125 countries, half from among its own staff."

After the survey was "checked for consistency and bias," the U.N. then came up with a set of measures that put 62.5 percent of the weight of the *entire study* on some type of "equality" (as defined by, you guessed it . . . the U.N.). Knowing the U.N. like we do, does that really sound like a recipe for an honest critique of the U.S. health-care system?

A.D.D. MOMENT

To translate: "How did we at Burger King come up with the category of 'Prominence of Flame Broiling'? We asked our own employees!"

A.D.D. MOMENT

Knowing Michael Moore like we do, does *Sicko* seem like it would be an honest critique of the U.S. health-care system?

But the WHO/U.N. doesn't *just* care about who has appropriately high taxes or whose system is the most socialized—they have other goals as well: "*better health*" (nice of them to include that) and "*responsiveness to people's expectations in regard to non-health matters.*" (Huh?)

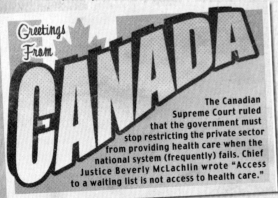

Greetings From CANADA

The Canadian Supreme Court ruled that the government must stop restricting the private sector from providing health care when the national system (frequently) fails. Chief Justice Beverly McLachlin wrote "Access to a waiting list is not access to health care."

The study reports that "several poor African and Asian countries rank fairly high on the level of responsiveness [to people's expectations]." I assume they mean that doctors respond to patients right away to tell them that they're screwed.

MOORE: "All independent health organizations in the world, and even our own CIA, believes that the Cubans have a pretty good health system. And they do, in fact, live longer than we do."

The climax of *Sicko* shows Michael Moore defying the laws of physics by remaining afloat in a boat to Cuba* as he accompanies 9/11 rescue workers who, he says, need health care and are unable to afford it in the United States.

*None of these are fat jokes. All just terrible coincidences.

While his actual point is ridiculous (see below), he does prove one important thing: A liberal filmmaker who brings a camera crew into a communist country with the intent to show that they are superior to the United States has a reasonably good chance of getting halfway decent health care. Shocking, I know. Fortunately, the idea that Cuba was giving an accurate picture of how the average Cuban is treated isn't taken seriously by anyone.

Except for those who really want to believe it's true . . . like Michael Moore. He told ABC's John Stossel, "I asked them to give us the same exact care they give their fellow Cuban citizens. No more, no less. And that's what they did."

Moore's stunt could be dismissed as a humorous attempt at exaggerating a point, except for one thing: He's not joking. In interview after interview he's made specific statements trying to back up the claims in his movie. For example, Moore has said that the CIA agrees with him. He couldn't be lying about that, right? *Riiiiiight?*

Well, unfortunately for Mike, the CIA isn't some mythical organization from another dimension that sends statistics about health care through secret telepathy. In fact, if you want to know their opinion, you can just ask them—which is exactly what *20/20* did after hearing Moore's claims. The CIA's response? "We don't say that Cuba has a pretty good system or that Cubans live longer than Americans."

I wish they would be a little less ambiguous. Maybe Moore was talking about a different CIA . . . like the "Cuban Information Agency," perhaps?

Maybe Moore could try the oh-so-convincing Nancy Pelosi technique of just accusing the CIA of lying?

But, misleading sources aside, is life expectancy even a fair way to judge a health-care system? Most people probably think yes. For example, if location A has a life expectancy of 78.7 years and location B has an expectancy of 75.8 years, you can reasonably assume that location A has a better overall health-care system, right?

Nope. In fact, the numbers in the above example are real, and they represent a much

starker difference than the one between America and other countries. Location A is actually Utah and location B is Nevada—two states that literally border each other. So why would one state have a life expectancy nearly three years longer than the other, especially considering that their health-care systems are essentially identical? Who knows (my guess is the killer Bs: buffets, booze, and brothels)—but one thing is for sure: Utah doesn't have a higher life expectancy because they have universal government health care.

Life expectancy is actually a *terrible* way to judge a health-care system. Why? Because a lot of people die for reasons that can't be controlled by doctors. To understand what I mean, let's look at the two things that come to mind when you think about Detroit: cars and murder.

We love our cars, and Detroit is (or at least *was*) the automobile capital of the world. Other countries don't drive nearly as much or as far as we do (or put on their makeup while texting, road raging, and eating an Egg McMuffin). More driving means more accidents, which unfortunately leads to more early deaths.

Detroit is unfortunately also illustrative of America's affinity for homicide. You're about eight times more likely to be murdered in Detroit than in America as a whole, and their 2007 murder rate was roughly equal to Venezuela's. Long-term corruption and incompetence in Detroit and other major cities drives America's national murder rate to a point that can be up to four times greater than that of some European countries.

In January of 2009, the average home price in Detroit was $7,000. I wonder why?

But neither murder nor car accidents, two factors that lower overall life expectancy, have anything to do with the quality of our health-care system. In fact, if you control for the higher number of homicides and accidents, some studies have shown that the U.S. ranks number one worldwide in life expectancy.

Unless countries like Cuba have somehow developed a way to un-slash the neck of a murder victim, or de-telephone-pole a car after an accident, it's clear that the longer-life-expectancy claim is as bogus as a photo of Michael Moore eating tofu.* Which brings us to another huge* factor affecting life expectancy that Michael Moore is very closely acquainted with:* *We have food.* Lots of it.

While Cubans eat to stay alive, we eat to kill ourselves. Dr. Robert N. Butler, a Pulitzer Prize–winning author, thinks the Cuban health-care system does some things well, but he admitted to *The New York Times* that "some of Cuba's shortcomings may actually improve its health profile." Sounds counterintuitive, right? Sure, but Butler had a good explanation. "Because they don't have up-to-date cars," he said, "they tend to have to exercise more by walking. And they may not have a surfeit of food, which keeps them from problems like obesity, but they're not starving, either."

*None of these are fat jokes. All just terrible coincidences.

Wow, what a glorious endorsement of communism! If only we could be so lucky as to have *just* enough food to survive and no ability to travel easily, maybe we too could be as happy and healthy as Cubans!

Does the fact that we are a rich country with new cars that likes to indulge in unhealthy things to the point that no one would flinch if we added a Big Mac to our flag really tell us anything about our health-care system? Of course not. We're a country that celebrates the hot dog and the apple pie as two of our national symbols. It's amazing we live past twelve.

The bottom line is that obesity might be the yummiest of all diseases, but the vast number of American fatties isn't easy on the eyes . . . or on our health-care statistics.

MOORE: "Cuba is a very poor country... yet, in spite of that, they are able to put together a health-care system that guarantees they have . . . . a better infant-mortality rate [than we do]."

On January 2, 2009, the Cuban government made a fascinating announcement: They had lowered their infant-mortality rate to 4.7 of every 1,000 births in 2008. That's one of the lowest in the world.

But what was truly amazing wasn't the *rate*, it was the *date*. How exactly did Cuba, a country that has approximately one calculator for the entire miserable island, compute and release an exact infant mortality rate for their entire country in less than 48 hours when it can take the United States about two years to put together theirs? Medical records from thousands of hospitals must be compiled, checked, and rechecked. If you've ever been stuck gathering a bunch of email addresses to put together a birthday party Evite for an annoying coworker, you know how impossible a task that must be. Yet Cuba is somehow able to magically become the world's most competent nation when it comes to this one singular task. How?

Maybe a better question is *why*? Why would Cuba be in such a rush to trumpet its low infant-mortality rate? The answer is that it's all about marketing. The world looks at infant mortality as one of the most important measures of a health-care system— which is exactly why Cuba spends so much

Greetings From CUBA

"A major Cuban health care issue is the prevalence of induced abortion, largely because abortion has been used as a means to minimize the incidence of infant mortality . . . and as the country's favorite birth control method."
—Sergio Diaz-Briquets, Cuban Communism 11th edition

time manipulating theirs. Whether it's direct misreporting or abortions at the first sign of possible trouble with a fetus, Cuba is about on par with Bernie Madoff when it comes to honest reporting.

But let's play the Michael Moore game for a minute and assume that the Castro brothers would welcome a PriceWaterhouseCoopers audit of their infant-mortality rate. Would a global game of "My Babies Die Less Often Than Your Babies" really be a legitimate way to fairly compare health-care systems?

Not at all. The problem with the infant-mortality rate lies in the incredible disparity in the ways by which the statistic is measured around the world. For example, while 40 percent of America's infant-mortality rate is attributable to infants who die on the day of their birth, some countries don't "reliably register" those deaths at all. In the U.S., a baby that shows any sign of life whatsoever is counted as a live birth, but other countries laugh at that crazy standard of "life" and instead use "size" or "weight" to determine whether a birth is "live." *US News and World Report* noted this phenomenon:

> "In Austria and Germany, fetal weight must be at least 500 grams (1 pound) to count as a live birth; in other parts of Europe, such as Switzerland, the fetus must be at least 30 centimeters (12 inches) long. In Belgium and France, births at less than 26 weeks of pregnancy are registered as lifeless."

> "Let me be the first to say that I would be thrilled if America's health-care system is anywhere near as functional as the post office."
>
> —Bill Maher

Perhaps you're a skeptic who doesn't trust *US News and World Report*. "It has the letters US right in its title . . . why should we trust what they say about European health care!?" Well, how about the Organization for Economic Cooperation and Development (OECD) instead? They're the ones that actually *collect* the European data and even they specifically warn against comparing infant-mortality rates around the world for precisely the same reasons.

In America, along with many developed nations, infant deaths don't have nearly as much to do with the merits of a health-care system as they did decades ago. For example, America has a higher rate of "very preterm" babies than most other countries. Very preterm babies are born at less than 32 weeks, and die at about 30 times the rate of our average. While they account for only two percent of births, they total *more than half* of all infant deaths. That's

CELEBRITY GUEST IDEEOT

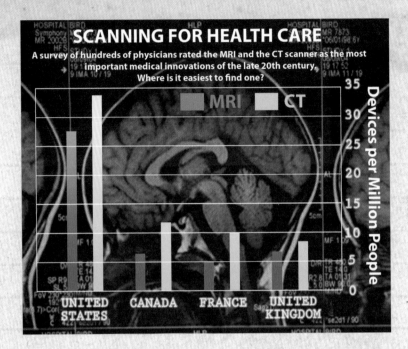

SCANNING FOR HEALTH CARE

A survey of hundreds of physicians rated the MRI and the CT scanner as the most important medical innovations of the late 20th century. Where is it easiest to find one?

MRI · CT

Devices per Million People

UNITED STATES · CANADA · FRANCE · UNITED KINGDOM

why, once you adjust for birth weight, the U.S. ends up with an infant-mortality rate that's about equal to Norway's—which has one of the lowest rates on the planet.

But *why* do we have so many more pre-term births in the first place? Is it because our health-care system is so bad? Nope—in some respects it's actually the other way around. Americans use far more fertility drugs than other countries and those drugs increase the possibility of multiple births and premature babies. In many other countries, couples don't have access to all of our drugs and treatments. If they can't conceive naturally, many people are forced to simply go without biological children.

If you asked an average "citizen of the world" (hat tip to President Obama for that) whether, after hearing the risks, they would choose to have advanced fertility options available, I have to believe that most would still say "yes." Again, the point is that the fact that the United States is a relatively wealthy country that chooses to spend its money on incredibly innovative drugs that produce a higher proportion of premature babies doesn't mean we have a bad health-care system. In fact, I would argue it means just the opposite.

One benefit of fertility drugs is that news channels get weeks of material every time a mother has a huge number of kids at once. Studies have shown that if "Octomom" didn't exist, cable news would have had to shut down for much of early 2009.

I don't blame Cuba for massaging their infant-mortality numbers a bit. I mean, their citizens are stuck dealing with the failure of their communist system, the bumbling brothers who have been running their country into the ground, defections of every kid with an ounce of baseball talent, and a daily UV index that would turn me into a dried cherry in nine minutes. (I don't tan well.) But, by announcing annual numbers before the New Year's champagne spoils, they are attempting to spread propaganda that Cuban health care, which was once an impressive and thriving system before it was destroyed by communism, is superior to America's. They spoon-feed (or trough feed*) this information to idiots who can't help but lap it up like a hungry pig in slop.*

I suppose the one morsel of solace we can take from *Sicko* is this: Michael Moore isn't shy about begging for total government control. Unlike most of our politicians, at least he's honest about it.

"SURE, GOVERNMENT MIGHT NOT BE THE PERFECT SOLUTION, BUT IT'S THE ONLY SOLUTION. YOUR PRECIOUS FREE-MARKET CAPITALISM HAS DONE NOTHING TO SOLVE THIS PROBLEM!"

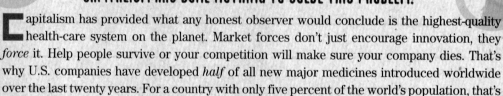

Capitalism has provided what any honest observer would conclude is the highest-quality health-care system on the planet. Market forces don't just encourage innovation, they *force* it. Help people survive or your competition will make sure your company dies. That's why U.S. companies have developed *half* of all new major medicines introduced worldwide over the last twenty years. For a country with only five percent of the world's population, that's not too bad.

Here is how it works: America develops new treatments, gets them first, and, yes, pays more for them. You know that fat, hairy rich guy with the hot young wife who was the first in town to buy a plasma screen when they still cost $30,000? That's America—we're the fat, hairy rich guy to the rest of the world. The left delights in vilifying the wealthiest one percent, but they forget the famous words of an anonymous fifth-grade philosopher: *When you're pointing at someone, there are three fingers pointing back at you.* To the rest of the world, *we are* the wealthiest one percent.

That leaves those who attack the American health-care system with only one main argument: quantity versus qual-

"The American health care system has done nothing more than any other to bring innovation to the world of medicine."

Someone from the U.S. has won the Nobel Prize for medicine in 36 of the last 43 years, or about 84% of the time.

*None of these are fat jokes. All just terrible coincidences.

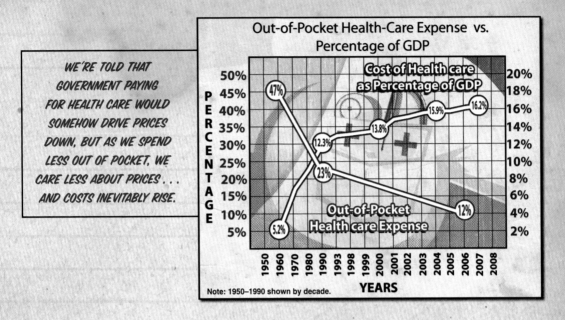

WE'RE TOLD THAT
GOVERNMENT PAYING
FOR HEALTH CARE WOULD
SOMEHOW DRIVE PRICES
DOWN, BUT AS WE SPEND
LESS OUT OF POCKET, WE
CARE LESS ABOUT PRICES . . .
AND COSTS INEVITABLY RISE.

ity. *Sure, America has the best health-care system,* they'll say. *For those who can afford it—but too many can't.*

Finally, an argument with some truth to it. For all of its unacknowledged virtue, our health-care system does still leave too many without coverage. The real question is what can rectify that more efficiently: a free market or a government monopoly?

Answer this question: What three letters can get you quality medical care for about half the price of a typical doctor's appointment and provide a 90-day supply of most prescription medications for less than a movie and popcorn, all while giving you the opportunity to pick up Cheetos, Mentos, Oreos, Pepto, and probably even this book-o.

The answer is W-A-L. You can get all of these things at your local Walgreens and/or Wal-Mart.

Walgreens is leading the way in the development of retail health clinics, which means that you can basically see a medical professional right in the pharmacy. Wait times are minimal, the cost is low, and you can grab a Whatchamacallit bar on the way out.

Despite the fact that the economic downturn has slowed the rapid expansion of the clinics and caused some providers to close shop, the number of retail clinics still increased by over 30 percent in 2008. Walgreens plans to have 400 clinics open by 2010 and CVS, the other market leader, plans on having almost 500. Anyone can walk into these clinics, regardless of health-insurance status, and get medical care for about one-sixth the cost of a trip to the emergency room, and one-half the cost of a normal trip to the doctor's office. The quality of care, usually

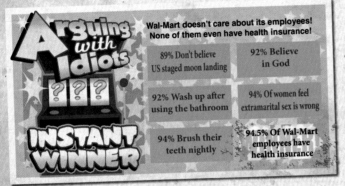

Wal-Mart doesn't care about its employees! None of them even have health insurance!

89% Don't believe US staged moon landing	92% Believe in God
92% Wash up after using the bathroom	94% Of women feel extramarital sex is wrong
94% Brush their teeth nightly	94.5% Of Wal-Mart employees have health insurance

given by a master's-degree-educated nurse practitioner, is so good that two-thirds of visits are paid for by insurance. The bulk of their business comes from people with insurance going there by choice, not the uninsured going there by necessity.

If you listen to the media, you probably think that, besides selling economy-sized bags of Triple Barbecue Cheddar Mega Crisps, Wal-Mart's main business line is assassinating helpless crippled runaway teenagers. Not so. Incredibly, they keep their profits churning with very little despotic evil or murder involved.

In 2006, Wal-Mart decided to lower their prescription drug prices to just $4 for a 30-day supply of most generic medications. That put the most popular vital medications within reach of just about everyone and launched what Bloomberg described as a "fierce" price war for prescription drugs, saving sick Americans literally billions of dollars.

In response to Wal-Mart's price cut, Target followed suit. And then Krogers. First Giant, Giant Eagle, Food Lion, Publix, and Safeway have all adopted similar plans to compete. Walgreens also now offers a 90-day supply of 400 different drugs for just $12.

In 2008, Wal-Mart made an announcement: They had saved customers $1 billion in prescription drug costs—a number that is undoubtedly underestimated because it doesn't count the savings at all of the other stores that followed their lead. So, what did Wal-Mart do next? They lowered prices again—this time to $10 for a 90-day supply. CVS jumped on the bandwagon too, offering hundreds of drugs for $9.99 for 90 days. The price war continued until Giant supermarkets actually began "selling" antibiotics for the unbeatable price of . . . nothing.

A.D.D. MOMENT

Given Wal-Mart's entrepreneurial spirit, why did they issue a letter in support of Obamacare? Well, besides fear of retribution from the government, *Reason Magazine* says they did it because it's "good from a competitive standpoint." About 99 percent of businesses the size of Wal-Mart's already offer their employees health care, while only 62 percent of smaller businesses do. Wal-Mart can handle the increased cost, smaller competitors can't.

Did all of these companies cut their prices so dramatically because their managements are filled with altruistic do-gooders with a furious desire to help their fellow humans? Well, partially, yes—not every business owner is Tony Soprano. But the real reason is that management understood that if they forged relationships with customers by conveniently providing them with vital medicine as inexpensively as possible, those customers would likely come back and buy their Cap'n Crunch, Mr. Clean, and Pringles Cheezums there too. And when times are better, they'll come back for their television, office furniture, and snowblower.

Charles Platt, a senior writer for *Wired* magazine, who has written about everything from cold fusion to nanotechnology, offered evidence of this kind of thinking when he applied for (and got) an entry-level job at a Wal-Mart in Flagstaff, Arizona. After an extremely thorough interview process, he had to give the Wal-Mart pledge: "If a customer comes within ten feet of me, I'm going to look him in the eye, smile, and greet him." As Platt wrote: "The reason was clearly articulated. On average, anyone walking into Wal-Mart is likely to spend more than $200,000 at the store during the rest of his life. Therefore, any clueless employee who alienates that customer will cost the store around a quarter-million dollars."

If Wal-Mart understands that one passing encounter with a customer is that important, imagine the value they see in curing someone's gout for $3.33 a month. Sure, low drug prices are good for you, but they're *great* for Wal-Mart, Walgreens, and CVS. Their motivation (outside of basic human decency) is capitalistic profit—and while it might not be popular to say this in today's America . . . that's *good.*

The pursuit of profits doesn't just lower prices, it also fuels impressive innovation and provides access to health care in ways never before thought possible. For example, you know that crazy idea called the internet? It was a small computer-networking thing used by universities and geeks before capitalism turned it into a way to buy, watch, listen to, look at, and create almost anything.

The internet is fueling technological solutions and widespread information-sharing that's acting like a massive health-care think tank. Here are just a few of the innovations now being developed *by the private sector* to serve those without insurance:

eHealthinsurance.com

The idea of buying your own health insurance has been so vilified that people tend to think that if you can't get it through their job, you can't get it at all. Enter ehealthinsurance.com. Put in your zip code and birth date and you'll have dozens of quotes from insurance companies that want your business. They feature plans for small businesses and individuals, and short-term plans if you're between jobs or just enjoy applying for health insurance every few months. I filled out the form and, believe it or not, there is a company out there willing to insure my 45-year-old-out-of-shape-coronary-in-waiting self for just $94 a month.

> **A.D.D. MOMENT**
>
> I assume that monthly rate would go up once they realize how much butter I actually consume.

Healthcarebluebook.com

Let's say you walk into an electronics store, go right up to the manager, and say: "Hello, I want to buy a flat-screen TV. I have no idea what anything in this place costs and I don't care because

I'm not paying for it. Please remove all the price tags, and don't give me a receipt after I buy." Do you think he'd give you a good deal on the price?

That, of course, is basically the current state of health care in America. When you have insurance, you simply don't care how much anything costs. Doctors don't have to compete on price, so why would they bother trying to keep prices low?

Healthcarebluebook.com steps in to fill the void by disclosing reasonable prices for various procedures and treatments, thereby arming the patient with the ultimate medication for out-of-control costs: information. Once you know the going price, you can actually call around to find a doctor you like and then even negotiate the price with him or her. Believe me, when a doctor's office realizes that you won't be putting them through the nightmare of submitting claims to an insurance company (or worse, the government), they're very likely to give you a good deal.

> **A.D.D. MOMENT**
>
> To avoid government paperwork, a doctor's office quite possibly might throw in a pizza coupon, a Snuggie, and a few Vicodin, too.

Teladoc and American Well

Need to talk to a doctor at 3 AM because, after doing a few Google searches, you're absolutely convinced that you're afflicted with pseudopseudohypoparathyroidism? Good luck getting your actual doctor on the phone, insurance or not. Usually, the sort of phone services available at 3 AM include having an overweight, hairy woman with a raspy voice speak a collection of well-rehearsed and sexually explicit phrases in an unconvincing manner (so I'm told), or a quasi-German man soliciting the purchase of the most absorbent cloth ever created by scientists.

> **A.D.D. MOMENT**
>
> I don't know if I want my doctor texting me. Seeing "yo gb u got da clap 4 eva!" on my iPhone would be a tad disturbing.

If you've ever thought that you wasted an hour driving to the doctor's office just so they can ask you two questions and diagnose you with something they've seen 3,000 other times, then Teladoc is probably for you. For just $35 you can be on the phone with a licensed physician within 3 hours, guaranteed.

Two other companies go even further. For $45, American Well will let you talk with a doctor via webcam, instant message, phone, or text. And at Wal-Mart, some locations have now begun to offer "virtual clinics" where you not only get to talk to a medical professional—they can actually look into your ears, eyes, and throat remotely via a webcam.

> **A.D.D. MOMENT**
>
> Following the path of every technology on earth, the webcam became universal only after widespread (bad word in this context) usage in the porn industry. Consider the irony of that: The physical act originally intended by God to create life has popularized a technology now being used to help doctors extend it. Ahhhh . . . the circle of porn.

The No Insurance Club

While it might sound like the worst Facebook group in existence, The No Insurance Club is actually a way to prepay medical expenses and get an extremely low rate in return. For about $500 per year patients get priority access to up to 12 doctor appointments, extremely low-priced prescriptions, free tests and blood work, plus they pay no deductibles, no copays, and avoid all of the endless paperwork. Considering the average doctor's appointment can run as high as $130, that's a huge saving.

These are just some of the innovative ideas that capitalism is dreaming up even as we brainstorm ways to get rid of it. Some of these companies might revolutionize the way we think about our health, others will fail as miserably as Alex Rodriguez taking a steroid test. But, the truth is clear: Capitalism is in the middle of creating the tools that can alleviate many of our biggest health-care concerns. Isn't it quintessential government to pick right now as the time to step in and "save the day"?

For a little extra, patients can cover their entire family and get up to 16 visits per year. If you have unused appointments in December I guess you can just drop your kids off at the doctor's office, have them fake a cough, and save money on babysitters.

"COMPARED TO OUR OTHER PROBLEMS, HEALTH CARE IS EASY TO FIX. WE JUST NEED THE RIGHT LEGISLATION AND A LOT OF MONEY."

As we've looked at the state of health care in America, we've seen how things aren't quite as bad as we think, how government can make things worse, and how capitalism can make things better. But the truth is that no one solution, from either side of the debate, can make health care what it needs to be.

If you've been on YouTube over the past couple of years, then, in addition to watching ugly English women sing, some kid named Charlie biting fingers, and my guests fainting midinterview, you probably saw me half in a coma and looking worse than usual after a quite intimate and painful surgery.

But(t), as bad as my experience under the knife was, it was far worse out in the waiting room. Without getting into details you don't want, let's just say the surgery didn't go well, and no one seemed to care.

Greetings From

GREECE

Analysts believe Greece needs about 5,000 general practitioners to meet demand. They currently have about 600. The lack of doctors is so bad that it's common for patients to offer bribes for appointments.

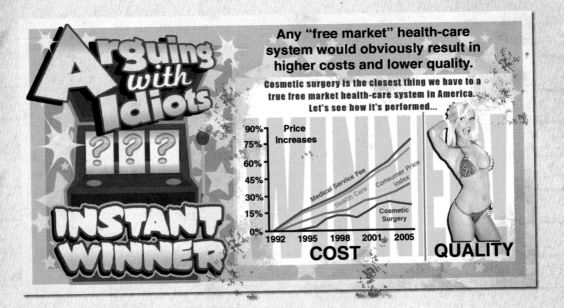

Any "free market" health-care system would obviously result in higher costs and lower quality.

Cosmetic surgery is the closest thing we have to a true free market health-care system in America. Let's see how it's performed...

Price Increases: 90%, 75%, 60%, 45%, 30%, 15%, 0%

Medical Service Fee, Health Care, Consumer Price Index, Cosmetic Surgery

1992, 1995, 1998, 2001, 2005

COST   QUALITY

The powerful lesson that I learned was that the system that is capable of transplanting a heart had lost something far more basic: its soul. It's not a lack of training, equipment, or technology that's the problem—we just have to put the *care* back in health care.

Our insurance system is designed, whether through the government or our employers, to cut out the relationship between doctors and patients. Doctors are so overcome with threatened legal action and bureaucracy that it's become expected that trips to the doctor's office are exercises in paperwork, patience, and rude staff. Encouraging competition and removing the needless levels of regulation can free up our doctors to once again worry about their patients instead of politicians and attorneys.

That brings me to Dr. John Muney, a New York physician who recently started an amazing program: unlimited doctor's appointments to anyone who wanted them for just $79 per month. His logic was simple: If he could avoid the mountains of paperwork that come with insurance, he could cut his costs and make sure health care was within reach of everyone.

That's when the government stepped in. You see, despite the speeches from politicians, the government doesn't really care if you're able to see a doctor. What they care about is *control*. The State Insurance Department told Dr. Muney that he had to stop offering his low-cost, fixed-rate plan because it was too similar to insurance. To put it another way, a doctor's effort to avoid the hassles of insurance could continue only if he started his own insurance company.

In the middle of the controversy, I brought Dr. Muney on the air to talk about it. After his appearance, the state told him that they would allow him to continue with a modified version of his plan, one that would, unfortunately, cover less and cost more. As Dr. Muney said: "I really don't want to charge more. They're forcing me."

While the situation is still far from optimal, the truth is that his entire plan would have been destroyed if it weren't for people all around America standing up and showing their outrage. That is why, despite how exhausting it is, we must continue arguing with every idiot at every opportunity.

When our freedoms aren't our focus, our country becomes dangerously ill. Our Founders might not have been doctors, but they still outlined the proper prescription to keep America healthy and vibrant: a commonsense approach focusing on rights and responsibilities.

Now, take the two of those, and call Washington in the morning.

THE U.S. CONSTITUTION

Lost in Translation

HOW many times have you argued with your idiot friends about what's constitutional and what isn't? You may even *show* them the Constitution, but the disagreement continues. That made me think that maybe the problem is that the entire Constitution is written in *English*—a language that is very difficult for the average idiot to comprehend. In addition, there are several words in the document longer than three letters, making it a tougher read than the "Dick and Jane" books they normally struggle through.

What follows is a translation (from English to Idiot) of several important parts of the U.S. Constitution, leaving no doubt as to what our Founding Fathers really intended.

Constitution for the United States of America

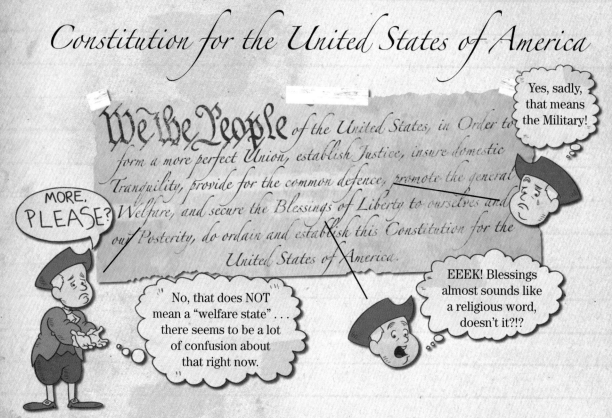

On July 24, 1787, delegates established a "Committee of Detail" to generate a rough draft of the Constitution, synergizing their debates. The preamble of their first draft read as follows:

We the People of the States of New Hampshire, Massachusetts, Rhode-Island and Providence Plantations, Connecticut, New York, New Jersey, Pennsylvania, Delaware, Maryland, Virginia, North-Carolina, South-Carolina, and Georgia, do ordain, declare, and establish the following Constitution for the Government of Ourselves and our Posterity.

Then, on September 8, the "Committee of Style" was established to refine and revise the Articles that had been agreed upon. After four days of work, they presented a digest version of the Constitution that included this new preamble:

We, the People of the United States, in order to form a more perfect union, to establish justice, insure domestic tranquility, provide for the common defence, promote the general welfare, and secure the blessings of liberty to ourselves and our posterity, do ordain and establish this Constitution for the United States of America.

Over 22 decades later, it has become easy for us to forget that the three million or so inhabitants of the country at that time considered themselves to be citizens of their own state first, and only then a citizen of the country. It was a far more localized environment, meaning that unifying the various states under the banner of "the United States" was a revolutionary way of thinking.

Article 1.

Section. 1. All legislative Powers herein granted shall be vested in a Congress of the United States, which shall consist of a Senate and House of Representatives.

Notice that it isn't the Supreme Court that is granted the right to make laws! Shocking.

Section. 2. The House of Representatives shall be composed of Members chosen every second Year by the People of the several States, and the Electors in each State shall have the Qualifications requisite for Electors of the most numerous Branch of the State Legislature.

In retrospect, a term-limit clause might not have been a bad idea here. Say, two or three terms, max? In Federalist Paper #53, James Madison, who also authored the majority of the Constitution, wrote, "A few of the members, as happens in all such assemblies, will possess superior talents; will, by frequent re-elections, become members of long standing; will be thoroughly masters of the public business, and perhaps not unwilling to avail themselves of those advantages. The greater the proportion of new members of Congress, and the less the information of the bulk of the members, the more apt they be to fall into the snares that may be laid before them."

Madison seemed to favor experience and know-how, but perhaps time has proven that he may have given our politicians far too much rope with which to hang themselves. He may have also assumed that people like Strom Thurmond and Robert Byrd would have the good sense to retire before reaching their early hundreds. Or, maybe he just didn't count on people living as long as they do now. After all, the life expectancy of someone born in Philadelphia from 1754 to 1790 was just 13 years.

> *No Person shall be a Representative who shall not have attained to the Age of twenty five Years, and been seven Years a Citizen of the United States, and who shall not, when elected, be an Inhabitant of that State in which he shall be chosen.*

In summary: We vote for House members every two years, they have to be 25 years old, have been a citizen for seven years, and live in the state where they were elected. I think Wal-Mart greeters have stricter hiring guidelines than we do.

> *Representatives and direct Taxes shall be apportioned among the several States which may be included within this Union, according to their respective Numbers, which shall be determined by adding to the whole Number of free Persons, including those bound to Service for a Term of Years, and excluding Indians not taxed, three-fifths of all other Persons.*

Idiots point to this line as "proof" that the Founders were racist Klansmen who wore powdered wigs instead of white sheets—but nothing could be farther from the truth. This whole section deals with counting Americans (a census) for the purpose of representation. It does not deal with placing value on human life.

Many of the Founders actually wanted to eliminate slavery, but knew they couldn't push for it right away and still keep the Union together. For instance, in the 1790 census, which took place three years after the ratification of the Constitution, the slave population of South Carolina alone was 77 percent of the white population. By 1820, slaves outnumbered whites 265,000 to 237,000, give or take, and, by 1860, the slave population had grown to over 412,000, compared to just 291,000 for whites. Georgia and Virginia also had an enormous number of slaves.

By including the slave population in the census on a one-to-one basis, the South would have had all the representation it needed to outvote the North on the slavery issue . . . indefinitely. So, in order to keep representation of the South down (thereby keeping the elimination of slavery on the table), the Founding Fathers devised this counting method to limit the power the South could wield, thus ensuring that one day this new nation would be able to abolish slavery.

For example, Gouverneur Morris, who assisted James Madison throughout the entire process of drafting the Constitution and was on the committee that decided on its final draft, described slavery as a "nefarious institution . . . The curse of heaven on states where it prevailed." He also argued that congressional representation should be based on "one for every 40,000 free inhabitants." As a vehement opponent of slavery, Morris opposed the "three-fifths" compromise because he felt it would still allow the southern states enough representatives to keep slavery going indefinitely.

Founders like George Washington and Thomas Jefferson are often described by critics as "hypocrites" when it comes to slavery. Yes, Washington and Jefferson both owned slaves, but both also opposed the slave trade. Is that "hypocrisy"? Well, let's think of it in modern-day terms: 200 years from now, if people decide that hiring illegal aliens is immoral, will all those who currently have their lawns mowed or children cared for by people who "lack documentation" be looked back on as racist hypocrites? Maybe, and it will certainly be easy to make those accusations, but no one is making them now . . . and that's exactly how it was in the late eighteenth century.

So, were the Founders who opposed slavery but acquiesced to the three-fifths clause heroes or hypocrites? Here are some of their actual thoughts on slavery; decide for yourself:

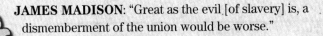

JAMES MADISON: "Great as the evil [of slavery] is, a dismemberment of the union would be worse."

GEORGE WASHINGTON: "There is not a man living who wishes more sincerely than I do, to see a plan adopted for the abolition of [slavery]."

JOHN ADAMS: "Every measure of prudence, therefore, ought to be assumed for the eventual total extirpation of slavery from the United States. . . . I have, through my whole life, held the practice of slavery in . . . abhorrence."

BENJAMIN FRANKLIN: "Slavery is . . . an atrocious debasement of human nature."

ALEXANDER HAMILTON: "The laws of certain states . . . give an ownership in the service of negroes as personal property. . . . But being men, by the laws of God and nature, they were capable of acquiring liberty—and when the captor in war . . . thought fit to give them liberty, the gift was not only valid, but irrevocable."

Idiots who argue with our Founders' compromise have no concept of how important this nation was, and still is. But our Founders knew. They had such a clear understanding of what they were creating that they knew it would be better to establish an imperfect Union, rather than risk having the great American experiment fail before it ever got started.

> Section. 3. The Senate of the United States shall be composed of two Senators from each State, chosen by the Legislature thereof, for six Years; and each Senator shall have one Vote.

It's amazing how many seemingly antidemocratic provisions can be found in the Constitution—but it was all by design. This section directed that senators were to be elected by state legislatures, not the people. Why? Two reasons: (1) The Founders felt that creating a direct connection between state governments and the federal government would help the document to be ratified, and (2) They wanted senators to be able to vote their conscience without worrying about pandering to specific groups of voters.

Unfortunately, it didn't work out the way they'd hoped. Instead of special-interest groups fighting among themselves, state legislators began to fight each other, resulting in postponed elections and, ultimately, empty Senate seats. The process was eventually changed by the Seventeenth Amendment, which, after being ratified in 1913, ensured senators were elected directly by the people. Unfortunately, they once again left out anything about term limits.

> *No Person shall be a Senator who shall not have attained to the Age of thirty Years, and been nine Years a Citizen of the United States, and who shall not, when elected, be an Inhabitant of that State for which he shall be chosen.*

Another summary: Two senators per state, each serving six-year terms. A senator has to be thirty years old, a citizen for nine years, and a resident of the state in which he or she is elected. What's not mentioned: A senator may grow up in Illinois, attend college in Connecticut, move to Arkansas with her husband, move on to Washington, D.C., and then claim to have been a Yankee fan her whole life in order to get elected in New York State. Another loose interpretation would be that a senator could go to a party, drive an Oldsmobile into a river, leave his 19-year-old female companion (who happens to not be his wife) inside the car, go home, sit around for 9 hours before finally calling police, and still be reelected to his Senate seat for the next 40+ years.

> *The Vice President of the United States shall be President of the Senate, but shall have no Vote, unless they be equally divided.*

At all other times he'll be sequestered in an undisclosed location, kept from the view of the citizenry. Until his term is over, then you won't be able to get rid of him.

> *Section. 6. No Senator or Representative shall, during the Time for which he was elected, be appointed to any civil Office under the Authority of the United States, which shall have been created, or the Emoluments whereof shall have been increased during such time; and no Person holding any Office under the United States, shall be a Member of either House during his Continuance in Office.*

This shows the amazing foresight of our Founders. They went to great lengths to limit the ways in which the system and, by default, the people in that system, could become corrupted.

As many people have noticed, the "emoluments" (i.e., salary) for the secretary of state were increased during Clinton's most recent Senate term. That made her constitutionally ineligible to be appointed to that office—but, since Congress didn't like the outcome, they simply changed the rules of the game.

By using the "Saxbe fix" (named after William Saxbe, whose appointment to attorney general by Republican president Richard Nixon was also unconstitutional), Congress was able to revert the salary for the secretary of state position back to the level it was before Clinton's latest term. That "fix" allegedly made her eligible for the position, but I think our Founders would disagree, especially considering there wasn't exactly any ambiguity in their wording of this section.

Besides Clinton and Saxbe, this clause was also violated by Jimmy Carter and Bill Clinton with their appointments of Ed Muskie as secretary of state and Lloyd Bentsen as treasury secretary, respectively.

To those who care about both the letter *and* spirit of our laws, the "Saxbe fix" is an abomination. You can't change history by passing a bill. If you don't like the emoluments clause, or believe it needs to be better defined, then use the tools our Founders gave us by *passing a constitutional amendment.*

Section. 7. Every Order, Resolution, or Vote to which the Concurrence of the Senate and House of Representatives may be necessary (except on a question of Adjournment) shall be presented to the President of the United States; and before the Same shall take Effect, shall be approved by him, or being disapproved by him, shall be repassed by two thirds of the Senate and House of Representatives, according to the Rules and Limitations prescribed in the Case of a Bill.

Notice that there is nothing in here about the presidential practice of "signing statements"—which are pronouncements made by a president upon signing a bill, used to detail some specific issue the president has with it. In some cases, a signing statement can actually modify a bill's intent. It's a practice that has been employed by presidents going all the way back to James Monroe, but it was used extensively by Bill Clinton and George W. Bush (who expressed opposition to 1,200 items over his two terms) and has continued under Barack Obama. The Supreme Court has never directly ruled on this practice, but the Constitution makes a president's options very clear: Veto a bill or "faithfully execute" the laws. Signing statements attempt to carve out middle ground where none was meant to exist.

Section. 8. The Congress shall have Power To lay and collect Taxes, Duties, Imposts and Excises, to pay the Debts and provide for the common Defence and general Welfare of the United States; but all Duties, Imposts and Excises shall be uniform throughout the United States;

Here's what's not in Section 8: "Congress shall also have the power to retaliate against executives at AIG, a company that will one day be founded, grow extremely large, fall on hard times, receive a government bailout, be allowed by Congress to give bonuses to their executives anyway, then have them taken away via a 90-percent tax levy. Congress shall also have the power to 'level the playing field' by imposing extraordinary taxes against successful people and shall at all times endeavor to 'redistribute wealth' to the less fortunate."

To borrow Money on the credit of the United States;

Congress seems to have no problem following this clause.

To regulate Commerce with foreign Nations, and among the several States, and with the Indian Tribes;

It's amazing how one small word can change everything. In this case, it's "among." The Constitution allows the federal government to regulate commerce *among* the states, not *within* them—but that line in the sand is long gone . . . as are states' rights. If we are serious about returning America to the principles laid out in this document, then it all starts by getting the federal government out of things they don't belong in. Fortunately, people are finally beginning to understand that—see the Tenth Amendment for one effort that's under way.

By the way, I wonder if we owe as much to the Indian tribes as we do to China?

To establish an uniform Rule of Naturalization, and uniform Laws on the subject of Bankruptcies throughout the United States;

"Uniform" means "always the same"—a concept that was shredded when the federal government single-handedly chose which companies would survive and which ones would fail.

To coin Money, regulate the Value thereof, and of foreign Coin, and fix the Standard of Weights and Measures;

Believe me, there's going to be a lot of "coining" coming our way very soon.

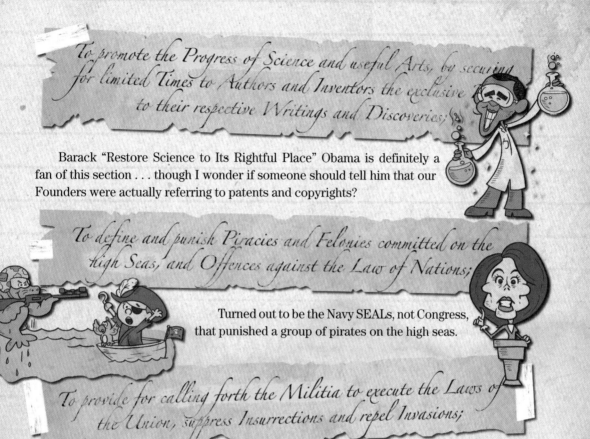

To promote the Progress of Science and useful Arts, by securing for limited Times to Authors and Inventors the exclusive to their respective Writings and Discoveries;

Barack "Restore Science to Its Rightful Place" Obama is definitely a fan of this section . . . though I wonder if someone should tell him that our Founders were actually referring to patents and copyrights?

To define and punish Piracies and Felonies committed on the high Seas, and Offences against the Law of Nations;

Turned out to be the Navy SEALs, not Congress, that punished a group of pirates on the high seas.

To provide for calling forth the Militia to execute the Laws of the Union, suppress Insurrections and repel Invasions;

A good question to ask your Idiot friend is: "What was the first 'insurrection' put down by a militia called forth by Congress?"

Very likely you will get a blank stare back. An extra-idiotic idiot might claim it was the "tea parties" of 2009, when a bunch of rich people financed by the GOP got together to complain about the president (at least that's what you were told happened if you listened to the main-stream media). But the new republic's first insurrection following ratification of the Constitution was actually started by whiskey drinkers and producers. (I know, drunks getting into a fight . . . shocking.)

In 1791, a tax on whiskey was imposed to help pay for the Revolutionary War: 6 cents per gallon for large whiskey producers and 9 cents per gallon for small producers. Of course, the tax not only affected farmers, but also those who drank the whiskey. By 1794, the tension created by this tax gave rise to an armed rebellion, which was quickly extinguished by a U.S.

Army force of over 13,000, led by President George Washington himself. No shots were ever fired.

This is a perfect illustration of what eventually happens when the federal government becomes oppressive and nonresponsive to the will of the people. In 1803, the government got the message and repealed the whiskey tax . . . will they get the message this time?

> To provide for organizing, arming, and disciplining, the Militia, and for governing such Part of them as may be employed in the Service of the United States, reserving to the States respectively, the Appointment of the Officers, and the Authority of training the Militia according to the discipline prescribed by Congress;

Obama Sub-Article 1a: "We also need a civilian force, just as strong, just as powerful and just as well funded as the military" . . . since our Founders were obviously not insightful enough to provide this. Also, let's not forget three months of mandatory "voluntary service" for all 18- to 25-year-olds.

> Section. 9. The Migration or Importation of such Persons as any of the States now existing shall think proper to admit, shall not be prohibited by the Congress prior to the Year one thousand eight hundred and eight, but a Tax or duty may be imposed on such Importation, not exceeding ten dollars for each Person.

Also referred to as the "Twenty Year Clause," this wasn't about taxing immigrants, it was about phasing out slavery. While the Thirteenth Amendment wouldn't come for 78 years, the Founders attempted, within the political realities of the time, to expedite the process.

The Privilege of the Writ of Habeas Corpus shall not be suspended, unless when in Cases of Rebellion or Invasion the public Safety may require it.

See, there it is, the smoking gun! You can't suspend Habeas Corpus ever, under any . . . wait, what? You *can* suspend Habeas Corpus when the *public safety* may require it? Wow, I guess this document is a little more accurate than the blogs, huh?

No Bill of Attainder or ex post facto Law shall be passed.

"Attainder" isn't exactly an everyday word, so allow me to quote Justice Hugo Black's interpretation of it from a 1946 case, *U.S. v. Lovett*: "Legislative acts, no matter what their form, that apply either to named individuals or to easily ascertainable members of a group in such a way as to inflict punishment on them without a judicial trial are bills of attainder prohibited by the Constitution." Now, I'm no constitutional scholar, but I am a thinker—wouldn't the law that Congress tried to pass targeting the bonuses of certain executives (primarily from AIG) fit that definition almost exactly?

No Money shall be drawn from the Treasury, but in Consequence of Appropriations made by Law; and a regular Statement and Account of the Receipts and Expenditures of all public Money shall be published from time to time.

From "time to time" apparently means that we get to see an account of those receipts once every 250 years. Maybe they've used up all the available paper to print money?

> *No Title of Nobility shall be granted by the United States: And no Person holding any Office of Profit or Trust under them, shall, without the Consent of the Congress, accept of any present, Emolument, Office, or Title, of any kind whatever, from any King, Prince, or foreign State.*

I believe this would also include the titles of "Messiah," "Chosen One," "All-Powerful Potentate," and "Savior of the Universe."

It's too bad they didn't include a provision for the unfortunate "gifts" *given* to other heads of state. That oversight means that the 25 DVDs (that were incompatible with European standards and couldn't be played) President Obama gave to UK Prime Minister Gordon Brown are apparently *not* unconstitutional.

> *Section. 10. No State shall enter into any Treaty, Alliance, or Confederation; grant Letters of Marque and Reprisal; coin Money; emit Bills of Credit; make any Thing but gold and silver Coin a Tender in Payment of Debts; pass any Bill of Attainder, ex post facto Law, or Law impairing the Obligation of Contracts; or grant any Title of Nobility.*

"Ex post facto" means "after the fact"—so the intent of this seems pretty clear, right? *Hey, States, no retroactive laws!* Unfortunately, the Supreme Court didn't see it that way. In their infinite wisdom, they decided that that clause doesn't pertain to taxes. Don't be surprised if states take advantage of that (Connecticut and New York already tried) by attempting to retroactively increase tax rates or retroactively create new ones.

No State shall, without the Consent of the Congress, lay any Imposts or Duties on Imports or Exports, except what may be absolutely necessary for executing it's inspection Laws: and the net Produce of all Duties and Imposts, laid by any State on Imports or Exports, shall be for the Use of the Treasury of the United States; and all such Laws shall be subject to the Revision and Controul of the Congress.

Oops! There are a lot of things in this document that people think are mistakes that really aren't (i.e., the word "choose" is often spelled "chuse," but that's how they rolled back then) . . . but this one actually is an error. It's kind of funny that, centuries later, most of us *still* can't get *its* vs. *it's* right.

Article II

Section. 1. The executive Power shall be vested in a President of the United States of America. He shall hold his Office during the Term of four Years, and, together with the Vice President, chosen for the same Term, be elected, as follows:

Wait, I'm still looking for the part specifying that the Power of the President shall also extend to him serving as the CEO of GM, Chrysler, Citi, Wachovia, Bear Stearns, AIG, etc. It must come later . . . . I'll keep looking.

In Case of the Removal of the President from Office, or of his Death, Resignation, or Inability to discharge the Powers and Duties of the said Office, the Same shall devolve on the Vice President, and the Congress may by Law provide for the Case of Removal, Death, Resignation or Inability, both of the President and Vice President, declaring what Officer shall then act as President, and such Officer shall act accordingly, until the Disability be removed, or a President shall be elected.

Want a chill to run down your spine? Here's the current presidential line of succession:

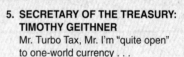

1. **VICE PRESIDENT: JOE BIDEN**
   Yes, the same guy who's been eating regularly at "Katie's Restaurant" in downtown Wilmington, even though it's been out of business since the '80s.

2. **SPEAKER OF THE HOUSE: NANCY PELOSI**
   This has you praying hard for the health and well-being of the president and vice president, doesn't it?

3. **PRESIDENT PRO-TEMPORE OF THE SENATE: ROBERT BYRD**
   Not just the former grand-pooba of the KKK . . . but also approximately 4,892 years old. On the plus side, his ascension to president would make an easy case for congressional term limits.

4. **SECRETARY OF STATE: HILLARY RODHAM CLINTON**
   It would take a village . . . to die for her to get in, but it would somehow be fitting if, after being rejected by her own party, she got into the Oval Office without ever winning an election.

5. **SECRETARY OF THE TREASURY: TIMOTHY GEITHNER**
   Mr. Turbo Tax, Mr. I'm "quite open" to one-world currency . . .

6. **SECRETARY OF DEFENSE: ROBERT GATES**
   So far . . . I'll take him!

7. **ATTORNEY GENERAL: ERIC HOLDER**
   America is a "nation of cowards."

8. **SECRETARY OF THE INTERIOR: KEN SALAZAR**
   Who?

9. **SECRETARY OF AGRICULTURE: TOM VILSACK**
   WHO??

10. **SECRETARY OF COMMERCE: GARY LOCKE**
    No clue.

11. **SECRETARY OF LABOR: HILDA SOLIS**
    An open-borders, pro-amnesty, pro-big-labor leftist, whose nomination was opposed in committee by just two Republicans. Two. At least she's eleventh in line.

The President shall, at stated Times, receive for his Services, a Compensation, which shall neither be increased nor diminished during the Period for which he shall have been elected, and he shall not receive within that Period any other Emolument from the United States, or any of them.

Presidential compensation started out at $25,000. The president's current compensation is $400,000, or about what the third-string right-fielder for the Toronto Blue Jays makes. I believe the current president is also about as qualified as the third-string right-fielder for the Toronto Blue Jays.

Article III.

Section. 1. The judicial Power of the United States shall be vested in one supreme Court, and in such inferior Courts as the Congress may from time to time ordain and establish. The Judges, both of the supreme and inferior Courts, shall hold their Offices during good Behaviour, and shall, at stated Times, receive for their Services a Compensation, which shall not be diminished during their Continuance in Office.

Supreme Court Justice Ruth Bader Ginsburg has been running around talking about why "international law" is okay to use as precedent when deciding Supreme Court rulings. That's "good behavior"?

In a speech given at Ohio State, Ginsburg asked: *"Why shouldn't we look to the wisdom of a judge from abroad with at least as much ease as we would read a law review article written by a professor?"* Well, maybe because of the oath of office she took when she became a Supreme Court Justice?

"I, [NAME], do solemnly swear (or affirm) that I will administer justice without respect to persons, and do equal right to the poor and to the rich, and that I will faithfully and impartially discharge and perform all the duties incumbent upon me as [TITLE] under the Constitution and laws of the United States. So help me God."

Hmm, that's interesting . . . the "Constitution and laws of the United States," huh? No mention of Germany, France, Switzerland, Lichtenstein, or Rwanda. Weird.

Chief Justice John Roberts put it this way: "If we're relying on a decision from a German judge about what our Constitution means, no president accountable to the people appointed that judge and no Senate accountable to the people confirmed that judge. And yet he's playing a role in shaping the law that binds the people in this country."

Maybe it's just me, but I'm thinking it might be time to redefine exactly what the "good behavior" clause really means.

> *Section. 3. Treason against the United States shall consist only in levying War against them, or in adhering to their Enemies, giving them Aid and Comfort. No Person shall be convicted of Treason unless on the Testimony of two Witnesses to the same overt Act, or on Confession in open Court.*

It seems as though it is now nearly impossible to rise to the level of "treason" in this country. You can be an American citizen, from, just as an example . . . California . . . and be carrying an AK-47 on a foreign battlefield, firing at U.S. troops, and, when caught, the worst charge you're likely to face is "jaywalking in a war zone."

Rushing to his defense will be idiots with questions like: "What kind of childhood did he have? What drove him to do this? Did his teachers use 'red ink' when they marked up his test papers? Did other children call him fatso or doofus at recess? Maybe he couldn't get a date for prom? Perhaps he had zits?"

When idiots factor in all of that, the perpetrator can't *possibly* be responsible for his treasonous actions. In fact, it's *our* fault. American society is to blame. Forget what the Constitution says, those men in powdered wigs had no idea how complex our culture would eventually become. The penalty for treason is no longer death, it's government-sponsored therapy.

Article. IV.

A Person charged in any State with Treason, Felony, or other Crime, who shall flee from Justice, and be found in another State, shall on Demand of the executive Authority of the State from which he fled, be delivered up, to be removed to the State having Jurisdiction of the Crime.

GET OUT!

N.Y.
C.T.

We take all of this unity among states for granted because, due to the wisdom of our Founders, it's been ingrained in our society for over 200 years—but things didn't start out that way. New Yorkers had no tolerance for the ways of Virginians, who, in turn, were leery of people from Massachusetts, etc. But now, we're all one big happy family. *Void in Massachusetts, Vermont, New York, California, and all other states where idiotic ideology has taken root.*

Section. 3. New States may be admitted by the Congress into this Union; but no new State shall be formed or erected within the Jurisdiction of any other State; nor any State be formed by the Junction of two or more States, or Parts of States, without the Consent of the Legislatures of the States concerned as well as of the Congress.

57?

This has me very concerned about the "57 states" mentioned by then-candidate Obama during his election campaign. Were those widely unknown seven states admitted by the Congress? He also mentioned that he had "one left to go," which would make 58, plus he hadn't visited Alaska or Hawaii yet. Are there, in fact, 60 states? If so, did Congress formally admit all ten? I DEMAND ANSWERS!

Article. VI.

All Debts contracted and Engagements entered into, before the Adoption of this Constitution, shall be as valid against the United States under this Constitution, as under the Confederation.

So we decided to honor our contracts even though we were going through a time of massive change? Wow, someone should tell Congress.

This Constitution, and the Laws of the United States which shall be made in Pursuance thereof; and all Treaties made, or which shall be made, under the Authority of the United States, shall be the supreme Law of the Land; and the Judges in every State shall be bound thereby, any Thing in the Constitution or Laws of any State to the Contrary notwithstanding.

This is the article that makes many people so uneasy with the U.N. The idiots in your life probably know nothing more about the U.N. than their "Trick or Treat for UNICEF" campaign. They don't pay attention to things like the "Convention on the Rights of the Child," which could give some international body of "experts" control over education, or the "Law of the Sea Treaty" which could give the U.N. control over U.S. territorial waters. (Sing to the tune of the "Chicken of the Sea" jingle) . . . "Ask any mermaid you happen to see, what's the worst treaty . . . Treaty of the Sea!" Hmm . . . maybe that doesn't work so well in print?

Bill of Rights

First Amendment

Congress shall make no law respecting an establishment of religion, or prohibiting the free exercise thereof; or abridging the freedom of speech, or of the press; or the right of the people peaceably to assemble, and to petition the Government for a redress of grievances.

That doesn't seem so hard to understand, does it? There's no problem as long as Congress doesn't make a law that tells Americans that Frisbetarianism (the belief that when you die, your soul goes up on the roof and you can't get it back down . . . like a Frisbee) is the official state religion to which all people must belong or pass a law that prohibits us from worshipping or *not* worshipping.

Given that straightforward definition, why are your idiot friends always screaming, "Separation of church and state!!"? Maybe you should ask them to point out those five words to you in this document.

They're not there.

That phrase was actually contained in a *letter* written by Thomas Jefferson to the Danbury Baptists Association in 1802, *fifteen years after* the Constitution was written. The Danbury Baptists were a minority religious group that feared that they had no "inalienable" right granted them by the state of Connecticut to worship as they chose. Instead, they felt they were allowed to worship only as a "favor" granted to them by the state. So, they wrote to President Jefferson seeking his guidance and comfort that they could continue to worship as they would.

Jefferson responded with the exact words from the Constitution to allay their fears. He then mentioned the "establishment clause" created a "wall of separation between church and state."

AHA, the smoking gun!! Actually, no, if you read the letter, Jefferson's clear meaning was that *religions were protected from the state*, not the other way around. "The legitimate powers of government," he told them, "reach actions only, & not opinions."

You'll also notice that there is no mention of constitutional protection from "being offended." If a person is offended by a religious display on government property, a nativity scene, for example . . . tough. We are all sorry for you, but we have every confidence that you'll get over it. If not, oh well—there's always France.

Second Amendment

A well regulated Militia, being necessary to the security of a free State, the right of the people to keep and bear Arms, shall not be infringed.

Here's a loose translation: If you break into my house in the middle of the night, you'll be shot dead. I won't be yelling, "Do anything you want with my wife and kids, but leave me alone . . . please!" A much more academic translation, along with a loooooooong response to idiots who like to talk about our Founders' use of grammar, can be found in our "Second Amendment" chapter.

Third Amendment

No Soldier shall, in time of peace be quartered in any house, without the consent of the Owner; nor in time of war, but in a manner to be prescribed by law.

This one hasn't really come up much recently, but I'm sure next time it does we'll have plenty of activist groups trying to keep soldiers away by debating the location of the comma. In the meantime, should a soldier knock on your door and ask for a room, please call your nearby constitutional lawyer for immediate assistance.

Fourth Amendment

The right of the people to be secure in their persons, houses, papers, and effects, against unreasonable searches and seizures, shall not be violated, and no Warrants shall issue, but upon probable cause, supported by Oath or affirmation, and particularly describing the place to be searched, and the persons or things to be seized.

At this point, your idiot friend is likely screaming, "George Bush's warrantless wiretapping program!" I don't know of a single American citizen (who's never had a conversation with an Osama wannabe in some musty cave in Pakistan) that is actually affected by this program . . . and neither does your idiot friend. Oh, and by the way, Barack Obama has not only defended the Bush program, he's broadened the government's legal argument for it.

Fifth Amendment

No person shall be held to answer for a capital, or otherwise infamous crime, unless on a presentment or indictment of a Grand Jury, except in cases arising in the land or naval forces, or in the Militia, when in actual service in time of War or public danger; nor shall any person be subject for the same offence to be twice put in jeopardy of life or limb; nor shall be compelled in any criminal case to be a witness against himself, nor be deprived of life, liberty, or property, without due process of law; nor shall private property be taken for public use, without just compensation.

"Twice put in jeopardy" The Founders worded this much more eloquently than we do. We just call it "double jeopardy" or "The O.J. Clause." Unfortunately for O.J., the Framers never mentioned anything about not being convicted for a completely unrelated crime and then having the mistaken verdict from your first trial used against you in the second.

"Witness against himself" Thus the familiar refrain, "I take the Fifth." That doesn't mean the person is asking for a fifth of whiskey (though many people who take the Fifth could certainly *use* a fifth at that point), it means that he is claiming his right to not bear witness against himself, granted to him by this clause, the Fifth Amendment.

This simple term was actually the result of much debate among the Founders. After seeing the lack of respect that the tyrannical British government had for private property, they wanted to include language to ensure that wouldn't happen here—but they disagreed on the exact wording. Some wanted to use the term "public *purpose*," or "public *benefit*"—a concept that would have made it much easier to seize property. ("Hey there, Joe, sorry, but we're gonna need your land to build a new Department of Motor Vehicles.")

"Public use" James Madison struck a compromise with the far more restrictive term "public use" and also included "just compensation" for victims of what we now call "eminent domain." Of course, the debate among our Founders turned out to be pointless, given the recent Supreme Court decision that allowed a Connecticut city to seize private property just so they could make money by selling it to a developer. Madison must be rolling over in his grave.

Sixth Amendment

In all criminal prosecutions, the accused shall enjoy the right to a speedy and public trial, by an impartial jury of the State and district wherein the crime shall have been committed, which district shall have been previously ascertained by law, and to be informed of the nature and cause of the accusation; to be confronted with the witnesses against him; to have compulsory process for obtaining witnesses in his favor, and to have the Assistance of Counsel for his defence.

With our court system so jammed up with frivolous lawsuits (it's only a matter of time before the Slanket sues the Snuggie) the right to a "speedy" trial is somewhat subjective. I would also argue that the whole "public" aspect has really been run through the shredder. I think our Founders would be quite disappointed to find out that we have high-def TVs hanging on walls broadcasting live feeds from around the world and we *still* have to fight to get cameras into the courtroom.

Seventh Amendment

In Suits at common law, where the value in controversy shall exceed twenty dollars, the right of trial by jury shall be preserved, and no fact tried by a jury, shall be otherwise re-examined in any Court of the United States, than according to the rules of the common law.

Since our Founders could never have known the insane rate at which we'd be "coining" money, they probably also didn't realize the effect that inflation would have on the value of a dollar. That's a likely reason why the "twenty dollars" wasn't indexed for inflation. But, if we're looking for original intent, the value of $20 back in 1787 was, well, who knows because the Bureau of Labor Statistics wasn't even created until the late 1800s. But given that $20 in 1913 would be worth $432 today, you can guess that the Founders didn't intend every jaywalking ticket to be decided by a jury.

Eighth Amendment

Excessive bail shall not be required, nor excessive fines imposed, nor cruel and unusual punishments inflicted.

Apologies to the idiots, but battle-field terrorists don't qualify.

Ninth Amendment

The enumeration in the Constitution, of certain rights, shall not be construed to deny or disparage others retained by the people.

While some of our Founders, like Thomas Jefferson, insisted on a Bill of Rights, others did not want to include them in the Constitution for fear that if certain rights were specified, then the people could be denied other rights that were not specifically listed. This amendment was the agreed-upon compromise.

Tenth Amendment

The powers not delegated to the United States by the Constitution, nor prohibited by it to the States, are reserved to the States respectively, or to the people.

This is a profound and critical amendment, widely ignored by the federal government. *Everything* that is not specifically spelled out here (abortion, for example) *is decided by the states.* Instead, the federal government has unconstitutionally overstepped its boundaries in almost every way possible. They're so far over the line that it would be difficult, if not impossible, to ever rein them back in—but one state is trying anyway.

Montana recently passed a bill asserting that guns manufactured in Montana and sold in Montana to people who intend to keep their weapons in Montana are exempt from all federal gun regulations, including registration requirements, background check, and dealer-licensing rules. Why? Because Article I, Section 3 gives the federal government the right to regulate commerce only *between* states, not *within* them.

While this bill is specifically written to pertain to firearms, it's really about the much larger concept of state rights. "It's a gun bill," said *Democratic* Governor Brian Schweitzer, "but it's another way of demonstrating the sovereignty of the state of Montana."

It's also a sign of hope. This bill is being crafted specifically to pick a fight with the federal government—a fight that I believe is long overdue. The theory goes that once someone from Montana attempts to exercise their rights under this legislation, a federal agency will intervene. At that point a lawsuit would be filed that, since the case involves the constitutionality of a law, could make it all the way to the U.S. Supreme Court.

If that happens, and if the Supreme Court were to rule in favor of Montana (Scalia, Thomas, Alito, Roberts, Kennedy, but you better act fast), it would be a major victory for state rights, and one that could extend far beyond guns to virtually every aspect of our lives. Texas and Alaska have similar laws pending—but more states have to get on the bandwagon if this is ever to succeed as a national issue.

Even with enough Supreme Court justices seemingly open to reestablishing state rights, they're not going to take this argument lightly. In 2005, they ruled in favor of the federal government being able to regulate marijuana grown and used in California. That means any new effort will have to navigate through the faults of California's attempt and present a clear, cohesive, and compelling case that the federal government has needlessly overstepped its bounds. If that happens—and that's a Montana-sized "if"—we may have finally found the kryptonite that can be used against the progressives' relentless attack on this document.

Thirteenth Amendment

Section. 1. Neither slavery nor involuntary servitude, except as a punishment for crime whereof the party shall have been duly convicted, shall exist within the United States, or any place subject to their jurisdiction.

It took 78 years and the deaths of 618,000 people during the Civil War (including deaths due to disease), but the long effort to abolish the blight of slavery had finally ended. Article 1, Section 9 had allowed twenty years of further slave trade, a length of time that many Founders hoped would be sufficient for the South to wean itself from the horrendous practice. But even after the importation of *new* slaves stopped in 1808, the South was so dependent upon slavery that it was unwilling to let it go. (Sound a little like businesses relying on illegal immigration today?) Thus, it became necessary to end slavery by expending unthinkable amounts of blood and treasure.

Fourteenth Amendment

Section. 1. All persons born or naturalized in the United States, and subject to the jurisdiction thereof, are citizens of the United States and of the State where-in they reside. No State shall make or enforce any law which shall abridge the privileges or immunities of citizens of the United States; nor shall any State deprive any person of life, liberty, or property, without due process of law; nor deny to any person within its jurisdiction the equal protection of the laws.

Perhaps no amendment has been twisted and turned as much as this one. The "birth-right citizenship" clause was originally meant to ensure that children of freed slaves would be American citizens. Of course, we don't really have that problem anymore, so here's the 21st-century revision:

"All persons who successfully sneak into the country will be allowed to stay indefinitely. All crimes committed by those lawbreakers (i.e., identity theft, fraud, and tax evasion) shall be ignored. These non-American Americans will be afforded free health care at emergency rooms, free education, and special in-state tuition deals at colleges, not afforded legal citizens. All children born of these lawbreakers shall immediately become citizens of the United States. Any persons attempting to thwart this revision of Section 1 will be labeled racists, hatemongers, xenophobes, and all-around bad people."

Section. 3. No person shall be a Senator or Representative in Congress, or elector of President and Vice President, or hold any office, civil or military, under the United States, or under any State, who, having previously taken an oath, as a member of Congress, or as an officer of the United States, or as a member of any State legislature, or as an executive or judicial officer of any State, to support the Constitution of the United States, shall have engaged in insurrection or rebellion against the same, or given aid or comfort to the enemies thereof. But Congress may by a vote of two-thirds of each House, remove such disability.

Does shaking hands with and accepting books from our enemies give them comfort? If so, then this section should be looked at a little more closely.

Fifteenth Amendment

Section. 1. The right of citizens of the United States to vote shall not be denied or abridged by the United States or by any State on account of race, color, or previous condition of servitude.

Oops . . . they "forgot" age . . . see the 26th Amendment. It took only 101 years to fix that.

Sixteenth Amendment

The Congress shall have power to lay and collect taxes on incomes, from whatever source derived, without apportionment among the several States, and without regard to any census or enumeration.

It was President Woodrow Wilson who finally got the progressive income tax passed in this country. Of course, his rhetoric would sound nothing like that of today's politicians, right? You decide. Here are Wilson's words from an address he gave in 1913:

> "You are here in order to enable the world to live more amply, with greater vision, with a finer spirit of hope and achievement. You are here to enrich the world . . ."

Such was the rhetoric of the new progressives in America,

as they began their campaign of "social justice" and "equity" in our country, all for the "greater good." Naturally, only the meanest, most evil one percent of wage earners would be affected by this new income tax, so 99 percent of the country didn't need to worry . . . at least until it was expanded a couple of decades later.

Twenty-second Amendment

Section. 1. No person shall be elected to the office of the President more than twice, and no person who has held the office of President, or acted as President, for more than two years of a term to which some other person was elected President shall be elected to the office of the President more than once. But this Article shall not apply to any person holding the office of President when this Article was proposed by the Congress, and shall not prevent any person who may be holding the office of President, or acting as President, during the term within which this Article becomes operative from holding the office of President or acting as President during the remainder of such term.

It's interesting that this amendment was proposed just two years (and ratified six years) after the death of FDR, a president who was allegedly so beloved that he was elected to four terms. I guess we loved him so much that we wanted to make sure no one would ever stay in office that long again. Makes sense. One interesting side note: Harry Truman was specifically excluded from this amendment. He could have run for a third term but wisely chose not to.

> ## Twenty-fourth Amendment
>
> Section. 1. The right of citizens of the United States to vote in any primary or other election for President or Vice President, for electors for President or Vice President, or for Senator or Representative in Congress, shall not be denied or abridged by the United States or any State by reason of failure to pay any poll tax or other tax.

Younger Americans probably skip right past this amendment, but it was actually pretty important . . . and controversial. Around the turn of the twentieth century, several states, unhappy about the end of slavery, instituted poll taxes as a way of keeping African-Americans out of the voting booth. By the time 1962 came around, five states (Alabama, Arkansas, Mississippi, Virginia, and Texas) still used the taxes as a means of discrimination.

This amendment made federal poll taxes a crime (and state taxes were also outlawed under the equal-protection clause)—but it had a hard time getting out of the Senate. Southern Democrats, intent on keeping the amendment from coming up for a vote, filibustered for ten straight days. Then, according to one account, "they ran out of words." The Senate jumped into action, but, since the wording of the amendment was stuck in the Judiciary Committee (headed by a senator from poll-tax-friendly Mississippi), they had to rely on an old political trick instead.

After the filibuster ended, Florida conservative Spessard Holland introduced a resolution to make Alexander Hamilton's former home a national monument. Once it was approved, Holland then moved to exchange the proposed language of the Twenty-fourth Amendment with the Hamilton resolution. That passed as well and the final vote was a landslide. The amendment was ratified by the states 514 days later, though Mississippi stuck to its guns; it was the only state to outright reject it.

Twenty-fifth Amendment

Section. 1. In case of the removal of the President from office or of his death or resignation, the Vice President shall become President.

Joe Biden was actually 25 years old when this amendment, precipitated by the assassination of JFK, was ratified. If they only knew then what we know now . . .

Twenty-sixth Amendment

Section. 1. The right of citizens of the United States, who are eighteen years of age or older, to vote shall not be denied or abridged by the United States or by any State on account of age.

Does that mean we *can* deny them on account of stupidity?

CITATIONS

Just the Facts, Man

CHAPTER 1: IN DEFENSE OF CAPITALISM

PAGE 1 ★ **"'is the system I represented.'"** Forrest McDonald, *Insull: The Rise and Fall of a Billionaire Utility Tycoon*, (Frederick, MD: Beard Books, 2004), http://books.google.com/books?id=eHjcrOi2hZkC. ★ **"In 1881 . . . named Thomas Edison."** Forrest McDonald, *Insull: The Rise and Fall of a Billionaire Utility Tycoon*, (Frederick, MD: Beard Books, 2004), http://books.google.com/books?id=eHjcrOi2hZkC. **PAGE 2** ★ **"market value of over $3 billion"** "Death of an Era," *Time*, July 25, 1938, www.time.com/time/magazine/article/0,9171,883008,00.html. ★ **"estimated to be $100 million"** "Death of an Era," *Time*, July 25, 1938, www.time.com/time/magazine/article/0,9171,883008,00.html. ★ **"on their cover in 1929"** "Samuel Insull," *Time*, November 4, 1929, www.time.com/time/covers/0,16641,19291104,00.html. ★ **"'planet to extinction'"** "The Declaration of Cumaná: Capitalism 'Threatens Life on the Planet,'" *rabble.ca*, April 24, 2009, http://rabble.ca/news/2009/04/ declaration-cumaná-capitalism-threatens-life-planet. ★ **"eight cents in his pocket"** Forrest McDonald, *Insull: The Rise and Fall of a Billionaire Utility Tycoon*, (Frederick, MD: Beard Books, 2004), http://books.google.com/books?id=eHjcrOi2hZkC. **PAGE 3** ★ **List of items from 1949 Sears catalogue**, Mark J. Perry, "Young Americans: Luckiest Generation in History," *Carpe Diem: Professor Mark J. Perry's Blog for Economics and Finance*, March 13, 2009, http://mjperry.blogspot.com/2009/03/ good-old-days-are-now.html. ★ **List of items purchased in 2009**, Mark J. Perry, "Young Americans: Luckiest Generation in History," *Carpe Diem: Professor Mark J. Perry's Blog for Economics and Finance*, March 13, 2009, http://mjperry.blogspot.com/2009/03/good-old-days-are-now.html. **PAGE 5** ★ **"'It has to end.'"** Nasser Karimi, "Venezuelan Leader: 'Capitalism Needs to Go Down,'" *breitbart.com*, April 3, 2009, www.breitbart.com/article.php?id=D97B37LO0. **PAGE 6** ★ **"just six of them were complete"** John Stossel, Chris Kilmer, Sarah Netter, "Wal-Mart, Private Sector Moved Faster After Katrina Than FEMA," *ABC News*, October 15, 2008, http://abcnews,go,com/Politics/Vote2008/story?id=6031025. ★ **"up and running within ten days"** John Stossel, Chris Kilmer, Sarah Netter, "Wal-Mart, Private Sector Moved Faster After Katrina Than FEMA," *ABC News*, October 15, 2008. http://a.abcnews.com/Politics/Vote2008/Story?id=6031025. ★ **"surpassed the $1 billion mark"** Charisse Jones, "Local Charities Fear Hurricane Relief Will Siphon Donations," *USA Today*, September 19, 2005, www.usatoday.com/money/2005-09-19-charities -donations_x.htm. ★ **"According to a GAO report . . . paid for by FEMA"** Jeff Jacoby, "FEMA's Follies," *Boston Globe*, June 18, 2006, www.boston.com/news/globe/editorial_opinion/oped/articles/2006/06/18/femas_follies. ★ **"did not appear to meet legitimate disaster needs"** U.S. Government Accountability Office, "Hurricane Katrina and Rita Disaster Relief: Improper and Potentially Fraudulent Individual Assistance Payments Estimated to Be Between $600 Million and $1.4 Billion," *gao.gov*, June 14, 2006, www.gao.gov/htext/d06844t.html. ★ **"Counting Down the Fraud"** U.S. Government Accountability Office, "Hurricane Katrina and Rita Disaster Relief: Improper and Potentially Fraudulent Individual Assistance Payments Estimated to Be Between $600 Million and $1.4 Billion," *gao.gov*, June 14, 2006, www.gao.gov/htext/d06844t.html. ★ **"debit cards worth $762,000"** Jeff Jacoby, "FEMA's Follies," *Boston Globe*, June 18, 2006, http://www.boston.com/news/globe/editorial_opinion/oped/articles/2006/06/18/femas_follies. **PAGE 7** ★ **Instant Win Card**, Charles Murray, *Losing Ground: American Social Policy, 1950-1980* (New York: Crown, 2008), 8, http://books.google.com/books?id=WVOwye55tlwC. ★ **"Government should not support the people."** Grover Cleveland, George Frederick Parker, *The Writings and Speeches of Grover Cleveland,* 450, http://books.google.com/books?id=toH4pXJPahkC. ★ **"bonds of a common brotherhood."** Grover Cleveland, George Frederick Parker, *The Writings and Speeches of Grover Cleveland,* 450, http://books.google.com/books?id=toH4pXJPahkC. ★ **"vetoed three times more bills"** J.F. Watts, Fred L. Israel, *Presidential Documents,* 164, http://books.google.com/books?id=Upv2CSXysq0C. ★ **"ten times more money"** John Robson, "Grover Cleveland: A Model for President Obama?," MercatorNet, January 24, 2009, http://www.mercatornet.com/articles/view/grover_cleveland_a_model_for_president_obama. **PAGE 8** ★ **"'public welfare may require it.'"** Ronald J. Pestritto, William J. Atto, *American Progressivism*, 220, http://books.google.com/books?id=8HSIXIUVa7IC. ★ **"'regulated by the public needs'"** James D. Richardson, *A Compilation of the Messages and Papers of the Presidents, 1789-1908, Vol. VIII*, (New York: Bureau of National Literature and Art, 1908), 557, http://books.google.com/books?id=9flMAAAAIAAJ. ★ **"'there is room for the state'"** Emma Vandore, "Sarkozy, Merkel, Blair, Call for New Capitalism," *foxnews.com*, January 8, 2009, http://www.foxnews.com/wires/2009Jan08/0,4670,EUFranceNewCapitalism,00.html. **PAGE 9** ★ **"'really the right economic system'"** Peter Gumbel, "Rethinking Marx," *Time*, February 2, 2009, www.time.com/time/specials/packages/article/

Note: Web links often change or are removed. While all were working at press time, they are provided here for convenience only.

301

0,28804,1873191_ 1873190_1873188,00.html. ★ **"'swift and orderly restructuring'"** Andrew Ross Sorkin, ed., "Greenspan Said to Support Some Bank Nationalizations," *Dealbook* blog at *nytimes.com*, February 18, 2009, http://dealbook.blogs.nytimes.com/2009/02/18/greenspan-said-to-support-some-bank-nationalizations. ★ **"'We Are All Socialists Now'"** Joe Meacham and Evan Thomas, "We Are All Socialists Now," *Newsweek*, February 7, 2009, www.news-week.com/ id/183663. ★ **"and massive tax rates"** Richard Heller, "The New Face of Swedish Socialism," *Forbes*, March 19, 2001, www.forbes.com/global/ 2001/0319/034.html. ★ **"'not prepared to own car factories'"** Sarah Lyall, "Sweden Says No to Saving Saab," *New York Times*, March 22, 2009, http:// www.nytimes.com/2009/03/23/world/europe/23saab.html. **PAGE 10** ★ **"'and a key partner'"** Jeffery R. Immelt, "GE 2008 Annual Report Letter: Cash Flow, Revenues, Portfolio," *ge.com*, February 6, 2009, www.ge.com/ ar2008/letter.html. ★ **"$5 trillion in mortgage liabilities"** Ken Sweet, "Government Seizes Fannie Mae, Freddie Mac," *Fox News*, September 7, 2008, www.foxbusiness.com/story/markets/government-seied-fannie-mae-freddie-mac. ★ **"lost money every single year since."** Alan Wirzbicki, "Senate Votes to Increase Funding for Amtrak Service," *Boston Globe*, October 31, 2007, www.boston .com/news/nation/washington/articles/2007/10/31/senate_votes_to_increase_funding_for_amtrak_service. ★ **"$30 billion in federal subsidies"** Shailagh Murray, "House Rejects Cuts in Amtrak Budget: Vote More Than Doubles Funding Approved By Appropriations Committee," *Washington Post*, June 30, 2005, www.washingtonpost.com/wp-dyn/content/article/2005/06/29/AR2005062902723.html. ★ **"not including another $1.3 billion"** Lisa Desjardins, "Winners and Losers in the Final Stimulus Bill," *cnn.com*, February 13, 2009, www.cnn.com/2009/ POLITICS/02/13/stimulus.winners.losers. **PAGE 11** ★ **"$466 in government subsidies"** Shailagh Murray, "House Rejects Cuts in Amtrak Budget: Vote More Than Doubles Funding Approved By Appropriations Committee," *Washington Post*, June 30, 2005, www.washingtonpost.com/wp-dyn/content/article/2005/06/29/AR2005062902723.html. ★ **"'less than $15 million'"** Shailagh Murray, "House Rejects Cuts in Amtrak Budget: Vote More Than Doubles Funding Approved By Appropriations Committee," *Washington Post*, June 30, 2005, www.washingtonpost.com /wp-dyn/content/article/2005/06/29/AR2005062902723.html. ★ **"fired by Amtrak seven months later"** National Railroad Passenger Corporation, "Amtrak Board Releases Gunn: Railroad Begins Search for Experienced Reform Leader, David Hughes Will Run Amtrak Until Successor Is Found," news release, November 11, 2005, www.amtrak.com/servlet/ContentServer?pagename=Amtrak/am2Copy/News_Release_Page&c=am2Copy&cid=10 93554026306. **PAGE 12** ★ **"support cram-down legislation after all,"** Elizabeth Williamson and David Enrich, "Citigroup, Senators in Talks to Let Judges Modify Mortgages," *Wall Street Journal*, January 8, 2009, http://online.wsj.com/article/SB123137932114363115.html?mod=testMod. **PAGE 13** ★ **"into a quasi-governmental corporation"** James Wilson, *Bureaucracy: What Government Agencies Do and Why They Do It* (New York: Basic Books, 1991), 123. ★ **"processing 90 million pieces"** James Wilson, *Bureaucracy: What Government Agencies Do and Why They Do It* (New York: Basic Books, 1991), 123. **PAGE 14** ★ **"save $100 million a year"** Robert D. Behn, "Closing a Government Facility," *Public Administration Review*, July/August, 1978, www.jstor.org/pss/975815. ★ **"more of a priority than 'profit'"** James Wilson, *Bureaucracy: What Government Agencies Do and Why They Do It* (New York: Basic Books, 1991), 124. ★ **"in the price of a basic stamp"** Nick Abraham, Joshua Hall, and Ben VanMetre, "First Class Inefficiency: We Protest the Postal Service's Monopoly Over the Mail," *Forbes*, April 16, 2009, www.forbes.com/2009/04/16/usps-postal-service-mail-opinions-contributors-monopoly.html. ★ **"*preferred* the loss of Saturday delivery***"** James Wilson, *Bureaucracy: What Government Agencies Do and Why They Do It* (New York: Basic Books, 1991), 124. ★ **"$2.8 billion in fiscal year 2008"** United States Postal Service, "Economy-Driven Mail Volume Decline Contributes to Postal Service $2.8 Billion Year-End Loss: FY 2008 Marked by Record On-Time Mail Delivery," news release, November 13, 2008, www.usps.com/communications/newsroom/2008/ pr08_118.htm. ★ **"$3 billion to $6 billion in 2009"** Gregg Carlstorm, "Long Recession Could Stymie USPS Struggle for Solvency," *Federal Times*, February 10, 2009, http://federaltimes.com/index.php?S=3939859. ★ **"'our situation is critical'"** Associated Press, "Postal Service Could Run Out of Money in '09: Postmaster General Seeking Permission to Cut Mail Delivery Service," *msnbc.com*, March 25, 2009, www.msnbc.msn.com/id/29877702. ★ **"five-day delivery again"** Gregg Carlstorm, "Long Recession Could Stymie USPS Struggle for Solvency," *Federal Times*, February 10, 2009, http://federaltimes.com/index .php?S=3939859. ★ **"both said they would oppose it"** Gregg Carlstorm, "Long Recession Could Stymie USPS Struggle for Solvency," *Federal Times*, February 10, 2009, http://federaltimes.com/index.php?S=3939859. ★ **"politicians don't like that either"** Gregg Carlstorm, "Long Recession Could Stymie USPS Struggle for Solvency," *Federal Times*, February 10, 2009, http://federaltimes.com/index.php?S=3939859. **PAGE 16** ★ **"over 6,000 pages of rules"** James Wilson, *Bureaucracy: What Government Agencies Do and Why They Do It* (New York: Basic Books, 1991), 127. ★ **"belong to at least four of them"** Jonathan Rauch, *Demosclerosis: The Silent Killer of American Government* (New York: Times Books, 1994). ★ **"largest public works project in American history"** Richard F. Weingroff, "Creating the Interstate System," *Public Roads* 60, no. 1 (Summer 1996), www.tfhrc.gov/pubrds/summer96/p96su10.htm. ★ **"just 28 pages long"** James Wilson, *Bureaucracy: What Government Agencies Do and Why They Do It* (New York: Basic Books, 1991), xiv. ★ **"It was 293 pages long"** James Wilson, *Bureaucracy: What Government Agencies Do and Why They Do It* (New York: Basic Books, 1991), xiv. List of government agencies Hannah Sistare, *Government Reorganization: Strategies and Tools to Get It Done*, (Washington, DC: IBM Center for the Business of Government, 2004), www.businessofgovernment.org/pdfs/ SistareReport.pdf. ★ **"'among other things'"** James Wilson, *Bureaucracy: What Government Agencies Do and Why They Do It* (New York: Basic Books, 1991), xv. **PAGE 17** ★ **"on the books since 1995"** Daniel J. Mitchell, "Does Big Government Breed Corruption and Sleaze?" *Cato@Liberty*, April 21, 2009, www.cato-at-liberty.org/2009/04/21/does-big-government-breed-corruption-and-sleaze. **PAGE 18** ★ **"Reorganizing Our Reorganizations"** Peri E. Arnold, "Reform's Changing Role," *Public Administration Review* 55, no. 5 (September-October, 1995), 407-417. ★ **"eleven (mostly unsuccessful) major attempts"** James Wilson, *Bureaucracy: What Government Agencies Do and Why They Do It* (New York: Basic Books, 1991). ★ **"'should be perpetually on his guard'"** "Roosevelt for Reform by Order of Executive: Warns the Keep Commission Not to Ask for Much Legislation," *New York Times*, March 24, 1906, http://query.nytimes.com/mem/archivefree/pdf?_r=1&res=9C07EFD91531E733A25757C2A9659C946797D6C F. ★ **"'nothing could be more foolish'"** "Roosevelt for Reform by Order of Executive: Warns the Keep Commission Not to Ask for Much Legislation," *New York Times*, March 24, 1906, http://query.nytimes.com/mem/archive-free/pdf?_r=1&res=9C07EFD91531E733A25757C2A9659C946797D6CF. ★ **"'Government were run on a businesslike basis'"** "Taft Will Submit Budget to Congress: Plan Under Way to Embody All Government Estimates In This Form," *New York Times*, September 29, 1912, http://query.nytimes.com/mem/archive-free/pdf?res=9A01EFD9113AE633A2575AC2A96F9C946396D6CF. **PAGE 19** ★ **"a first for any American president"** Hannah Sistare, *Government Reorganization: Strategies and Tools to Get It Done*, (Washington, DC: IBM Center for the Business of Government, 2004), www.businessofgovernment.org/pdfs/ SistareReport.pdf. ★ **"'off the backs' of the American people'"** Grace Commission, *President's Private Sector Survey on Cost Control: A Report to the President, Volume 1*, special report prepared at the request of the Executive Committee, January 15, 1984, www.uhuh.com/taxstuff/gracecom.htm. ★ **"necessary social welfare programs'"** Grace Commission, *President's Private Sector Survey on Cost Control: A Report to the President, Volume 1*, special report prepared at the request of the Executive Committee, January 15, 1984, www .uhuh.com/taxstuff/gracecom.htm. **PAGE 20** ★ **"estimated at over $40 million"** "Drinkers Still Pay Flood Relief Tax Enacted in 1936," *wgal.com*, July 12, 2005, www.wgal.com/news/4711497/detail.html?subid=22100741&qs=1;bp=t. ★ **"an absurd 18 percent"** Mike Faher, "Customers Still Paying 'Johnstown Flood Tax,'" *Johnstown Tribune-Democrat*, December 15, 2007, www.tribunedemocrat.com/local/local_story_349235951.html. ★ **"net about $283 million"**

Pennsylvania Office of the Governor, *2009-10 Budget*, (Harrisburg, 2009), www.portal.state.pa.us/portal/server.pt/ gateway/PTARGS_0_113914_350146_0_0 _18/2009_10_Budget_Document.pdf. ★ **"'with the workplace and factory'"** Bruce Crumley, "The Protests in France Get Personal," *Time*, March 19, 2009, www.time.com/time/world/article/ 0,8599,1886519,00.html. ★ **"'economic opportunity to trickle up'"** Lori Montgomery, "In Obama Tax Plan, a Shift of Wealth From the Top Down," *Washington Post*, March 7, 2009, www.washingtonpost.com/wp-dyn/content/article/2009/03/06/ AR2009030603367.html. **PAGE 21** ★ **"sporting event in Massachusetts"** Mac Daniel, "Black and Blue: Largely Ignored, Puritan Laws Like 'Common Day of Rest' Revisited for the Holidays," *Boston Globe*, December 4, 2005, www.boston.com/news/local/massachusetts/articles/2005/12/04/back_and_blue. ★ **"set up in the 1930s"** Dan Morgan, Sarah Cohen, and Gilbert M. Gaul, "Dairy Industry Crushed Innovator Who Bested Price-Control System," *Washington Post*, December 10, 2006, www.washingtonpost.com/wp-dyn/content/article/2006/12/09/AR2006120900925.html. ★ **"we need some regulation now"** Jeff Poor, "CNBC Contributor Howard Dean: 'I Think We Had Quite Enough Capitalism,'" *newsbusters.org*, May 8, 2009, http://newsbusters.org/blogs/jeff-poor/2009/05/08/cnbc-contributor-howard-dean-i-think-we-had-quite-enough-capitalism. ★ **"over $1.5 billion a year"** Citizens Against Government Waste, "Milk Marketing Orders," *cagw .org*, accessed May 13, 2009, www.cagw.org/site/Page Server?pagename=policy_Milk_Marketing_Orders. ★ **"$12.5 billion in annual revenues"** Dean Foods, "Shareholder Information 2009," *deanfoods.com*, accessed May 13, 2009, www.deanfoods.com/our-company/investor-relations/shareholder-information.aspx. ★ **"competitors were also forced to slash prices"** Dan Morgan, Sarah Cohen, and Gilbert M. Gaul, "Dairy Industry Crushed Innovator Who Bested Price-Control System," *Washington Post*, December 10, 2006, www.washingtonpost.com/wp- dyn/content/article/2006/12/09/AR2006120900925.html. **PAGE 22** ★ **"passed the bill by 13 votes"** Morgan, Sarah Cohen, and Gilbert M. Gaul, "Dairy Industry Crushed Innovator Who Bested Price-Control System," *Washington Post*, December 10, 2006, www.washingtonpost.com/wp-dyn/content/article/2006/12/09/AR2006120900925.html. ★ **"member companies and their employees"** Dan Morgan, Sarah Cohen, and Gilbert M. Gaul, "Dairy Industry Crushed Innovator Who Bested Price-Control System," *Washington Post*, December 10, 2006, www.washingtonpost.com/wp-dyn/content/article/2006/12/09/AR2006120900925.html. ★ **"contributions received from dairy interests"** Dan Morgan, Sarah Cohen, and Gilbert M. Gaul, "Dairy Industry Crushed Innovator Who Bested Price-Control System," page 5, *Washington Post*, December 10, 2006, www.washingtonpost.com/wp-dyn/content/article/2006/12/09/AR2006120900925.html. ★ **"up to $400,000 a month,"** Dan Morgan, Sarah Cohen, and Gilbert M. Gaul, "Dairy Industry Crushed Innovator Who Bested Price-Control System," page 5, *Washington Post*, December 10, 2006, www.washingtonpost.com/wp-dyn/content/article/2006/12/09/AR2006120900925.html. ★ **"reversed that decision"** Hein Hettinga, et. al v. U.S., 07-5403 F. 06cv01637 (D.C. Cir. 2009), http://caselaw.lp.findlaw.com/data2/circs/dc/075403p.pdf. ★ **"free enterprise in the United States"** Dan Morgan, Sarah Cohen, and Gilbert M. Gaul, "Dairy Industry Crushed Innovator Who Bested Price-Control System," *Washington Post*, December 10, 2006, www.washingtonpost.com/wp-dyn/content/article/2006/12/09/AR2006120900925.html. **PAGE 23** ★ **"a real economic system'"** Breitbart, "Ahmadinejad Rips Capitalism," *breitbart .com*, April 6, 2009, www.breitbart.com/article.php?id=CNG.15148f36e80f2222604c174cd120fa19.5b1. ★ **"about $2.7 billion"** Kirk Johnson, "Weicker Income-Tax Plan Dying As Bipartisan Opposition Grows," *New York Times*, May 16, 1991, www.nytimes.com/1991/05/16/nyregion/weicker-income-tax-plan-dying-as-bipartisan-opposition-grows.html. ★ **"'facing toward the future"** Kirk Johnson, "Budget Is Passed for Connecticut with Income Tax," *New York Times*, August 23, 1991, www.nytimes.com/1991/08/23/nyregion/budget-is-passed-for-connecticut-with-income-tax.html. ★ **"over $7.5 billion a year"** Connecticut Office of the Governor, *2010-2011 Biennial Budget*, (Hartford, 2009), www.ct.gov/opm/lib/opm/budget/ 2010_2011_biennial_budget/bigbook/bigbook-part1_fob_final_schedules.pdf. **PAGE 24** ★ **"$6 billion to $8 billion over the next two years"** Associated Press, "Rell Says Jobs, Revenue Not as Bad as Once Thought," *Associated Press*, March 4, 2009. ★ **"projected to be $18.8 billion"** Connecticut Office of the Governor, *2010-2011 Biennial Budget*, (Hartford, 2009), www.ct.gov/opm/lib/opm/budget/ 2010_2011_biennial_budget/bigbook/bigbookpart1_fob_final_schedules.pdf. ★ **"'and our environment were destroyed'"** Robert Higgs, "Results of Still Another Fifty-Year Experiment in Political Economy," *Independent Review* 12, no.1 (Summer 2007): 151-2, www.independent.org/pdf/tir/ tir_12_01_09_higgs.pdf. **PAGE 25** ★ **"to 18 percent within a few years"** Daniel J. Mitchell, "Baltic Beacon," *cato.org*, June 20, 2007, www.cato.org/pub_display.php?pub_id=8378. ★ **"average of just 10-15 minutes to file their returns online"** Daniel J. Mitchell, "Estonia's Flat Tax Leads to Economic Boom," *Cato@Liberty*, April 18, 2007, www.cato-at-liberty.org/2007/04/18/estonias-flat-tax-leads-to-economic-boom. ★ **"virtually identical to Finland's"** Craig M. Newmark, "Estonia and Finland, Updated," *Independent Review* 13, no. 4 (Spring 2009): 624-5. ★ **"to 7.5 per thousand"** Craig M. Newmark, "Estonia and Finland, Updated," *Independent Review* 13, no. 4 (Spring 2009): 624-5. ★ **"cut . . . almost in half"** Craig M. Newmark, "Estonia and Finland, Updated," *Independent Review* 13, no. 4 (Spring 2009): 624-5. ★ **"5.8 percent over the same time period"** Craig M. Newmark, "Estonia and Finland, Updated," *Independent Review* 13, no. 4 (Spring 2009): 624-5. ★ **"127 cellular phones for every hundred people"** Craig M. Newmark, "Estonia and Finland, Updated," *Independent Review* 13, no. 4 (Spring 2009): 624-5. ★ **"'Silicon Valley on the Baltic Sea'"** Mark Landler, "Hot Technology for Chilly Streets in Estonia," *New York Times*, December 13, 2005, www.nytimes.com/2005/12/13/technology/13skype.html. **PAGE 28** ★ **"poverty line is still over 40 percent"** Mark Weisbrot, Luis Sandoval, and David Rosnick, "Poverty Rates in Venezuela: Getting the Numbers Right," (Washington, D.C.: Center for Economic and Policy Research, 2006), www.rethinkvenezuela.com/downloads/ceprpov.htm. ★ **"rate is over 30 percent"** U.S. Central Intelligence Agency, "Field Listing: Population Below Poverty Line," in *The World Factbook* (Washington, D.C.: CIA, 2008), www.cia.gov/library/publications/the-world-fact book/fields/2046.html. **PAGE 31** ★ **"'more attractive not to work than to work'"** Roger Cohen, "One France Is Enough," *New York Times*, March 4, 2009, www.nytimes.com/2009/03/05/ opinion/05Cohen.html. **PAGE 32** ★ **"'created before it can be shared'"** The Economist, "France's Troubles: A Tale of Two Frances," *The Economist*, March 30, 2006. ★ **"as 23 percent of young people in France are unemployed"** The Economist, "France's Troubles: A Tale of Two Frances," *The Economist*, March 30, 2006. ★ **"64 percent of all French youths"** The Economist, "France's Troubles: A Tale of Two Frances," *The Economist*, March 30, 2006. ★ **"'say in their protests, 'institutionalizes insecurity'"** The Economist, "France's Troubles: A Tale of Two Frances," *The Economist*, March 30, 2006. ★ **"25 percent of all jobs in France"** The Economist, "France's Troubles: A Tale of Two Frances," *The Economist*, March 30, 2006. ★ **"three schools in the top hundred"** Academic Ranking of World Universities, "Top 500 World Universities," *Center for World Class Universities*, 2008, www.arwu.org/rank2008/ARWU2008_A(EN).htm. **PAGE 33** ★ **"from 66 percent of GDP today"** AFX News Limited, "France's Breton Says Debt Could Fall to 60 pct of GDP by 2012," *forbes.com*, December 14, 2005, www.forbes.com/feeds/afx/2005/12/14/afx2390783.html. ★ **"catastrophic 100 percent in 2014"** The Economist, "France's Troubles: A Tale of Two Frances," *The Economist*, March 30, 2006. ★ **"17 different schools in the top 20"** Academic Ranking of World Universities, "Top 500 World Universities," *Center for World Class Universities*, 2008, www.arwu.org/rank2008/ARWU2008_A(EN).htm.

CHAPTER 2: THE SECOND AMENDMENT

PAGE 35 ★ **"'fear the government, there is tyranny'"** Walter E. Williams, *Do the Right Thing: The People's Economist Speaks* (Stanford, CA: Hoover Institution Press, 1995), 149, http://books.google.com/books?id=SxGurfTCNZcC. **PAGE 36** ★ **"militia clause were actually quite common"** Eugene Volokh, *The Commonplace Second Amendment*, 73 N.Y.U.L. Rev. 793, 794-95 (1998). ★ **"'right to service in a "militia"'"** "Lock and Load," *New York*

Times, June 27, 2008, www.nytimes.com/2008/06/27/opinion /27fri1.html. **PAGE 37** ★ **"'shall ever be debarred the use of arms'"** Thomas Jefferson, *The Writings of Thomas Jefferson*, ed. Paul Leicester Ford (New York: G. P. Putnam's Sons, 1893): 2: 27. ★ **"'a ridiculous notion'"** *Copeman v. Gallant*, 1 P. Wms. 314, 320 (1716). **"decision 'with some heat'"** *Copeman v. Gallant*, 1 P. Wms. 314, 320 (1716). ★ **"'must not be had to the preamble'"** James Kent, *Commentaries on American Law*, vol. 4 (Boston: Little, Brown, 1858). **PAGE 38** ★ **"'not really a right'"** Alicia Colon, "A Case for Guns," New York Sun, November 17, 2006, www.nysun.com/new-york/case-for-guns/43736/. ★ **"'used to create doubt or uncertainty'"** Norman Singer, *2A Sutherland on Statutory Constructions*, sect. 47.04 at 224-25 (6th ed., Clark Boardman Callaghan 2000). ★ **"'shall forever be encouraged'"** U.S. Congress, *Act of August 7, 1789*, ch.8, 1 stat. 50, 52. ★ **"'Progress of Science and the useful Arts'"** U.S. Constitution, art. 1, sect. 8, cl. 8. ★ **"don't limit copyright and patent protection"** *Scnapper v. Foley*, 667 F.2d 102, 112 (D.C. Cir. 1981) and *Eldred v. Ashcroft*, 537 U.S. 186, 212 (2003). **PAGE 39** ★ **"'and know when they are violated'"** St. George Tucker, *Blackstone's Commentaries* app. 308 (William Birch Young & Abraham Small 1803). ★ **"report done by the Missouri Information Analysis Center"** Joshua Rhett Miller, "'Fusion Centers' Expand Criteria to Identify Militia Members," foxnews.com, March 23, 2009, www.fox news.com/politics/first100days/2009/03/23/fusion-centers-expand-criteria-identify-militia-members. **PAGE 40** ★ **"'and also to organize 'the Militia'"** *Perpich v. Department of Defense*, 496 U.S. 334, 340 (1990) and U.S. Constitution, art. 1, sect. 8. ★ **"asked 'Who are the Militia?'"** Jonathan Elliott, *The Debates in the Several State Conventions of the Adoption of the Federal Constitution* 425, (2nd ed., J.B. Lippincott 1836). ★ **"'consist now of the whole people'"** Jonathan Elliott, *The Debates in the Several State Conventions of the Adoption of the Federal Constitution* 425, (2nd ed., J.B. Lippincott 1836). ★ **"'cooperate in the work of defence'"** *United States v. Miller*, 307 U.S. 174, 179-80 (1939). ★ **"'acting in concert for the common defense'"** *United States v. Miller*, 307 U.S. 174, 179-80 (1939). ★ **"'citizens with arms in their hands'"** James Madison, "The Federalist Number 46," in *The Federalist Papers*, eds. George W. Carey and James McClellan (Indianapolis, IN: Liberty Fund, 2001): 244. ★ **"'afraid to trust the people with arms'"** James Madison, "The Federalist Number 46," in *The Federalist Papers*, eds. George W. Carey and James McClellan (Indianapolis, IN: Liberty Fund, 2001): 244. ★ **"who all have and can use arms"** *Boston Evening Post*, November 21, 1768, at 2, col. 3. ★ **"spirit and ability of Americans'"** *New York Packet and American Advertiser*, April 4, 1776, at 2, cols. 1-2. **PAGE 41** ★ **"law defines 'the militia of the United States'"** U.S. Code Title 10, sect. 311-313. ★ **"'expected to appear bearing arms supplied by'"** *United States v. Miller*, 307 U.S. 174, 179-80 (1939). ★ **"'rendering themselves useless—by disarming them'"** Kate Mason Rowland, *The Life of George Mason: 1725-1792* (New York: G. P. Putnam's Sons, 1892): 2:408. ★ **"'suitable to their Conditions and as allowed by Law'"** Bill of Rights 1 William & Mary, Sess. 2, c. 2, sect. 1 (1689). ★ **"defence of his house and family"** *Mallock v. Eastly*, 87 Eng. Rep. 1370, 1374, Mod. Rep. 482 (C.P. 1744). **PAGE 42** ★ **"'for their defence, not for offence'"** John Adams, *The Adams Papers: Legal Papers of John Adams*, L. Kinvin Wroth and Hiller B. Zobel eds. (Cambridge, MA: Belknap Press of Harvard University Press, 1965), 3:149 and 3:248. ★ **"disarmament of the people of Boston provoked outrage"** *Journals of the Continental Congress, 1774-1789* (Washington, D.C., 1905): 2: 136-7. **PAGE 43** ★ **"'regulated means 'properly disciplined'"** *Oxford English Dictionary*, 1st ed., under the word "Regulated." ★ **"means 'training in the practice of arms'"** *Oxford English Dictionary*, 1st ed., under the word "Discipline." ★ **"'well-regulated militia'"** Kate Mason Rowland, *The Life of George Mason: 1725-1792* (New York: G. P. Putnam's Sons, 1892): 1:428. ★ **"the world as well as property'"** Thomas Paine, *The Writings of Thomas Paine*, ed. Moncure Daniel Conway (New York: G. P. Putnam's Sons, 1894): 1:56. **PAGE 44** ★ **"Newburn . . . Gazette reported that 'a Demoniac'"** *North Carolina Gazette* (Newburn), July 7, 1775, at 3, col.1. ★ **"'After the 1996 'Dunblane Massacre'"** "Handgun Crime 'Up' Despite Ban," news.bbc.co.uk, July 16, 2001, http://news.bbc.co.uk/1/hi/uk/1440764.stm. ★ **"John Adams confidently quoted from it"** John Adams, *The Adams Papers: Legal Papers of John Adams*, L. Kinvin Wroth and Hiller B. Zobel eds., (Cambridge, MA: Belknap Press of Harvard University Press, 1965): 3:242. ★ **"not by thoughtful consideration"** Thomas Jefferson, *The Commonplace Book of Thomas Jefferson*, Gilbert Chinard ed. (Baltimore: Johns Hopkins University Press, 1926). See also Cesare Beccaria, *An Essay on Crimes and Punishments*, trans. Edward D. Ingraham (Philadelphia: P.H. Nicklin, 1819). ★ **"'prepared with Weapons for his Defense'"** *North Carolina Gazette* (Newburn), July 7, 1775, at 2, col.3. **PAGE 46** ★ **"husband to death with a two-slice toaster."** Pat Hathcock and Jason Collins, "Harris County Charges Victoria Woman with Murder," *Victoria Advocate*, November 18, 2002, www.dadi.org/ toaster.htm. ★ **"pushed the hearse forward into her head, killing her."** Fox News "Widow Killed by Husband's Coffin on Way to Bury Him," *foxnews.com*, November 11, 2008, www.foxnews .com/story/0,2933,449919,00 .html. ★ **"StarCraft online for almost 50 consecutive hours."** "S. Korean Dies After Games Session," news.bbc.co.uk, August 10, 2005, http://news.bbc .co.uk/1/hi/technology/4137782.stm. ★ **"watching pornography on his laptop computer."** David Watkinson, "Popular Blackburn Comedian Died of Accidental Gas Overdose," *thisislancashire.co.uk*, April 15, 2009, www.thisislancashire.co.uk/news/4293113. ★ **"considered a violation of your Fourth Amendment rights"** *Kyllo v. United States*, 533 U.S. 27 (2001). **PAGE 47** ★ **"the rest of us will be cannibals"** Mike Morris, "Ted Turner: Global Warming Could Lead to Cannibalism," *Atlanta Journal-Constitution*, April 3, 2008, www.ajc.com/metro/content/news/stories/2008/04/03/turner_0404.html. **PAGE 48** ★ **"restricted in the United States since the mid-1930s"** *National Firearms Act, U.S. Code* 26 (1934), sec. 5801, www.atf.gov/pub/fire-explo_ pub/nfa.htm. ★ **"subject to government health and safety regulations"** Violence Policy Center, "About the Violence Policy Center," vpc.org, accessed June 17, 2009, www.vpc.org/aboutvpc.htm. ★ **"'support for restrictions on these weapons'"** Violence Policy Center, "Conclusion," in "Assault Weapons and Accessories in America," *vpc.org*, Accessed June 17, 2009, www.vpc.org/studies/awaconc.htm. **PAGE 50** ★ **"'different enough to remain on the market'"** Violence Policy Center, "Conclusion," in "Assault Weapons and Accessories in America," *vpc.org*, Accessed June 17, 2009, www.vpc.org/studies/ awaconc.htm. ★ **"deemed to be 'assault weapons'"** *Crimes and Criminal Procedure, U.S. Code* 18, sec. 921, (a) (30) (A). ★ **"'evil features' was banned'"** *Crimes and Criminal Procedure, U.S. Code* 18, sec. 921, (a) (30) (B). ★ **"'safe Defence of a free state'"** Merrill Jensen, John P. Kaminski, and Gaspare J. Saladino, eds., *The Documentary History of the Ratification of the Constitution* (Madison: State Historical Society of Wisconsin, 1976): 440. **PAGE 51** ★ **"a shoulder thing that goes up'"** Bill Gavin, Keith Ablow, and Carolyn McCarthy, interview by Tucker Carlson, *Tucker*, MSNBC, April 19, 2007, www.msnbc.msn.com/id/18200226. **PAGE 52** ★ **"husband was killed and son injured"** Peter Marks, "Train Shooting Victim Speaks for First Time Since Injury," *New York Times*, December 15, 1993, www.nytimes.com/1993/12/15/nyregion /train-shooting-victim-speaks-for-first-time-since-injury.html. ★ **"'with a gun and I don't have one'"** Philip Morris, "Anti-Gun Politician Switches Sides After Being Made Victim in Mugging," *Cleveland Plain Dealer*, May 16, 2007. ★ **"Nothing seemed to work very well"** Robert A. Hahn et al. for the Task Force on Community Preventative Services, *First Reports Evaluating the Effectiveness of Strategies for Preventing Violence: Firearms Laws* (Atlanta: Centers for Disease Control and Prevention, 2003), http://cdc.gov/mmwr/preview/ mmwrhtml/ rr5214a2.htm. ★ **"'getting more conservative about gun control'"** Richard S. Dunham, "Support Waning for New Gun Laws," *Houston Chronicle*, May 5, 2009, www.chron.com/disp/ story.mpl/politics/6409891.html. ★ **"reduce violent crime, suicide, or accidents? Zero"** National Research Council Committee on Law and Justice, Charles F. Wellford, John V. Pepper, and Carol V. Petrie eds., *Firearms and Violence: A Critical Review* (Washington, D.C.: National Academies Press, 2004): 98. **PAGE 53** ★ **"skyrocketed 340 percent"** David Leppard, "Ministers 'Covered Up' Gun Crime," *London Times*, August 26, 2007, www.timesonline.co.uk/tol/ news/uk/crime/article2328368.ece. ★ **"'no significant correlations'"** Martin Killias, John van Kesteren, and

Martin Rindlisbacher, "Guns, Violent Crime, and Suicide in 21 Countries," *Canadian Journal of Criminology* 43, no. 4 (2001): 429-48. ★ **"between 1990-1995, reached the same conclusion"** Gary Kleck, *Targeting Guns: Firearms and Their Control* (Piscataway, N.J.: Aldine Transaction, 1997): 254. ★ **"widespread gun ownership had fewer murders"** Don B. Kates and Barry Mauser, "Would Banning Firearms Reduce Murder and Suicide? A Review of International and Some Domestic Evidence," Harvard Journal of Law and Public Policy 30, no. 2 (2007): 651-94. ★ **"in crimes rose by 40 percent"** "Handgun Crime 'Up' Despite Ban," *news.bbc.co.uk*, July 16, 2001, http://news.bbc.co.uk/2/hi/uk_news/1440764.stm. ★ **"rather than criminals"** "Handgun Crime 'Up' Despite Ban," *news.bbc.co.uk*, July 16, 2001, http://news.bbc.co.uk/2/hi/uk_news/1440764.stm. ★ **"response time was . . . 8 minutes, 25 seconds"** Matthew Cella, "Police Response to 911s Slowing," *Washington Times*, May 10, 2004, www.washington times.com/news/2004/may/10/20040510-122711-8996r. **PAGE 54** ★ **"so tired of waiting that they gave up"** Jim Keary, "Need Police? Call 911 and Wait: Sick-Leave Abuse Retards Responses," *Washington Times*, June 24, 1998. ★ **"the 911 system is a joke'"** "Time to Police the Chief," *Washington Post*, June 1, 2003, http://pqasb.pqarchiver.com/washingtonpost/ access/342376461.html?dids=342376461:342376461&FMT=ABS&FMTS=ABS:FT&fmac=&date=Jun+1,+2003&author=&desc=Time+to+Police+the+Chief. ★ **"even after all the money we've put into this"** Michael Neibauer, "Councilman Claims He Was Badgered During 911 Call," *examiner.com*, December 15, 2007, www.examiner.com/a-1106755~Councilman_ claims_he_was_badgered_during_911_call.html. ★ **"gun rights over human life."** "Lock and Load," *New York Times*, June 27, 2008, http://www.nytimes.com/2008/06/27/ opinion/27fri1.html. ★ **"recording with some calming music"** Shelly Feuer Domash, "Nassau 911 Callers Are Being Put on Hold," *New York Times*, September14, 2003, www.nytimes.com/2003/09/14/nyregion/nassau-911-callers-are-being-put-on-hold.html. ★ **"911 calls in New York City: 7.2 minutes"** "Mayor Bloomberg Releases Fiscal 2005 Mayor's Management Report," *U.S. States News*, September 12, 2005. ★ **"Los Angeles, 10.5 minutes"** "L.A. Police Average Over Ten Minutes in Responding to 911 Calls," *Associated Press*, July 1, 2003. ★ **"Atlanta and three neighboring counties, 11.1 minutes"** Fox 5 Atlanta, "911 Response Times: An I-Team Investigation," *Fox News*. ★ **"Philadelphia, almost 7 minutes"** Howard Goodman, "A System Geared to Preventing 'Another Polec'," *Philadelphia Inquirer*, August 3, 1998. ★ **"Florida, just over 7 minutes"** Leanora Minai, "Is That Enough? There are 505 Sworn Officers on St. Petersburg's Force. 97 Work the Street," *St. Petersburg Times*, April 7, 2002, www.sptimes.com/2002/04/07/TampaBay/Is_that_enough.shtml. ★ **"highest police officer to citizen ratio"** Michael Powell, Sari Horwitz, and Cheryl W. Thompson, "Problems in D.C. Police Dept. Festered for Decades," *Washington Post*, October 12, 1997. ★ **"values gun rights over human life'"** "Lock and Load," *New York Times*, June 27, 2008, www.nytimes.com/2008/06/27/opinion/ 27fri1.html. ★ **"you get hammered for it"** David A. Fahrenthold, "D.C. Police Cut Goal on Closing Homicides: Ramsey Calls New Target for Solving Cases Realistic," *Washington Post*, June 26, 2002, www.washingtonpost.com/ ac2/wp-dyn/A45064-2002Jun25. **PAGE 55** ★ **"solved, it counts towards the department's success"** Charles C. Maddox, Esq., *Audit of Contract Performance Measures and the Mayor's Scorecard Measures*, Government of the District of Columbia Office of the Inspector General, 2001, Audit Report No. OIG-00-2-12MA, http://oig.dc.gov/news/view2.asp?url=2001_March_20/part_one_30201.pdf&mode=audit&archived=1&month=20012. ★ **"it's 6 percent"** Charles C. Maddox, Esq., *Audit of Contract Performance Measures and the Mayor's Scorecard Measures*, Government of the District of Columbia Office of the Inspector General, 2001, Audit Report No. OIG-00-2-12MA, http://oig.dc.gov/news/view2.asp?url=2001_March_20/part_one_30201.pdf&mode=audit&archi ved=1&month=20012. ★ **"rated only a 'code 2'"** *Warren v. District of Columbia*, 444 A.2d 1 (D.C. 1981). **PAGE 56** ★ **"the police left"** *Warren v. District of Columbia*, 444 A.2d 1 (D.C. 1981). ★ **"investigate the trouble'—and nobody ever did"** *Warren v. District of Columbia*, 444 A.2d 1 (D.C. 1981). ★ **"brutalized them for another fourteen hours"** *Warren v. District of Columbia*, 444 A.2d 1 (D.C. 1981). ★ **"especially when young, how to use them'"** Robert J. Cottrol, ed., *Gun Control and the Constitution: Sources and Explorations of the Second Amendment* (New York: Garland, 1994): 27. ★ **"reasonable means to enforce this restraining order"** *Town of Castle Rock v. Gonzales*, 545 U.S. 748 (2005). **PAGE 57** ★ **"again told to wait until 10 pm"** *Town of Castle Rock v. Gonzales*, 545 U.S. 748 (2005). ★ **"then went to get something to eat"** *Town of Castle Rock v. Gonzales*, 545 U.S. 748 (2005). ★ **"three little girls . . . were already dead"** *Town of Castle Rock v. Gonzales*, 545 U.S. 748 (2005). ★ **"Jessica had no constitutional interest"** *Town of Castle Rock v. Gonzales*, 545 U.S. 748 (2005). **PAGE 58** ★ **"from 760,000 to over 3 million defensive gun uses"** Gary Kleck, "Guns and Self Defense," in *Targeting Guns: Firearms and Their Control* (Piscataway, N.J.: Aldine Transaction, 1997). ★ **"no shots were ever fired"** Gary Kleck and Marc Gertz, "Armed Resistance to Crime: The Prevalence and Nature of Self-Defense with a Gun," *Journal of Criminal Law and Criminology* 86, no. 1 (1995). ★ **"at most, one percent"** Gary Kleck, *Targeting Guns: Firearms and Their Control* (Piscataway, N.J.: Aldine Transaction, 1997): 168-9. ★ **"reduced the chance of being injured"** Lawrence Southwick, Jr., "Self-Defense with Guns: The Consequences," *Journal of Criminal Justice* 28, no. 5 (2000): 351, 362, 367. ★ **"789 accidental deaths from firearms"** Centers for Disease Control and Prevention, "Age-Adjusted Death Rates for 113 Selected Causes by Race and Sex: United States, 2005," *disastercenter.com*, January 16, 2008, www.disastercenter.com/cdc/Age%20adjusted%20death%20rates%20for%20113%20selected% 20causes%20by%20race%20and%20sex%202005.html. ★ **"as dying in a plane crash or from bronchitis"** Centers for Disease Control and Prevention, "Age-Adjusted Death Rates for 113 Selected Causes by Race and Sex: United States, 2005," *disastercenter.com*, January 16, 2008, www.disastercenter.com/ cdc/Age%20adjusted%20death%20rates%20for%20113%20selected%20causes%20by%20race%20and%20sex%202005.html. ★ **"prepared their own downfall by so doing'"** Hugh-Redwald Trevor-Roper, *Hitler's Secret Conversations: 1941-1944* (New York: Farrar, Strauss and Young, 1953): 345. ★ **"285 children drowned in pools in 2003"** National Safety Council, *Injury Facts 2007* (Itasca, IL: National Safety Council, 2007). **PAGE 59** ★ **"death by gun . . . isn't even close'"** Steven D. Levitt and Stephen J. Dubner, *Freakonomics: A Rogue Economist Explores the Hidden Side of Everything (Revised and Expanded Edition)* (New York: William Morrow, 2006): 135-6. ★ **"because other methods would be chosen'"** World Health Organization, *Changing Patterns in Suicide Behavior* (Copenhagen: World Health Organization, 1982). ★ **"or overdosing on pills"** Gary Kleck, *Targeting Guns: Firearms and Their Control* (Piscataway, N.J.: Aldine Transaction, 1997): 266. ★ **"an average rate of suicide"** James B. Jacobs, *Can Gun Control Work?* (New York: Oxford University Press, USA, 2002): 6. ★ **"often at far greater rates"** Gary Kleck, *Targeting Guns: Firearms and Their Control* (Piscataway, N.J.: Aldine Transaction, 1997): 254, 265-89. See also Martin Killias, John van Kesteren, and Martin Rindlisbacher, "Guns, Violent Crime, and Suicide in 21 Countries," *Canadian Journal of Criminology* 43, no. 4 (2001): 429-48. ★ **"rates of suicide and homicide in . . . America, combined"** World Health Organization, "Suicide Rates (Per 100,000), by Gender, Japan, 1950-2006," who.int, accessed May 28, 2009, www.who.int/mental_health/ media/japa.pdf. See also, Centers for Disease Control and Prevention, "Suicide: Facts at a Glance," cdc.gov, accessed May 28, 2009, www.cdc.gov/ncipc/ dvp/suicide/SuicideData Sheet.pdf and Centers for Disease Control and Prevention, "Faststats: Assault or Homicide," cdc.gov, accessed May 28, 2009, www.cdc.gov/nchs/fastats/ homicide.htm.

CHAPTER 3: EDUCATION

PAGE 62 ★ **"four times more money at public schools"** Neal McCluskey, "No Federal Failure Left Behind," cato.org, July 12, 2004, www.cato.org/pub_ display.php?pub_id=4574. ★ **"over one million incoming college students"** PR Newswire, "Strong American Schools Unveils New Research on the Cost of

College Remediation for Unprepared U.S. Students and Taxpayers," *PR Newswire-US Newswire*, September 15, 2008. ★ **"$2.5 billion a year"** PR Newswire, "Strong American Schools Unveils New Research on the Cost of College Remediation for Unprepared U.S. Students and Taxpayers," *PR Newswire-US Newswire*, September 15, 2008. ★ **"32 million Americans who can't read or write"** Chris Davies, "Illiteracy Rates Worsening in U.S.," *Daily Vidette*, January 20, 2009, www.dailyvidette.com/media/storage/paper420/news/2009/01/20/News/Illiteracy.Rates.Worsening.In.U.s-3589202.shtml. **PAGE 63** ★ **"couldn't even locate New York State"** Shradhha Sharma, "Know Your Astoria From Your Erie? Many Young People Are Woefully Ignorant of National, World Geography," *Mobile Register*, April 15, 2007. ★ **"four votes in the House"** *Department of Education Organization Act*, HR 2444, 96th Cong., 1st sess. (February 27, 1979). **PAGE 64** ★ **"objected to expanding federal influence"** Edward B. Fiske, "Some Republicans Oppose Efforts to Abolish U.S. Education Dept.," *New York Times*, December 26, 1981. ★ **"NYPD corruption was dealt a death blow"** Clyde Haberman, "Serpico Steps Out of the Shadows to Testify," *New York Times*, September 24, 1997, www.nytimes.com/1997/09/24/nyregion/serpico-steps-out-of-the-shadows-to-testify.html. ★ **"'education is the motor-force of revolution'"** Andy McCarthy, "What Kind of Education Reform Did Ayers & Obama Have in Mind?" *National Review*, October 11, 2008. **PAGE 67** ★ **"purple . . . is in"** Naomi Aoki, "Harshness of Red Marks Has Students Seeing Purple," *Boston Globe*, August 23, 2004, www.boston.com/news/education/k_12/articles/2004/08/23/harshness_of_red_marks_has_students_seeing_purple. ★ **"'the improvements progressives sought'"** Ronald J. Pestritto, *American Progressivism: A Reader*, (Lanham, MD: Lexington, 2008), 13. ★ **"'doesn't look as scary as red'"** Naomi Aoki, "Harshness of Red Marks Has Students Seeing Purple," *Boston Globe*, August 23, 2004, www.boston.com/news/education/k_12/articles/2004/08/23/harshness_of_red_marks_has_students_seeing_purple ★ **"'I use purple a lot'"** Naomi Aoki, "Harshness of Red Marks Has Students Seeing Purple," *Boston Globe*, August 23, 2004, www.boston.com/news/education/k_12/articles/2004/08/23/harshness_of_red_marks_has_students_seeing_purple. ★ **"'purple is a more approachable color'"** Sherry Parmet, "Teachers Starting to Shun Red Pens: Color May Lower Kids' Confidence," *San Diego Union-Tribune*, October 4, 2004, www.signonsandiego.com/uniontrib/20041004/news_1m4pens.html. **PAGE 69** ★ **"'unduly specialized or else disintegrated'"** Ronald J. Pestritto, *American Progressivism: A Reader*, (Lanham, MD: Lexington, 2008), 120. ★ **"'properly responding to these influences'"** Ronald J. Pestritto, *American Progressivism: A Reader*, (Lanham, MD: Lexington, 2008), 120. ★ **"'red is not one of those colors'"** Associated Press, "Parents to Teachers: No More Red Pencils," *msnbc.com*, April 3, 2005, www.msnbc.msn.com/id/ 7374218. ★ **"'here's what you can do better'"** Sherry Parmet, "Teachers Starting to Shun Red Pens: Color May Lower Kids' Confidence," *San Diego Union-Tribune*, October 4, 2004, www.signonsandiego.com/uniontrib/20041004/news_1m4pens.html. ★ **"'it's the color of Barney'"** Sherry Parmet, "Teachers Starting to Shun Red Pens: Color May Lower Kids' Confidence," *San Diego Union-Tribune*, October 4, 2004, www.signonsandiego.com/uniontrib/20041004/ news_1m4pens.html. ★ **"'let down generations of children'"** Polly Curtis, "Children Being Failed by Progressive Teaching, Say Tories," *The Guardian*, May 9, 2008, www.guardian.co.uk/education/2008/may/09/schools.uk. **PAGE 70** ★ **"'unlike their fathers as we can.'"** Michael E. McGerr, *A Fierce Discontent*, (Simon & Schuster, 2003), 111. ★ **"'flawed assumptions of the past.'"** Glenn Beck Radio Program, February, 4, 2009. ★ **"all aspects of the child's nature"** Nicholas O'Han, "Who We Are: LREI: A Leader in Progressive Education," *lrei.org*, accessed May 21, 2009, www.lrei.org/whoweare/index.html. ★ **"to get the same jobs as their liberal peers"** States News Service, "Professors More Likely to Be Liberal than Conservative: Socially Conservative Professors Must Publish More to Get Same Jobs as Liberal Peers," *States News Service*, November 14, 2007. ★ **"'Star Trek and Religion' (Indiana Bloomington University)'"** Careers and Education, "Top 6 Absurd College Courses for 2008!" *careersandeducation.com*, accessed May 21, 2009, www.careersandeducation.com/top-6-absurd-college-courses-for-2008. ★ **"'The American Vacation' (U. Iowa)"** University of Phoenix, "Strangest College Degrees and Classes—University of Phoenix Online Respects Your Time," *phoenix.19gi.com*, January 16, 2009, http://phoenix.19gi.com/uop/strangest-college-degrees-and-classes-university-of-phoenix-online. ★ **"'Learning from YouTube' (Pitzer)"** University of Phoenix, "Strangest College Degrees and Classes—University of Phoenix Online Respects Your Time," *phoenix.19gi.com*, January 16, 2009, http://phoenix.19gi.com/uop/strangest-college-degrees-and-classes-university-of-phoenix-online. ★ **"Feminist Critique of Christianity' (U. Penn)"** Accuracy in Academia, "America's Most Ridiculous College Courses," *academia.org*, accessed May 21, 2009, www.academia.org/campus_reports/2001/sept_2001_4.html. ★ **"Blackness' (Occidental)"** Charlotte Allen, "I Got an A in Phallus 101," *Los Angeles Times*, January 7, 2007, www.latimes.com/ news/opinion/la-opallen7jan07,0,6765169.story?coll=la-opinion-center. ★ **"'Queer Musicology' (UCLA)"** Charlotte Allen, "I Got an A in Phallus 101," *Los Angeles Times*, January 7, 2007, www.latimes.com/news/opinion/la-op-allen7jan07,0,6765169.story. **PAGE 71** ★ **"'The Phallus' and 'Native American Feminisms'"** Charlotte Allen, "I Got an A in Phallus 101," *Los Angeles Times*, January 7, 2007, www.latimes.com/news/opinion/la-op-allen7jan07,0,6765169.story. ★ **"than they did in the 1960s"** Neal McCluskey, "No Federal Failure Left Behind," *cato.org*, July 12, 2004, www.cato.org/pub_display.php?pub_id=4574. ★ **"Have math and reading skills improved?"** Pete Chagnon, "U.S. Education Model Needs More than Money," *onenewsnow.com*, May 5, 2009, www.onenewsnow.com/Education/Default.aspx?id=516014. ★ **"Have graduation rates improved?"** James J. Heckman and Paul A. LaFontaine, "The Declining American High School Graduation Rate: Evidence, Sources, and Consequences," *NBER Reporter Online*, no. 1 (2008), www.nber.org/reporter/2008number1/heckman.html. ★ **"Nation's Report Card, 2008 Assessment"** U.S. Department of Education, National Center for Education Statistics, *NAEP 2008 Trends in Academic Progress*, (Washington, D.C.: National Center for Education Statistics, 2008) http://nces.ed.gov/nationsreportcard/pdf/main2008/2009479.pdf. ★ **"$9,138 per public school student"** U.S. Census Bureau, *Public Education Finances: 2006*, (Washington, D.C.: U.S. Census Bureau, 2008) http://ftp2.census.gov/govs/school/06f33pub.pdf. ★ **"at least double that amount"** Andrew J. Coulson, "The Real Cost of Public Schools," *cato.org*, April 6, 2008, www.cato.org/pub_display.php?pub_id=9319. **PAGE 72** ★ **"each of these states: . . . NY"** U.S. Department of Education, National Center for Education Statistics, "State Education Data Profiles: New York," *nces.ed.gov*, accessed May 21, 2009, http://nces.ed.gov/programs/stateprofiles. ★ **"each of these states: . . . UT"** U.S. Department of Education, National Center for Education Statistics, "State Education Data Profiles: Utah," *nces.ed.gov*, accessed May 21, 2009, http://nces.ed.gov/programs/stateprofiles. ★ **"each of these states: . . . U.S. Avg."** U.S. Department of Education, National Center for Education Statistics, "State Education Data Profiles: Utah," *nces.ed.gov*, accessed May 21, 2009, http://nces.ed.gov/programs/stateprofiles. ★ **"social, emotional, personal, physical, and intellectual'"** Prairie Creek Community School, "Progressive Education," *prairiecreek.org*, accessed May 21, 2009, www.prairiecreek.org. **PAGE 73** ★ **"35 percent of Democrats in Congress"** USA Today Opinion Blog, "Our View on Improving Education: Despite Success, School Choice Runs into New Barriers," *blogs.usatoday.com*, May 19, 2009, http://blogs.usatoday.com/oped/2009/05/our-view-on-improving-education-despite-success-school-choice-runs-into-new-barriers.html. ★ **"'most of us will never forget'"** David W. Magill, "Communications from the Director: On the Same Page: A Fall to Remember," *ucls.uchicago.edu*, December 2008, www.ucls.uchicago.edu/about/message/1208.shtml. **PAGE 74** ★ **"lowest high school graduation rate"** "Learning (and Succeeding) on Jump Street," *Wall Street Journal*, June 10, 2008, http://online.wsj.com/article/ SB121306417113859741.html. ★ **"went on to college"** "Learning (and Succeeding) on Jump Street," *Wall Street Journal*, June 10, 2008, http://online.wsj.com/article/ SB121306417113859741.html. ★ **shut down funding for the D.C. voucher program"** "Democrats and Poor Kids: Sitting on Evidence of Voucher Success, and the Battle of New York," *Wall Street Journal*, April 5, 2009, http://online.wsj.com/article/SB123897492702491099.html. **PAGE 75** ★ **"'a unionized monopoly'"** John Stossel, "Teachers

Unions Are Killing the Public Schools," realclearpolitics.com, February 15, 2006, www.realclearpolitics.com/Commentary/com-2_15_06_JS.html. ★ **"minimal accountability for their failure"** Amy Fagan, "Lessons Learned: Former Education Secretary Sees Union Excess at the Crux of School Failures," *Washington Times*, March 16, 2007. ★ **"105 page Memorandum of Understanding"** Neal McClusky, "Corruption in the Public Schools: The Market Is the Answer," *Policy Analysis*, no. 542, April 20, 2005, www.policyarchive.org/bitstream/handle/10207/6723/pa542.pdf. ★ **"'one student's progress with that of another'"** Wingra School, "Is Wingra a Good Choice for Your Family?" *wingraschool.org*, Accessed May 21, 2009, www.wingraschool.org/wingra_rightfit.html. **PAGE 77** ★ **"fire just 21 a year"** Jason Song, "Failure Gets a Pass: Firing Tenured Teachers Can Be a Costly and Tortuous Task," *Los Angeles Times*, May 3, 2009, www.latimes.com/news/local/la-me-teachers3-2009may03,0,679507.story. ★ **"students were actually getting injured in it"** Jason Song, "Failure Gets a Pass: Firing Tenured Teachers Can Be a Costly and Tortuous Task," *Los Angeles Times*, May 3, 2009, www.latimes.com/news/local/la-me-teachers3-2009may03,0,679507.story. **PAGE 78** ★ **"Dissatisfaction with academic instruction at schools"** U.S. Department of Education, National Center for Education Statistics, "1.5 Million Homeschooled Students in the United States in 2007," *Issue Brief*, December 2008, http://nces.ed.gov/pubs2009/2009030.pdf. ★ **"social development of home-schooled children'"** Isabel Shaw, "Social Skills and Homeschooling: Myths and Facts," *school.familyeducation.com*, Accessed May 21, 2009, http://school.familyeducation.com/home-schooling/human-relations/56224.html. ★ **"by 30-37 percentile points"** Brian D. Ray, *Strengths of Their Own—Home Schoolers Across America: Academic Achievement, Family Characteristics, and Longitudinal Traits*, (Salem, OR: National Home Education Research Institute, 1999). ★ **"above public school averages on the Stanford Achievement Test"** Christopher J. Klicka, *Home School Heroes: The Struggle and Triumph of Home Schooling in America*, (Nashville, TN: B&H Publishing Group, 2006), 52, http://books.google.com/books?id=gTc16uQVm1wC. ★ **"Louisa May Alcott"** Stacy Conradt, "10 Homeschooled Celebrities," *cnn.com*, April 23, 2009, www.cnn.com/2009/LIVING/04/22/mf.home.schooled. ★ **"Venus and Serena Williams"** Theresa Willingham, "Homeschooled Alumni Impressive and Growing: Famous Homeschoolers Can Be Proud of Their Rank," *suite101.com*, September 29, 2009, http://homeschooling.suite101.com/article.cfm/homeschooled_alumni_impressive_and_growing. **PAGE 80** ★ **"and allowing extra time to finish"** Kris Axtman, "When Tests' Teachers Are the Cheaters," *Christian Science Monitor*, January 11, 2005, www.csmonitor.com/2005/0111/p01s03-ussc.html. ★ **"even more cheating than they originally thought"** Nanette Asimov and Todd Wallack, "The Teachers Who Cheat" *San Francisco Chronicle*, May 13, 2007, www.sfgate.com/cgi-bin/article.cgi?file=/c/a/2007/05/13/MNGMSPPIU91.DTL. ★ **"lower the passing score *from 75 to* 42"** Marie Gryphon, "Education Law Encourages Fuzzy Math," *cato.org*, February 18, 2005, www.cato.org/pub_display.php?pub_id=3694. ★ **"lower standards . . . will be able to keep up"** Tamar Lewin, "States Found to Vary Widely on Education," *New York Times*, June 8, 2007, www.nytimes.com/2007/06/08/education/08scores.html. ★ **"teacher's annual salary at $52,570"** U.S. Department of Labor, Bureau of Labor Statistics, "Occupational Employment and Wages, May 2008: 25-2022 Middle School Teachers, Except Special and Vocational Education," *bls.gov*, May 4, 2009, www.bls.gov/oes/current/oes252022.htm. ★ **"policemen at $52,480"** U.S. Department of Labor, Bureau of Labor Statistics, "Occupational Employment and Wages, May 2008: 33-3051 Police and Sheriff's Patrol Officers," *bls.gov*, May 4, 2009, www.bls.gov/oes/current/oes333051.htm. ★ **"short-order cooks at $20,230"** U.S. Department of Labor, Bureau of Labor Statistics, "Occupational Employment and Wages, May 2008: 35-2015 Cooks, Short Order," *bls.gov*, May 4, 2009, www.bls.gov/oes/current/oes352015.htm. **PAGE 82** ★ **"way to protect their academic pursuits and research"** M.J. Stephey, "A Brief History of Tenure," *Time*, November 17, 2008, www.time.com/time/nation/article/0,8599,1859505,00.html. ★ **"were becoming far easier to achieve"** M.J. Stephey, "A Brief History of Tenure," *Time*, November 17, 2008, www.time.com/time/nation/article/0,8599,1859505,00.html. ★ **"up to a decade of probation"** M.J. Stephey, "A Brief History of Tenure," *Time*, November 17, 2008, www.time.com/time/nation/article/0,8599,1859505,00.html. ★ **"two years for a teacher to get tenure"** Robert Gammon, "The Case Against Tenure: How Job Protection for K-12 Educators Penalizes Students," *East Bay Express*, December 7, 2005, www.eastbayexpress.com/gyrobase/the_case_against_tenure/Content?oid=290281. ★ **"efforts to try and make tenure . . . more reasonable"** Robert Gammon, "The Case Against Tenure: How Job Protection for K-12 Educators Penalizes Students," *East Bay Express*, December 7, 2005, www.eastbayexpress.com/gyrobase/the_case_against_tenure/Content?oid=290281. ★ **"'reflection on our role as its stewards'"** The School in Rose Valley, "Educational Mission/Philosophy," *theschoolinrosevalley.org*, accessed May 21, 2009. **PAGE 83** ★ **"pummel white students in the SATs"** Anya Sostek, "Asian-American Achievements Mask Disparity," *Pittsburgh Post-Gazette*, June 10, 2008, www.post-gazette.com/pg/08162/888704-85.stm.

CHAPTER 4: AMERICA'S ENERGY FUTURE

PAGE 85 ★ **"whopping 6.7 percent of our total"** Neil King, Jr., "A Past President's Advice to Obama: Act With Haste," *Wall Street Journal*, December 11, 2008, http://online.wsj.com/article/SB122894725018995935.html. **PAGE 86** ★ **"emissions by 734,000 tons every year"** Patrick Cassidy, "Report Big Wind for Cape Cod Wind Farm," *Cape Cod Times*, January 17, 2009, www.capecodonline.com/apps/pbcs.dll/article?AID=/20090117/NEWS/901170316. ★ **"we import 70 percent now"** Neil King, Jr., "A Past President's Advice to Obama: Act With Haste," *Wall Street Journal*, December 11, 2008, http://online.wsj.com/article/SB122894725018995935.html. ★ **"with $23.9 billion in profit"** Ronald D. White "Exxon Mobil Shatters U.S. Record for Annual Profit," *Los Angeles Times*, January 31, 2009, http://articles.latimes.com/2009/jan/31/business/fi-oilearns31. **PAGE 87** ★ **"skyrocketed to $72.30"** Robert Murphy, "On Those Oil Profits," *townhall.com*, March 8, 2008, http://townhall.com/columnists/RobertMurphy/2008/03/08/on_those_oil_profits. ★ **"all-time high of $147.27 per barrel"** Ronald D. White "Exxon Mobil Shatters U.S. Record for Annual Profit," *Los Angeles Times*, January 31, 2009, http://articles.latimes.com/2009/jan/31/business/fi-oilearns31. ★ **"'Future generations are depending on it'"** Daily Mail Reporter, "The Prince and the Frog: Charles Signs Up Hollywood Stars in Fairytale Mission to Save the World's Rainforests," *Daily Mail*, May 6, 2009, www.dailymail.co.uk/news/article-1177524/Prince-Charles-Harrison-Ford-star-film-save-worlds-rainforests-needs-happy-ending.html. ★ **"322 tons of CO2 were emitted"** Rebecca English, "The Prince of Hypocrites: Charles Embarks on a 16,000 Mile 'Green' Crusade . . . Aboard a Private Jet," *Daily Mail*, February 14, 2009, www.dailymail.co.uk/news/article-1145127/The-Prince-hypocrites-Charles-embarks-16-000-mile-green-crusade--aboard-private-jet.html. ★ **"oil consumption increased seven percent"** Energy Information Administration, "Brazil Energy Profile," *tonto.eia.doe.gov*, April 10, 2009, http://tonto.eia.doe.gov/country/country_energy_data.cfm?fips=BR. ★ **"increased by 12 percent"** "China Oil Consumption Up 12% in 2008," *China Daily*, January 27, 2009, www.chinadaily.com.cn/china/2009-01/27/content_7429805.htm. ★ **"to 2.72 million a day in 2007"** Energy Information Administration, "India Energy Profile," *tonto.eia.doe.gov*, May 15, 2009, http://tonto.eia.doe.gov/country/country_energy_data.cfm?fips=IN. ★ **"increase of over 17 percent"** Robert Murphy, "On Those Oil Profits," *townhall.com*, March 8, 2008, http://townhall.com/columnists/RobertMurphy/2008/03/08/on_those_oil_profits. **PAGE 88** ★ **"and many other beloved American corporations"** Yahoo! Finance, see esp. "Microsoft," "Apple," "Google," "Johnson & Johnson," "Coca-Cola," and "Nike," accessed May 15, 2009, http://finance.yahoo.com/. ★ **"than the average large U.S. public company"** Robert Murphy, "On Those Oil Profits," *townhall.com*, March 8, 2008, http://townhall.com/columnists/RobertMurphy/2008/03/08/on_those_oil_profits. ★ **"less than one percent of the company"** Ben Stein, "Exxon Mobil Needs a Hug," *New York Times*, March 2, 2008, www.nytimes.com/2008/03/02/business/02every.html. ★ **"by investing in growing companies"** Ben Stein, "Exxon Mobil Needs a Hug," *New York Times*, March 2, 2008, www.nytimes.com/2008/03/02/business/ 02every.html. ★ **Chart: Too Big to Profit?** Search performed via Yahoo Finance, *biz.yahoo.com*, accessed May 15, 2009, http://biz.yahoo.com. **PAGE 89** ★ **"with a 9.5 percent margin"** Yahoo Finance, "Industry Summary," *biz.yahoo.com*, accessed May 15, 2009, http://biz.yahoo.com/p/sum_qpmd.html. ★ **"paid $81 billion in income taxes"** Robert Murphy, "On Those Oil Profits," *townhall.com*, March 8, 2008, http://townhall.com/columnists/RobertMurphy/2008/03/08/on_those_oil_profits. ★ **"income taxes skyrocketed 170 percent"** Moira Herbst, "Exxon: Profit Pirate or Tax Victim?" *Business Week*, May 2, 2008, http://www.businessweek.com/bwdaily/dnflash/content/may2008/db2008051_596535.htm. ★ **"94.2 billion in three years"** Yahoo Finance, "Exxon Mobil Corp. (XOM) Income Statement," *finance.yahoo.com*, accessed May 15, 2009, http://finance.yahoo.com/q/is?s=XOM&annual. ★ **"GDP of Ecuador"** Ecuador Explorer, "Ecuador Facts and Statistics," *ecuadorexplorer.com*, accessed May 15, 2009, www.ecuadorexplorer.com/html/vital_stats.html. ★ **"and Guatemala"** U.S. Central Intelligence Agency, "Guatemala," in *The World Factbook*, (Washington, D.C.: CIA, 2009), www.cia.gov/library/publications/the-world-factbook/print/gt.html. ★ **"about $318 million in taxes per day"** Robert Bryce, "Exxon, Big Oil Profits Evil Only Until You Weigh Their Tax Bills," *U.S. News and World Report*, February 11, 2009, www.usnews.com/articles/opinion/2009/02/11/exxon-big-oil-profits-evil-only-until-you-weigh-their-tax-bills.html. ★ **"on American families by Big Oil"** H. Josef Hebert, "Congress Slams Oil Chiefs on Profits," *Seattle Times*, April 3, 2008, http://seattletimes.nwsource.com/html/ politics/2004319229_apcongressoil.html. ★ **"energy companies are recording record profits"** FCDH e-Media, "U.S. Senate Committee on Commerce, Science and Transportation and U.S. Senate Committee on Energy and Natural Resources Hold a Joint Hearing on Energy Pricing and Profits (Part 1 of 3)" *Washington Post*, November 9, 2005, www.washingtonpost.com/wp-dyn/content/article/2005/11/09/AR2005110901070.html. ★ **"your sacrifice, gentlemen, appears to be nothing"** FCDH e-media, "U.S. Senate Committee on Commerce, Science and Transportation and U.S. Senate Committee on Energy and Natural Resources Hold a Joint Hearing on Energy Pricing and Profits (Part 1 of 3)" *Washington Post*, November 9, 2005, www.washingtonpost.com/wp-dyn/content/article/2005/11/09/AR2005110901070.html. ★ **"middle class and hard-working families"** Senate Committee on the Judiciary, *Exploring the Skyrocketing Price of Oil*, 110th cong., 2nd sess., May 21, 2008, http://frwebgate.access.gpo.gov/cgibin/getdoc.cgi?dbname=110_senate_ hearings&docid=f:43354.pdf. **PAGE 90** ★ **"small compared to their large revenues"** Tom Doggett, "US Treasury Secretary Attacks Oil, Gas Tax Breaks," *Reuters*, March 5, 2009, http://in.reuters.com/article/oilRpt/idINN0454844120090304. ★ **"profit they can take in this economy"** "What Is a 'Windfall' Profit?" *Wall Street Journal*, August 4, 2008, http://online.wsj.com/article/SB121780636275808495.html. ★ **"and implementing new taxes"** Claudia Cattaneo, "Obama Seeks More Revenue From Oil and Gas," *Financial Report*, February 26, 2009, www.financialpost.com/news-sectors/story.html?id=1332570. ★ **"silly to have a solar project [there]"** Jennifer Bowles, "Renewable Energy Projects Meet Opposition From Environmentalists," *Press-Enterprise*, June 2, 2008, www.pe.com/localnews/inland/stories/PE_News_Local_S_renewable 03.3cc481c.html. ★ **"running all of your companies"** A. Barton Hinkle, "Democrats Know How to Fix Economy: Take it Over," *Richmond Times-Dispatch*, December 23, 2008, www.timesdispatch.com/rtd/news/opinion/ columnists/article/HINKLE23_20081222-205320/160304. ★ **"$1.2 billion over the coming decade"** Tom Doggett, "US Treasury Secretary Attacks Oil, Gas Tax Breaks," *Reuters*, March 5, 2009, http://in.reuters.com/article/oilRpt/idINN0454844120090304. ★ **"will inevitably cause prices to rise"** Robert Murphy, "On Those Oil Profits," *townhall.com*, March 8, 2008, http://townhall.com/columnists/RobertMurphy/2008/03/08/on_those_oil_profits. **PAGE 91** ★ **"$50–$300 billion per year by 2020"** AFP, "Obama Wants to Raise Money Via Pollution Caps: Reports," hosted by *Google News*, February 26, 2009, www.google.com/hostednews/afp/article/ALeqM5gud46bd54cMtA3pIXmBT9PSNQiqg. ★ **"Instant Win Taxes"** Scott A. Hodge, "Number of Americans Paying Zero Federal Income Tax Grows to 43.4 Million," *taxfoundation.org*, March 30, 2006, www.taxfoundation.org/research/show/1410.html. **PAGE 92** ★ **"or $80 billion"** Salvatore Lazzari, *The Crude Oil Windfall Profit Tax of the 1980s: Implications for Current Energy Policy*, CRS Report for Congress, March 9, 2009, http://blog.nam.org/CRS%20Report%20on%20Windfall%20Profits%20Tax.pdf. ★ **"none of this is needed"** Peter Maloney, "Solar Project Draws New Opposition," *New York Times*, September 23, 2008, www.nytimes.com/2008/09/24/business/businessspecial2/24shrike.html **PAGE 93** ★ **"Reality Check Arena"** U.S. Department of Energy, Energy Information Administration, "Table 1.3: Primary Energy Consumption by Source, Selected Years, 1949-2008," in *Annual Energy Review 2008*, *eia.doe.gov*, accessed July 7, 2008, www.eia.doe.gov/aer/pdf/pages/sec1_9.pdf. **PAGE 94** ★ **"range from 2 billion"** Arctic National Wildlife Refuge, "Top Ten Reasons to Support ANWR Development," *anwr.org*, accessed May 15, 2009, www.anwr.org/ANWR-Basics/Top-ten-reasons-to-support-ANWR-development.php. ★ **"to 16 billion barrels"** Energy Information Administration, *Analysis of Crude Oil Production in the Arctic National Wildlife Refuge*, (Washington, D.C.: EIA, 2008), 14, www.eia.doe.gov/oiaf/servicerpt/anwr/pdf/sroiaf (2008)03.pdf. ★ **"anywhere from 500,000 to 1.5 million barrels"** Energy Information Administration, *Analysis of Crude Oil Production in the Arctic National Wildlife Refuge*, (Washington, D.C.: EIA, 2008), 14, www.eia.doe.gov/oiaf/servicerpt/anwr/pdf/sroiaf (2008)03.pdf. ★ **"saving us $135 billion to $327 billion"** Arctic National Wildlife Refuge, "Top Ten Reasons to Support ANWR Development," *anwr.org*, accessed May 15, 2009, www.anwr.org/ANWR-Basics/Top-ten-reasons-to-support-ANWR-development.php. ★ **"an estimated 60,000 to 130,000 jobs"** Bernard A. Gelb, *ANWR Development: Economic Impacts*, CRS Report for Congress, December 3, 2001, http://digital.library.unt.edu/govdocs/crs/permalink/meta-crs-1408:1. ★ **"$700 million a year in royalties"** M. Lynne Corn, *Arctic National Wildlife Refuge: Background and Issues*, CRS Report for Congress, May 15, 2003, http://digital.library.unt.edu/govdocs/crs/permalink/meta-crs-3775:1. ★ **"only disturb 2,000 acres of them"** Douglas Waller, "Some Shaky Figures on ANWR Drilling," *Time*, August 13, 2001, www.time.com/time/columnist/waller/article/0,9565,170983,00.html. ★ **"size of the University of Florida Campus"** University of Florida, "About UF," *ufl.edu*, March 19, 2009, www.ufl.edu/aboutUF. ★ **"as healthy as those in surrounding areas"** Arctic National Wildlife Refuge, "Top Ten Reasons to Support ANWR Development," *anwr.org*, accessed May 15, 2009, www.anwr.org/ANWR-Basics/Top-ten-reasons-to-support-ANWR-development.php. ★ **"President Clinton vetoed it"** Charles Pope, "Senate OKs Oil Drilling in Alaska's ANWR," *Seattle Post-Intelligencer*, March 17, 2005, www.seattlepi.com/local/216352_anwr17.html. **PAGE 95** ★ **"on hold for further review"** Zachary Coile, "White House Puts Costal Drilling Plans on Hold," *San Francisco Gate*, February 11, 2009, www.sfgate.com/cgi-bin/article.cgi?f=/c/a/2009/02/10/MNB015R7TQ. DTL&tsp=1. ★ **"would have been tapped under the plan"** Zachary Coile, "White House Puts Costal Drilling Plans on Hold," *San Francisco Gate*, February 11, 2009, www.sfgate.com/cgi-bin/article.cgi?f=/c/a/2009/02/10/MNB015R7TQ. DTL&tsp=1. ★ **"from offshore oil and gas development"** U.S. Department of the Interior, Minerals Management Service, "OCS Oil Spills Facts," *mms.gov*, September 2002, www.mms.gov/stats/PDFs/2002OilSpillFacts.pdf. ★ **"61 percent of all oil spilled in U.S. waters"** U.S. Department of the Interior, Minerals Management Service, "OCS Oil Spills Facts," *mms.gov*, September 2002, www.mms.gov/stats/PDFs/2002OilSpillFacts.pdf. ★ **"two percent of the total oil spillage"** U.S. Department of the Interior, Minerals Management Service, "OCS Oil Spills Facts," *mms.gov*, September 2002, www.mms.gov/stats/PDFs/2002OilSpillFacts.pdf. **PAGE 96** ★ **"ancient American Native burial sites"** Glenn G. Wattley, "Glenn G. Wattley: R.I. Does Offshore Wind Right," *Providence Journal*, November 5, 2008, www.projo.com/opinion/contributors/content/CT_wattley5_11-05-08_9SC3LA8_v12.3e2d674.html. ★ **"taking 175,000 cars off the road per year"** Stephen Power, "First Offshore Wind Farm Is Meeting Stiff Resistance," *Wall Street Journal*, January 13, 2009, http://online.wsj.com/article/SB123181056426575945.html. ★ **"about 734,000 tons annually"** Cape Wind, "Project at a Glance," *capewind.org*, accessed May 20, 2009, www.capewind.org/modules.php?op=modload&name=Sections&file=index&req=viewarticle&artid=24. ★ **"would've killed Cape Wind"** Jeff Jacoby, "Kennedy

Doesn't Play by the Rules," *Boston Globe*, May 7, 2006, www.boston.com/news/globe/editorial_opinion/oped/articles/2006/05/07/kennedy_doesnt_play_ by_the_rules. **PAGE 97** ★ **"double the nation's solar capacity"** Paul Davidson, "Pacific Gas Deal Will Nearly Double USA's Solar Power," *USA Today*, August 18, 2008, www.usatoday.com/money/industries/energy/2008-08-17-solar-electric_N.htm. ★ **"and the burrowing owl"** Peter Maloney, "Solar Project Draws New Opposition," *New York Times*, September 23, 2008, www.nytimes.com/2008/09/24/business/businessspecial2/24shrike.html. ★ **"'where the hell we can put it'"** Richard Simon, "Feinstein Wants Desert Swat Off-Limits to Solar, Wind Projects," *Los Angeles Times*, March 25, 2009, www.latimes.com/news/nationworld/nation/la-na-desert25-2009mar25,0,6168582.story. ★ **"'other planets and dome cities'"** "With Five Private Jets, Travolta Still Lectures on Global Warming," *London Evening Standard*, March 3, 2007, www.thisislondon.co.uk/showbiz/article-2339084details/ Air+miles+Travolta+urges+fans+to+'do+their+bit'+for+the+environment/article.do. ★ **"estimated 800 tons of carbon emissions"** "With Five Private Jets, Travolta Still Lectures on Global Warming," *London Evening Standard*, March 3, 2007. ★ **"case to the state Supreme Court"** The Economist, "Tree-Huggers v. Nerds: As the Planet Heats Up, So Do Disputes Between Environmentalists," *The Economist*, February 12, 2009, www.economist.com/world/unitedstates/ displaystory.cfm?story_id=13109915. ★ **"'for $660 million in 2000'"** Tim Doyle, "Koch's New Fight," *Forbes*, September 21, 2006, www.forbes.com/ 2006/09/21/koch-gordon-nantucket-biz_cz_td_06rich400_0921nantucket.html. **PAGE 98** ★ **"ridership was at a 50 year high"** CNN, "As Gas Goes Up, Driving Goes Down," *cnn.com*, May 27, 2008, www.cnn.com/2008/US/05/26/gas.driving/index.html. ★ **"gave to politicians from 2005-2008"** Open Secrets Center for Responsive Politics, "Lobbying: Crop Production and Basic Processing," *opensecrets.org*, accessed May 15, 2009, www.opensecrets.org/lobby/ indusclient.php? year=2006&lname=A01&id=. ★ **"$56.1 billion from 1995-2006"** Robert Bryce, "The Corn Ethanol Juggernaut," *Yale Environment 360*, September 15, 2008, http://e360.yale.edu/content/feature.msp?id=2063. ★ **"Who killed the flying car?"** Edward Carr, "Who Killed the Flying Car? A Case of Technological Murder Mystery," *Excelsior*, November 11, 2008, http://media.www.brooklynexcelsior.com/media/storage/paper901/news/2008/11/11/Columns/ Who-Killed.The.Flying.Car.A.Case.Of.Technological.Murder.Mystery-3538032.shtml. **PAGE 99** ★ **"corn crop being used for ethanol"** Adrienne Lewis, "Our View on Energy: Ethanol Production Soars, But Its Allure Plummets," *USA Today*, July 25, 2008, http://blogs.usatoday.com/oped/2008/07/our-view-on-ene.html. ★ **"cows that eat, yes, corn feed"** Michael S. Rosenwald, "The Rising Tide of Corn: Ethanol-Driven Demand Felt Across the Market," *Washington Post*, June 15, 2007, www.washingtonpost.com/wp-dyn/content/article/2007/06/14/AR2007061402008.html. ★ **"drove the price of other crops higher"** Michael S. Rosenwald, "The Rising Tide of Corn: Ethanol-Driven Demand Felt Across the Market," *Washington Post*, June 15, 2007, www.washingtonpost .com/wp-dyn/content/article/2007/06/14/AR2007061402008.html. ★ **"expense of soybeans, wheat, and other grains"** Ariana Eunjung Cha, "Rising Grain Prices Panic Developing World," *Washington Post*, April 4, 2008, www.washingtonpost.com/wp-dyn/content/article/2008/04/03/AR2008040304054.html. **PAGE 100** ★ **"'if we don't do something about it' "** Laurie David interviewed by HBO, *hbo.com*, accessed May 15, 2009, www.hbo.com/docs/programs /toohot/interview.html. ★ **"jet to Texas A&M campus"** Richard Pawlik, "Laurie David Is a Hypocrite," *Texas A&M Battalion*, April 12, 2007, www.thebatt.com/ media/storage/paper657/news/2007/04/12/MailCall/Laurie.David.Is.A.Hypocrite-2837056.shtml. ★ **"home in Martha's Vineyard"** David Frum, "The Hypocrisy of Celebrity Environmentalists," *American Enterprise Institute*, August 4, 2007, www.aei.org/article/26610. ★ **"'notice of apparent violations'"** "Laurie David Curbs Her Environmentalism," *Radar*, January 30, 2008, www.radarmagazine.com/exclusives/2005/11/laurie-david-curbs-her-environmentalism.php. ★ **"30 percent less efficient than gasoline"** Duke University Office of News and Communications, "Study Critiques Corn-for-Ethanol's Carbon Footprint," *news .duke.edu*, March 2, 2009, http://news.duke.edu/2009/03/ethcarbon.html. ★ **"yields about half as much fuel"** Eric Reguly, "It's Time to Kill Corn Subsidies and Go Brazilian," *Globe and Mail*, May 12, 2008, http://www.theglobeandmail.com/report-on-business/its-time-to-kill-corn-subsidies-and-go-brazilian/ article685537. ★ **"made those kind of connections"** "Half Gas, Half Electric, Total California Cool: Hollywood Gets a Charge Out of Hybrid Cars," *Washington Post*, June 6, 2002, www.washingtonpost.com/ac2/wp-dyn?pagename=article&node=&contentId=A2587-2002Jun5. ★ **"worse for the environment than regular gas"** Jason Hill, Stephen Polasky, Erik Nelson, David Tilman, Hong Huo, Lindsay Ludwig, James Neumann, Haochi Zheng, and Diego Bonta, "Climate Change and Health Costs of Air Emissions from Biofuels and Gasoline," *Proceedings of the National Academy of Sciences* 106, no. 6 (February 10, 2009): 2077-82, www.pnas.org/content/early/2009/02/02/0812835106.full.pdf. ★ **"'get a tax credit up to$3,400'"** U.S. Department of Energy, "New Energy Tax Credits for Hybrids," *fueleconomy.gov*, accessed June 15, 2009, http://fueleconomy.gov/feg/tax_hybrid.shtml. ★ **"only two percent of car buyers are signing up"** Ken Bensinger, "Hybrid Car Sales Go From 60 to 0 at Breakneck Speed," *Los Angeles Times*, March 17, 2009, http://articles.latimes .com/2009/mar/17/business/fi-hybrid17. **PAGE 101** ★ **"government's 'cash for clunkers' program"** Trish Turner, "Senate Poised to Pass 'Cash for Clunkers' Bill," *foxnews.com*, June 2, 2009, www.foxnews.com/politics/2009/06/02/senate-poised-pass-cash-clunkers. ★ **"emissions come from manufacturing it"** The Editors of *E Magazine*, "EarthTalk: When Is It Best to Buy a More Fuel Efficient Car?" *Christian Science Monitor*, January 16, 2009, http://features.csmonitor.com/environment/2009/01/16/earthtalk-when-is-it-best-to-buy-a-more-fuel-efficient-car. ★ **"better indicator of household wealth than a doctorate"** U.S. Bureau of the Census, *The Big Payoff: Educational Attainment and Synthetic Estimates of Work-Life Earnings* (Washington, D.C.: Bureau of the Census, 2002), www.census.gov/prod/2002pubs/p23-210.pdf. ★ **"household earns $113,400 a year"** J. D. Power and Associates, "Honda, Toyota, Ford, and Volkswagen Land the Most Vehicles at the Top of the Inaugural Automotive Environmental Index," *jdpower.com*, August 31, 2006, www .jdpower.com/corporate/news/releases/pressrelease.aspx?ID=2006147. ★ **"median household income in America"** U.S. Bureau of the Census, "Household Income Rises, Poverty Rate Unchanged, Number of Uninsured Down," press release, *census.gov*, August 26, 2008, www.census.gov/Press-Release/www/ releases/archives/income_wealth/012528.html. ★ **"more than six times the poverty line"** U.S. Department of Health and Human Services, *The 2009 HHS Poverty Guidelines: One Version of the [U.S.] Federal Poverty Measure* (Washington, D.C.: Department of Health and Human Services, 2009), http://aspe. hhs.gov/POVERTY/09poverty.shtml. ★ **"'Why is it you guys can't do this?'"** Eva Rodriguez, "Detroit's CEO in Chief," *Washington Post*, May 3, 2009, www .washingtonpost.com/wp-dyn/content/article/2009/05/01/AR2009050103395_pf.html. **PAGE 102** ★ **"'of the sort our president detests'"** ABC News, "'This Week' Transcript: Senators Leahy and Hatch,'" *abcnews.go.com*, May 3, 2009, http://abcnews.go.com/ThisWeek/Story?id=7491153. ★ **"'losing money on each one sold'"** Steven Mufson, "The Car of the Future—But at What Cost?: Hybrid Vehicles Are Popular, but Making Them Profitable Is a Challenge," *Washington Post*, November 25, 2008, www.washingtonpost.com/wpdyn/content/article/2008/11/24/AR2008112403211.html. ★ **"'not a very viable economic proposition'"** Ken Thomas, "Hybrids 'Still Unprofitable Proposition," *drive.com*, December 11, 2006, http://www.drive.com.au/Editorial/ArticleDetail. aspx?ArticleID=22167&vf=1. ★ **"'subsidize the price of hybrid technology'"** Justin Hyde, "Ford to Subsidize Hybrid Technology in Escape SUV," *San Jose Mercury News*, March 14, 2003. ★ **"'years of bleeding red ink ahead'"** Christian Caryl and Akiko Kashiwagi, "Get Your Green Motor Running," *Newsweek*, September 15, 2008, www.newsweek.com/id/157508. ★ **"'won't make a dime on this car for years'"** Chuck Squatriglia, "Can Automakers Build a 100-MPG Car?" *Wired*, April 4, 2008, www.wired.com/autopia/tag/chevrolet-volt/page/3. ★ **"'we weren't making a lot'"** Ken Bensinger, "For Carmakers, Hybrids Drive Thin Line Between Hope, Hype," *nj.com*, March 21, 2009, www.nj.com/business/index.ssf/2009/03/for_carmakers_hybrids_drive_th.html. ★ **"best selling hybrids in 2008"** Electric Drive Transportation Association, "Hybrid Sales Figures/Tax Credits for Hybrids," *electricdrive.org*, accessed June 11, 2009, www.electricdrive.org/index.php?ht=d/Articles/cat_id/5514/pid/2549. ★ **"outsold the Nissan Altima hybrid 18 to 1"** Electric Drive Transportation Association, "Hybrid Sales Figures/Tax Credits for Hybrids," *electricdrive.org*, accessed June 11, 2009, www.electricdrive.org/index.php?ht=d/Articles/cat_ id/5514/pid/2549. ★ **"it 'makes a statement about me'"** Micheline Maynard, "Say 'Hybrid' and Many People Will Hear 'Prius,'" *New York Times*, July 4, 2007, www.nytimes.com/2007/07/04/business/04hybrid.html. ★ **"mostly rich . . . people buying hybrids"** E. Kinney Zalesne, "Where Are the Republican Hybrid Buyers?: A Closer Look Into the Accelerated Trend of Buying Hybrid Vehicles," *Wall Street Journal*, May 2, 2009, http://online.wsj.com/ article/SB124118913906577389.html. **PAGE 103** ★ **"'parting the smug from their money'"** Jeremy Clarkson, "Honda Insight 1.3 IMA SE Hybrid," *London Times*, May 17, 2009, www.timesonline.co.uk/tol/driving/jeremy_clarkson/article6294116.ece. ★ **"the Ford F-150 and the Chevrolet Silverado"** Jacqueline Mitchell, "The Year's Best-and Worst-Selling Cars," *Forbes*, December 3, 2008, www.forbes.com/2008/12/03/2008-car-sales-forbeslife-cx_jm_1203cars.html. **PAGE 104** ★ **"outsold the Prius by 16 percent"** Jacqueline Mitchell, "The Year's Best- and Worst-Selling Cars," *Forbes*, December 3, 2008, www.forbes.com/2008/12/03/2008-car-sales-forbeslife-cx_jm_1203cars.html. ★ **"drove off the lot in the Camry"** Drive Transportation Association, "Hybrid Sales Figures/Tax Credits for Hybrids," *electricdrive.org*, accessed June 11, 2009, www.electricdrive.org/index.php?ht=d/Articles/cat_id/5514/pid/2549. See also "Best Selling Cars of 2008," *autos.aol.com*, accessed June 15, 2009, http://autos.aol.com/gallery/2008-top-ten-best-selling. ★ **"89 out of every 100 people who bought a Camry"** Drive Transportation Association, "Hybrid Sales Figures/Tax Credits for Hybrids," *electricdrive.org*, accessed June 11, 2009, www.electricdrive.org/index.php?ht=d/Articles/cat_id/5514/pid/2549. See also "Best Selling Cars of 2008," *autos.aol.com*, accessed June 15, 2009, http://autos.aol.com/gallery/2008-top-ten-best-selling. ★ **"hybrid that looks exactly the same"** "Best Selling Cars of 2008," *autos.aol.com*, accessed June 15, 2009, http://autos.aol.com/gallery/2008-top-ten-best-selling. ★ **"only 9 percent of buyers"** Drive Transportation Association, "Hybrid Sales Figures/Tax Credits for Hybrids," *electricdrive.org*, accessed June 11, 2009, www.electricdrive.org/index.php?ht=d/Articles/cat_id/5514/pid/2549. ★ **"fell by 12 percent from 2007 to 2008"** Drive Transportation Association, "Hybrid Sales Figures/Tax Credits for Hybrids," *electricdrive.org*, accessed June 11, 2009, www.electricdrive.org/index.php?ht=d/Articles/cat_id/5514/pid/2549. ★ **"down 45 percent compared to the same period"** Andrew Donoghue, "U.S. Sales Stall, But Prius Still Big in Japan," *businessgreen.com*, June 5, 2009, www.businessgreen.com/business-green/news/2243569/sales-stall-prius-big-japan. ★ **"faster than their gas-powered competition"** Ken Bensinger, "Hybrid Car Sales Go From 60 to 0 at Breakneck Speed," *Los Angeles Times*, March 17, 2009, http://articles.latimes.com/2009/mar/17/business/fi-hybrid17. ★ **"will employ 1,000 people"** "Ford Adds Third Dearborn Shift to Crank Out F-150s," *Detroit Free Press*, February 10, 2009, ★ **"and annoy 1,000,000 environmentalists"** Conservatively . . . ★ **"'these projects are built on suitable lands'"** Richard Simon, "Feinstein Wants Desert Swath Off-Limits to Solar, Wind," *Los Angeles Times*, March 25, 2009, http://articles.latimes.com/2009/mar/25/nation/na-desert25. **PAGE 105** ★ **"mentioned the Camry hybrid and the Nissan Altima hybrid"** Ken Thomas, "Apology for Promoting Japanese Cars," *USA Today*, September 20, 2007, www.usatoday.com/news/washington/2007-09-20-60972752_x.htm. ★ **"159,000 miles to break even"** Dan Strumph, "48 MPG Is Nice, but Hybrids Don't Add Up Right Now," *Associated Press*, January 11, 2009. ★ **"'even at . . . record gas prices'"** Dan Strumph, "48 MPG Is Nice, but Hybrids Don't Add Up Right Now," *Associated Press*, January 11, 2009. ★ **"still NOT a vegetarian"** Henning Steinfeld, Pierre Gerber, Tom Wassenaar, Vincent Castel, Mauricio Rosales, and Cees de Haan, *Livestock's Long Shadow: Environmental Issues and Opinions* (Rome: Food and Agriculture Organization of the United Nations, 2006), ftp://ftp.fao.org/docrep/fao/010/a0701e/A0701E00.pdf. **PAGE 106** ★ **"claiming that it 'addressed climate change'"** U.S. Department of Transportation, National Highway Traffic Safety Administration, *Average Fuel Economy Standards: Passenger Cars and Light Trucks, Model Years 2011-2015* (Washington, D.C.: Department of Transportation, 2009), http://keithhennessey.com/wp-content/uploads/2009/05/NHTSA_analysis.pdf. ★ **"in the atmosphere by the year 2100"** U.S. Department of Transportation, National Highway Traffic Safety Administration, *Average Fuel Economy Standards: Passenger Cars and Light Trucks, Model Years 2011-2015* (Washington, D.C.: Department of Transportation, 2009), 624, http://keithhennessey.com/wp-content/uploads/2009/05/NHTSA_analysis.pdf. See also Keith Hennessey, "Understanding the President's CAFE Announcement," *keithhennessey.com*, May 19, 2009, http://keithhennessey.com/2009/05/19/understanding-the-presidents-cafe-announcement. ★ **"is 970 parts per million"** Intergovernmental Panel on Climate Change, *Summary for Policymakers: A Report of Working Group I of the Intergovernmental Panel on Climate Change* (New York: Intergovernmental Panel on Climate Change, 2001), www.ipcc.ch/pdf/press-releases/20january2001-spm.pdf. ★ **"'line dry (your clothes) as much as possible'"** James Barron, "Boldface Names," *New York Times*, June 20, 2001, www.nytimes.com/2001/06/20/nyregion/boldface-names-887340.html. ★ **"uses $22,000 a year in water"** Peter Schweizer, *Do As I Say (Not As I Do): Profiles in Liberal Hypocrisy* (New York: Anchor, 2006), 173-190, http://books.google.com/books?id=rsQ14C2MX7EC. ★ **"'One (1) limousine (artist)'"** *Barbra Streisand Tour—Technical Manual*, September 12, 2006, posted on *thesmokinggun.com*, http://www.thesmokinggun.com/backstagetour/barbra/barbra1.html. ★ **"'it necessarily applied to her'"** James Barron, "Boldface Names," *New York Times*, June 20, 2001, www.nytimes.com/2001/06/20/nyregion/boldface-names-887340.html. **PAGE 107** ★ **"(0.0072 degrees Fahrenheit) by 2100"** U.S. Department of Transportation, National Highway Traffic Safety Administration, *Average Fuel Economy Standards: Passenger Cars and Light Trucks, Model Years 2011-2015* (Washington, D.C.: Department of Transportation, 2009), http://keithhennessey.com/wp-content/uploads/2009/05/NHTSA_analysis.pdf. ★ **"save us 1/1,600th of the doomsday-level global warming"** U.S. Department of Transportation, National Highway Traffic Safety Administration, *Average Fuel Economy Standards: Passenger Cars and Light Trucks, Model Years 2011-2015* (Washington, D.C.: Department of Transportation, 2009), http://keithhennessey.com/wp-content/uploads/2009/05/NHTSA_analysis.pdf. ★ **"only 1/45th of the margin of error"** Intergovernmental Panel on Climate Change, *Summary for Policymakers: A Report of Working Group I of the Intergovernmental Panel on Climate Change* (New York: Intergovernmental Panel on Climate Change, 2001), 5, www.ipcc.ch/pdf/press-releases/20january2001-spm.pdf. ★ **"past century's temperature change"** Steven Milloy, "U.N. Climate Distractions," *foxnews.com*, November 21, 2007, www.foxnews.com/story/0,2933,312490,00.html. ★ **"total is 0.04 centimeters by 2100"** Intergovernmental Panel on Climate Change, *Summary for Policymakers: A Report of Working Group I of the Intergovernmental Panel on Climate Change* (New York: Intergovernmental Panel on Climate Change, 2001), www.ipcc.ch/pdf/press-releases/20january2001-spm.pdf. ★ **"waned about in An Inconvenient Truth"** FoxNews.com, "Scientists: Gore Goes Too Far in 'An Inconvenient Truth,'" *foxnews.com*, March 13, 2007, www.foxnews.com/story/0,2933,258462,00.html. ★ **"'avoiding dangerous climate change'"** Monash University Newsline, "Car Is Doomed, Energy Experts Warn," *monash.edu*, February 28, 2008, www.monash.edu.au/news/newsline/story/1253. ★ **"'shift from private car to public transport"** Monash University Newsline, "Car Is Doomed, Energy Experts Warn," *monash.edu*, February 28, 2008, www.monash.edu.au/news/newsline/story/1253. ★ **"'The car,' they said 'is doomed'"** Monash University Newsline, "Car Is Doomed, Energy Experts Warn," *monash.edu*, February 28, 2008, www.monash.edu.au/news/newsline/story/1253. ★ **"reaction to the Arab oil embargo of 1973-74"** Mike Allen and Eamon Javers, "Obama Announces New Fuel Standards," *politico.com*, May 18, 2009, www.politico.com/news/stories/0509/22650.html. **PAGE 108** ★ **"depending on the poll"** Lymari Morales, "Americans Green-Light Higher Fuel Efficiency Standards," *Gallup*, May 19, 2009, www.gallup.com/poll/ 118543/Americans-Green-Light-Higher-Fuel-Efficiency-Standards.aspx. ★ **"between 78"** William Branigin, Juliet Eilperin, and Steven Mufson, "Obama Announces New Energy, Environmental Policies," *Washington Post*, January 26, 2009, www.washingtonpost.com/wp-dyn/content/

article/2009/01/26/AR2009012601157_pf.html. ★ **"and 92 percent of Americans"** New York Times and CBS News, "New York Times-CBS News Poll April 20-24, 2007," *nytimes.com*, April 2007, http://graphics8.nytimes.com/packages/pdf/national/20070424_poll.pdf. ★ **"average of 35 miles per gallon"** Steve Hargreaves, "Bush Signs Energy Bill," *money.cnn.com*, December 19, 2007, http://money.cnn.com/2007/12/19/news/economy/energy_bill. ★ **"Toyota Prius and the Honda Civic hybrid"** Marlo Lewis, Jr., "Miles to Go: How Many Vehicles Actually Meet Speaker Pelosi's 35-MPG Fuel Economy Standard?" http://cei.org/gencon/019,06290.cfm. ★ **"We have to find a way to do both'"** Michael Rothfeld, "A Powerful Champion of a Power Line," *Los Angeles Times*, April 27, 2008, http://articles.latimes.com/p/2008/apr/27/local/me-park27. **PAGE 109** ★ **"tougher standards four years earlier"** Stephen Power and Christopher Conkey, "U.S. Orders Stricter Fuel Goals for Autos," *Wall Street Journal*, May 19, 2009, http://online.wsj.com/article/SB124266939482331283.html. ★ **"$1,300 to the price of every new car"** Associated Press, "Automakers, Obama Announce Mileage, Pollution Plan," *Boston Herald*, May 19, 2009, www.bostonherald.com/news/us_politics/view.bg?articleid=1173289. ★ **"at $6,000 per vehicle"** David Shepardson, "New Fuel Rules Will Hike GM Vehicle Prices By an Average $6,000," *Detroit News*, January 13, 2008. ★ **"cost over 11,000 jobs by 2015"** U.S. Department of Transportation, National Highway Traffic Safety Administration, *Average Fuel Economy Standards: Passenger Cars and Light Trucks, Model Years 2011-2015* (Washington, D.C.: Department of Transportation, 2009), 586, http://keithhennessey.com/wp-content/uploads/2009/05/NHTSA_analysis.pdf. ★ **"almost 49,000 lost jobs"** U.S. Department of Transportation, National Highway Traffic Safety Administration, *Average Fuel Economy Standards: Passenger Cars and Light Trucks, Model Years 2011-2015* (Washington, D.C.: Department of Transportation, 2009), 586, http://keithhennessey.com/wp-content/uploads/2009/05/NHTSA_analysis.pdf. ★ **"97,000 to 195,000 additional overall injuries"** Committee on Effectiveness and Impact of Corporate Average Fuel Economy (CAFE) Standards, *Effectiveness and Impact of Corporate Average Fuel Economy (CAFÉ) Standards* (Washington, D.C.: National Academies Press, 2002), 26, http://books.nap.edu/html/cafe/ch2.pdf. ★ **"that was only through 1999"** "Are Lives Really an Acceptable Price for Fuel Efficiency?" *USA Today*, July 8, 1999. **PAGE 110** ★ **"most secure findings in the safety literature'"** Robert W. Crandall and John D. Graham, "The Effect of Fuel Economy Standards on Automobile Safety," *Journal of Law and Economics* 32 (April 1989). ★ **"in the peer-reviewed scientific literature'"** Ken Adelman, "Road Regs: Wrongs that Don't Make Rights," *National Review Online*, January 17, 2002, www.nationalreview.com/comment/comment-adelman011702.shtml. ★ **"three times the chance of dying in a light car"** Insurance Institute for Highway Safety, "Driver Deaths by Make and Model: Fatality Risk in One Vehicle Versus Another," *Status Report* 42, no. 4 (2007), www.iihs.org/externaldata/srdata/docs/sr4204.pdf.

CHAPTER 5: UNIONS

PAGE 113 ★ **"recent Rasmussen survey"** Rasmussen Reports, "Just 9% of Non-Union Workers Want to Join Union," *rasmussenreports.com*, March 16, 2009, www.rasmussenreports.com/public_content/business/jobs_employment/just_9_of_non_union_workers_want_to_join_union. **PAGE 114** ★ **"same prounion percentage as the general population"** Rasmussen Reports, "Just 9% of Non-Union Workers Want to Join Union," *rasmussenreports.com*, March 16, 2009, www.rasmussenreports.com/public_content/business/jobs_employment/just_9_of_non_union_workers_want_to_join_union. ★ **"private-sector workers belonged to a union"** Barry T. Hirsch and Jeffrey M. Hirsch, "The Rise and Fall of Private Sector Unionism: What Comes Next?" paper presented at "The NLRA After Seventy Years: An Assessment," Allied Social Science Association Meetings, Boston, January 9, 2009, www.aeaweb.org/annual_mtg_papers/2006/0107_1015_1702.pdf. ★ **"private-sector jobs were still unionized"** U.S. Department of Labor, Bureau of Labor Statistics, "Union Membership (Annual)," *bls.gov*, January 28, 2009, www.bls.gov/news.release/union2.toc.htm. ★ **"7.6 percent of non-government workers"** U.S. Department of Labor, Bureau of Labor Statistics, "Union Members Summary," *bls.gov*, January 28, 2009, www.bls.gov/news.release/union2.nr0.htm. ★ **"five times higher"** U.S. Department of Labor, Bureau of Labor Statistics, "Union Members Summary," *bls.gov*, January 28, 2009, www.bls.gov/news.release/union2.nr0.htm. ★ **"declined from 14.3 to 8.2 million"** Barry T. Hirsch and Jeffrey M. Hirsch, "The Rise and Fall of Private Sector Unionism: What Comes Next?" paper presented at "The NLRA After Seventy Years: An Assessment," Allied Social Science Association Meetings, Boston, January 9, 2009, www.aeaweb.org/annual_mtg_papers/2006/0107_1015_1702.pdf. **PAGE 115** ★ **"saying the word "union'"** Abdon M. Pallasch, "Obama Applauds Unions at Convention," *Chicago Sun-Times*, April 25, 2008, www.suntimes.com/news/politics/obama/915251,CST-NWS-union25.article. ★ **"and we're proud of it'"** Michael Mishak, "Unplugged: The SEIU Chief on the Labor Movement and the Card Check," *Las Vegas Sun*, May 10, 2009, www.lasvegassun.com/news/2009/may/10/stern-unplugged-seiu-chief-labor-movement-and-card. ★ **"twelve of the twenty top donors from 1989 to 2008"** Open Secrets, "Top All-Time Donors 1989-2008 Summary," *opensecrets.org*, March 2, 2009, www.opensecrets.org/orgs/list.php?order=A. *Beck Rights* Communications Workers of America et al. v. Beck et al., 487 U.S., no. 86-673 (1988), www.law.stanford.edu/publications/projects/campaignfinance/collection/487us735.pdf. **PAGE 117** ★ **"60 percent of workplace elections"** National Labor Relations Board, *Seventy Third Annual Report of the National Labor Relations Board for the Fiscal Year Ended September 30, 2008*, (Washington, D.C.: U.S. Government Printing Office, 2008), www.nlrb.gov/nlrb/shared_files/brochures/AnnualReports/Entire2008Annual.pdf. ★ **"restraint and coercion of employees'"** National Labor Relations Board, *Seventy Third Annual Report of the National Labor Relations Board for the Fiscal Year Ended September 30, 2008*, (Washington, D.C.: U.S. Government Printing Office, 2008), www.nlrb.gov/nlrb/shared_files/brochures/Annual%20Reports/Entire2008Annual.pdf. ★ **"rightful share of the economic pie'"** New York Times Editorial Board, "A Hopeful Year for Unions," February 7, 2008, www.nytimes.com/2008/02/07/opinion/07thu3.html. ★ **"positions taken by our editorial boards'"** Carrie Sheffield, "NYT: Do As I Say, Not As I Do With Unions," *Washington Times*, May 4, 2009, www.washingtontimes.com/weblogs/politics-101/2009/may/04/nyt-do-as-a-i-say-not-as-i-do-when-it-comes-to-uni. **PAGE 118** ★ **"to have a secret ballot'"** Brendan Sasso, "McGovern Joins Business Groups' Push to Defeat Labor-Backed 'Card Check' Bill," *The Hill*, October 7, 2008, http://thehill.com/business--lobby/mcgovern-joins-business-groups-push-to-defeat-labor-backed-card-check-bill-2008-10-07.html. ★ **"groundswell from unrepresented employees;'"** Peter J. Hurtgen, Testimony in front of U.S. Senate Committee, March 27, 2007, http://help.senate.gov/Hearings/2007_03_27_a/Hurtgen.pdf. **PAGE 119** ★ **"the only requirement"** James Sherk and Ryan O'Donnell, "EFCA: High-Pressure Spin Selling and Creative Organizing for Labor Unions," *The Heritage Foundation*, March 11, 2009, www.heritage.org/research/labor/wm2335.cfm. ★ **"binding government arbitration"** Newt Gingrich, "Arbitration the Real Threat in EFCA," *Politico*, April 22, 2009, www.politico.com/news/stories/0409/21509.html. ★ **"a particularly bad time"** Josh Drobnyk, "Specter Pulls Back Support of Card Check Law," *Los Angeles Times*, March 25, 2009, www.latimes.com/news/nationworld/nation/la-na-specter25-2009mar25,0,2212293.story ★ **"when the economy returns to normalcy"** Josh Drobnyk, "Specter Pulls Back Support of Card Check Law," *Los Angeles Times*, March 25, 2009, www.latimes.com/news/nationworld/nation/la-na-specter25-2009mar25,0,2212293.story ★ **"proposed a compromise"** Alec MacGillis, "Executives Detail Labor Bill Compromise" *Washington Post*, March 22, 2009, www.washingtonpost.com/wp-dyn/content/article/2009/03/21/AR2009032101449.html. **PAGE 120** ★ **"fired 75 of its 220 employees"** Alec MacGillis, "Union in Dispute Over Layoffs," March 19, 2009, www.washingtonpost.com/wp-dyn/content/article/2009/03/18/AR2009031800709.html ★ **"filed unfair labor practices charges"** Alec MacGillis, "Union in Dispute Over Layoffs," March 19, 2009, www.washingtonpost.com/wp-dyn/content/article/2009/03/18/AR2009031800709.html ★ **"Union of Union Representatives"** Alec

MacGillis, "Union in Dispute Over Layoffs," March 19, 2009, www.washingtonpost.com/wp-dyn/content/article/2009/03/18/AR2009031800709.html ★ **"'by reducing its membership'"** Steven Greenhouse, "Union is Accused of Violations," *New York Times,* March 18, 2009, http://query.nytimes.com/gst/fullpage.ht ml?res=950CEFDC1530F934A25750C0A96F9C8B63. ★ **"by helping elect President Obama"** Alec MacGillis, "Union in Dispute Over Layoffs," March 19, 2009, www.washingtonpost.com/wp-dyn/content/article/2009/03/18/AR2009031800709.html **PAGE 121** ★ **"A More Perfect Union . . . "** SEIU website, Biography, "Anna Burger Chair, Change to Win; International Secretary-Treasurer Service Employees International Union, CLC," www.seiu.org/a/ourunion/anna-burger.php. See also Service Employees International Union, "Our Union: Anna Burger," *seiu.org,* accessed July 1, 2009, www.seiu.org/a/ourunion/anna-burger.php. See also "Unions benefit from Obama decisions: President enacts labor-friendly policies, waits on card check," by S.A. Miller, Washington Times, May 5, 2009, http://washingtontimes.com/news/2009/may/05/unions-benefit-from-obamas-early-decisions; http://online.wsj.com/article/SB124226652880418035.html. See also S.A. Miller, "Unions Benefit from Obama Decisions: President Enacts Labor-Friendly Policies, Waits on Card Check," *Washington Times,* May 5, 2009, http://washingtontimes.com/news/2009/may/05/unions-benefit-from-obamas-early-decisions. See also "Andy Stern's Go-To Guy: Meet Craig Becker, Labor's Secret Weapon," *Wall Street Journal,* May 14, 2009, http://online.wsj.com/article/SB124226652880418035.html. 3. "Mixed reviews for W.H.'s surprise FEC pick," By KENNETH P. VOGEL, Politico, May 1, 2009, www.politico.com/news/stories/0509/22009.html. See also White House press release, "President Obama Announces More Key Administration Posts," March 19, 2009, www.whitehouse.gov/the_press_office/President-Obama-Announces-More-Key-Administration-Posts-3/19/09. See also SEIU, "Former SEIU Political Leader Appointed as Obama's Political Director," www.seiu.org/2008/11/former-seiu-political-leader-appointed-as-obamas-political-director.php. See also Kate Thomas, "Former SEIU Political Leader Appointed as Obama's Political Director," *seiu.org,* November 21, 2008, www.seiu.org/2008/11/former-seiu-political-leader-appointed-as-obamas-political-director.php. See also GAO, "GAO Announces Appointments to Health Information Technology Policy Committee," April 3, 2009, www.gao.gov/press/health_it_committee2009apr03.pdf **PAGE 122** ★ **"how we can fix our economy"** Artists for Workers Choice, "The Stars Come Out in Support of Employee Free Choice Act," media release, May 11, 2009, www.artists4workerschoice.org/mediareleases.cfm. ★ **"gave a key endorsement to Obama"** Kathleen Hennessey, "SEIU Nevada Endorses Obama," *USA Today,* January 9, 2008, www.usatoday.com/news/ politics/2008-01-09-1792078901_x.htm. ★ **"threatened with the loss of $6.8 billion"** Evan Halper, "U.S. Threatens to Rescind Stimulus Money Over Wage Cuts," *Los Angeles Times,* May 8, 2009, www.latimes.com/news/local/la-me-health-cuts8-2009may 08,0,4592200.story. ★ **"SEIU was given 'unprecedented access'"** Russell Goldman, "State Suggests Union May Have Tried to Block Federal Funds," *ABC News,* May 13, 2009, www.abcnews.go.com/Business/Story?id=7570203. ★ **"'have stakeholders on a call like this'"** Russell Goldman, "State Suggests Union May Have Tried to Block Federal Funds," *ABC News,* May 13, 2009, www.abcnews.go.com/Business/Story?id=7570203. ★ **"threatened Wells Fargo"** Sandra M. Jones, "Hartmarx Union Protest Puts Pressure on Wells Fargo," May 8, 2009, www.chicagotribune.com/business/chi-fri-factory-battles2-0508-may08,0,2515792.story ★ **"'State of Illinois any longer'"** Sandra M. Jones, "Hartmarx Union Protest Puts Pressure on Wells Fargo," May 8, 2009, www.chicagotribune.com/business/chi-fri-factory-battles2-0508-may08,0,2515792.story ★ **"before I was elected to anything"** Political Radar blog, "Obama Parties Post- Debate with SEIU," *ABC News,* January 16, 2008, http://blogs.abcnews .com/politicalradar/2008/01/obama-parties-p.html. **PAGE 123** ★ **"unspecified cuts to wage and benefits"** U.S. Office of the Press Secretary, "Obama Administration Auto Restructuring Initiative: Chrysler-Fiat Alliance," April 30, 2009, http://online.wsj.com/public/resources/documents/autoplan20090430.pdf. ★ **"waive Chrysler's $8 billion payment"** John Lippert and Mike Ramsey, "UAW Said to Get 55% Chrysler Ownership, Board Seats (Update1)" *Bloomberg,* April 28, 2009, www.bloomberg.com/apps/news?pid=20601082&sid=aRyHgTljlyFI. ★ **"55 percent equity stake"** U.S. Office of the Press Secretary, "Obama Administration Auto Restructuring Initiative: Chrysler-Fiat Alliance," April 30, 2009, http://online.wsj.com/public/resources/documents/autoplan20090430.pdf. ★ **"99 percent of their 2008 election-cycle donations"** Center for Responsive Politics via Open Secrets, "United Auto Workers," *opensecrets.org,* accessed May 20, 2009, www.opensecrets.org/orgs/summary.php?id=D000000070. ★ **"Daimler waived the $2 billion"** U.S. Office of the Press Secretary, "Obama Administration Auto Restructuring Initiative: Chrysler-Fiat Alliance," April 30, 2009, http://online.wsj.com/public/resources/documents/autoplan20090430.pdf. ★ **"an additional $600 million"** U.S. Office of the Press Secretary, "Obama Administration Auto Restructuring Initiative: Chrysler-Fiat Alliance," April 30, 2009, http://online.wsj.com/public/resources/documents/autoplan20090430.pdf. **PAGE 125** ★ **"gave up all of its assets"** Jones Day Law Firm, "Affidavit of Ronald E. Kolka in Support of First Day Pleadings," United States Bankruptcy Court, Southern District of New York, May 1, 2009, http://online.wsj.com/public/resources/documents/20090430_chrysler_affidavit.pdf . ★ **"*absolutely nothing* in return"** U.S. Office of the Press Secretary, "Obama Administration Auto Restructuring Initiative: Chrysler-Fiat Alliance," April 30, 2009, http://online.wsj.com/public/resources/documents/autoplan20090430.pdf. ★ **"it's all gone"** Chris Isidore, "Chrysler Won't Repay Bailout Money," *cnnmoney.com,* May 6, 2009, http://money.cnn.com/2009/05/05/news/companies/chrysler_loans. ★ **"another $4.7 billion"** Chris Isidore, "Chrysler Won't Repay Bailout Money," *cnnmoney.com,* May 6, 2009, http://money.cnn.com/2009/05/05/news/companies/chrysler_loans. ★ **"20 Worst CEOs Ever"** Portfolio Staff, "The Best (and Worst) CEOs. Ever.," *Portfolio,* April 22, 2009, www.portfolio.com/executives/2009/04/22/20-Worst-CEOs. ★ **"'more than enough to do'"** Stephanie Condon, "Obama: 'I Don't Want to Run Auto Companies'" *CBS News,* Political Hotsheet blog, April 29, 2009, www.cbsnews.com/blogs/2009/04/29/politics/politicalhotsheet/entry4979228.shtml. ★ **"handed over $3 billion in loans"** Hugo Miller and Alexander Deslongchamps, "Chrysler to Receive $10.5 Billion From Canada, U.S. (Update 3)," *Bloomberg,* April 30, 2009, www.bloomberg.com/apps/news?pid=20601082&sid=aqGtF27fAJHA. ★ **"Chrysler won't ever be repaying"** Sinclair Stewart and Shawn McCarthy, "'Low Likelihood' Chrysler Loans Will Be Repaid," *Globe and Mail,* May 15, 2009, www.theglobeandmail.com/report-on-business/article1139608.ece. ★ **"$195 more per week than non-union workers"** U.S. Department of Labor, Bureau of Labor Statistics, "Median Weekly Earnings of Full-Time Wage and Salary Workers by Union Affiliation and Selected Characteristics," *bls.gov,* January 28, 2009, www.bls.gov/news.release/union2.t02.htm. ★ **"'Nobody's even close'"** Micheline Maynard, "Union Takes Rare Front Seat in Deal For Chrysler," *New York Times,* May 1, 2009, www.nytimes.com/2009/05/02/business/02bankrupt .html. **PAGE 126** ★ **"private-sector job growth"** U.S. Labor Department, Drs. Barry Hirsch and David Macpherson, "Private Sector Employment Growth, 2003-2008," accessed May 22, 2009, http://2.bp.blogspot.com/_otfwl2zc6Qc/SghMi5dchqI/ AAAAAAAAKEs/PsMZt9QZ-BI/s1600-h/jobs.bmp. ★ **"Chart: Private Sector Employment Growth"** Dr. Barry Hirsch and Dr. David Macpherson, "Private-Sector Employment Growth, 2003-2008," *U.S. Labor Department,* accessed July 1, 2009, http://2.bp.blogspot.com/_otfwl2zc6Qc/ SghMi5dchqI/AAAAAAAAKEs/PsMZt9QZ-BI/s1600-h/jobs.bmp. **PAGE 127** ★ **"at $73 an hour"** Mark J. Perry, "GM Paid $73.26 Per Hour for Labor Costs in 2006," *Carpe Diem: Professor Mark. J. Perry's Blog for Economics and Finance,* November 21, 2008, http://mjperry.blogspot.com/2008/11/gm-paid-7326-per-hour-for-labor-costs.html. ★ **"earn $48 an hour"** Mark J. Perry, "GM Paid $73.26 Per Hour for Labor Costs in 2006," *Carpe Diem: Professor Mark. J. Perry's Blog for Economics and Finance,* November 21, 2008, http://mjperry .blogspot.com/2008/11/gm-paid-7326-per-hour-for-labor-costs.html. ★ **"Amounted to $1,800"** Jenny Gold, "Cutting Worker Costs Key to Automakers' Survival," *NPR,* December 23, 2008, http://www.npr.org/templates/story/story.php?storyId=98643230. ★ **"around $3,000 per car"** Jenny Gold, "Cutting Worker Costs Key to Automakers' Survival," *NPR,* December 23, 2008, http://www.npr.org/templates/story/story.php?storyId=98643230. ★ **"fired General**

Motors Chairman and CEO Rick Wagoner" Mike Allen and Josh Gerstein, "GM CEO Resigns at Obama's Behest," *Politico*, March 30, 2009, www.politico .com/news/stories/0309/20625.html. ★ **"slash wages in half for new workers"** Judson Berger, "With GM's Wagoner Ousted, Should Union Head Have Met the Same Fate," *Fox News*, March 31, 2009, www.foxnews.com/politics/first100days/2009/03/31/union-head-met-fate-general-motors-ceo. ★ **"is down 50 percent"** Bree Fowler, "GM Cuts 10,000 Salaried Jobs, Trims Employees' Pay," *newsvine.com*, February 10, 2009, www.newsvine.com/_ news/2009/02/10/2416422-gm-cuts-10000-salaried-jobs-trims-employees-pay. ★ **"paid for their labor fairly."** Associated Press, "West Wing Stars Stump for Union Bill," *msnbc.com*, March 31, 2009, www.msnbc.msn.com/id/29980172. **PAGE 128** ★ **"paid nearly their full salary"** Lou Ann Hammond, "Job Banks—Protecting the People, Not the Jobs," *carlist.com*, accessed May 20, 2009, www.carlist.com/autonews/2005/autonews_164.html. ★ **"over 72 percent of their full-time pay"** Robert Schoenberger, "GM and UAW Will Drop Jobs Bank Program That Paid Employees When There Was No Work," *Cleveland Plain Dealer*, January 28, 2009, http://blog.cleveland.com/business/2009/01/gm_and_uaw_agree_to_drop_jobs.html **PAGE 129** ★ **"only 112 were terminated"** Associated Press, "Superintendant: Bad Teachers Hard to Fire," *msnbc.com*, June 28, 2008, www.msnbc.msn.com/id/25430476. ★ **"'Unless they commit a lewd act'"** CashCopywriter, "Organization Holds Contest That Will Pay Bad Teachers to Quit: Why Poor Performing School Teachers Are Almost Impossible to Fire," *associatedcontent.com*, March 17, 2008, www.associatedcontent.com/article/653231/organization_holds_contest_that_will.html. ★ **"lewd act may not be enough"** Teachers Union Facts, "Protecting Bad Teachers," *Center for Union Facts*, 2008, http://teachersunionexposed.com/ protecting.cfm. ★ **"It's almost impossible'"** John Stossel, "Teachers Unions Are Killing the Public Schools," *realclearpolitics.com*, February 15, 2006, www .realclearpolitics.com/Commentary/com-2_15_06_JS.html. ★ **"more than $300,000 in salary"** John Stossel, "Teachers Unions Are Killing the Public Schools," *realclearpolitics.com*, February 15, 2006, www.realclearpolitics.com/Commentary/com-2_15_06_JS.html. ★ **decline an average of 10 percent"** David Lee and Alexandre Mas, "Long-Run Impacts of Unions on Firms: New Evidence from Financial Markets 1961-1999" (working paper, National Bureau of Economic Research, Cambridge, MA, 2009), www.princeton.edu/~davidlee/wp/w14709.pdf. **PAGE 130** ★ **"How to Fire a Tenured Teacher in NYC"** John Stossel, "How to Fire an Incompetent Teacher: An Illustrated Guide to New York's Public School Bureaucracy," *Reason*, October 2006, www.reason .com/news/show/36802.html.

CHAPTER 6: ILLEGAL IMMIGRATION

PAGE 133 ★ **"approximately two-thousand people willfully ignore"** Fred Ebel for The American Resistance, "How Many Illegal Aliens Are in the U.S.?" *theamericanresistance.com*, www.theamericanresistance.com/ref/illegal_alien_numbers.html (accessed May 4, 2009). ★ **"range from 10-20 million"** Brad Knickerbocker, "Illegal Immigrants in the US: How Many Are There?" *Christian Science Monitor*, May 16, 2006, www.csmonitor.com/2006/0516/p01s02-ussc. html. **PAGE 134** ★ **"'promoting racial hatred'"** Associated Press, "Some Hispanics Decry Group's Border Patrols," *kvoa.com*, June 12, 2005, www.kvoa .com/Global/ story.asp?S=3464545. ★ **"'without question, a racist'"** David Edwards and Mike Sheehan, "Lou Dobbs Protested as 'Racist' at Book Signing," *rawstory.com*, November 12, 2007, http://rawstory.com/news/2007/Lou_Dobbs_protested_as_racist_at_1112.html. ★ **"'Nothing short of base racism'"** Peter Nicholas and Robert Salladay, "Gov. Praises 'Minuteman' Campaign," *Los Angeles Times*, April 29, 2005, http://articles.latimes.com/2005/apr/29/local/ me-governor29. ★ **"'that's just not going to fly'"** Susan Carroll, "Border Watch to Widen: Minuteman Project Plans to Patrol More States," *azcentral.com*, April 19, 2005, www.azcentral.com/arizonarepublic/news/articles/0419minuteman19.html. ★ **"'punished—or destroyed—for existing"** Clara Reyes, "Jeers to KMBC-TV for Promoting a Police State," *Dos Mundos* 25, no. 4. ★ **"'scare Latinos out of the state'"** Marcelo Ballvé, New America Media, "Immigrant Rights Activists Battle Harsh Laws Across U.S." *alternet.org*, December 23, 2008, www.alternet.org/immigration/114785/immigrant_rights_activists_battle_ harsh_laws_across_u.s. ★ **"'incoherent, distracted mass.'"** Thomas Jefferson, "Notes on Virginia," 1782, F. III., 190. **PAGE 135** ★ **"'tell the bigots to shut up'"** The Brownsville Herald, "GOP Senator Hangs Tough on Immigration," *The Brownsville Herald*, May 29, 2007, www.brownsvilleherald.com/articles/ immigration-76854-graham-issue.html. ★ **"less than $2.50 a day"** Anup Shah, "Poverty Facts and Stats," *globalissues.org*, March 22, 2009, www.global issues.org/article/26/poverty-facts-and-stats. ★ **"'translate belief into policy'"** Amy Gershkoff and Shana Kushner, "Shaping Public Opinion: The 9/11-Iraq Connection in the Bush Administration's Rhetoric," *Perspectives on Politics* 3 (2005): 525-537. **PAGE 136** ★ **"Wages dropped to $3.35 an hour"** Federation for American Immigration Reform "Immigration Issues: Immigration and Job Displacement," *fairus.org*, September 2006, www.fairus.org/site/News2 ?page=NewsArticle&id=16983. **PAGE 137** ★ **"between four and six million jobs . . . since 1990."** Robert Justich and Betty Ng, CFA, "The Underground Labor Force Is Rising to the Surface," *Bear Stearns*, January 3, 2005, www.bearstearns.com/bscportal/pdfs/underground.pdf. ★ **"'moving walls'"** Indiana General Assembly, State Chambers Senate Committee on Pensions and Labor, Michael W. Cutler, *Hearing on IN Senate Bill 0580* (Indianapolis, 2009), www.cis.org/testimony/CutlerIndiana0580. ★ **"hundreds of residents lined up"** Randall Parker, "Illegal Alien Meat Packing Plant Raids Raise Wages," *parapundit.com*, December 23, 2006, www.parapundit.com/archives/003974.html. **PAGE 138** ★ **"one woman who drove 40 miles"** Tom Blumer, "'Jobs Americans Won't Do' Meme Takes Another Hit in Mississippi," *newsbusters.org*, September 6, 2008, http://newsbusters.org/blogs/tom-blumer/2008/09/06/ jobs-americans-wont-do-meme-takes-another-hit-mississippi. ★ **"half of whom were subsequently hired"** Evan Perez and Corey Dade, "An Immigration Raid Aids Blacks for a Time," *Pittsburgh Post-Gazette*, January 17, 2007, www.post-gazette.com/pg/07017/754517-28.stm. ★ **"it's free, web-based, 99.5 percent accurate"** Janice Kephart, "If It's Fixed, Don't Break It: Moving Forward with E-Verify," *Center for Immigration Studies*, September 2008, www.cis .org/Everify. ★ **"off the ships at Ellis Island"** Steven Camarota, "Our New Immigration Predicament," *American Enterprise*, December 1, 2001. ★ **"average of 34 percent less by 1998"** Robert Rector, "Amnesty and Continued Low Skill Immigration Will Substantially Raise Welfare Costs and Poverty," Center for Immigration Studies *Backgrounder*, May 2006, www.heritage.org/research/immigration/bg1936.cfm. ★ **"the requested five years"** Omnibus Appropriations Act of 2009, HR 1105, 111th Cong. (March 11, 2009), www.govtrack.us/congress/bill.xpd?bill=h111-1105. **PAGE 139** ★ **"50 percent more likely to use welfare than citizens"** Steven Camarota, "Senate Amnesty Could Strain Welfare System: Newest Data Shows Latin American Immigrants Make Heavy Use of Welfare," *Center for Immigration Studies*, June 6, 2007, www.cis.org/articles/2007/welfarerelease.html. ★ **"twelve percent of our nation's poor"** Robert Rector, "Illegal Alien Amnesty Bill Bloats Welfare: Largest Expansion in 35 Years," *humanevents.com*, June 5, 2006, www.humanevents.com/article.php?id =15343. ★ **"'liberty enlightening the world'"** Elizabeth Koed, "A Symbol Transformed—The Statue of Liberty," *Social Contract Journal* 2, no. 3 (Spring 1992): 134-42. www.thesocialcontract.com/artman2/publish/tsc0203/article_147.shtml. ★ **"income taxes become significantly less positive"** Bernard Wasow, "Illegal Immigrants, Our Low-Income Taxpayers," *Mother Jones*, May 26, 2006, www.motherjones.com/politics/2006/05/illegal-immigrants-our-low- income-taxpayers. ★ **"in California for about $150"** Eduardo Porter, "Illegal Aliens Are Bolstering Social Security With Billions," *New York Times*, April 5, 2005, www.nytimes.com/2005/04/05/business/05immigration.html. ★ **"Our nation spends more than $4.7 billion a year on healthcare for illegal aliens"** Steven Camarota, "The High Cost of Cheap Labor: Illegal Immigration and the Federal Budget," *Center for Immigration Studies*, August, 2004, www.cis.org/ articles/2004/fiscal.html. ★ **"close over 70 hospitals"** Reuters, "Barry Arbuckle, PhD, MemorialCare Medical Centers CEO and Immediate Past Chair,

California Hospital Association, Speaks Out on California Budget Passage," *reuters.com*, February 20, 2009, www.reuters.com/article/pressRelease/idUS27 3333+20-Feb-2009+PRN20090220. ★ **"three percent of the population"** Carl Limbacher, "Justice Dept. Figures on Incarcerated Illegals," *freerepublic.com*, March 27, 2006, www.freerepublic.com/focus/f-news/1604385/posts. ★ **"spending about $30 billion each year"** Federation for American Immigration Reform, "Breaking the Piggy Bank: How Illegal Immigration Is Sending Schools Into the Red," *fairus.org*, June 2005, www.fairus.org/site/DocServer/piggybank 05.pdf?docID=2301. ★ **"'more on alcoholic beverages than fresh fruits and vegetables"** Philip Martin, "Farm Labor Shortages: How Real? What Response?" *Center for Immigration Studies*, September 2007, www.cis.org/articles/2007/back907.html. **PAGE 140** ★ **"425,000 'anchor babies' born in the U.S. each year"** Federation for American Immigration Reform, "Anchor Babies: Part of the Immigration-Related American Lexicon," *fairus.org*, April 2008, www.fairus.org/site/PageServer?pagename=iic_immigrationissuecenters4608. ★**"Dallas taxpayers another $31.3 million"** John Reiniers, "Anchor Babies Weigh Down Economy," *Hernando Today*, January 26, 2008, www2.hernandotoday.com/content/2008/jan/26/ha-anchor-babies-weigh-down-economy. ★ **"don't even know what we know"** Majority Staff of the House Committee on Homeland Security, "A Line in the Sand: Confronting the Threat at the Southwest Border," Washington, D.C., 2006, www.firecoalition.com/ downloads/A_Line_In_The _Sand_Report.pdf. ★ **"almost 70 percent of illegal aliens are Mexican"** Pia M. Orreniou, "Illegal Immigration and Enforcement along the U.S.-Mexico Border: An Overview," *Economic and Financial Review*, January 2001, http://findarticles.com/p/articles/mi_m0DKI /is_1_2001/ai_75891496/pg_6. **PAGE 141** ★ **"over 13 million unemployed Americans"** U.S. Department of Labor, Bureau of Labor Statistics, "The Employment Situation: June 2009," news release, July 2, 2009, www.bls.gov/news.release/empsit .nr0.htm. ★ **"85 percent of 'catch-and-release"** Kris Axtman, "Illegal Entry by Non-Mexicans Rises," *USA Today*, July 25, 2005, www.usatoday.com/news/ nation/2005-07-25-csm-otm_x.htm. ★ **"'any law enforcement officer'"** Kris Axtman, "Illegal Entry by Non-Mexicans Rises," *USA Today*, July 25, 2005, www.usatoday.com/news/nation/2005-07-25-csm-otm_x.htm. ★ **"currently 554,000 illegal-alien fugitives on the loose"** Rural Migration News, "DHS: Border, ICE, USCIS," *Rural Migration News* 15, no.2 (April 2009), http://migration.ucdavis.edu/rmn/more.php?id=1428_0_4_0. **PAGE 142** ★ **"sued him for $32 million"** Michael Cutler, "Exclusive: Illegal Alien Suit against Arizona Rancher Should Signal a Call to Action by Citizens," *Family Security Matters*, February 19, 2009, www.familysecuritymatters.org/publications/id.2563/pub_detail.asp. ★ **"the second-highest number of kidnappings in the world"** Brian Ross, Richard Esposito, and Asa Eslocker, "Kidnapping Capital of the U.S.A.," *ABC News*, February 11, 2009, http://abcnews.go.com/Blotter/story? id=6848672. ★ **"rapid and sudden collapse"** Fox News, "Military Report: Mexico, Pakistan at Risk of 'Rapid and Sudden Collapse,'" *foxnews.com*, January 14, 2009, www.foxnews.com/story/0,2933,479906,00.html. ★ **"'makes Al-Qaeda look like Sunday-schoolers'"** Joseph Myers and Patrick Poole, "Hezbollah, Illegal Immigration, and the next 9/11," *Front Page*, April 28, 2006, www.frontpagemag.com/readArticle.aspx?ARTID=4639. ★ **"note of our messy southern border"** Joseph Myers and Patrick Poole, "Hezbollah, Illegal Immigration, and the next 9/11," *Front Page*, April 28, 2006, www.frontpagemag.com/readArticle. aspx?ARTID=4639. **Graph: Historical levels of illegal immigrants** Jeffery S. Passel, "Background Briefing Prepared for Task Force on Immigration and America's Future" (Pew Hispanic Center, Washington, D.C., June 14, 2005), http://pewhispanic.org/files/reports/46.pdf. **PAGE 144** ★ **"experts as the drug cartels'"** Sara A. Carter, "Exclusive: Hezbollah Uses Mexican Drug Routes into U.S.," *Washington Times*, March 27, 2009, www.washingtontimes.com/ news/2009/mar /27/hezbollah-uses-mexican-drug-routes-into-us. ★ **"'pretending to be Hispanic immigrants'"** Robert S. Mueller, testimony to the U.S. House of Representatives Committee of Appropriations Subcommittee on Science, State, Justice, and Commerce, and Related Issues, March 8, 2005, www.fbi.gov/congress/congress05/mueller030805.htm. ★ **"he did it over and over again"** Majority Staff of the House Committee on Homeland Security, "A Line in the Sand: Confronting the Threat at the Southwest Border," Washington, D.C., 2006, www.firecoalition.com/downloads/A_Line_In_The_Sand_Report. pdf. ★ **"'written on the Statue of Liberty'"** Darragh Johnson, "Immigration Is Not in the Script for Hollywood's Cause Celebs," Washington Post, April 20, 2006, www.washingtonpost.com/wp-dyn/content/article/ 006/04/19/AR2006041902937.html. **PAGE 145** ★ **"settled for a mere $100,000"** Ted Poe, "Free Gilmer," *poe.house.gov*, February 9, 2007, http://poe.house.gov/News/DocumentSingle.aspx?DocumentID=60369. ★ **"into a real celebration"** Sara A. Carter, "Al Qaeda Eyes Bio Attack From Mexico," *Washington Times*, June 3, 2009, www.washingtontimes.com/news/2009/jun/03/al-qaeda-eyes-bio-attack-via-mexico-border. ★ **"train and arm all of their guards by 2017"** Christopher Mason, "Canada to Arm Its Border Guards," *New York Times*, September 1, 2006, http://query.nytimes.com/gst/fullpagehtml?res=9903E4D91E3EF932A3575AC0A9609C8B63. ★ **"with 800,000 illegal immigrants a year"** N.C. Aizenman, "Number of Illegal Immigrants to U.S. Is Down, Report Finds," *Washington Post*, October 3, 2008, www.washingtonpost.com/wp-dyn/content/ story/2008/10/02/ST200 8100203040.html. **PAGE 146** ★ **"it's proposed to be only 670 miles long"** Stephanie Simon, "Border-Fence Project Hits a Snag," *Wall Street Journal*, February 4, 2009, http://online.wsj.com/article/SB123370523066745559.html. **PAGE 147** ★ **"three years to even start . . . just 23 miles"** Ginger Thompson "Work Under Way on 'Virtual Fence,'" *New York Times*, May 8, 2009, www.nytimes.com/2009/05/09/us/09border.html. ★ **"'to be addressed later'"** Ginger Thompson "Work Under Way on 'Virtual Fence,'" *New York Times*, May 8, 2009, www.nytimes.com/2009/05/ us/09border.html. ★ **"'written by a professor'"** Adam Liptak "Ginsburg Shares Her Views on Influence of Foreign Law on Her Court, and Vice Versa," *New York Times*, April 11, 2009, www.nytimes.com/2009/04/12/us/12ginsburg.html. **PAGE 148** ★ **"opinions of mankind'"** Stuart Taylor, Jr. and Evan Thomas, "The Long Arm of the Law: A Looming Battle Over the Role Foreign Judges Should Play in U.S. Courts," *Newsweek*, April 18, 2009. ★ **"30 percent of a restaurant's operating costs"** Drew DeSilver, "Low-Paid Illegal Workforce Has Little Impact on Prices," *Seattle Times*, September 19, 2006, http:// seattletimes.nwsource.com/html/localnews/2003265139_imprices19.html. ★ **"'handshake or anything like that'"** Kurt Nimmo, "Obama Feigns Ignorance of CFR, NAU," *infowars.com*, April 1, 2008, www.infowars.com/obama-feigns-ignorance-of-cfr-nau. **"weapons and violence"** Associated Press, "Mexico's Ex-President Fox Says Racism Dictates U.S. Immigration Policy," Arizona Daily Star, October 9, 2007, www.azstarnet.com/allheadlines/205318.php. **PAGE 149** ★ **"Chicago Branch of the CFR"** Chicago Council on Global Affairs, "Board of Directors," *thechicagocouncil.org*, www.thechicagocouncil.org/chicago_ council_board_directors.php. ★ **"'outer security perimeter'"** Task Force on the Future of North America, *Building a North American Community*, (New York: Council on Foreign Relations, 2005), www.cfr.org/content/publications/attachments/NorthAmerica_TF_final.pdf. ★ **"'and I am proud of it'"** David Rockefeller, *Memoirs*, (New York: Random House, 2002), 405. ★ **"'Immigrant Mother Describes Terror'"** Susan Donaldson James, "Immigration Raids Cripple Small Towns," *ABC News*, August 29, 2008, http://abcnews.go.com/TheLaw/Story?id=5679696. **PAGE 150** ★ **"'and a private nurse'"** Miriam Jordan, "Flight on This 'Airline' Is One-Way Ticket Home for Illegal Immigrants," *pantagraph.com*, October 20, 2008, www.pantagraph.com/articles/2008/10/20/news/doc48f8 e1c8f4102072249437.txt. ★ **"'treat us like animals'"** Jordana Hart, "ICE Air Flying Undocumented Immigrants Home in Larger Numbers," *immigrateusa.com*, February 12, 2009, www.immigrateusa.us/content/view/1778/48. ★ **"'spread terror'"** Audrey Hudson, "Napolitano's Priority: Canada Border," *Washington Times*, January 26, 2009, http://www.washingtontimes.com/news/2009/jan/26/canadian-border-key-priority-in-napolitano-securit. ★ **"In 1986 . . . was about 5 million"** William Branigin, "Illegal Immigrant Population Grows to 5 Million," Washington Post, February 8, 1997, http://www.washingtonpost.com/wp-srv/ national/daily/march/31/immig6.htm. **PAGE 151** ★ **"as many as 90 percent"** Matt Hayes, "Bush Amnesty Sparks Surge in Border Crossings," *FOX News*, February 19, 2004, www.foxnews.com/story/0,2933,111818,00.html.

CHAPTER 7: THE NANNY STATE

PAGE 153 ★ **"punitive 'sin' taxes"** Supermarket News, "New York Retailers to Protest Beverage Tax," *supermarketnews.com*, February 26, 2009, http://supermarketnews.com/news/ny_bevtax_0226. ★ **laws dictating your house's paint color"** Stephanie Sandoval, "Farmers Branch Residents in a Paint Brawl," *Dallas News*, October 9, 2007, www.dallasnews.com/sharedcontent/dws/news/localnews/stories/101007dnmetfbpaint.3641f66.html. ★ **"regulations aimed at smoking"** Jesse McKinley, "Smoking Ban Hits Home. Truly," *New York Times*, January 26, 2009, www.nytimes.com/2009/01/27/us/27belmont.html. ★ **"drinking"** Inigo Figuracion, "About San Diego Profile: Beach Alcohol Ban," *about.com: San Diego*, January 15, 2008, http://sandiego.about.com/od/outdoorrecreatio1/p/booze_ban.htm. ★ **"dancing"** Lynh Bui, "San Tan Flat Wins Dancing Duel," *azcentral.com*, April 30, 2008, www.azcentral.com/arizonarepublic/local/articles/0430santanflat0430-on.html. ★ **"eating"** Elena Schor, "Los Angeles City Council Issues Fast-Food Ban for Poor Neighbourhoods," *gaurdian.co.uk*, July 30, 2008, www.guardian.co.uk/world/2008/jul/30/usa2. ★ **"washing your car in the driveway"** William M. Welch, "No Driveway Carwashes, Wash. State Says," *USA Today*, September 28, 2008, www.usatoday.com/news/nation/2008-09-28-car-wash_N.htm. ★ **"keeping a cat in your store"** Kate Hammer, "Guess Who's Minding the Store," *New York Times*, December 21, 2007, http://query.nytimes.com/gst/fullpage.html?res=9A05E4DC103EF932A15751C1A9619C8B63. ★ **"smiling for your driver's license"** UPI, "Smiles Banned on Indiana Driver's License," *upi.com*, December 9, 2008, www.upi.com/Odd_News/2008/12/09/Smiles-banned-on-Indiana-drivers-license/UPI-35581228851121. ★ **"playing tag"** Associated Press, "Northern Va. Pupils Told to End Tag; 'Intense Aggression' cited," *Associated Press State and Local Wire*, McLean, Va, April 15, 2008. ★ **"pants are too baggy"** Neil Conan, "Baggy Pants Banned Signed into Law in Louisiana," *Talk of the Nation*, NPR, September 4, 2007, www.npr.org/templates/story/story.php?storyId=14157759. ★ **"helmet for soccer"** CBS News, "Soccer Helmet Bill Kicked Around on Beacon Hill," *wbztv.com*, December 14, 2005, http://wbztv.com/local/Soccer.Helmets.Beacon.2.574933.html. ★ **"trick-or-treating when you were 12"** Portsmouth Police Department, *City Code Regarding Curfew and Trick or Treat Activities*, by S.D. White, October 11, 2008, http://portsmouthpd.us/?p=901. ★ **"sat on a milk crate"** Peter Gauvin, "Sidewalk Standoff," *paloaltoonline.com*, May 21, 1997, www.paloaltoonline.com/news_features/homeless/homeless.story1.php. **PAGE 155** ★ **"Capone made millions"** Eric Burns, *The Spirits of America: A Social History of Alcohol*, (Philadelphia: Temple University Press, 2004), 205-6. ★ **"DUI's increased after smoking was banned in bars"** Science Daily, "Increase in Drunk Driving Fatalities Followed Ban on Smoking in Bars," *sciencedaily.com*, May 21, 2008, www.sciencedaily.com/releases/2008/05/080521120216.htm. ★ **"potluck dinner illegal"** Radley Balko, "Nanny-State Lawmakers Abuse Power," *foxnews.com*, March 10, 2005, www.foxnews.com/story/0,2933,149955,00.html. ★ **"my pocket nor breaks my leg."** Henry Stephens Randall, *The Life of Thomas Jefferson*, (New York: Derby & Jackson, 1858), 621. ★ **"requiring ignition-locking breathalyzers in all cars"** Jayne O'Donnell, "Will Autos Some Day Have Breathalyzers?" *USA Today*, April 28. 2006, www.usatoday.com/money/autos/2006-04-24-breathalyzer-usat_x.htm. **PAGE 156** ★ **"'deal with the issue of drunk driving'"** Radley Balko, "When Drunk Driving Deterrence Becomes Neo-Prohibition," *foxnews.com*, October 6, 2005, www.foxnews.com/story/0,2933,171383,00.html. **Graph: A Toast to Success?** Century Council, *2007 State of Drunk Driving Fatalities in America* (Arlington, VA: Century Council, 2007), www.centurycouncil.org/files/2007%20State%20of%20Drunk%20Driving%20Fatalities%20in%20America_3.pdf. **PAGE 157** ★ **"don't believe in the technology."** Jayne O'Donnell, "Will Autos Some Day Have Breathalyzers?" *USA Today*, April 28. 2006, www.usatoday.com/money/autos/2006-04-24-breathalyzer-usat_x.htm. **PAGE 159** ★ **"from repeat offenders"** National Highway Traffic Safety Administration, "You Drink & Drive. You Lose: Driving Home the Facts about Repeat Offenders," *nhtsa.com*, www.nhtsa.dot.gov/people/outreach/SafeSobr/ydydyl/repeatOff.html. ★ **"60 crimes punishable by death"** Regan McTarsney, "Amnesty Report Says China Leads the World in Executions," *aol.co.nz*, April 15, 2008, www.aol.co.nz/sport/story/Amnesty-report-says-China-leads-the-world-in-executions/351731/index.html. ★ **"a car that didn't have it"** Chrissie Cole, "New York Man With Anti-DUI Device Crashes Rental Car," *injuryboard.com*, February 16, 2009, http://newyorkcity.injuryboard.com/automobile-accidents/new-york-man-with-antidui-device-crashes-rental-car-.aspx. ★ **"alcohol-free breath"** Gina Barton, "Drunken Driver Beats Ignition Lock: Six-Time Offender Used Balloon to Blow into Car's Device, Police Say," *Milwaukee Journal Sentinel*, October 8, 2008. **PAGE 160** ★ **"lobsters out of supermarkets"** PETA, "Lobster Liberation," *lobsterlib.com*, www.lobsterlib.com. **PAGE 161** ★ **"dare to bring candy to school"** Associated Press, "Honor Student Suspended for Buying Skittles," *chron.com*, March 13, 2008, www.chron.com/disp/story.mpl/bizarre/5613051.html. **PAGE 164** ★ **"prone to feeling angry and confused"** Hara Estroff Marano, "A Nation of Wimps," *Psychology Today Magazine*, (November/December, 2004): 3484, www.psychologytoday.com/articles/pto-20041112-000010.html. **PAGE 165** ★ **"Actual toll: 25,000"** News-Medical.net, "New Study Challenges CDC's 400,000 Obesity Deaths Figure," *news-medical.net*, April 20, 2005, www.news-medical.net/news/2005/04/20/9348.aspx. ★ **"force-fed pounds of it"** National Cancer Institute, "Artificial Sweeteners and Cancer: Questions and Answers," *cancer.gov*, October 5, 2006, www.cancer.gov/cancertopics/factsheet/Risk/artificial-sweeteners. **PAGE 166** ★ **"bladder cancer in rats"** John Henkel, "Sugar Substitutes: Americans Opt for Sweetness and Lite," *FDA Consumer Magazine*, (November/December, 1999), http://vm.cfsan.fda.gov/~dms/fdsugar.html. ★ **"800 diet sodas . . . a day"** John Henkel, "Sugar Substitutes: Americans Opt for Sweetness and Lite," *FDA Consumer Magazine*, (November/December, 1999), http://vm.cfsan.fda.gov/~dms/fdsugar.html. ★ **"75 children a year"** United States Consumer Product Safety Commission, "Consumer Product Safety Alert: Prevent Child In-Home Drowning Deaths," *cpsc.gov*, www.cpsc.gov/cpscpub/pubs/drown.html. ★ **"Repeal Day"** Allen Katz, "Now Toasting: Happy Repeal Day," *The New York Times*, December 5, 2008, http://themoment.blogs.nytimes.com/2008/12/05/now-toasting-happy-repeal-day. **PAGE 167** ★ **"connected to bad moonshine"** Michael Klein, "Raising a Toast on the Anniversary of Prohibition," *Philadelphia Inquirer*, December 5, 2008. ★ **"4,100 died nationwide in 1925"** Thomas M. Coffey, *The Long Thirst: Prohibition in America, 1920-1933*, (New York: W.W. Norton & Co., 1975), 196-8. ★ **including Joseph Kennedy, Sr."** Encyclopedia Britannica Online, entry entitled "Kennedy, Joseph P," www.britannica.com/EBchecked/topic/314858/Joseph-P-Kennedy (accessed May 4, 2009). ★ **"increased nearly 80 percent"** Thomas M. Coffey, *The Long Thirst: Prohibition in America, 1920-1933*, (New York: W.W. Norton & Co., 1975), 196-8. **PAGE 168** ★ **"$1 billion in lost state tax revenue"** Marina Walker Guevara and Kate Willson, "Big Tobacco's New York Black Market: How America's Top Cigarette Firms Fueled a Billion-Dollar Underground Trade," *publicintegrity.org*, December 19, 2008, www.publicintegrity.org/articles/entry/1098. ★ **"pulled in another $500 million"** Marina Walker Guevara and Kate Willson, "Big Tobacco's New York Black Market: How America's Top Cigarette Firms Fueled a Billion-Dollar Underground Trade," *publicintegrity.org*, December 19, 2008, www.publicintegrity.org/articles/entry/1098. ★ **"rival bootleggers didn't appreciate"** Patrick Fleenor, "No: Smugglers and Thieves Await Passage," *San Diego Union-Tribune*, October 12, 2006, www.signonsandiego.com/uniontrib/20061012/news_lz1e12fleenor.html. **PAGE 169** ★ **"never have gotten into this business"** Jim O'Grady, "Neighborhood Report: New York Smoking; Shared Misery: Newsstands Feel the Tax's Pinch Too," *New York Times*, August 18, 2002, www.nytimes.com/2002/08/18/nyregion/neighborhood-report-new-york-smoking-shared-misery-newsstands-feel-tax-s-pinch.html. ★ **"no morning traffic at all"** Jim O'Grady, "Neighborhood Report: New York Smoking; Shared Misery: Newsstands Feel the Tax's Pinch Too," *New York Times*, August 18, 2002, www.nytimes.com/2002/08/18/nyregion/neighborhood-report-new-york-smoking-shared-misery-newsstands-feel-tax-s-pinch.html. ★ **"trafficking bootleg cigarettes"** Tim Whitmire, "Prosecution Rests in North

Carolina Case Linking Cigarette Smuggling to HezbollahTerrorists," *Associated Press*, June 14, 2002, www.highbeam.com/doc/1P1-53618974.html. ★ **"except in Houston"** Lee McGuire, "Houston Deflates Attention Getting Balloons," *KHOU 11*, November 12, 2008, www.khou.com/business/stories/khou081112_jj_attention-getting-balloons.1a7a736ab.html. **PAGE 170** ★ **"wanted a smoke-free establishment"** Karri Peifer and Sheri Trice, "Smoking or Non Smoking?" *richmond.com*, February 9, 2005, www.richmond.com/news-features/5113. ★ **"government in their business"** Karri Peifer and Sheri Trice, "Smoking or Non-Smoking?" *richmond.com*, February 9, 2005, www.richmond.com/news-features/5113. **PAGE 171** ★ **"$93 billion a year"** Matthew Herper, "The Hidden Cost of Obesity," *forbes.com*, November 24, 2006, www.forbes.com/2006/07/19/obesity-fat-costs_cx_mh_0720obesity.html. ★ **"over their life spans than a smoker"** Jan J. Barendregt, M.A. Luc Bonneux, M.D. and Paul J. van der Maas, Ph.D., "The Health Care Costs of Smoking," *New England Journal of Medicine*, 337, no. 15 (1997): 1052-1057, http://content.nejm.org/cgi/content/full/337/15/1052. **PAGE 172** ★ **"because she was unbuckled"** Philip Terzian, "Police and Soccer Moms," *Washington Times*, December 17, 2000. ★ **"$27 million in revenue a year"** Stephen Majors, "Cash-Strapped States Mull Seatbelt Law Changes," *myway.com*, February 4, 2008, http://abcnews.go.com/US/wireStory?id=6800880. **PAGE 173** ★ **"'Click it or Ticket' in 2008"** National Highway Traffic Safety Administration, "Click It or Ticket," *nhtsa.gov*, www.nhtsa.gov/portal/site/nhtsa/menuitem.ce4a601cdfe97fc239d17110cba046a0.

CHAPTER 8: OWNING A HOME

PAGE 176 ★ **"any kind of financial crisis."** Stephen Labaton, "New Agency Proposed to Oversee Freddie Mac and Fannie Mae," *New York Times*, September 11, 2003, www.nytimes.com/2003/09/11/business/new-agency-proposed-to-oversee-freddie-mac-and-fannie-mae.html. ★ **Graph: U.S. Home Prices**, Financial Wisdom, "Median Home Prices Inflation Adjusted," *newfinancialwisdom.com*, September 30, 2008, www.newfinancialwisdom.com/median-home-prices-inflation-adjusted. **PAGE 177** ★ **Graph: Existing Home Prices**, Vikas Bajal and Bill Marsh, "Looking for the Bottom: Three Indicators," *New York Times*, March 15, 2009, www.nytimes.com/interactive/2009/03/15/weekinreview/20090315_VIKAS_MM.html **PAGE 178** ★ **"renters actually spend, on average, about 26 percent less"** Nick Timiraos, "Renters Lose Edge on Homeowners," *Wall Street Journal*, February 25, 2009, http://online.wsj.com/article/SB123552129423664663.html. ★ **"an incredible 66 percent less"** Nick Timiraos, "Renters Lose Edge on Homeowners," *Wall Street Journal*, February 25, 2009, http://online.wsj.com/article/SB123552129423664663.html. ★ **"millions of homeowners upside down on their mortgages"** Associated Press, "12% of Homeowners Behind on Mortgages," *cbsnews.com*, March 5, 2009, www.cbsnews.com/stories/2009/03/05/business/main4844773.shtml. ★ **"closing costs and other transaction fees"** Rebecca Tuhus-Dubrow, "Rethinking Rent: Maybe We Should Stop Trying to Be a Nation of Homeowners," *Boston Globe*, March 22, 2009, www.boston.com/bostonglobe/ideas/articles/2009/03/22/rethinking_rent. ★ **"about 2 to 4 percent per year"** Rebecca Tuhus-Dubrow, "Rethinking Rent: Maybe We Should Stop Trying to Be a Nation of Homeowners," *Boston Globe*, March 22, 2009, www.boston.com/bostonglobe/ideas/articles/2009/03/22/rethinking_rent/. ★ **"approach 2 percent of the home's value"** Forbes.com staff, "Table: Who Pays America's Highest Property Taxes?" *forbes.com*, January 23, 2009, www.forbes.com/2009/01/22/taxes-homes-property-forbeslife-cx_mw_0122realestate_table.html. ★ **"8 percent of the area's median salary"** Forbes.com staff, "Who Pays America's Highest Property Taxes?" *forbes.com*, January 23, 2009, www.forbes.com/2009/01/23/taxes-homes-property-forbeslife-cx_mw_0123realestate.html. ★ **"about 35 times higher"** National Association of Realtors, "Social Benefits of Homeownership and Stable Housing," *realtor.org*, January 2006, www.realtor.org/research/research/homeownershipbenefits. ★ **"you can always sell a few shares"** The Economist, "Home Ownership: Shelter, or Burden?" *The Economist*, April 16, 2009, www.economist.com/businessfinance/displayStory.cfm?story_id=13491933. **PAGE 179** ★ **"twice as likely to be married as renters"** Denise DiPasquale and Edward L. Glaeser, "Incentives and Social Capital: Are Homeowners Better Citizens?" *Journal of International Economics* 50, no. 2 (2000), 497-517. ★ **"homeowners are generally older"** Grace W. Bucchianeri, "The American Dream or the American Delusion? The Private and External Benefits of Homeownership" (working paper, Wharton School of Business, University of Pennsylvania, Pennsylvania, 2009), 9, http://real.wharton.upenn.edu/~wongg/research/The%20American%20Dream.pdf. ★ **"going forward are very solid."** Barney Frank, interview by Bill O'Reilly, *The O'Reilly Factor*, Fox News, October 2, 2008, www.foxnews.com/story/0,2933,432173,00.html. **PAGE 180** ★ **"shortages that artificially increase prices"** Randal O'Toole, "Don't Hobble Houston with Land Planning," *cato.org*, January 19, 2008, www.cato.org/pub_display.php?pub_id=9107. ★ **"which I do not see."** "What They Said About Fan and Fred," *Wall Street Journal*, October 2, 2008, http://online.wsj.com/article/SB122290574391296381.html. ★ **"no zoning restrictions at all"** City of Houston, "Deed Restrictions: Frequently Asked Questions," *houstontx.gov*, accessed June 23, 2009, http://www.houstontx.gov/legal/dr-faq.html. ★ **"most affordable housing of any major city"** Randal O'Toole, "Don't Hobble Houston with Land Planning," *cato.org*, January 19, 2008, www.cato.org/pub_display.php?pub_id=9107. ★ **"saved yourself 82 percent"** G. Scott Thomas, "Home Affordability Rankings for Top 50 Markets," *bizjournals.com*, March 10, 2008, www.bizjournals.com/specials/pages/160.html. ★ **"better shielded from the very real collapse"** Nancy Sarnoff, "Houston Home Sales, Prices Down Again," *Houston Chronicle*, April 21, 2009, www.chron.com/disp/story.mpl/front/6384403.html. ★ **"driving up the price of property ownership"** Randal O'Toole, "Don't Hobble Houston with Land Planning," *cato.org*, January 19, 2008, www.cato.org/pub_display.php?pub_id=9107. ★ **"without massive economic intervention"** Loren Steffy, "Lack of Zoning has Paid Off for Houston," *Houston Chronicle*, May 27, 2008, www.chron.com/disp/story.mpl/business/steffy/5804649.html. ★ **"twice the rate as heavily regulated states"** Randal O'Toole, "Don't Hobble Houston with Land Planning," *cato.org*, January 19, 2008, www.cato.org/pub_display.php?pub_id=9107. ★ **"every other state in the country . . . combined"** Arthur Laffer and Stephen Moore, "Soak the Rich, Lose the Rich," *Wall Street Journal*, May 18, 2009, http://online.wsj.com/article/SB124260067214828295.html. **PAGE 181** ★ **"largest population increase in the entire country"** U.S. Bureau of the Census, "New Orleans Population Continues Katrina Recovery; Houston Leads in Numerical Growth," *census.gov*, July 10, 2008, www.census.gov/Press-Release/www/releases/archives/population/012242.html. ★ **"perceived happiness mostly disappears"** Grace W. Bucchianeri, "The American Dream or the American Delusion? The Private and External Benefits of Homeownership" (working paper, Wharton School of Business, University of Pennsylvania, Pennsylvania, 2009), 1, http://real.wharton.upenn.edu/~wongg/research/The%20American%20Dream.pdf. ★ **"active leisure' than their renting counterparts"** Grace W. Bucchianeri, "The American Dream or the American Delusion? The Private and External Benefits of Homeownership" (working paper, Wharton School of Business, University of Pennsylvania, Pennsylvania, 2009), 5, http://real.wharton.upenn.edu/~wongg/research/The%20American%20Dream.pdf. ★ **"spend more time commuting"** Rebecca Tuhus-Dubrow, "Rethinking Rent: Maybe We Should Stop Trying to Be a Nation of Homeowners," *Boston Globe*, March 22, 2009, www.boston.com/bostonglobe/ideas/articles/2009/03/22/rethinking_rent/. ★ **"towards subsidized housing."** "What They Said About Fan and Fred," *Wall Street Journal*, October 2, 2008, http://online.wsj.com/article/SB122290574391296381.html. **PAGE 182** ★ **"20 million Americans change jobs every year"** Michael Gregory, "Is Your Dream Job a Reality?" *careerbuilder.com*, October 7, 2008, www.careerbuilder.com/Article/CB-885-Job-Search-Is-Your-Dream-Job-a-Reality. ★ **"about ten times before age 40"** Dawn Rosenberg McKay, "How Often Do People Change Careers?" *Dawn's Career Planning Blog* at *careerplanning.about.com*, July 28, 2006, http://careerplanning.about.com/b/2006/07/28/how-often-do-people-change-careers.htm. ★ **"average person now moves about 12 times"** U.S. Bureau of the Census, "Geographical Mobility/Migration: Calculating Migration Expectancy," *census.gov*, October 21, 2008, www.census.gov/population/www/socdemo/migrate/cal-mig-exp.html. ★ **"same unemployment rate as the rest of the country"** U.S. Department of Labor, Bureau of Labor Statistics, "Labor Force Statistics from the Current Population Survey," *bls.gov*, May 6, 2009, www.bls.gov/cps/cps_htgm.htm. **PAGE 183** ★ **"when the country had 120 million fewer people"** Sam Roberts, "Slump Creates Lack of Mobility for Americans," *New York Times*, April 22, 2009, www .nytimes.com/2009/04/23/us/23census.html. **PAGE 184** ★ **"Switzerland had the lowest rate in both"** Rebecca Tuhus-Dubrow, "Rethinking Rent: Maybe We Should Stop Trying to Be a Nation of Homeowners," *Boston Globe*, March 22, 2009, www.boston.com/bostonglobe/ideas/articles/2009/03/22/rethinking_ rent. ★ **"where they live rather than what they do best"** Rebecca Tuhus-Dubrow, "Rethinking Rent: Maybe We Should Stop Trying to Be a Nation of Homeowners," *Boston Globe*, March 22, 2009, www.boston.com/bostonglobe/ideas/articles/2009/03/22/rethinking_rent. ★ **"than, in fact, exists."** "What They Said About Fan and Fred," *Wall Street Journal*, October 2, 2008, http://online.wsj.com/article/SB122290574391296381.html. **PAGE 185** ★ Graph: U.S. Home Ownership "Table 5. Homeownership Rates for the United States: 1968 to 2008," U.S. Census Bureau, www.census.gov/hhes/www/housing/hvs/ qtr208/q208tab5.html. **PAGE 186** ★ **"pay more for those homes"** Steven Slivinski, "House Bias: The Economic Consequences of Subsidizing Homeownership," *Region Focus*, Fall 2008, www.richmondfed.org/publications/research/region_focus/2008/fall/pdf/cover_story.pdf. ★ **"12 pounds heavier than those who rent."** Grace W. Bucchianeri, "The American Dream or the American Delusion? The Private and External Benefits of Homeownership" (paper, Wharton School of Business, University of Pennsylvania, Philadelphia, 2003), http://real.wharton.upenn.edu/~wongg/research/The%20American%20 Dream.pdf. **PAGE 187** ★ **"billions of tax dollars disappear"** Nick Timiraos, "Mortgage Deduction Looks Less Sacred," *Wall Street Journal*, February 27, 2009, http://online.wsj.com/article/SB123569898005989291.html. ★ **"the number of gardens"** Steven Slivinski, "House Bias: The Economic Consequences of Subsidizing Homeownership," *Region Focus*, Fall 2008, www.richmondfed.org/publications/research/region_focus/2008/fall/pdf/cover_story.pdf. ★ **"buy mulch and leave it at that"** Steven Slivinski, "House Bias: The Economic Consequences of Subsidizing Homeownership," *Region Focus*, Fall 2008, www .richmondfed.org/publications/research/region_focus/2008/fall/pdf/cover_story.pdf. ★ **"full 65 percent of American homeowners"** Grace W. Bucchianeri, "The American Dream or the American Delusion? The Private and External Benefits of Homeownership" (working paper, Wharton School of Business, University of Pennsylvania, Pennsylvania, 2009), 2, http://real.wharton.upenn.edu/~wongg/research/The%20American%20Dream.pdf.

CHAPTER 9: ECONOMICS 101

PAGE 190 ★ **"success of our voluntary tax system"** Charles B. Rangel, "The AMT Must Go: Stop the Middle-Class Tax Raid," *Wall Street Journal*, October 30, 2007, www.opinionjournal.com/editorial/?id=110010800. ★ **"39.9 percent of the country's total income tax"** U.S. Department of the Treasury, Internal Revenue Service, "Table 5," in *SOI Tax Stats: Individual Statistical Tables by Tax Rate and Income Percentile*, March 27, 2009, www.irs.gov/taxstats/ indtaxstats/article/0,,id=133521,00.html. ★ **"paid 71 percent of the tab"** U.S. Department of the Treasury, Internal Revenue Service, "Table 5," in *SOI Tax Stats: Individual Statistical Tables by Tax Rate and Income Percentile*, March 27, 2009, www.irs.gov/taxstats/indtaxstats/ article/0,,id=133521,00.html. ★ **"less than three percent of the income taxes"** U.S. Department of the Treasury, Internal Revenue Service, "Table 5," in *SOI Tax Stats: Individual Statistical Tables by Tax Rate and Income Percentile*, March 27, 2009, www.irs.gov/taxstats/indtaxstats/article/0,,id=133521,00.html. **PAGE 191** ★ Chart: Who Pays the Taxes? Congressional Budget Office, *Historical Effective Tax Rates, 1979to 2005: Supplement with Additional Data on Sources of Income and High-Income Households* (Washington, D.C.: U.S. Congress, 2008), www.cbo.gov/ftpdocs/98xx/doc9884/12-23-EffectiveTaxRates_Letter.pdf. ★ **"who makes just $60,000 a year"** Tom Bawden, "Buffett Blasts System that Lets Him Pay Less Tax than Secretary," *London Times*, June 28, 2007, www.timesonline.co.uk/tol/ money/tax/article1996735.ece. ★ **"the richest man in the world"** CNN, "Buffett Named World's Richest Man," *cnn.com*, March 6, 2008, http://edition.cnn .com/2008/WORLD/europe/03/06/money.forbes. ★ **"effective federal tax burden is 31.5 percent"** Congressional Budget Office, *Historical Effective Tax Rates, 1979to 2005: Supplement with Additional Data on Sources of Income and High-Income Households* (Washington, D.C.: U.S. Congress, 2008), www .cbo.gov/ftpdocs/98xx/doc9884/12-23-EffectiveTaxRates_Letter.pdf. ★ **"disproportionate share of federal taxes"** Congressional Budget Office, *Historical Effective Tax Rates, 1979to 2005: Supplement with Additional Data on Sources of Income and High-Income Households* (Washington, D.C.: U.S. Congress, 2008), www.cbo.gov/ftpdocs/98xx/doc9884/12-23-EffectiveTaxRates_Letter.pdf. **PAGE 192** ★ **"bottom twenty percent only pay 0.4 percent"** Tax Policy Center, "Table T07-0294: Distribution of Federal Taxes Under Pre-EGTRRA Individual Income and Estate Tax Law, By Cash Income Percentiles, 2007," *taxpolicycenter.org*, August 24, 2007, http://www.taxpolicycenter.org/numbers/displayatab.cfm?Docid=1655. ★ Chart: Distribution of All Federal Taxes by Income Tax Policy Center, "Table T07-0294: Distribution of Federal Taxes Under Pre-EGTRRA Individual Income and Estate Tax Law, By Cash Income Percentiles, 2007," *taxpolicycenter.org*, August 24, 2007, www.taxpolicycenter.org/numbers/displayatab.cfm?Docid=1655. **PAGE 193** ★ **"65 percent reductions in median income"** U.S. Department of the Treasury, *Income Mobility in the U.S. From 1996-2005* (Washington, D.C.: Department of the Treasury, 2007), www.treas.gov/offices/tax-policy/library/ incomemobilitystudy03-08revise.pdf. ★ **"still in that group a decade later"** *65 percent reductions in median income* U.S. Department of the Treasury, *Income Mobility in the U.S. From 1996-2005* (Washington, D.C.: Department of the Treasury, 2007), www.treas.gov/offices/tax-policy/library/incomemobilitystudy03-08revise.pdf. **"higher income group by 2005"** "65 percent reductions in median income" U.S. Department of the Treasury, *Income Mobility in the U.S. From 1996-2005* (Washington, D.C.: Department of the Treasury, 2007), www.treas.gov/offices/ tax-policy/library/incomemobilitystudy03-08revise.pdf. ★ **"only 32 of them are still there today"** John Tamny, "The Forbes 400 as a Lesson in Economics," *realclearpolitics.com*, September 28, 2007, www.realclearpolitics.com/articles/2007/09/the_forbes_400_as_a_lesson_in.html. **PAGE 194** ★ **"average of 233 percent by 2006"** "65 percent reductions in median income" U.S. Department of the Treasury, *Income Mobility in the U.S. From 1996-2005* (Washington, D.C.: Department of the Treasury, 2007), www.treas.gov/offices/tax-policy/library/incomemobilitystudy03-08revise.pdf. ★ **"higher increases in income"** Congressional Budget Office, *Changes in the Economic Resources of Low-Income Households with Children* (Washington, D.C.: U.S. Congress, 2007), www.cbo.gov/doc.cfm?index=8113. ★ **"second study by the Treasury Department"** "65 percent reductions in median income" U.S. Department of the Treasury, *Income Mobility in the U.S. From 1996-2005* (Washington, D.C.: Department of the Treasury, 2007), www.treas.gov/offices/tax-policy/library/ incomemobilitystudy03-08revise.pdf. ★ Chart: The Poor Get Richer . . . U.S. Department of the Treasury, "Income Mobility in the U.S. from 1996-2005," *treas.gov*, November 13, 2007, www.treas.gov/offices/tax-policy/library/incomemobilitystudy03-08revise.pdf. **PAGE 195** ★ **"George Bush doesn't care about black people"** The Associated Press, "Kanye West Rips Bush at Telethon," *Reuters*, May 26, 2009, www.reuters.com/article/entertainmentNews/ idUSTRE54P5L820090526. ★ **"proud non-reader of books"** Mark Egan, "'Proud Non-Reader' Kayne West Turns Author," *foxnews.com*, September 5, 2005, www.foxnews.com/story/0,2933,168387,00.html. ★ Chart: Real Median Income Growth U.S. Bureau of the Census, "Table P-5B: Regions of Black People by Median Income and Sex: 1953-2007" and "Table P-5W: Regions of White People by Median Income and Sex: 1953-2007" in *Historical Income Data* (Washington, D.C.: U.S. Bureau of the Census, 2008), www.census.gov/hhes/www/income/histinc/p05B.html and www.census.gov/hhes/www/income/ histinc/p05W.html. **PAGE 196** ★ **"impact 45-55 percent of all small business income"** "The 2% Illusion: Take Everything They Earn and It Still Won't

Be Enough," *Wall Street Journal*, February 27, 2009, http://online.wsj.com/article/SB123561551065378405.html. ★ **"'a bunch of corrupt politicians'"** Huffington Post, "Rush Limbaugh To New York: Drop Dead," *huffingtonpost.com*, March 30, 2009, www.huffingtonpost.com/2009/03/30/rush-limbaugh-to-new-york_n_181005.html. ★ **"'thought about the taxes earlier'"** David M. Halbfinger, "Paterson Bids Rush Limbaugh Farewell," *City Room* blog at *nytimes.com*, April 2, 2009, http://cityroom.blogs.nytimes.com/2009/04/02/paterson-bids-rush-limbaugh-farewell/. ★ **"forcing agencies to produce 'Doomsday Budgets'"** Glenn Blain, "Gov. Paterson to MTA: Go Ahead with Doomsday Budget," *New York Daily News*, March 23, 2009, www.nydailynews.com/ny_local/2009/03/23/2009-03-23_gov_paterson_to_mta_go_ahead_with_doomsd.html. ★ **"guy who makes $54 million a year"** Forbes, "The 2009 Celebrity 100: #23 Rush Limbaugh," *forbes.com*, June 3, 2009, www.forbes.com/lists/2009/53/celebrity-09_Rush-Limbaugh_YNXQ.html. ★ **"audited him for twelve straight years"** Neil Cavuto, "Rush Limbaugh Speaks Out on 'Millionaires' Tax,'" *Your World With Neil Cavuto* on Fox News, April 9, 2009, www.foxnews.com/story/0,2933,513695,00.html. **PAGE 197** ★ **"a 66 percent increase in just eight years"** U.S. Office of Management and Budget, "Table 1," in *FY 2010 President's Budget: Historical Tables* (Washington, D.C.: White House, 2009), www.whitehouse.gov/omb/budget/Historicals. ★ **"over this period was 22 percent"** Federal Reserve Bank of Minneapolis, "Consumer Price Index, 1913-," *minneapolisfed.org*, accessed June 9, 2009, www.minneapolisfed.org/community_education/teacher/calc/hist1913.cfm. ★ **"transportation spending was up 43 percent"** U.S. Office of Management and Budget, "Table 3.2," in *FY 2010 President's Budget: Historical Tables* (Washington, D.C.: White House, 2009), www.whitehouse.gov/omb/budget/Historicals. ★ **"Health care spending was up 46 percent"** U.S. Office of Management and Budget, "Table 3.2," in *FY 2010 President's Budget: Historical Tables* (Washington, D.C.: White House, 2009), www.whitehouse.gov/omb/budget/Historicals. ★ **"Department of Education budget was up more than 85 percent"** U.S. Office of Management and Budget, "Table 4.1," in *FY 2010 President's Budget: Historical Tables* (Washington, D.C.: White House, 2009), www.whitehouse.gov/omb/budget/Historicals. ★ **"Welfare spending was up 60 percent"** U.S. Office of Management and Budget, "Table 3.2," in *FY 2010 President's Budget: Historical Tables* (Washington, D.C.: White House, 2009), www.whitehouse.gov/omb/budget/Historicals. ★ **"four, five, or six times the rate of inflation"** U.S. Office of Management and Budget, "Table 3.1" and "Table 3.2," in *FY 2010 President's Budget: Historical Tables* (Washington, D.C.: White House, 2009), www.whitehouse.gov/omb/budget/Historicals. ★ **"increase in government spending of 48 percent"** U.S. Office of Management and Budget, "Table 4.1," in *FY 2010 President's Budget: Historical Tables* (Washington, D.C.: White House, 2009), www.whitehouse.gov/omb/budget/Historicals. ★ **"30 times the rate of inflation"** Federal Reserve Bank of Minneapolis, "Consumer Price Index, 1913-," *minneapolisfed.org*, accessed June 9, 2009, www.minneapolisfed.org/community_education/teacher/calc/hist1913.cfm. ★ **Chart: Beltway Bonanza...** U.S. Office of Management and Budget, "Table 3.2," in *FY 2010 President's Budget: Historical Tables* (Washington, D.C.: White House, 2009), www.whitehouse.gov/omb/budget/Historicals, See Also, U.S. Office of Management and Budget, "Table 4.1," in *FY 2010 President's Budget: Historical Tables* (Washington, D.C.: White House, 2009), www.whitehouse.gov/omb/budget/Historicals. ★ **"and Dance Theater Etcetera in Brooklyn"** Citizens Against Government Waste, "Earmarks Rise to $19.6 Billion in CAGW's *2009 Pig Book*," cagw.org, April 14, 2009, www.cagw.org/site/News2?page=NewsArticle&id=11994. **PAGE 198** ★ **"combined economies of Norway"** U.S. Central Intelligence Agency, "Norway," in *The World Factbook* (Washington, D.C.: CIA, 2008), https://www.cia.gov/library/publications/the-world-factbook/geos/NO.html. ★ **"and Austria"** U.S. Central Intelligence Agency, "Austria," in *The World Factbook* (Washington, D.C.: CIA, 2008), https://www.cia.gov/library/publications/the-world-factbook/geos/AU.html. ★ **"gaining jobs in government"** U.S. Department of Labor, Bureau of Labor Statistics, "Government Employment: Employment, Hours, and Earnings from the Current Employment Statistics Survey (National)," *bls.gov*, accessed June 15, 2009, http://data.bls.gov/cgi-bin/surveymost. ★ **"1) government, 2) education, and 3) health care"** U.S. Department of Labor, Bureau of Labor Statistics, "Education and Health Services: Employment, Hours and Earnings from the Current Employment Statistics Survey (National)," and "Health *bls.gov*, accessed June 15, 2009, http://data.bls.gov/PDQ/servlet/SurveyOutputServlet?series_id=CES6561000001&data_tool=XGtable. ★ **"'areas where we can save taxpayer dollars' "** Barack Obama, "Obama's Remarks on $17 Billion Spending Reductions," *realclearpolitics.com*, May 7, 2009, www.realclearpolitics.com/articles/2009/05/07/obamas_remarks_on_17_billion_spending_reductions_96385.html. **PAGE 199** ★ **"exactly the same: 0.8"** Robert J. Barro, "Government Spending Is No Free Lunch: Now the Democrats Are Peddling Voodoo Economics," *Wall Street Journal*, January 22, 2009, http://online.wsj.com/article/SB123258618204604599.html. ★ **"wartime spending probably increases the multiplier"** Robert J. Barro, "Government Spending Is No Free Lunch: Now the Democrats Are Peddling Voodoo Economics," *Wall Street Journal*, January 22, 2009, http://online.wsj.com/article/SB123258618204604599.html. ★ **"average spending . . . increased by about 50 percent"** U.S. Office of Management and Budget, "Table 4.1," in *FY 2010 President's Budget: Historical Tables* (Washington, D.C.: White House, 2009), www.whitehouse.gov/omb/budget/Historicals. ★ **"cats and dogs . . . in foreign countries"** Great Cats and Rare Canids Act of 2009, HR 411, 111th Cong., 1st sess. (January 9, 2009), http://thomas.loc.gov/cgi-bin/bdquery/z?d111:h.r.00411:. ★ **"wants to give to the International Monetary Fund"** Naftali Bendavid, "Lawmakers Pave the Way for an IMF Contribution," *Wall Street Journal*, May 13, 2009, http://online.wsj.com/article/SB124217345624213065.html. ★ **"photos in exchange for votes"** Sarah O'Connor, "Obama's IMF Boost Exacts Heavy Toll," *Financial Times*, June 14, 2009. **PAGE 200** ★ **"repercussions of recent fiscal irresponsibility"** Charles B. Rangel, "The AMT Must Go: Stop the Middle-Class Tax Raid," *Wall Street Journal*, October 30, 2007, www.opinionjournal.com/editorial/?id=110010800. ★ **"'occurred under this administration's watch'"** Associated Press, "Senate Passes $2.8 Trillion Spending Plan for 2007," *USA Today*, March 17, 2006, www.usatoday.com/news/washington/2006-03-16-debt-ceiling_x.htm. ★ **"'not burden them with mountains of debt' "** Nancy Pelosi, "Pelosi Calls for a New America, Built on the Values that Made Our Country Great," *speaker.gov*, January 4, 2007, http://speaker.gov/newsroom/speeches?id=0006. ★ **"cut earmark spending in half"** Heritage Foundation, "Pelosi Formally Rejects GOP's Earmark Moratorium," *The Foundry* blog at *heritage.org*, February 6, 2008, http://blog.heritage.org/2008/02/06/pelosi-formally-rejects-gops-earmark-moratorium-2. See also, Nancy Pelosi, "Pelosi: President's Assertions on the Economy Just Don't Hold Up," *speaker.gov*, August 8, 2007, http://speaker.gov/newsroom/pressreleases?id=0281. ★ **"...$1.8 trillion"** U.S. Office of Management and Budget, "Table 1.1," in *FY 2010 President's Budget: Historical Tables* (Washington, D.C.: White House, 2009), www.whitehouse.gov/omb/budget/Historicals. ★ **"ratio of more than 35-to-1"** Roddy Boyd, "The Last Days of Bear Stearns," *money.cnn.com*, March 31, 2008, http://money.cnn.com/2008/03/28/magazines/fortune/boyd_bear.fortune. **PAGE 201** ★ **"pay-as-you-go' budgeting"** "The 'Paygo' Coverup," *Wall Street Journal*, June 12, 2009, http://online.wsj.com/article/SB124467627264104053.html. ★ **"unemployment rate stayed high throughout the decade"** U.S. Office of Management and Budget, "Table 1.2," in *FY 2010 President's Budget: Historical Tables* (Washington, D.C.: White House, 2009), www.whitehouse.gov/omb/budget/Historicals. ★ **"still hovering around 15 percent"** U.S. Department of Labor, Bureau of Labor Statistics, "Employment Status of the Civilian Noninstitutional Population, 1940 to Date," *bls.gov*, Accessed June 15, 2009, ftp://ftp.bls.gov/pub/special.requests/lf/aat1.txt. **PAGE 202** ★ **Graph: New Deal Spending vs. Unemployment Rates, 1928-1944** U.S. Department of Commerce, Bureau of the Census, "Series D 85-86 Unemployment: 1890-1970" in *Historical Statistics of the United States: Colonial Times to 1970, Part 1*, census.gov, Accessed July 2, 2009, 185, www2.census.gov/prod2/statcomp/documents/CT1970p1-01.pdf. See also, U.S. Department of Commerce, Bureau of the Census, "Series Y 466-471 Outlays of the Federal Government, by Major Function: 1900-1939" in *Historical Statistics of the United States: Colonial Times to 1970, Part 2*, *census.gov*, Accessed July 2, 2009, 1115, www2.census.gov/prod2/statcomp/documents/CT1970p2-01.pdf. See also, U.S. Department of Commerce, Bureau of the Census, "Series Y 472-487 Outlays of the Federal Government, by Major Function: 1940-1970" in *Historical Statistics of the United States: Colonial Times to 1970, Part 2*, *census.gov*, Accessed July 2, 2009, 1116, www2.census.gov/prod2/statcomp/documents/CT1970p2-01.pdf. ★ **"'And enormous debt to boot'"** John Morton Blum, *From the Morgenthau Diaries: Years of Urgency, 1938-1941* (Boston: Houghton Mifflin, 1959), 2:24. ★ **"government actually burned fields of crops"** Jim Powell, *FDR's Folly: How Roosevelt and His New Deal Prolonged the Great Depression* (New York: Three Rivers Press, 2003), 133-5. ★ **"thousands of Americans who were going to bed hungry"** Jim Powell, *FDR's Folly: How Roosevelt and His New Deal Prolonged the Great Depression* (New York: Three Rivers Press, 2003), 129. ★ **"eight fiscal stimulus plans"** "Barack Obama-San," *Wall Street Journal*, December 16, 2008, http://online.wsj.com/article/SB122938932478509075.html. ★ **"'the world's most expensive airport'"** James Sterngold, "Costly Airport to Be Opened Near Osaka," *New York Times*, August 30, 1994, www.nytimes.com/1994/08/30/business/costly-airport-to-be-opened-near-osaka.html. **PAGE 203** ★ **"Of at least $1.4 trillion"** Anthony Randazzo, Michael Flynn and Adam B. Summers, "Turning Japanese," *Reason*, July 2009, www.reason.com/news/show/133862 .html. ★ **"the Nikei was at 12,000"** "Barack Obama-San," *Wall Street Journal*, December 16, 2008, http://online.wsj.com/article/SB122938932478509075 .html. **Chart: The Bailouts: Putting it all on Red** "Big Budget Events, Milestones in Government Spending," *cnbc.com* (accessed July 19, 2009), www.cnbc .com/id/27717424. **PAGE 204** ★ **"future of $15 to $16 trillion of debt"** U.S. Office of Management and Budget, "Table S-14," in *Updated Summary Tables May, 2009: Budget of the U.S. Government Fiscal Year 2010* (Washington, D.C.: White House, 2009), 31, www.whitehouse.gov/omb/budget/fy2010/ assets/summary.pdf. ★ **"below the Canadian dollar in value for the first time"** Federal Reserve Bank of Atlanta, "Dollar Index History Charts," *frbatlanta .org*, accessed June 9, 2009, http://www.frbatlanta.org/dollarindex/user/dsp_chart_menu.cfm. ★ **"the figure is near $3 trillion"** David Goldman, "CNNMoney .com's Bailout Tracker," *money.cnn.com*, accessed June 9, 2009, http://money.cnn.com/news/storysupplement/economy/bailouttracker. ★ **"about $1 trillion in new spending"** David Goldman, "CNNMoney.com's Bailout Tracker," *money.cnn.com*, accessed June 9, 2009, http://money.cnn.com/news/storysupple ment/economy/bailouttracker. ★ **Chart: Solving One Crisis . . .** Federal Reserve Bank of St. Louis, "Series: BASE, St. Louis Adjusted Monetary Base," *research.stlouisfed.org*, accessed July 1, 2009, http://research.stlouisfed.org/fred2/series/BASE. **PAGE 205** ★ **"and spend another trillion"** David Goldman, "CNNMoney.com's Bailout Tracker," *money.cnn.com*, accessed June 9, 2009, http://money.cnn.com/news/storysupplement/economy/bailouttracker. ★ **"$80 billion bailing out GM, Chrysler, and GMAC"** James Pethokoukis, "FACTBOOK: Where Has the U.S. Bailout Money Gone?" *Reuters*, June 17, 2009, http://www.reuters.com/article/businessNews/idUSTRE55G4TS20090617. ★ **"save roughly 320,000 jobs"** "Number 9: General Motors," in "Fortune's Global 500, 2008," *money.cnn.com*, accessed June 9, 2009, http://money.cnn.com/magazines/fortune/global500/2008/snapshots/175.html. See also Chrysler, "Chrysler Group Corporate Overview," *media.chrysler.com*, accessed June 9, 2009, http://media.chrysler.com/newsrelease.do;jsessionid=5CDF2512CB4EBF0 14AFE1000B9FAFC19?id=866&mid=175. ★ **"should be put on hold"** Paul Krugman, "Let's Get Fiscal," *New York Times*, October 16, 2008, www.nytimes .com/2008/10/17/opinion/17krugman.html. **PAGE 206** ★ **"supposed to create three and a half million jobs"** Whitehouse.gov, "Issues: Economy," *whitehouse.gov*, accessed June 9, 2009, http://www.whitehouse.gov/issues/economy. ★ **"Among the biggest donors . . . were the unions"** Open Secrets, "2008 Overview: Business-Labor-Ideology Split in PAC & Individual Donations to Candidates and Parties," *opensecrets.org*, May 12, 2009, www.opensecrets .org/overview/blio.php. See also Open Secrets, "Top Overall Donors: Election Cycle 2006," *opensecrets.org*, accessed June 9. 2009, www.opensecrets.org/ bigpicture/topcontribs.php?cycle=2006. **PAGE 207** ★ **"raised about $1.45 trillion"** U.S. Office of Management and Budget, "Table 2.1," in *FY 2010 President's Budget: Historical Tables* (Washington, D.C.: White House, 2009), www.whitehouse.gov/omb/budget/Historicals/. ★ **"over 40 million unemployed homeless people."** *Letters to the President*, DVD, directed by Petr Lom (Paris, ARTE France, 2008). **PAGE 208** ★ **"increased over 250 percent since 1980"** U.S. Office of Management and Budget, "Table 1.1," in *FY 2010 President's Budget: Historical Tables* (Washington, D.C.: White House, 2009), www.whitehouse.gov/omb/budget/Historicals. ★ **"state and local spending is up 495 percent"** U.S. Department of Commerce, Bureau of Economic Analysis, "Table 3.3: State and Local Government Current Receipts and Expenditures," *bea.gov*, accessed June 9, 2009, www.bea.gov/national/nipaweb/ TableView.asp?SelectedTable=86&ViewSeries=NO&Java=no&Request3Place=N&3Place=N&FromView=YES&Freq=Year&FirstYear=1960&LastYear=2008& 3Place=N&Update=Update&JavaBox=no#Mid. ★ **"it's $2.2 trillion now"** U.S. Department of Commerce, Bureau of Economic Analysis, "Table 3.3: State and Local Government Current Receipts and Expenditures," *bea.gov*, accessed June 9, 2009, http://www.bea.gov/national/nipaweb/TableView.asp?SelectedTable =86&ViewSeries=NO&Java=no&Request3Place=N&3Place=N&FromView=YES&Freq=Year&FirstYear=1960&LastYear=2008&3Place=N&Update=Update&Ja vaBox=no#Mid. ★ **"chief among them Medicare...(AFDC)"** Robert Pear, "Welfare Debate Will Reexamine Old Assumptions," *New York Times*, January 2, 1995, http://www.nytimes.com/1995/01/02/us/welfare-debate-will-re-examine-old-assumptions.html. ★ **"the actual cost? $107 billion."** Steven Hayward and Erik Peterson, "The Medicare Monster," *Reason*, January, 1993, www.reason.com/news/show/29339.html. **PAGE 209** ★ **"get money back from the government every year"** U.S. Congressional Budget Office, "Table 1," in *Historical Effective Federal Tax Rates: 1979 to 2006* (Washington, D.C.: Congressional Budget Office, 2009), www.cbo.gov/ftpdocs/100xx/doc10068/effective_tax_rates_2006.pdf. ★ **"one of every six dollars"** Dennis Cauchon, "Benefit Spending Soars to New High," *USA Today*, June 4, 2009, www.usatoday.com/news/washington/2009-06-03-benefits_N.htm. ★ **"started keeping records in 1929"** Dennis Cauchon, "Benefit Spending Soars to New High," *USA Today*, June 4, 2009, www.usatoday.com/news/washington/2009-06-03- benefits_N.htm. ★ **"expenditures were $33 billion"** U.S. Office of Management and Budget, "Table 1.1," in *FY 2010 President's Budget: Historical Tables* (Washington, D.C.: White House, 2009), www.whitehouse.gov/omb/budget/Historicals. ★ **"a nearly $3 trillion government"** U.S. Office of Management and Budget, "Table 1.1," in *FY 2010 President's Budget: Historical Tables* (Washington, D.C.: White House, 2009), www.whitehouse.gov/omb/budget/Historicals. ★ **"less than 5 percent of total output"** U.S. Office of Management and Budget, "Table 1.1," in *FY 2010 President's Budget: Historical Tables* (Washington, D.C.: White House, 2009), www.whitehouse.gov/omb/budget/Historicals. ★ **"roughly 15 percent of total output"** U.S. Office of Management and Budget, "Table 1.1," in *FY 2010 President's Budget: Historical Tables* (Washington, D.C.: White House, 2009), http://www.whitehouse.gov/omb/budget/Historicals. ★ **"roughly 19 percent of total output"** U.S. Office of Management and Budget, "Table 1.1," in *FY 2010 President's Budget: Historical Tables* (Washington, D.C.: White House, 2009), http://www.whitehouse.gov/omb/budget/Historicals. ★ **"spend 28.1 percent of total output"** U.S. Office of Management and Budget, "Table 1.1," in *FY 2010 President's Budget: Historical Tables* (Washington, D.C.: White House, 2009), http://www.whitehouse.gov/omb/budget/ Historicals. **PAGE 210** ★ **"as economist Walter Williams . . . has noted"** Walter E. Williams, "Social Justice," *The Freeman* 48, no. 7 (July 1998), www.thefreemanonline.org/featured/social-justice-2. ★ **"allocating 10.5 trillion"** David Goldman, "CNNMoney.com's Bailout Tracker," *cnnmoney.com*, http:// money.cnn.com/news/storysupplement/economy/bailouttracker. ★ **"a $6 trillion national debt"** U.S. Office of Management and Budget, "Table S-14," in *Updated Summary Tables May, 2009: Budget of the U.S. Government Fiscal Year 2010* (Washington, D.C.: White House, 2009), 31, www.whitehouse.gov/omb/ budget/fy2010/assets/summary.pdf. ★ **"will climb to $16 trillion"** U.S. Office of Management and Budget, "Table S-14," in *Updated Summary Tables May, 2009: Budget of the U.S. Government Fiscal Year 2010* (Washington, D.C.: White House, 2009), 31, www.whitehouse.gov/omb/budget/fy2010/assets/

summary.pdf. ★ **"$50 plus trillion in unfunded liabilities"** Peter G. Peterson Foundation, "What Is the Real National Debt?" *pgpf.org*, accessed June 15, 2009, www.pgpf.org/about/nationaldebt. ★ **"inflow was $655 billion"** U.S. Office of Management and Budget, "Table S-3," in *Updated Summary Tables May, 2009: Budget of the U.S. Government Fiscal Year 2010* (Washington, D.C.: White House, 2009), 6, www.whitehouse.gov/omb/budget/fy2010/assets/summary.pdf. ★ **"contributing to the massive $1.8 trillion deficit"** U.S. Office of Management and Budget, "Table S-4," in *Updated Summary Tables May, 2009: Budget of the U.S. Government Fiscal Year 2010* (Washington, D.C.: White House, 2009), 8, www.whitehouse.gov/omb/budget/fy2010/assets/summary.pdf. **PAGE 211** ★ **"'a fearsome master'"** About.com, "Great Government Quotes," *usgovinfo.about.com*, accessed June 9, 2009, http://usgovinfo.about.com/blquotes2.htm.

CHAPTER 10: U.S. PRESIDENTS

PAGE 213 ★ **"'Would you use this word to describe yourself?'"** CNN Election Center 2008, "Part I: CNN/YouTube Democratic Presidential Debate Transcript," *cnn.com*, July 24, 2007, www.cnn.com/2007/POLITICS/07/23/debate.transcript. ★ **"'need to bring back to American politics'"** CNN Election Center 2008, "Part I: CNN/YouTube Democratic Presidential Debate Transcript," *cnn.com*, July 24, 2007, www.cnn.com/2007/POLITICS/07/23/debate. transcript. **PAGE 214** ★ **"'the change that needs to be brought'"** CNN Election Center 2008, "Part I: CNN/YouTube Democratic Presidential Debate Transcript," *cnn.com*, July 24, 2007, www.cnn.com/2007/POLITICS/07/23/debate.transcript. ★ **"fired off 40 lawsuits"** Scott Green, *Sarbanes-Oxley and the Board of Directors: Techniques and Best Practices for Corporate Governance* (Indianapolis: Wiley, 2005), 12, http://books.google.com/books?id=kqGuom3GFEEC ★ **"federally control large corporations"** Timothy P. Carney, "Big Business and Big Government," *cato.org*, July 21, 2006, www.cato.org/research/ articles/cpr28n4-1.html. ★ **"Roosevelt is his political idol"** Dan Nowicki, "A McCain Cabinet Could Bear Shades of Teddy Roosevelt," *USA Today*, February 19, 2008, www.usatoday.com/news/politics/election2008/2008-02-18-mccain-roosevelt_N.htm. **PAGE 215** ★ **"'all corporations doing an interstate business'"** Theodore Roosevelt, "The New Nationalism Speech," *teachingamericanhistory.org*, accessed June 15, 2009, http://teachingamericanhistory.org/library/index.asp?document=501. ★ **"'realize that desire to do well'"** Theodore Roosevelt, "The New Nationalism Speech," *teachingamericanhistory.org*, accessed June 15, 2009, http://teachingamericanhistory.org/library/index.asp?document=501. ★ **"'Our next question is for Senator Biden'"** CNN Election Center 2008, "Part I: CNN/YouTube Democratic Presidential Debate Transcript," *cnn.com*, July 24, 2007, www.cnn.com/2007/POLITICS/07/23/debate.transcript. ★ **"if you were worth your salt"** Theodore Roosevelt, *The New Nationalism* (New York: Outlook, 1910), 13, http://books.google.com/books?id=qRaGAAAAMAAJ. **PAGE 218** ★ **"'for equally good service.'"** Theodore Roosevelt, *The New Nationalism* (New York: Outlook, 1910), 11, http://books.google.com/books?id=qRaGAAAAMAAJ. ★ **"'represents benefit to the community'"** Theodore Roosevelt, *The New Nationalism* (New York: Outlook, 1910), 17, http://books.google.com/books?id=qRaGAAAAMAAJ. ★ **"'increase in government control is now necessary'"** Theodore Roosevelt, *The New Nationalism* (New York: Outlook, 1910), 18, http://books.google.com/books?id=qRaGAAAAMAAJ. **PAGE 219** ★ **"'degree the public welfare may require it'"** Theodore Roosevelt, *The New Nationalism* (New York: Outlook, 1910), 23, http://books.google.com/books?id=qRaGAAAAMAAJ. ★ **"with 'just and reasonable' rates"** S. E. Forman, *Advanced American History* (New York: Century, 1922), 578, http://books .google.com/books?id=mnIAAAAAYAAJ. ★ **"what was 'just and reasonable'"** S. E. Forman, *Advanced American History* (New York: Century, 1922), 578, http://books.google.com/booksid=mnIAAAAAYAAJ. ★ **"helping cause the bank panic of 1907"** Michael Chapman, "TR: No Friend of the Constitution," *CATO Policy Report* 24, no. 6, (November/December 2002), www.cato.org/pubs/policy_report/v24n6/chapman.pdf. **PAGE 220** ★ **"led to the creation of the Federal Reserve"** Milton Friedman and Anna Jacobson Schwartz, *A Monetary History of the United States* (Princeton, NJ: Princeton University Press, 1971), 171. ★ **"by J.P. Morgan and his efforts"** John Spence, "Bear Stearns' Bailout Has Echoes of 1907 Panic," *marketwatch.com*, March 14, 2008, www.marketwatch.com/story/jp-morgans-role-in-bailout-harks-back-to-panic-of-1907. ★ **"about five percent of its true market value"** Brian Tumbore, "J.P. Morgan—Savior—The Panic of 1907," *buyandhold.com*, accessed June 15, 2009, www.buyandhold.com/bh/en/education/history/2000/122499.html. ★ **"'Social Security Insurance' program"** Theodore Roosevelt, "Platform of the Progressive Party," *pbs.org*, accessed June 15, 2009, www.pbs.org/wgbh/amex/presidents/26_t_roosevelt/psources/ps_trprogress.html. ★ **"'the conditions of labor and living'"** Theodore Roosevelt, "Platform of the Progressive Party," *pbs.org*, accessed June 15, 2009, www.pbs.org/wgbh/amex/presidents/26_t_roosevelt/psources/ps_trprogress.html. ★ **"a 'more easy and expeditious' method"** Theodore Roosevelt, "Platform of the Progressive Party," *pbs.org*, accessed June 15, 2009, www.pbs.org/wgbh/amex/presidents/26_t_roosevelt/psources/ps_trprogress.html. **PAGE 221** ★ **"rather than simply a 'man'"** Ronald J. Pestritto, *Woodrow Wilson and the Roots of Modern Liberalism* (New York: Rowman & Littlefield, 2009), 11, http://books.google.com/books?id=B_5xhT1CvXAC ★ **"political principles in 'historical reality'"** Ronald J. Pestritto, *Woodrow Wilson and the Roots of Modern Liberalism* (New York: Rowman & Littlefield, 2009), 11, http://books.google.com/books?id=B_5xhT1CvXAC. ★ **"the thing I had been waiting for"** Woodrow Wilson, *The New Freedom: A Call for the Emancipation of the Generous Energies of a People* (Charleston, SC: BiblioBazaar, 2007). **PAGE 222** ★ **"'not a machine, but a living thing'"** Woodrow Wilson, *Constitutional Government in the United States* (Washington, D.C.: Wilson, 2007), 56, http://books.google.com/books?id=C1-85GjNgfkC. **PAGE 223** ★ **"'or enlistment service of the United States'"** *Military Laws of the United States 1915: Supplement* (Washington, D.C.: Government Printing Office, 1918), 277, http://books .google.com/books?id=FjBCAAAAIAAJ. **PAGE 224** ★ **"amendment to it called The Sedition Act"** "Sedition Act of 1918," *u-s-history.com*, accessed June 15, 2009, www.u-s-history.com/pages/h1345.html. ★ **"'not more than twenty years, or both'"** Thomas F. Carroll, "Freedom of Speech and the Press in Wartime—The Espionage Act," *Michigan Law Review* 17, (1918-1919), 649, http://books.google.com/books?id=XVUWAAAAYAAJ. ★ **"'non-interventionist policy in his second term'"** Nico Hines, "The Top Ten: The Times US Presidential Rankings," *London Times*, October 31, 2008, www.timesonline.co.uk/tol/news/world/us_and_americas/us_elections/article5048771.ece. ★ **"deny mail delivery to dissenters"** Thomas F. Carroll, "Freedom of Speech and the Press in Wartime—The Espionage Act," *Michigan Law Review* 17, (1918-1919), 629, http://books.google.com/books?id=XVUWAAAAYAAJ. ★ **"crimes in violation of Wilson's Sedition Act"** Peter Richardson, review of *Democracy's Prisoner: Eugene V. Debs, the Great War, and the Right to Dissent* by Ernest Freeberg, *Los Angeles Times*, June 15, 2008, www.latimes.com/features/printedition/books/la-bk-richardson15-2008jun15,0,2418054.story. **PAGE 225** ★ **"'better not monkey with the buzzard'"** Geoffrey R. Stone, *Perilous Times: Free Speech in Wartime from the Sedition Act of 1798 to the War on Terrorism*, (New York: W.W. Norton & Company, 2004), 202, http://books.google.com/books?id=S7ScI3Ia25sC. ★ **"America's entry into World War I"** Peter Richardson, review of *Democracy's Prisoner: Eugene V. Debs, the Great War, and the Right to Dissent* by Ernest Freeberg, *Los Angeles Times*, June 15, 2008, www.latimes.com/features/printedition/books/la-bk-richardson15-2008jun15,0,2418054.story. **PAGE 226** ★ **"'never let a crisis go to waste'"** Jeff Zeleny, "Obama Weighs Quick Undoing of Bush Policy," *New York Times*, November 9, 2008, www.nytimes.com/2008/11/10/us/politics/10obama.html. ★ **"'the same failed Republican policies"** Political Bulletin, "Campaign News: Clinton Touts Obama at Joint Florida Appearances," *usnews.com*, October 21, 2008, www.usnews.com/usnews/politics/bulletin/bulletin_081021.htm. ★ **"high unemployment rate (25 percent)"** Robert VanGiezen and Albert E. Schwenk, Bureau of Labor Statistics, "Compensation From Before World War I Through the Great Depression," *bls.gov*, January 30, 2003, www.bls.gov/opub/cwc/

cm20030124ar03p1.htm. ★ **"Pennsylvania, Vermont, New Hampshire, Maine, and Connecticut"** "Election of 1932," *u-s-history.com*, accessed June 15, 2009, www.u-s-history.com/pages/h894.html. **PAGE 227** ★ **"agencies, administrations, authorities, and acts"** Franklin D. Roosevelt Presidential Library and Museum, "Frequently Asked Questions: Q. What Did All the Letters in Those Alphabet Agencies Stand For?" *fdrlibrary.marist.edu*, accessed June 15, 2009, www.fdrlibrary.marist.edu/alphab6.html. ★ **"Unemployment during the New Deal and New Deal II"** Robert VanGiezen and Albert E. Schwenk, Bureau of Labor Statistics, "Compensation From Before World War I Through the Great Depression," *bls.gov*, January 30, 2003, www.bls.gov/opub/cwc/cm20030124ar03p1.htm. ★ **"'the only American principal'"** Joslyn Pine, *Wit and Wisdom of the American Presidents: A Book of Quotations* (Mineola, NY: Dover, 2000). **PAGE 228** ★ **"'reduction in federal expenditures'"** Jesse Walker, "The New Franklin Roosevelts: Don't Count on a Candidate's Campaign Stance to Tell You How He'll Behave in Office," *reason.com*, April 10, 2008, www.reason.com/news/show/125921.html. ★ **"'any form of tax increase'"** Barack Obama, posted by taxreformer, "President Obama's Pledge Never to Raise Taxes on Anyone Making Less than $250,000 a Year," *youtube.com*, February 4, 2009, www.youtube.com/watch?v=Q8erePM8V5U. **PAGE 229** ★ **"U.S. off of the 'gold standard'"** The White House, "Presidents: 32. Franklin D. Roosevelt, 1933-1945," *whitehouse.gov*, accessed June 15, 2009, www.whitehouse.gov/about/presidents/franklindroosevelt. ★ **"'right to a good education'"** Cass R. Sunstein, *The Second Bill of Rights: FDR's Unfinished Revolution and Why We Need It More Than Ever* (New York: Basic Books, 2006), 243, http://books.google.com/books?id=cj00Zjh1XlkC ★ **"'and gold certificates now owned by them'"** Franklin D. Roosevelt, *Executive Order 6102: Requiring Gold Coin, Gold Bullion, and Gold Certificates to Be Delivered to the Government*, issued April 5, 1933, *presidency.ucsb.edu*, accessed June 15, 2009, www.presidency.ucsb.edu/ws/index.php?pid=14611. **PAGE 230** ★ **"urgent need of shelter is denied it"** Leslie Kaufman and David W. Chen, "City Reaches Deal on Shelter for Homeless," *New York Times*, September 17, 2008, www.nytimes.com/2008/09/18/nyregion/18homeless.html. ★ **"'operate 24/7—so please come by'"** New York City Department of Homeless Services, "Single Adult Services," *nyc.gov*, accessed June 15, 2009, www.nyc.gov/html/dhs/html/homeless/adultserv.shtml. **PAGE 231** ★ **"'carried into practice for our citizens'"** Franklin Delano Roosevelt, "State of the Union Message to Congress—January 11, 1944," *fdrlibrary.marist.edu*, accessed June 15, 2009, www.fdrlibrary.marist.edu/011144.html. ★ **"'stuff of which dictatorships are made'"** Barack Obama, *The Audacity of Hope: Thoughts on Reclaiming the American Dream* (New York: Knopf, 2008), 183, http://search.barnesandnoble.com/booksearch/isbninquiry.asp?r=1&ean=0307455874. ★ **"'quantity of their goods'"** President Lyndon B. Johnson Remarks at the University of Michigan, May 22, 1964, www.lbjlib.utexas.edu/johnson/archives.hom/speeches.hom/640522.asp. ★ **"good for everybody.'"** David R. Francis, "How Obama's Tax Plans Would 'Spread the Wealth Around'," *The Christian Science Monitor*, October 27, 2008, www.csmonitor.com/2008/1027/p16s01wmgn.html. ★ **"'most important national investment.'"** President Jimmy Carter, Department of Education Organization Act Statement on Signing S. 210 Into Law, October 17, 1979, www.presidency.ucsb.edu/ws/index.php?pid=31543. **PAGE 232** ★ **"'generation is fulfilling our duty.'"** President George W. Bush Remarks at Signing of the Medicare Prescription Drug, Improvement and Modernization Act of 2003, December 8, 2003, www.cms.hhs.gov/History/Downloads/BushSignMMA2003.pdf ★ **"remained neutral as states began trying to secede"** Jay Tolson, "Worst Presidents: James Buchanan (1857–1861)," *U.S. News & World Report*, February 16, 2007, www.usnews.com/articles/news/history/2007/02/16/worst-presidents-james-buchanan.html.

CHAPTER 11: UNIVERSAL HEALTH CARE

PAGE 238 ★ **"rose by 7 percent' . . . costs rose by 18 percent."** Liz Kowalczyk, "ER Visits, Costs in Mass. Climb," *Boston Globe*, April 24, 2009, www.boston.com/news/local/massachusetts/articles/2009/04/24/er_visits_costs_in_mass_climb. **PAGE 239** ★ **"'pegged by the Census at 46 million in 2007, is swelling.'"** Susan Page, "Hurdles Remain in Obama's Push to Revamp Health Care," USA Today, May 31, 2009, www.usatoday.com/news/health/2009-05-31-hurdles_N.htm. ★ **"10 million illegal aliens and other non-citizens"** Dennis Keegan and David West, *Reality Check: The Unreported Good News About America* (Washington, D.C.: Regnery, 2008): 186. ★ **"household income of over $50,000 a year"** Carmen DeNavas-Walt, Bernadette D. Proctor, and Jessica C. Smith for the U.S. Bureau of the Census, *Income, Poverty, and Health Insurance Coverage in the United States: 2007* (Washington D.C.: Bureau of the Census, 2008), www.census.gov/prod/2008pubs/p60-235.pdf. ★ **"household income of over $75,000"** Carmen DeNavas-Walt, Bernadette D. Proctor, and Jessica C. Smith for the U.S. Bureau of the Census, *Income, Poverty, and Health Insurance Coverage in the United States: 2007* (Washington D.C.: Bureau of the Census, 2008), www.census.gov/prod/2008pubs/p60-235.pdf. • **"make too little or too much"** Governor Edward G. Rendell, "Governor's Message from Pennsylvania's CHIP, February 2008," *chipcoverskids.com*, accessed June 1, 2009, www.chipcoverspakids.com/chip-resources/resources-for-organizations-community-partners-and-school-districts/promotional-materials/governors-message-february-2008. **PAGE 240** ★ **"pay 19% of earnings . . . 90% purchase"** Michael Tanner, "The Grass Is Not Always Greener: A Look at National Health Care Systems Around the World," Policy Analysis, no. 613 (March 18, 2008), www.cato.org/pubs/pas/pa-613.pdf. ★ **"83 million people already benefit"** Carmen DeNavas-Walt, Bernadette D. Proctor, and Jessica C. Smith for the U.S. Bureau of the Census, *Income, Poverty, and Health Insurance Coverage in the United States: 2007* (Washington D.C.: Bureau of the Census, 2008): 27, www.census.gov/prod/2008pubs/p60-235.pdf. ★ **"they just haven't applied for it yet"** Blue Cross and Blue Shield Association, "The Uninsured in America," *coverageforall.org*, accessed May 30, 2009, www.coverageforall.org/pdf/BC-BS_Uninsured-America.pdf. See also, Reuters, "Internet Comes to Rescue of 14 Million Uninsured in U.S.; Providing Access to Gov. Health Programs They're Not Aware of : Pioneering Nonprofit Simplifies Enrollment Process," *reuters.com*, January 16, 2008, www.reuters.com/article/pressRelease/idUS219580+16-Jan-2008+PRN20080116. ★ **"likely in the area of 3 percent"** Blue Cross and Blue Shield Association, "The Uninsured in America," *coverageforall.org*, accessed May 30, 2009, www.coverageforall.org/pdf/BC-BS_Uninsured-America.pdf. ★ **"problem as 'worse than an epidemic'"** Jennifer Pifer-Bixler, "Study: 86.7 Million Americans Uninsured Over Last Two Years," *cnn.com*, March 4, 2009, www.cnn.com/2009/HEALTH/03/04/uninsured.epidemic.obama/index.html. **PAGE 241** ★ **"How to Build a Headline for the Media"** Families USA, "New Report Finds 86.7 Million Americans Were Uninsured at Some Point in 2007-2008," press release, March 4, 2009, www.familiesusa.org/resources/newsroom/press-releases/2009-press-releases/one-of-three-uninsured.html. **PAGE 242** ★ **"major advocacy groups"** Families USA, *Americans At Risk: One in Three Uninsured* (Washington, D.C.: Families USA, 2009), www.familiesusa.org/assets/pdfs/americans-at-risk.pdf. ★ **"'millions of uninsured' in America"** Jennifer Pifer-Bixler, "Study: 86.7 Million Americans Uninsured Over Last Two Years," *cnn.com*, March 4, 2009, www.cnn.com/2009/HEALTH/03/04/uninsured.epidemic.obama/index.html. ★ **"are 'uninsured' for less than a year"** U.S. Department of Health and Human Services, Office of the Assistant Secretary for Planning and Evaluation, *Overview of the Uninsured in the United States: An Analysis of the 2005 Current Population Survey* (Washington, D.C.: Department of Health and Human Services, 2005), http://aspe.hhs.gov/health/reports/05/uninsured-cps/index.htm. ★ **"between the ages of 18-34"** Carmen DeNavas-Walt, Bernadette D. Proctor, and Jessica C. Smith for the U.S. Bureau of the Census, *Income, Poverty, and Health Insurance Coverage in the United States: 2007* (Washington D.C.: Bureau of the Census, 2008), www.census.gov/prod/2008pubs/p60-235.pdf. ★ **"for around $50 a month"** M. P. McQueen, "Health Insurers Target the Individual Market," *Wall Street Journal*, August 21, 2007, http://online.wsj.com/article/SB118765356072903507.html. **PAGE 243** ★ **"15 percent of drivers have no auto insurance"** M. P. McQueen, "Road Risks Rise as More Drivers Drop

Insurance," *Wall Street Journal*, December 17, 2008, http://online.wsj.com/article/SB122947388659212351.html. ★ **"average wait is 70 days"** Michael Tanner, "The Grass Is Not Always Greener: A Look at National Health Care Systems Around the World," Policy Analysis, no. 613 (March 18, 2008), www .cato.org/ pubs/pas/pa-613.pdf. **PAGE 244** ★ **"patients be seen in less than four hours"** Daniel Martin, "Four-Hour Wait for a Lifesaving Ambulance Trip," *London Daily Mail*, January 12, 2009, www.dailymail.co.uk/health/article-1112207/Four-hour-wait-lifesaving-ambulance-trip.html. ★ **"sometimes for five hours or more"** Daniel Martin, "A&E Patients Left in Ambulances for up to FIVE Hours 'So Trusts Can Meet Government Targets,'" *London Daily Mail*, February 18, 2008, www.dailymail.co.uk/news/article-515332/A-E-patients-left-ambulances-FIVE-hours-trusts-meet-government-targets.html. ★ **"literally smell the tourists coming into the Capitol"** Sharyl Attkisson, "Visitor Center a $621M Boondoggle?" *cbsnews.com*, December 2, 2008, www.cbsnews.com/ stories/2008/12/02/cbsnews_investigates/main4644086.shtml. **PAGE 246** ★ **"another interminable wait once inside"** Nigel Hawkes, "Patients Admitted to Hospital Simply to Hit Targets," *London Times*, December 24, 2007, www.timesonline.co.uk/tol/life_and_style/health/article3090643.ece. ★ **"ten times the cost"** Nigel Hawkes, "Patients Admitted to Hospital Simply to Hit Targets," *London Times*, December 24, 2007, www.timesonline.co.uk/tol/life_and_style/ health/article3090643.ece. ★ **"close to $1,000 for every patient admitted"** Michael Blastland and Andrew Dilnot, *The Numbers Game: The Commonsense Guide to Understanding Numbers in the News, in Politics, and in Life* (New York: Penguin, 2008): 86. ★ **"Don't wash the sheets in between visitors"** Daniel Martin, "Hard-Up Hospital Orders Staff: Don't Wash Sheets—Turn Them Over," *London Daily Mail*, April 13, 2007, www.dailymail.co.uk/ healtharticle-448395/Hard-hospital-orders-staff-Dont-wash-sheets--turn-over.html. ★ **"asking patients to bring drugs in from home"** Daniel Martin, "Hard-Up Hospital Orders Staff: Don't Wash Sheets—Turn Them Over," *London Daily Mail*, April 13, 2007, www.dailymail.co.uk/health/article-448395/Hard-hospital-orders-staff-Dont-wash-sheets--turn-over.html. ★ **"almost half of dentists"** Matthew Moore, "Sufferers Pull Out Teeth Due to Lack of Dentists," *London Telegraph*, April 19, 2008, www.telegraph.co.uk/news/uknews/1566241/Sufferers-pull-out-teeth-due-to-lack-of-dentists.html. ★ **"led to about 1 in 5 people"** Matthew Moore, "Sufferers Pull Out Teeth Due to Lack of Dentists," *London Telegraph*, April 19, 2008, www.telegraph.co.uk/news/uknews/1566241/ Sufferers-pull-out-teeth-due-to-lack-of-dentists.html. ★ **"using superglue to reattach crowns"** Daily Mail Reporter, "Man Pulls Out 13 of His Own Teeth With Pliers 'Because He Couldn't Find an NHS Dentist,'" *London Daily Mail*, February 6, 2009, www.dailymail.co.uk/news/article-1135582/Man-pulls-13-teeth-pliers-NHS-dentist.html. ★ **"84 percent said it didn't get any easier to find a dentist"** Matthew Moore, "Sufferers Pull Out Teeth Due to Lack of Dentists," *London Telegraph*, April 19, 2008, www.telegraph.co.uk/news/uknews/1566241/Sufferers-pull-out-teeth-due-to-lack-of-dentists.html. **PAGE 247** ★ **"waiting times . . . are 'shorter than ever'"** United Kingdom Department of Health, *Chief Executive's Report to the NHS: June 2006*, (London, 2006), http://news.bbc.co.uk/ 1/shared/bsp/hi/pdfs/07_06_06_nhs.pdf. ★ **"within . . . just six months"** United Kingdom Department of Health, *Chief Executive's Report to the NHS: June 2006*, (London, 2006), http://news.bbc.co.uk/1/shared/bsp/hi/pdfs/07_06_06_nhs.pdf. ★ **"were waiting several years for surgeries"** Celia Hall, "Patients Wait Year for Hip Surgery," *London Telegraph*, December 21, 2006, www.telegraph.co.uk/news/uknews/1537385/Patients-wait-year-for-hip-surgery.html. ★ **"wait times increased by about 20 percent"** Michael Blastland and Andrew Dilnot, *The Numbers Game: The Commonsense Guide to Understanding Numbers in the News, in Politics, and in Life* (New York: Penguin, 2008): 74-6. ★ **"increasing by 143 percent"** Michael Blastland and Andrew Dilnot, *The Numbers Game: The Commonsense Guide to Understanding Numbers in the News, in Politics, and in Life* (New York: Penguin, 2008): 74-6. ★ **"a standard method of rationing'"** Gardiner Harris, "The Evidence Gap: British Balance Benefit vs. Cost of Latest Drugs," *New York Times*, December 2, 2008, www.nytimes.com/2008/12/03/health/03nice.html. ★ **"delay the progression of the disease"** Sarah Rubenstein, "U.K. Says Tykerb Isn't Worth Cost, Even With 12 Free Weeks," *Wall Street Journal*, March 5, 2009, http://blogs.wsj.com/health/2009/03/05/uk-says-tykerb-isnt-worth-cost-even-with-12-free-weeks. ★ **"worth more than your life"** Sarah Rubenstein, "U.K. Says Tykerb Isn't Worth Cost, Even With 12 Free Weeks," *Wall Street Journal*, March 5, 2009, http:// blogs.wsj.com/health/2009/03/05/uk-says-tykerb-isnt-worth-cost-even-with-12-free-weeks. See also, United Kingdom National Institute for Health and Clinical Excellence, "Breast Cancer (Advanced or Metastatic)—Lapatinib: Final Appraisal Determination," *nice.org.uk*, March 5, 2009, www.nice.org.uk/guidance/index .jsp?action=download&o=43476. ★ **"watch the decisions and mimic the procedures of NICE"** Victoria E. Knight, "As NICE and the UK Go, So Goes the Globe in Evaluating Drugs," *Wall Street Journal*, December 3, 2008, http://blogs.wsj.com/health/2008/12/03/as-nice-and-the-uk-go-so-goes-the-globe-in-evaluating-drugs. ★ **"Chart: Life Worth vs. Apartment Rent"** Daniel Baum, "March 2009 Manhattan Rental Market Report," *tregny.com*, March 1, 2009, www.tregny.com/content/rental_market_reports/march-2009-manhattan-rental-market-report. See also, Associated Press, "Some U.K Patients Denied Costly Cancer Meds," *msnbc.com*, April 8, 2009, www.msnbc.msn.com/id/30106986. **PAGE 248** ★ **"and medicine for people who were already dead"** Carl Campanile, "Medicaid Cops Bare Eye-Popping 'Scams,'" *New York Post*, February 23, 2009, www.nypost.com/seven/02232009/news/regionalnews/medicaid_ cops_bare_eye_popping_scams_ 156496.htm. ★ **"wasting time and money on those that are neither'"** GOP.gov, "Question and Answer: Government-Rationed Health Care," *gop.gov*, February 10, 2009, www.gop.gov/policy-news/09/02/10question-and-answer-government-rationed. ★ **"covered benefits and payment incentives"** Tom Daschle, with Jeanne M. Lambrew and Scott S. Greenberger, *Critical: What We Can Do About the Health-Care Crisis* (New York: Thomas Dunne, 2008): 158, http://books.google.com books?id=b4ZOip6AqK8C. ★ **"About 20 percent . . . are considered incurable"** Michael Tanner, "The Grass Is Not Always Greener: A Look at National Health Care Systems Around the World," Policy Analysis, no. 613 (March 18, 2008), www.cato.org/pubs/ pas/pa-613.pdf. ★ **"Daschle was Barack Obama's first choice"** CNN, "Obama: 'I Screwed Up' on Daschle Appointment," *cnn.com*, February 3, 2009, www .cnn.com/2009/POLITICS/02/03/obama.dashle/index.html. ★ **"learning about NICE . . . and we just couldn't'"** Gardiner Harris, "The Evidence Gap: British Balance Benefit vs. Cost of Latest Drugs," *New York Times*, December 2, 2008, www.nytimes.com/2008/12/03/health/03nice.html. **PAGE 249** ★ **"Set up the single-payer system"** Mark Halperin, "McCain Camp Debate Release on Obama and Health Care," *The Page* blog at cnn.com, May 30, 2009, http:// thepage.time.com/mccain-camp-debate-release-on-obama-and-health-care/. ★ **"I don't want to wait for that perfect system'"** Jamie Mulligan, "Seniors Town Hall in Ames, "Community Blog at iowa.barackobama.com, September 21, 2007, http://iowa.barackobama.com/page/community/tag/ames. ★ **"and we have to take back the House' "** Bill Moyers, "Bill Moyers and Michael Winship: Rx and the Single Payer," *Bill Moyers Journal* blog at pbs.org, May 21, 2009, www.pbs.org/moyers/journal/blog/2009/05/bill_moyers_ michael_winship_rx.html. ★ **"That's the single biggest thing'"** Glenn Beck, "Interview with Daniel Hannan: Brits Running Out of $$$," *glennbeck.com*, March 26, 2009, www.glennbeck.com/content/articles/article/196/23233. ★ **Chart: Medicare Spending** Steven Hayward and Erik Peterson, "The Medicare Monster," Reason, January, 1993, www.reason.com/news/show/29339.html. **PAGE 250** ★ **"Of the six biggest documentaries of all time"** Box Office Mojo, "Documentary: 1982-Present," *boxofficemojo.com*, accessed May 30, 2009, www.boxofficemojo.com/ genres/chart/?id=documentary.htm ★ **"just slightly ahead of Slovenia'"** Associated Press, "Little Defense for U.S. Health Care in 'Sicko,'" *msnbc.msn.com*, July 2, 2007, www.msnbc.msn.com/id/19552132. ★ **"developed [data] through a variety of techniques'"** World Health Organization, "Message from the Director-General," *who.int*, accessed May 30, 2009, www.who.int/whr/2000/media_centre/dgmessage/en/index.html. **PAGE 251** ★ **"for not having a progressive enough tax system"** World Health Organization, "World Health Organization Assesses the World's Health Systems," *who.int*, accessed May 30, 2009, www.who.int/whr/2000/media_centre/press_release/en. ★ **"differences among individuals and groups'"** World Health Organization, "World Health

Organization Assesses the World's Health Systems," *who.int*, accessed May 30, 2009, www.who.int/whr/2000/media_centre/press_release/en. ★ **"from New Jersey Governor Jon Corzine"** Jon Corzine, testifying before the U.S. Senate Committee on House Energy and Subcommittee on Health, *America's Need for Healthcare Reform*, 110th Cong., 2nd sess., September 18, 2008. ★ **"Tom Daschle"** Tom Daschle, testifying before the Senate Health, Education, Labor and Pensions Committee, *Nomination of Tom Daschle*, January 8, 2009. "*NPR*" Joseph Shapiro, "Health Care Lessons From France," *Day to Day* on *NPR*, July 11, 2008, www.npr.org/templates/story/story.php?storyId=92419273. ★ **"CNN"** Paula Zahn et al., "Fixing America's Broken Health Care System: YouTube Generation's Top Priorities," *CNN*, July 18, 2007, http://transcripts.cnn.com/TRANSCRIPTS/0707/18/se.01.html. ★ **"the New York Times"** "World's Best Medical Care?" *New York Times*, August 12, 2007, www.nytimes.com/2007/08/12/opinion/12sun1.html. ★ **"and the San Francisco Chronicle"** Victoria Colliver, "We Spend Far More, But Our Health Care Is Falling Behind: Australia, Canada, Germany, New Zealand, U.K. Spend Less and Do Better Job, Studies Say," *San Francisco Chronicle*, July 10, 2007, www.sfgate.com/cgi-bin/article.cgi?file=/c/a/2007/07/10/MNGNUQTQJB1.DTL. **PAGE 252** ★ **"half from among its own staff"** World Health Organization, "How Well Do Health Systems Perform?" in *The World Health Report 2000* (Geneva: World Health Organization, 2000), www.who.int/whr/2000/en/whr00_ch2_en.pdf. ★ **"'checked for consistency and bias'"** World Health Organization, "How Well Do Health Systems Perform?" in *The World Health Report 2000* (Geneva: World Health Organization, 2000), www.who.int/whr/2000/en/whr00_ch2_en.pdf. ★ **"put 62.5 percent of the weight"** World Health Organization, "How Well Do Heal Systems Perform?" in *The World Health Report 2000* (Geneva: World Health Organization, 2000): 39, www.who.int/whr/2000/en/whr00_ch2_en.pdf. ★ **"'expectations in regard to non-health matters'"** World Health Organization, "How Well Do Health Systems Perform?" in *The World Health Report 2000* (Geneva: World Health Organization, 2000): 37, www.who.int/whr/2000/en/whr00_ch2_en.pdf. ★ **"'level of responsiveness [to people's expectations]'"** World Health Organization, "How Well Do Health Systems Perform?" in *The World Health Report 2000* (Geneva: World Health Organization, 2000): 35, www.who.int/whr/2000/en/whr00_ch2_en.pdf. ★ **"'not access to health care.'"** CBC News, "Indepth: Health Care," *cbc.ca*, August 22, 2006, www.cbc.ca/news/background/healthcare. ★ **"live longer than we do"** Melissa Scott, "Healthy in Cuba, Sick in America? John Stossel Takes on Michael Moore, Examines Government-Run Health Care," *ABC News*, September 7, 2006, http://abcnews.go.com/2020/Story?id=3568278. **PAGE 253** ★ **"'No more, no less. And that's what they did'"** Melissa Scott, "Healthy in Cuba, Sick in America? John Stossel Takes on Michael Moore, Examines Government-Run Health Care," *ABC News*, September 7, 2006, http://abcnews.go.com/2020/Story?id=3568278. ★ **"that the C.I.A. agrees with him"** Melissa Scott, "Healthy in Cuba, Sick in America? John Stossel Takes on Michael Moore, Examines Government-Run Health Care," *ABC News*, September 7, 2006, http://abcnews.go.com/2020/Story?id=3568278. ★ **"'that Cubans live longer than Americans'"** Melissa Scott, "Healthy in Cuba, Sick in America? John Stossel Takes on Michael Moore, Examines Government-Run Health Care," *ABC News*, September 7, 2006, http://abcnews.go.com/2020/Story?id=3568278. ★ **Chart: When Free Health Care Isn't Free** Elizabeth Docteur and Howard Oxley, "Health-Care Systems: Lessons from the Reform Experience" (working paper, Organization for Economic Co-Operation and Development, Directorate for Employment, Labour, and Social Affairs, Paris, 2003), www.oecd.org/ dataoecd/5/53/22364122.pdf. **PAGE 254** ★ **"illustrative of America's affinity for homicide"** Federal Bureau of Investigation, "Murder," in *Crime in the United States 2007* (Washington, D.C.: Federal Bureau of Investigation, 2007), www.fbi.gov/ucr/cius2007/offenses/violent_crime/murder_homicide.html. ★ **"roughly that of Venezuela's"**, Sarah Miller Llana, "Will Venezuela's Murder Rate Hurt Chávez?" *Christian Science Monitor*, December 3, 2008, www.csmonitor.com/2008/1203/p06s01-woam.html. ★ **"four times greater than some European countries"** Adam Liptak, "Inmate Count in U.S. Dwarfs Other Nations'," *The New York Times*, April 23, 2008. ★ **"average home price in Detroit was $7,000"** Cynthia Bowers, "Housing Crisis Upside: $1 Homes?" *CBS News*, February 24, 2009, www.cbsnews.com/stories/2009/02/24/eveningnews/main4826433.shtml. ★ **"number one worldwide in life expectancy"** David Gratzer, "A Canadian Doctor Describes How Socialized Medicine Doesn't Work," *Investor's Business Daily*, July 26, 2007 www.ibdeditorials.com/IBDArticles.aspx?id=270338135202343. ★ **"but they're not starving, either"** Anthony DePalma, "Sicko,' Castro, and the '120 Years Club'," *The New York Times*, May 27, 2007, www.nytimes.com/2007/05/27/weekinreview/27depalma.html. **PAGE 255** ★ **"'better infant mortality rate [than we do]'"** Rene Rodriguez, "Cuban Healthcare is Painted Rosy in 'Sicko,' Critics Say," *Miami Herald*, June 23, 2007, www.miamiherald.com/509/story/148897.html. ★ **"to 4.7 of every 1,000 births in 2008"** "Cuba Sees Lowest Ever Infant Mortality Rate," *Periodico 26*, January 3, 2009, www.periodico26.cu/english/health/jan2009/infant-mortality010309.html. ★ **"favorite birth control method."** Irving Horowitz and Jaime Suchlicki, eds., *Cuban Communism* (Piscataway, NJ: Transaction, 2000), 691. **PAGE 256** ★ **"abortions at the first sign of possible trouble"** Melissa Scott, "Healthy in Cuba, Sick in America? John Stossel Takes on Michael Moore, Examines Government-Run Health Care," *ABC News*, September 7, 2006, http://abcnews.go.com/2020/Story?id=3568278. ★ **"don't 'reliably register' those deaths"** Bernadine Healy, "Behind the Baby Count," *U.S. News and World Report*, September 24, 2006, http://health.usnews.com/usnews/health/articles/060924/2healy.htm. ★ **"standard of 'size' or 'weight'"** Bernadine Healy, "Behind the Baby Count," *U.S. News and World Report*, September 24, 2006, http://health.usnews.com/usnews/health/articles/060924/2healy.htm. ★ **"'are registered as lifeless'"** Bernadine Healy, "Behind the Baby Count," *U.S. News and World Report*, September 24, 2006, http://health.usnews.com/usnews/health/articles/060924/2healy.htm. ★ **"as functional as the post office."** Bill Maher, *Real Time with Bill Maher*, HBO, March 6, 2009, www.youtube.com/watch?v=aitvFZTOrp4. ★ **"warn against comparing infant mortality rates"** Organization for Economic Cooperation and Development, "Infant Mortality" in *OECD Health Data 2007* (Paris: Organization for Economic Cooperation and Development, 2008), www.oecd.org/dataoecd/4/36/40321504.pdf. ★ **higher rate of 'very pre-term' babies"** Marian F. MacDorman, PhD., and T.J. Matthews, M.S., *Recent Trends in Infant Mortality in the United States: NCHS Data Brief No. 9* (Hyattsville, MD: National Center for Health Statistics, 2008), www.cdc.gov/nchs/data/databriefs/db09.htm. **PAGE 257** ★ **Graph: Scanning for Healthcare** Organization for Economic Co-Operation and Development, "OCED Health Data 2009—Frequently Requested Data," *oced.org*, accessed July 2, 2009, www.oecd.org/document/16/0,3343,en_2649_34631_2085200_1_1_1_1,00.html. See also, Victor R. Fuchs and Harold C. Sox, Jr., "Physicians' Views of the Relative Importance of Thirty Medical Innovations," *Health Affairs* 20, no. 5 (2001), http://content.healthaffairs.org/cgi/reprint/20/5/30.pdf. ★ **"mortality rate that's about equal to Norway"** Bernadine Healy, "Behind the Baby Count," *U.S. News and World Report*, September 24, 2006, http://health.usnews.com/usnews/health/articles/060924/2healy.htm. ★ **"one of the lowest rates on the planet"** Marian F. MacDorman, PhD., and T.J. Matthews, M.S., *Recent Trends in Infant Mortality in the United States: NCHS Data Brief No. 9* (Hyattsville, MD: National Center for Health Statistics, 2008), www.cdc.gov/nchs/data/databriefs/db09.htm. ★ **"cable news would have had to shut down"** No study has ever shown this, but it's probably true. **PAGE 258** ★ **"half of all new major medicines"** The CATO Institute, "American Cancer Society Wants Gov't to Run Health Care," *opposingviews.com*, May 11, 2009, www.opposingviews.com/articles/opinion-american-cancer-society-wants-gov-t-to-run-health-care. ★ **"Nobel Prize...84% of the time."** The Nobel Foundation, "All Nobel Laureates in Medicine," *nobelprize.org*, accessed July 2, 2009, http://nobelprize.org/nobel_prizes/medicine/laureates. **PAGE 259** ★ **Chart: Out of Pocket Expense vs. GDP** U.S. Department of Health and Human Services, Centers for Medicare and Medicaid Services, "National Health Expenditure Data: Historical," *cms.hhs.gov*, accessed July 2, 2009, www.cms.hhs.gov/NationalHealthExpendData/02_NationalHealthAccountsHistorical.asp. See also, Organization for Economic Co-Operation and Development, "OCED Health Data 2009—Frequently Requested Data," *oced.org*, accessed July 2, 2009, www.oecd.org/document/ 16/0,3343,en_2649_34631_2085200_1_1_1_1,00.html. ★ **"medications for less than a movie and popcorn"** Wal-Mart, "Wal-Mart Launches Phase Three of $4 Prescription Program," *walmartstores.com*, May 5, 2008, http://walmartstores.com/FactsNews/NewsRoom/8248.aspx. ★ **"retail clinics still increased over 30 percent"** Merchant Medicine, "Retail Clinics: 2008 Year-End Review and 2009 Outlook," *merchantmedicine.com*, accessed May 30, 2009, www.merchantmedicine.com/News.cfm?view=21. ★ **"Walgreens plans to have 400 clinics"** Bruce Japsen, "Walgreens Leads Field in Retail Clinics: Retail Chain to Operate 400 Clinics in U.S. by August," *Chicago Tribune*, December 4, 2008, http://archives.chicagotribune.com/2008/dec/04/business/chi-thu-notebook-retail-clinics-dec04. ★ **"CVS, plans on having almost 500"** Parija B. Kavilanz, "Wal-Mart Wants Your Rash and Strep Throat," *cnnmoney.com*, April 14, 2009, http://money.cnn.com/2009/04/13/news/economy/healthcare_retailclinics/index.htm. ★ **"cost of a normal trip to the doctor's office"** BlueCross and BlueShield of Texas, "Doctor's Office Versus E.R. Visits," *bcbstx.com*, accessed May 30, 2009, www.bcbstx.com/employer/hccc/topic6.htm. **PAGE 260** ★ **"94.5% of Wal-Mart employees have health insurance."** Associated Press, "Wal-Mart to Create 22,000 Jobs in '09," *money.aol.com*, June 4, 2009, http://money.aol.com/article/wal-mart-says-it-will-create-22000-jobs/513230. ★ **"two-thirds of visits are paid for by insurance"** Jacob Goldstein, "Which Patients Are Going to Retail Clinics?" *Health* blog at *wsj.com*, September 11, 2008, http://blogs.wsj.com/health/2008/09/11/which-patients-are-going-to-retail-clinics. ★ **"just $4 for a 30-day supply"** Wal-Mart, "$4 Prescriptions Program," *walmart.com*, accessed May 30, 2009, www.walmart.com/4prescriptions. ★ **"literally billions of dollars"** Shannon Pettypiece, "Generic-Pill Spending Dips in 'Fierce' U.S. Price War (Update 3)," *bloomberg.com*, December 10, 2008, www.bloomberg.com/apps/news?pid=20601087&sid=amqGqBv07pkg. ★ **"400 different drugs for just $12"** Walgreens, "Welcome to Walgreens Prescription Savings Club," *walgreens.com*, accessed May 30, 2009, http://webapp.walgreens.com/MYWCARDWeb/servlet/walgreens.wcard.proxy.WCardInternetProxy/RxSavingsRH?. ★ **"saved customers $1 billion"** Associated Press, "Wal-Mart Expands Program Providing Drug Discounts," *New York Times*, May 6, 2008, http://query.nytimes.com/gst/fullpage.html?res=9B0CE5D71431F935A35756C0A96E9C8B63. ★ **"to $10 for a 90-day supply"** Associated Press, "Wal-Mart Expands Program Providing Drug Discounts," *New York Times*, May 6, 2008, http://query.nytimes.com/gst/fullpage.html?res=9B0CE5D71431F935A35756C0A96E9C8B63. ★ **"for $9.99 for 90 days"** Lisa Girion and Andrea Chang, "CVS Slashes Generic Drug Costs, Escalates Price War," *Los Angeles Times*, October 31, 2008, http://articles.latimes.com/2008/oct/31/business/fi-pricewar31. ★ **"the unbeatable price of . . . nothing"** Ylan Q. Mui, "Giant Food to Offer Free Prescription Antibiotics," *Washington Post*, December 31, 2008, www.washingtonpost.com/wp-dyn/content/article/2008/12/30/AR2008123002834.html. ★ **"good from a competitive standpoint"** Peter Suderman, "Wal-Mart Joins the Ranks of the Health-Care Corporatists," *Reason Magazine*, June 30, 2009, www.reason.com/blog/show/134470.html. ★ **99 percent of businesses . . . while only 62 percent"** Catherine Rampell "Who Gets Employer-Based Health Insurance?" Economix Blog, *nytimes.com*, June 30, 2009, http://economix.blogs.nytimes.com/2009/06/30/who-gets-employer-provided-health-insurance. **PAGE 261** ★ **"'cost the store around a quarter-million dollars'"** Charles Platt, "Fly on the Wall: Undercover at Wal-Mart, the Heartland Superstore that May Save the Economy," *New York Post*, February 7, 2009, www.nypost.com/seven/02072009/postopinion/opedcolumnists/fly_on_the_wal_154007.htm. **PAGE 263** ★ **"after quite an intimate and painful surgery"** Please, please, please—I beg you, do NOT go to YouTube and watch this, www.youtube.com/watch?v=bX1rLv_hNeI. ★ **"Greece needs about 5,000 general practitioners"** Michael Tanner, "The Grass Is Not Always Greener: A Look at National Health Care Systems Around the World," Policy Analysis, no. 613 (March 18, 2008), www.cato.org/pubs/pas/pa-613.pdf. **PAGE 264** ★ **Instant Win: Cosmetic Surgery Graph** Devon M. Herrick, "National Healthcare Entrepreneurs: The Changing Nature of Providers" (Policy Report no. 318, National Center for Policy Analysis, Dallas, December 2008), hwww.ncpa.org/pdfs/st318.pdf. **PAGE 265** ★ **"'They're forcing me'"** Jennifer Fermino, "State Slaps Dr. Do-Good: Insurance Bureaucrats Reject $79 Health Plan," *New York Post*, March 4, 2009, www.nypost.com/seven/03042009/news/regionalnews/state_slaps_dr__do_good_157907.htm.

CHAPTER 12: THE U.S. CONSTITUTION

PAGE 268 ★ **"'Committee of Detail' to generate a rough draft"** Library of Congress, "Report of the Committee of Detail: Introduction," in *American Treasures of the Library of Congress: Top Treasures Exhibit Object Focus*, *loc.gov*, December 5, 2005, www.loc.gov/exhibits/treasures/trt047.html. ★ **"'for the Government of Ourselves and our Posterity'"** Committee of Detail, *Broadside Annotated in the Hand of William Samuel Johnson*, (Philadelphia: Claypoole and Dunlap, 1787), www.loc.gov/exhibits/treasures/images/vc4.7.jpg. **PAGE 269** ★ **"'this constitution for the United States of America'"** Library of Congress, "Report of the Committee of Style: Introduction," in *American Treasures of the Library of Congress: Top Treasures Exhibit Object Focus*, *loc.gov*, December 26, 2007, www.loc.gov/exhibits/treasures/trt007.html. **PAGE 270** ★ **"'snares that may be laid before them'"** Alexander Hamilton, James Madison, and John Jay, *The Federalist Papers*, (St. Paul, MN: Wilder Publications, 2008), 214, http://books.google.com/books?id=ZJD7Q4Vn_t4C. • **"from 1754 to 1790 was just 13 years"** J. Worth Estes and Billy G. Smith, eds., *A Melancholy Scene of Devastation: The Public Response to the 1793 Philadelphia Yellow Fever Epidemic*, (Sagamore Beach, MA: Science History Publications, 1997), 173, http://books.google.com/books?id=Mfiwih28gIC. **PAGE 271** ★ **"was 77 percent of the white population"** U.S. Department of Commerce and Labor, Bureau of the Census, *Heads of Families at the First Census of the United States Taken in the Year 1790: South Carolina*, (Washington, D.C.: Government Printing Office, 1908), www2.census.gov/prod2/decennial/documents/1790k-01.pdf. ★ **"'curse of heaven on states where it prevailed'"** W. O. Blake, *History of Slavery and the Slave Trade, Ancient and Modern: The Forms of Slavery that Prevailed in Ancient Nations, Particularly in Greece and Rome: The African Slave Trade and the Political History of Slavery in the United States*, (Baltimore: Miller, 1859), 395, http://books.google.com/books?id=UgwZAAAAYAAJ. ★ **"'one for every 40,000 free inhabitants'"** W. O. Blake, *History of Slavery and the Slave Trade, Ancient and Modern: The Forms of Slavery that Prevailed in Ancient Nations, Particularly in Greece and Rome: The African Slave Trade and the Political History of Slavery in the United States*, (Baltimore: Miller, 1859), 395, http://books.google.com/books?id=UgwZAAAAYAAJ. ★ **"keep slavery going indefinitely"** William Howard Adams, *Gouverneur Morris: An Independent Life*, (New Haven, CT: Yale University Press, 2003), 159, http://books.google.com/books?id=2TbC9bQsI6MC. ★ **"'dismemberment of the union would be worse'"** U.S. Constitution, art. 1, sec. 9, cl. 1, http://press-pubs.uchicago.edu/founders/documents/a1_9_1s14.html. ★ **"'plan adopted for the abolition of (slavery)'"** W. B. Allen, ed., *George Washington: A Collection*, (Indianapolis, IN: Liberty Fund, 1988), 319. **PAGE 272** ★ **"'practice of slavery in . . . abhorrence'"** Adrienne Koch and William Peden, eds., *The Selected Writings of John and John Quincy Adams*, (New York: Knopf, 1946), 209-10. ★ **"'atrocious debasement of human nature'"** Benjamin Franklin, "An Address to the Public from the Pennsylvania Society for Promoting the Abolition of Slavery," in *Franklin: Writings*, ed. J.A. Leo Lemay, (New York, Library of America, 1987), 1154. ★ **"'not only valid, but irrevocable'"** Alexander Hamilton, "Philo Camillus no. 2," in *The Papers of Alexander Hamilton: Volume XIX*, ed. Harold C. Syrett, (New York: Columbia University Press, 1973) 101-2. ★ **"without pandering to specific groups of voters"** U.S. Senate, "Direct Election of Senators," *senate.gov*, accessed May 26, 2009, www.senate.gov/rtandhistory/history/common/briefing/Direct_Election_Senators.htm. ★ **"Seventeenth Amendment . . . were elected directly by the people"** U.S. Senate, "Direct Election of Senators," *senate.gov*, accessed May 26, 2009, www.senate.gov/rtandhistory/history/common/briefing/Direct_Election_Senators.htm. **PAGE 273** ★ **"Senator could go to a party" New York Times News Service, "Kennedy's Friends Face Quiz: Statements Sought on Island Party Before Accident," *Pittsburgh Post-Gazette*, July 24, 1969. ★ **"sit around for 9 hours"** UPI, "17 Calls Reported After Ted Mishap," *St. Petersburg Times*, August 14, 1969, http://news.google.com/newspapers?nid=888&dat=19690814&id=tg4OAAAAIBAJ&sjid=wnsDAAAAIBAJ&pg=5935,2228494. **PAGE 274 ★ "during Clinton's most recent Senate term"** Peter Barker, "Is Clinton Ineligible to Join the Cabinet?" *The Caucus* blog at *newyorktimes.com*, December 2, 2008, http://thecaucus.blogs.nytimes.com/2008/12/02/is-clinton-eligible-to-join-the-cabinet. ★ **"level it was before Clinton's latest term"** Rick Klein, "The Hillary Fix," *The Note* blog at *abcnews.com*, December 4, 2008, http://blogs.abcnews.com/thenote/2008/12/the-hillary-fix.html. **PAGE 275 ★ "all the way back to James Monroe"** John T. Woolley, "Presidential Signing Statements Hoover—G.W. Bush: Frequently Asked Questions," *presidency.ucsb.edu*, accessed May 26, 2009, www.presidency.ucsb.edu/signingstatements.php. ★ **"opposition to 1,200 items over his term"** Josh Gerstein, "Obama: Ignore Signing Statements," *politico.com*, March 9, 2009, www.politico.com/news/stories/0309/19795.html. ★ **"continued under Barack Obama"** Karen Travers and Sunlen Miller, "Obama Will Continue Signing Statements; Calls for Review of His Predecessor's," *Political Punch* blog at *abcnews.com*, March 9, 2009, http://blogs.abcnews.com/politicalpunch/200/03/obama-will-cont.html. **PAGE 278 ★ "led by President George Washington himself"** Gerald Carson, "A Tax on Whiskey? Never!" *American Heritage Magazine* 14, no.5 (August 1963), www.americanheritage.com/articles/magazine/ah/1963/5/1963_5_62.shtml. ★ **"'as well funded as the military'"** Ben Evans, "Georgia Congressman Warns of Obama Dictatorship," *abcnews.com*, November 10, 2008, http://abcnews.go.com/Politics/wireStory?id=6225433. **PAGE 279 ★ "'bills of attainder prohibited by the Constitution'"** James Taranto, "Attainder for Beginners: A 'Grenade' Is Constitutional. A Sniper Rifle Isn't," *Wall Street Journal*, March 23, 2009, http://online.wsj.com/article/SB123782896283015881.html. **PAGE 280 ★ "that clause doesn't pertain to taxes"** *United States v. Carlton*, 512 U.S. 26 (1994), http://supreme.justia.com/us/512/26/case.html. **PAGE 282 ★ "out of business since the 80s"** Patricia Talorico, "Joe Gives Delaware Shout-Outs: Updated," *Second Helpings* blog at *delawareonline.com*, October 2, 2008, www.delawareonline.com/blogs/secondhelpings/2008/10/joe-gives-delaware-shout-outs.html. ★ **"former grand-pooba of the KKK"** Eric Painin, "A Senator's Shame: Byrd, in His New Book, Again Confronts Early Ties to KKK," *Washington Post*, June 19, 2005, www.washingtonpost.com/wpdyn/content/article/2005/06/18/AR2005061801105.html. ★ **"'quite open' to one world currency"** Ben Smith, "Geithner 'Open' to China Proposal," *politico.com*, March 25, 2009, www.politico.com/blogs/bensmith/0309/Geithner_open_to_China_proposal.html. ★ **"a 'nation of cowards'"** Terry Frieden, "Holder: U.S. a 'Nation of Cowards' on Race Discussions," *cnn.com*, February 19, 2009, www.cnn.com/2009/POLITICS/02/18/holder.race.relations/index.html. ★ **"pro-amnesty"** On the Issues, "Hilda Solis on Immigration," *ontheissues.org*, February 2, 2009, http://ontheissues.org/CA/Hilda_Solis_Immigration.htm. ★ **"pro-big-labor"** Associated Press, "Obama's Pick for Labor Secretary Welcomed by Unions, Eyed Cautiously Among Business," *foxnews.com*, December 18, 2008, www.foxnews.com/politics/2008/12/18/rep-solis-tapped-labor-secretary-sources-say. ★ **"by just two Republicans"** Alex Isenstadt, "Solis Wins Easy Committee Approval," *politico.com*, February 11, 2009, www.politico.com/news/stories/0209/18751.html. **PAGE 283 ★ "started out at $25,000"** Marvin Kitman, *George Washington's Expense Account*, (New York: Grove, 2001), 285, http://books.google.com/books?id=PKPwykRxhhMC. ★ **"current compensation is $400,000"** Erik Holm, Linda Shen, and Peter Eichenbaum, "AIG May Find CEO Candidates Shun Obama Pay Parity (Update 2)," *bloomberg.com*, May 22, 2009, www.bloomberg.com/apps/news?pid=20601087&sid=a.hWKtnAQGPk. **PAGE 284 ★ "'binds the people in this country'"** Adam Liptak, "The Court at a Crossroads," *Columbia Law School Magazine*, March 2009, www.law.columbia.edu/magazine/1873/the-court-at-a-crossroads. **PAGE 285 ★ "'57 states' mentioned by then-candidate Obama"** ObamaGaffe, "Obama Claims He's Visited 57 States," *youtube.com*, May 9, 2008, www.youtube.com/watch?v=EpGH02DtIws. **PAGE 286 ★ "'experts' control over education"** David Crary, "UN Convention on the Rights of the Child Stirs Debate," *Chicago Tribune*, April 30, 2009, www.chicagotribune.com/news/nationworld/chi-unchildren30apr30,0,3313935.story. ★ **"U.N. control over U.S. territorial waters"** Nathanial Gronewold, "Rising Seabed Claims Swamp U.N. Commission," *New York Times*, April 13, 2009, www.nytimes.com/gwire/2009/04/13/13greenwire-rising-seabed-claims-swamp-un-commission-10511.html. **PAGE 287 ★ "fifteen years after the constitution was written"** Thomas Jefferson, "Jefferson's Letter to the Danbury Baptists, January 1, 1802" *Library of Congress Information Bulletin* 57, no.6 (June 1998), www.loc.gov/loc/lcib/9806/danpre.html. **PAGE 288 ★ "'wall of separation between church and state'"** Thomas Jefferson, "Jefferson's Letter to the Danbury Baptists, January 1, 1802" *Library of Congress Information Bulletin* 57, no.6 (June 1998), www.loc.gov/loc/lcib/9806/danpre.html. ★ **"'actions only, & not opinions'"** Thomas Jefferson, "Jefferson's Letter to the Danbury Baptists, January 1, 1802" *Library of Congress Information Bulletin* 57, no.6 (June 1998), www.loc.gov/loc/lcib/9806/danpre.html. **PAGE 289 ★ "broadened the government's legal argument for it"** "Obama Channels Cheney: Obama Adopts Bush View on the Powers of the Presidency," *Wall Street Journal*, March 6, 2009, http://online.wsj.com/article/SB123638765474658467.html. **PAGE 290 ★ "what we now call 'eminent domain'"** Bruce L. Benson, "The Evolution of Eminent Domain," *Independent Review* 12, no. 3 (winter 2008), 430, www.independent.org/pdf/tir/tir_12_03_04_benson.pdf. ★ **"allowed a city to seize private property"** Associated Press, "Homes May be 'Taken' for Private Projects: Justices: Local Governments Can Give OK if It's for Public Good," *msnbc.com*, June 23, 2005, www.msnbc.msn.com/id/8331097. **PAGE 292 ★ "more than that in 1787"** U.S. Department of Labor, Bureau of Labor Statistics, "CPI Inflation Calculator," *bls.gov*, accessed May 26, 2009, www.bls.gov/data/inflation_calculator.htm. ★ **"like Thomas Jefferson, insisted on a Bill of Rights"** University of Virginia Library, comp., "Thomas Jefferson on Politics and Government: 15. The Bill of Rights," *etext.virginia.edu*, accessed May 26, 2009, http://etext.Virginia.edu/jefferson/quotations/jeff0950.htm. **PAGE 293 ★ "exempt from all federal gun regulations"** Kahrin Deines, "Montana Gun Law Targets States' Rights Clash," *San Francisco Chronicle*, May 10, 2009, www.sfgate.com/cgi-bin/article.cgi?f=/c/a/2009/05/10/MN4V17BCF2.DTL. ★ **"'sovereignty of the state of Montana'"** Kahrin Deines, "Montana Gun Law Targets States' Rights Clash," *San Francisco Chronicle*, May 10, 2009, www.sfgate.com/cgibin/article.cgi?f=/c/a/2009/05/10/MN4V17BCF2.DTL. ★ **"regulate marijuana grown and used in California"** Associated Press, "Montana Fires a Warning Shot Over States' Rights," *msnbc.com*, April 29, 2009, www.msnbc.msn.com/id/30482736. **PAGE 294 ★ "deaths of 618,000 people during the Civil War"** Stig Förster and Jorg Nagler, eds. *On the Road to Total War: The American Civil War and the German Wars of Unification, 1861-1871*, (Cambridge, England: Cambridge University Press, 2002), 24, http://books.google.com/books?id=Qm4o2vsMTdYC. ★ **"importation of new slaves stopped in 1808"** Martin A. Klein, *Historical Dictionary of Slavery and Abolition*,(Lanham, MD: Scarecrow Press, 2002), 43, http://books.google.com books?id=Go3FnxcpjLUC. **PAGE 296 ★ "You are here to enrich the world'"** Woodrow Wilson, *The Politics of Woodrow Wilson: Selections from His Speeches and Writings*, (Freeport, NY: Books for Libraries Press, 1970), 239, http://books.google.com/books?id=rxC4IG60KTwC. **PAGE 297 ★ "could've run for a third term"** "The 22nd Amendment," *Time*, March 5, 1951, www.time.com/time/magazine/article/0,9171,805716,00.html. **PAGE 298 ★ "used the taxes as a means of discrimination"** "Friendly Filibuster," *Time*, April 6, 1962, www.time.com/time/magazine/article/0,9171,896015,00.html. ★ **"'they ran out of words'"** "Friendly Filibuster," *Time*, April 6, 1962, www.time.com/time/magazine/article/0,9171,896015,00.html. ★ **"Alexander Hamilton's former home a national monument"** "Friendly Filibuster," *Time*, April 6, 1962, www.time.com/time/magazine/article/0,9171,896015,00.html. ★ **"the only state to outright reject it"** Tyler Lewis, "Today in Civil Rights History: The 24th Amendment Prohibits Poll Taxes," *civilrights.org*, January 23, 2009, www.civilrights.org/archives/2009/01/027-24th-amendment.html.

FUSION

entertainment & enlightenment

"YOU REALLY THINK THAT A FEW HUNDRED PAGES OF MINDLESS DRIVEL WILL CHANGE MY MIND? NO WAY, I CAN EASILY DEAL WITH YOUR NONSENSE ONCE A YEAR."

I have some bad news for you: I also publish a magazine.

The key to winning America back is for each of us to stay informed and become authorities on the issues that will decide our future. This book is a great place to start, but if you want the latest facts, stats and winning arguments all year long, then check out my magazine, *Fusion*.

Since its launch in 2005, *Fusion* has combined intelligent and timely commentary with cutting edge humor and, above all, common sense. In other words, it's the *fusion* of entertainment and enlightenment.

Here's the kind of exclusive stuff we've featured in Fusion:

★ A one-on-one interview with the founder of the Minuteman Project.
★ A powerful column by the former U.S. Comptroller General David M. Walker on America's deficits.
★ Occasionally accurate "Predictive Obituaries." (Okay, Michael Jackson was the only one we ever got right.)
★ Exclusive jail-house interviews with Jose Compean and Ignacio Ramos
★ An Op/Ed by Congressman Ron Paul explaining why the FED is to blame for the economic crisis.
★ An essay by Penn Jillette on why he is a *Libertarian* nut and not just your average nut.

FUSION:
MORE PERSPECTIVE, MORE COMEDY, MORE HEART, MORE GLENN

Subscribe now and take advantage of an EXCLUSIVE offer for readers of *Arguing with Idiots*—find out more at www.glennbeck.com/arguing or by calling 1-888-GLENNBECK and mentioning the code "Arguing."